PUBLIC SOCIOLOGY

PUBLIC SOCIOLOGY

THE CONTEMPORARY DEBATE

Lawrence T. Nichols

editor

Transaction Publishers
New Brunswick (U.S.A.) and London (U.K.)

Library of Congress Catalog Number: 2007021251
ISBN: 978-0-7658-0387-0
Printed in the United States of America

Library of Congress Cataloging-in-Publication Data

Public sociology : the contemporary debate / Lawrence T. Nichols, editor.
    p. cm.
  Includes bibliographical references.
  ISBN 978-0-7658-0387-0
  1. Sociology--Methodology. 2. Sociology--Philosophy. I. Nichols, Lawrence T.

HM511.P84 2007
301--dc22

2007021251

Contents

Introduction

Lawrence T. Nichols

Within every field of learning, there are times of intense excitement, when particular ideas or emergent paradigms seem to be on everyone's mind. Such moments often release deep emotions, as practitioners enter into spirited debate or enlist in new movements and counter-movements. Thus, within the discipline of psychology there have been periodic upheavals in conjunction with such diverse developments as Freudian and Jungian analysis, Watsonian and Skinnerian behaviorism, the humanistic approaches of Gordon Allport and Carl Rogers, Victor Frankl and Erik Erikson, and, more recently, the "positive psychology" movement championed by Christopher Peterson and Martin Seligman. In the same way, economics has often experienced turmoil and transformation as its classical nineteenth-century paradigm gave way to the Keynesianism of the 1930s, which was eventually challenged by the "supply side" approaches of the 1970s and more recent "behavioral economics."

The field of sociology has provided a stage upon which a long series of intellectual movements have enacted their dramas. In the late nineteenth and early twentieth centuries, Social Darwinism (especially as formulated by Herbert Spencer and William Graham Sumner) gained widespread hegemony in the United States, but it was challenged by more humane "social ethics" approaches grounded in the Social Gospel movement and Progressive era politics (e.g., the writings of Jane Addams and her circle on urban life, or the early critique of white-collar crime by Edward A. Ross). The 1920s and 1930s witnessed efforts to promote a "hard science," even scientistic, approach related to the social planning emphasis of the times (e.g., the works of Franklin Giddings, F. Stuart Chapin, and William F. Ogburn). For two decades following World War II, a "systems" model (most often associated with functionalism, Talcott Parsons and Robert K. Merton) dominated professional discourse to an unusually

1

high degree, only to be supplanted by a "power elite" (championed by C. Wright Mills), "political economy," and "world systems" (associated with Immanuel Wallerstein) counter-movement in the 1960s and 1970s. Varieties of neo-Marxism (e.g. Richard Quinney), feminist theories (e.g., Patricia Hill Collins), and other conflict-oriented approaches (e.g., Jurgen Habermas, Anthony Giddens) also proliferated and prospered. From the late 1970s to the new millennium there was a resurgence of interpretive sociologies of meaning, including constructionism (e.g., Malcolm Spector and John Kitsuse, Joel Best) and deconstructionism (e.g., Stephen Pfohl), along with a reinvigorated symbolic interactionism (e.g., the works of Norman K. Denzin and Gary Alan Fine) which came to be known, collectively, as "the postmodern turn" in the field.

In August 2004, Professor Michael Burawoy of the University of California, Berkeley, delivered a presidential address to members of the American Sociological Association entitled, "For Public Sociology." As veterans of annual national conferences can attest, most speeches of this kind elicit, at best, polite applause and ephemeral discussion. On this occasion, however, the response was dramatically different. Somehow, Burawoy "struck a nerve" and initiated a spirited debate about the nature and possibilities of his concept of public sociology. Perhaps this heightened response is attributable, in part, to the quality of the ideas articulated in the four-part paradigm of professional, critical, policy, and public sociology, combined with the passion and charisma of their advocate. Or perhaps the intensely enthusiastic and sharply critical reactions of sociologists to the proposal should be understood in terms of a broader *zeitgeist* and the longing of sociologists to be regarded once again as experts on the most pressing issues of the times, as happened in the heady days of the 1960s. Very likely there is no final explanation. What is abundantly clear is that "public sociology" has now assumed center stage.

In my capacity as editor of *The American Sociologist*, I was pleased to facilitate and extend this discussion by bringing out a thematic issue (volume 36, numbers 3-4, winter 2005) on this topic. The project was deeply indebted to the organizational efforts and commitment of Professor Vince Jeffries, who solicited manuscripts and served as a liaison with individual authors. A broad range of scholars contributed conceptual and empirically grounded papers. Michael Burawoy also played a key role by engaging the papers and articulating an extensive rejoinder.

This might have remained the culmination of the project. At Transaction Publishers, however, Irving Louis Horowitz (long recognized for his writings on sociology and public policy) and President Mary Curtis envisioned greater possibilities and concluded that a book about public sociology, based on our *American Sociologist* issue, might reach a broader audience. Having been offered the opportunity to serve as editor of this volume, I suggested extending the discussion once more, by incorporating two additional articles from earlier issues of *The American Sociologist* and by soliciting two new contributions. Meanwhile, we decided to alter the arrangement of the materials, by interspersing the four new papers with the nine from the thematic issue. Michael Burawoy's essay, fittingly, will remain the final article. It should be noted, however, that this paper responds only to the eight papers from the winter 2005 issue. Professor Burawoy had hoped to expand his discussion to include the new materials as well, but the burden of other commitments finally precluded this.

Although, as noted, the topic of public sociology is a current and "hot button" issue, it also represents a longstanding impulse in the field of sociology that is easily traceable to such classical figures as Auguste Comte, Karl Marx, Harriet Martineau, Emile Durkheim, and Jane Addams. While limitations of space preclude an encyclopedic treatment, an effort has been made to provide a relatively broad historical perspective as necessary backdrop to the present debate.

We begin with three historical articles. "Back to the Future: Settlement Sociology, 1885-1930," by Patricia Madoo Lengerman and Jill Niebrugge-Brantley (originally published in *The American Sociologist*, volume 33, number 3, fall 2002) examines the pioneering studies by settlement-movement sociologists that focused especially on urban problems and the "neighborly relation." Sean McMahon follows with a discussion of selected public speeches of Edward Alsworth Ross, a fascinating and controversial figure in the early decades of academic sociology, whose engagement with the issues of the day would surely qualify him as a public sociologist in our contemporary sense. Chet Ballard next contributes an historical sketch of the founding of the Association for Humanist Sociology, a group committed to using sociology as a tool for social change and the building of a more just society.

The fourth and fifth articles in the volume report on the personal efforts of their authors to engage in public sociology. Edna Bonacich recounts her involvement with the organized labor movement over a period of several decades. Norella Putney, Dawn Alley, and Vern Bengtson likewise detail their work in social gerontology, which they characterize as "public sociology in action."

The remaining articles provide theoretical treatments of the issues, from both supportive and critical points of view. David Boyns and Jesse Fletcher engage the four-part Burawoy model, and argue for what they call the "strong program in professional sociology." Vincent Jeffries, meanwhile, seeks to extend the discussion by calling attention to the relevance of the work of the late Pitirim A. Sorokin (especially in the area of altruism) for developing a public sociology. Christopher Chase-Dunn articulates conceptual links between the Burawoy proposal and a global vision, arguing that sociologists must move beyond the role of "citizens" in the traditional nation-state sense and work toward a "global commonwealth." Robert Prus offers a broadly pragmatist perspective on the necessary foundations of a public sociology that addresses "humanly engaged realities."

Offering a "guide for the perplexed," Steven Brint expounds eleven theses that respond to the eleven major points in Burawoy's presidential address on public sociology, with an emphasis on the continual need to create new scientific knowledge in the field. Jonathan Turner questions the entire Burawoy project, and expresses concern about its potentially harmful effects on the discipline. Neil McLaughlin, Lisa Kowalchuk, and Kerry Turcotte stake out an intermediate position, arguing that the discipline does not need to be protected against the "public sociology" approach, but they also question Burawoy's treatment of what he calls "critical" sociology."*

In the final chapter, "Third-Wave Sociology and the End of Pure Science," Michael Burawoy offers a rejoinder to the majority of the papers. Demonstrating the spirit of genuine scholarly inquiry, he takes seriously the questions raised by critics and provides a thoughtful response that moves the dialogue forward. Wherever we stand, as individuals, on the large questions debated here, all of us should be grateful for the stimulus and challenge that Michael has provided.

It is our sincere hope that the essays in this volume will reach a variety of audiences, including students, professional sociologists, and interested readers from the general public. All of us should be concerned about the shape and relevance of the field of sociology; for all of us, in one way or another, are part of the story.

---

*For a partial response to McLaughlin et al., see Appendix: Letter to the Editor by Mathieu Deflem at the end of chapter 12.

References

Addams, Jane. 1893. *Philanthropy and Social Progress*. New York: Crowell.

Allport, Gordon W. 1950. *The Nature of Personality*. Cambridge, MA: Addison-Wesley.

Best, Joel (ed.). 1989. *Images of Issues*. New York: Aldine de Gruyter.

Burawoy, Michael. 2004. "Presidential Address: For Public Sociology," *American Sociological Review* 70 (1): 4-28.

Canto, Victor A., Douglas H. Jones, and Arthur B. Laffer. 1983. *Foundations of Supply-Side Economics*. New York: Academic Press.

Chapin, F. Stuart. 1935. *Contemporary American Institutions*. New York: Harper and Brothers.

Collins, Patricia Hill. 1991. *Black Feminist Thought*. New York: Routledge.

Comte, Auguste. 1875-1877. *System of Positive Polity*. London: Longmans, Green.

Denzin, Norman K. 1991. *Hollywood Shot by Shot: Alcoholism in American Cinema*. New York: Aldine de Gruyter.

Durkheim, Emile. 1956. *Education and Sociology*. Glencoe, IL: Free Press.

Erikson, Erik. 1958. *Young Man Luther: A Study in Psychoanalysis and History*. New York: Norton.

Fine, Gary Alan. 1995. *A Second Chicago School?* Chicago: University of Chicago Press.

Frankl, Victor E. 1963. *Man's Search for Meaning: An Introduction to Logotherapy*. New York: Pocket Books.

Freud, Sigmund. 1965. *The Interpretation of Dreams*. New York: Avon Books.

Giddens, Anthony and Philip Stanworth (eds.). 1974. *Elites and Power in British Society*. London: Cambridge University Press.

Giddings, Franklin. 1921. *The Principles of Sociology*. New York: Macmillan.

Habermas, Jurgen. 1979. *Communication and the Evolution of Society*. Boston: Beacon Press.

Horowitz, Irving Louis. 1967. *The Rise and Fall of Project Camelot: Studies in the Relationship between Social Science and Practical Politics*. Cambridge, MA: MIT Press.

-----. 1972. *Foundations of Political Sociology*. New York: Harper and Row.

Jung, Carl G. 1933. *Modern Man in Search of a Soul*. San Diego: Harcourt Brace Jovanovich.

Keynes, John Maynard. 1936. *The General Theory of Employment, Interest and Money*. New York: Harcourt Brace.

Martineau, Harriet. 1837. *Society in America*. London: Saunders and Otley.

Marx, Karl. 1961. *Economic and Philosophic Manuscripts of 1844*. Moscow: Foreign Language Publishing House.

Merton, Robert K. 1949. *Social Theory and Social Structure*. New York: Free Press.

Mills, C. Wright. 1959. *The Power Elite*. New York: Oxford University Press.

Ogburn, William F. 1937. *Social Characteristics of Cities*. Chicago: International City Managers' Association.

Parsons, Talcott. 1951. *The Social System*. New York: Free Press.

Peterson, Christopher and Martin Seligman. 2004. *Character Strengths and Virtues: A Handbook and Classification*. Washington, D.C.: American Psychological Association.

Pfohl, Stephen (ed.). 2006. *Culture, Power and History: Studies in Critical Sociology*. Boston: Brill.

Quinney, Richard. 1977. *Class, State, and Crime*. New York: McKay.

Rogers, Carl. 1961. *On Becoming A Person*. Boston: Houghton, Mifflin.

Ross, Edward A. 1907. *Sin and Society: An Analysis of Latter-Day Iniquity*. Boston: Houghton, Mifflin.

Seligman, Martin E. P. 2002. *Authentic Happiness: Using the New Positive Psychology to Realize Your Potential for Lasting Fulfillment*. New York: Free Press.

Skinner, B. F. 1938. *The Behavior of Organisms, An Experimental Analysis*. New York: Appleton-Century-Crofts.

Spector, Malcolm and John I. Kitsuse. 1977. *Constructing Social Problems*. Menlo Park, CA: Sage

Spencer, Herbert. 1904. *Principles of Sociology*. New York: Appleton.

Sumner, William Graham and Albert G. Keller. 1927. *The Science of Society*. New Haven: Yale University Press.

Wallerstein, Immanuel. 1974. *The Modern World-System*. New York: Academic Press.

Watson, John B. 1925. *Behaviorism*. New York: The People's Institute Publishing Co.

1

Back to the Future: Settlement Sociology, 1885–1930

Patricia Madoo Lengermann and Jill Niebrugge-Brantley

Between 1885 and 1930, as sociology was becoming an academic discipline, sociology was also being practiced intelligently, innovatively, and self-consciously outside the academy in the social settlements that grew up in America's major cities. In this paper, we first define and give a brief overview of the settlement movement in America; second, we show how the settlement workers were sociologists in their self-definition and action and in their relations with other sociologists; third, in the body of the paper, we describe the sociology done by the settlements in terms of the empirical research they undertook and the theory they created. Our argument is that settlement sociologists produced empirical studies that were both substantively significant and methodologically pioneering; that they did so in terms of a coherent social theory unique in its focus on "the neighborly relation"; and that both their research and theory were part of a critical, reflexive, and activist sociology.

This paper deals with a moment—largely forgotten by sociologists—when sociology in the United States played a vital role in improving the lives of individuals and groups and in shaping government policies to produce a more just society.[1] Between 1885 and 1930, as sociology was becoming an academic discipline, sociology was also being practiced intelligently, innovatively, and self-consciously outside the academy in the social settlements that grew up in America's major cities. Settlement sociology is important to sociologists today for what it tells about how sociology can function in the practical world, for lessons it teaches about social movements and social change, and for the evidence it gives of a forgotten continuity in the American sociological tradition. In what follows, we first define and give a brief overview of the settlement movement in America; second, we show how the settlement workers were sociologists in their self-definition and action and in their relations with other

7

sociologists; third, we describe the sociology done by the settlements in terms of the empirical research they undertook and the theory they created. We conclude with an observation about some essential continuities in the American sociological tradition.

Definition and Historical Overview

The first settlement is usually considered to have been Toynbee Hall, started in 1884 by Oxford students under the influence of Canon Samuel Barnett. It was named in honor of Arnold Toynbee, an early Oxford exponent of the idea of bridging class differences by having privileged class young men live among the working poor in the Whitechapel district where Barnett had a church. In 1886, Stanton Coit, after a brief stay at Toynbee Hall, started the first American settlement on the Lower East Side in New York City, known first as The Neighborhood Guild and later as University Settlement. In September 1889, unaware of Coit's efforts but also impressed by Toynbee Hall, Jane Addams and Ellen Gates Starr opened what became the archetype and dominant U.S. social settlement, Hull House, in Chicago's desperately poor 19th ward. That same year, in October, Vida Scudder and Jean Fine and other graduates of Smith College opened the College Settlement at 95 Rivington Street, in New York City. By 1890, the College Settlements Association had begun recruiting workers and getting funding. In 1891, Andover House (later South End House) was started in Boston by W. J. Tucker and Robert A. Woods; Lillian Wald established the Henry Street Settlement on the Lower East Side in 1893; Graham Taylor started the Chicago Commons on the West Side of Chicago in 1894. By 1897 there were seventy-four American settlements; 103 by 1900; 204 by 1905, and by about 1910 there were 413 U.S. organizations identified as settlements.[2]

In 1911, Robert A. Woods and Albert J. Kennedy published *The Handbook of Settlements*, which attempted to "present an outline of the material facts about every settlement in the United States" (Woods and Kennedy 1911: v). Woods and Kennedy claimed to have read "every publication issued by" the settlements included and to have "visited . . . the large majority of the houses and . . . discussed . . . their development and program . . . with their leading representatives" (1911: v). Looking at their report, we see that around 1910 the 413 U.S. settlements were in thirty-three states and Hawaii, with particularly dense concentrations in the major cities—New York, Chicago, Boston, Philadelphia, Los Angeles, San Francisco. There is an important gender component in settlement work in the United States; *The Handbook* shows 1,077 women residents and 322 men; 5,718 women volunteers and 1,594 men; 216 women as head residents and eighty-five men.[3] This gender pattern is significant because it shows a sociological enterprise in which women played a major role in the classic period and, perhaps, helps explain the resonances between settlement sociology and feminist sociology.

Settlement residents were themselves much interested in delineating the uniqueness of their venture. Samuel Barnett himself wrote: "Settlements . . . simply open a way by which the members of one class in society may live in the midst of another class. They have no platform, no program, and their members do not come to do their neighbors good. They represent the education which is by permeation" (S. Barnett, 1970 [1906]: 80-81). In the most famous expression of the settlement in America, Jane Addams, in the 1892 address which launched her as a major figure in the world of social reform, presented the following understanding at The School of Applied Ethics in Plymouth, Massachusetts:

The Settlement, then, is an experimental effort to aid in the solution of the social and industrial problems which are engendered by the modern conditions of life in a great city. It insists that these problems are not confined to any one portion of a city. It is an attempt to relieve, at the same time, the over-accumulation at one end of society and the destitution at the other; . . . . It should demand from its residents a scientific patience in the accumulation of facts and the steady holding of their sympathies as one of the best instruments for that accumulation. It must be grounded in a philosophy whose foundation is on the solidarity of the human race, a philosophy which will not waver when the race happens to be represented by a drunken woman or an idiot boy. Its residents must be . . . content to live quietly side by side with their neighbors until they grow into a sense of relationship and mutual interests . . . [,] to see the needs of their neighborhood as a whole, to furnish data for legislation, and use their influence to secure it . . . [,] to regard the entire life of their city as organic, to make an effort to unify it, and to protest against its over-differentiation. (Addams 1893: 21-23)

In a speech at the Chicago World's Fair in 1893, Robert A. Woods, the head resident at South End, Boston, explained:

A . . . settlement collects a group of men or women of trained minds and elevated moral sense, who reside together in one of the poorer and more crowded sections of a city or town for the sake, in the first place, of observing carefully from day to day the varied and shifting phases of the life of the people, particularly of those who live and work immediately around them; and in the second place, of bringing to bear at every different point of human need, particularly so far as the immediate district is concerned, such of the resources of society as are necessary to supply those needs. (Woods 1970 [1893]: 30)

And Mary Kingsbury Simkhovitch, who founded Greenwich Settlement in New York in 1902, reflected in her autobiography, significantly titled, *Neighborhood* (1938):

The realism of the settlement [is] its understanding that, before any help can be given, the situation must be felt, realized and understood at first hand. . . . Only that which is lived can be understood and translated to others. The chief mission of the settlement has always been its accenting of contact as fundamental. At the university, one learned that scholarship is a sincere effort to get at truth. . . . In the settlement one learned much the same thing, but in the first case it was through contact with minds and in the other by contact with people and situations. The settlement is, indeed, from this aspect a graduate school. (1938: 39)

Thus, we see six qualities distinguishing the settlement: (1) it is a movement across class lines; (2) it requires, as its name suggests, that people from a relatively privileged class attempt to live with people who are from disempowered classes; (3) it asks that that living be done in "a neighborly relation"; (4) it expects that the privileged class persons will learn from their experiences; (5) it suggests that that learning may be both informal and systematic; (6) it expects settlement residents to use what they learn to change society to effect a more just distribution of socially produced goods.

Settlement Work as Sociological Work

In this period, 1883–1930, when American sociology was being invented, what we now take for granted as the actual material conditions of being a sociologist—credentialing through degree, employment as a professor, publication in disciplinary journals, and use of specialized vocabulary—was only one possibility among many. Indeed, in the last two decades of the nineteenth century, sociology was as much a part of political discourse as it was an academic enterprise. Sociologists often acted as public intellectuals on both sides of the ideological spectrum—as social Darwinist apologists for the status quo, but more frequently in reform or progressive politics. The word "sociology" had the dual meaning that "psychology" has retained to this day; referring to both a field of study and the thing being so studied. A nineteenth century contemporary looking at "sociology" would have as easily turned to the settlement as to the university—indeed, we could argue perhaps more easily, because the university did not necessarily contain a sociology department (the first being founded at Chicago in 1892); but the settlement always acknowledged itself in some way as concerned with "sociology."

We are not here saying that all settlement workers were sociologists, but that the settlements as a collective enterprise and many settlement workers as individuals saw themselves as doing sociology. Scholars writing from the perspective of a new, i.e., inclusive, history of sociology must answer the challenge of whether what they describe is indeed sociology and whether the people they name are indeed sociologists. In making our claim for the settlements as part of sociology, we draw on criteria developed by Dirk Käsler (1981) and by Mary Jo Deegan (1991) which argue that individuals be considered as sociologists if they acted as members of a sociological community, engaging in at least one of the following activities: employment as a sociologist; membership in a national sociological association; publication framed by an explicit concern with sociological principles; self-identification as a "sociologist"; and recognition by contemporaries as a sociologist (Käsler, 1981; Deegan, 1991). Using these criteria, we trace the settlement's relationship to sociology in the careers and personal statements of settlement workers, in the programmatic statements by settlements, in the social science publication of settlement workers, and in the presence of academic sociologists in settlement sociology—as well as in the research and theoretical work of settlement sociologists which forms the focus of the third section of the paper.

A self-conscious sense of themselves as working in the field of sociology is present in many of the leading settlement residents' memoirs. Representative are those of Graham Taylor and Mary Kingsbury Simkhovitch. Taylor, the founder of the Chicago Commons settlement and a professor of sociology at the Chicago Theological Seminary, titled his autobiography *Pioneering on Social Frontiers*, referring to the new urban America and the academic development of sociology:

> Here then [in Chicago in 1893] I found myself between two frontiers. The one in the front faced me with its advancing lines of academic research and its picket lines of social pioneers, who were followed by the supporting ranks of the more progressive citizens. And there was that frontier in the rear, across which lived and labored the vastly outnumbering multitude of wage-earning people and commercial middle men and their families who constituted the mass life to which religion was also to be interpreted and applied. . . .
>   It seemed to me that the advancing frontier could be seen more clearly from the rear . . . . (1930: 5-6)

Taylor saw himself as a pioneer in teaching sociology and his autobiographical reflections on teaching in those early years illustrates what we have said about a discipline in its infancy with many possible paths before it. Noting that "I well remember how completely I was thrown back upon my own resources. For more than a decade there were no such reference texts available for sociological use in the classroom as there were in philosophy, of history, economics, and political science." Taylor recalls the significance of the settlement experience in clarifying this new discipline:

What I did not find in literature came to me unbidden from contemporary life. Voices rang out from very diverse fields of social action, bearing deeply home to me their incentive to more specialized study of social phenomena and effort. The new and impelling notes struck by these men and women who were working far apart from one another seemed to breathe the same spirit. They led me to realize that long before there was any scientific formulation of the social sciences or the philosophy of society there was a movement in life like that of a brooding spirit–the *Zeit Geist*. What they did or wanted done was long afterward recognized to have assumed a "sociological attitude" . . . . (Taylor 1930: 391-392)

A similar path is traced by Simkhovitch who identifies a key turning point in her undergraduate education at Boston University occurring about 1889 when she joined the Brotherhood of the Carpenter, an Anglican congregation led by the Reverend W. D. P. Bliss, the editor of the *Encyclopedia of Social Reform* and a Fabian Socialist. Simkhovitch was assigned

a club of girls called the Primrose Club. This was my first opportunity to know colored people well and also my first chance to lead a club. The members invited me to their homes, and when I saw the primitive wooden houses in the rear of Beacon Hill, with yard toilets and no bathing facilities, I was amazed. "Who owns this house?" I asked the mother of one of the club girls, and in reply I discovered that the owner was a senior warden in one of Boston's oldest parishes! . . . . How could this be?

I now began to be more interested in social studies and less absorbed in classical literature . . . . [I] had to find out for myself as best I could what was the matter with my colored friends' houses. (Simkhovitch 1938: 40-41)

Because of this turn to social studies, Simkhovitch went on to graduate work at Radcliffe, in Berlin—with Georg Simmel—and at Columbia; she studied Spencer, Marx, the Pragmatist philosophers, and Fabian Socialism, and had collegial relationships with Beatrice and Sidney Webb and Franklin Giddings. Simkhovitch calls "this course of study the first step necessary for the practical sociologist" (Simkhovitch 1938: 45-46).

Similar evidence could be offered for a host of settlement workers— Edith Abbott, Sophonisba Breckinridge, Anna Julia Cooper, Florence Kelley, Vida Scudder, Mary Roberts Smith, Ida B. Wells-Barnett, Robert Woods. Mary Jo Deegan's landmark study, *Jane Addams and the Men of the Chicago School, 1892–1918* (1988), offers a definitive analysis of Addams' relationship with key sociologists.

A consciousness of the importance of sociology in the work of the settlement is present in numerous reports and mission statements by the settlements. For instance, the College Settlement Association's *Second Annual Report* in 1892 argues that "the establishment of fellowships for women who seek to pursue sociological studies in college settlements would perhaps help our movement more than any other one thing" and subsequent annual reports detail the achievements of fellowship holders: Isabel Eaton, Frances Kellor, and Mary Van Kleeck—all now recognized as early women sociologists who did important empirical sociological research (Alchon, 1998; Aptheker, 1973; Fitzpatrick, 1990)—were among the fellowship holders. The College Settlement in Manhattan listed first among its Activities "Investigations": "The house has for many years carried on a series of sociological studies; largely into aspects of women's and children's life and labor. . . " (Woods and Kennedy, 1911: 193-194). South End House in Boston, under its listing of Activities in the *Handbook of Settlements,* reports: "The objective study of neighborhood, district, and city conditions constitutes an important part of its work, and a considerable body of material dealing with phases of city life and institutions has been published" (Woods and Kennedy, 1911: 125). The Calhoun Colored School and Settlement in Lowndes County, Alabama named among its activities "sociological study of the county "(Calhoun Colored School and Settlement, in Woods and Kennedy, 1911: 6-7). The Bethlehem Institute in Los Angeles described itself as seeking "to interpret social conditions sanely and to draw the widest attention to the unfilled needs of the city as illustrated in the neighborhoods with which it comes in touch…[and which] has annually gathered the sociology students of the Southern California colleges into a social institute extending through a week" (Woods and Kennedy, 1911: 10).

Settlement sociologists who published in the *American Journal of Sociology* and the *Annals of the American Academy of Political and Social Science* included: Edith Abbott, Addams, Florence Kelley, Julia Lathrop, Benjamin C. Marsh, Mary McDowell, Mary White Ovington, Simkhovitch, Taylor, and Woods. Their acceptance as part of the sociological community is reflected in the lead article in the first issue of the *AJS;* editor Albion Small called for a new journal to produce both scientific and practical knowledge: "no subject which pertains to men's pursuits is beneath the notice of sociology"; contributors were to be "men and women who are gathering the materials of social philosophy from the most diverse sources"; contents would range from "methodology" to "social amelioration" to "social conditions"; the purpose was to increase people's understanding so that they could form "more effective combinations for the promotion of the general welfare" (Small, 1895: 14).

The settlements also helped to found and support their own journal of social science research, *Survey,* which was published from 1897 to 1952 under a variety of titles—*Charities* (Dec. 1897-Oct. 1905*), Charities and the Commons* (Nov. 1905-March 1909), *Survey* (April 1909-1932),

Survey: Midmonthly Journal of Social Work (1933-1948), and *Survey Graphic* (which alternated with the *Midmonthly* between June 1922-1932). Under all its various titles, the journal attempted to reach a wider audience than the increasingly professionalizing *American Journal of Sociology*, counted in part on newsstand sales as well as subscriptions (its long-time editors Arthur and Paul Kellogg believed as late as 1920 that an article by Addams assured a sellout of a *Survey* issue [Davis, 1973]), and focused on placing sociological insights before the general public. A typical issue of *Survey* combined social science graphs and analysis with photos, drawings, and articles on such topics as the spreading effects of the automobile, homelessness, the pacifist movement, and to mark the anniversary of Lincoln's birth, a special issue on race relations with articles by Addams, Sophonisba Breckinridge, W. E. B. DuBois, and Ida B. Wells-Barnett.

Many academic sociologists did research in various ways connected with the settlement and clearly saw the settlement as part of the practice of sociology; these included: Emory Bogardus (Northwestern University Settlement), W. E. B. DuBois (Starr Centre and College Settlement, Philadelphia), Franklin Giddings (Greenwich House), Charles R. Henderson (see Henderson 1899/1902), George Herbert Mead (Hull-House and the University of Chicago), Mary Roberts Smith (San Francisco Settlement), and Charles Zeublin (Northwestern University Settlement and Hull-House).

Settlement Sociology—Research and Theory

The purest evidence of the practice of sociology at the settlements lies, of course, in the work they created.

Empirical Research

The most striking immediate feature of settlement sociology is the wealth of empirical research it produced and the ingenuity it showed in inventing methods of social research in an age when academic sociology was trying to become more than social philosophy. The settlement sociologists assumed that one contribution social scientists could make to the problem of class division was accurate descriptions of the conditions of the working classes and of all groups living in dire poverty—immigrants, domestic servants, African-Americans, and the indigent old, sick, and mentally ill. They sought empirical evidence on the depth and dimensions of poverty in order to formulate policy and to persuade a general public of the need for social change. Woods (1893a) articulated this faith in the importance and utility of research:

The close, scientific study of the social conditions in the neighborhood about a Settlement is indispensable to its successes. . . . The movement of the Settlements will be false to its promise, it will cut off its own future, if it does not know for itself, and tell thinking people, and by its absolute statement of facts compel thinking people to hear, how the other half lives. The residents should become familiar with all that goes to make up the life about them,—what homes the people have . . . ; what food and drink . . . ; what clothes . . .; what work . . . .

After the study of the social statics of the neighborhood comes the study of its social dynamics. What the people are accomplishing for themselves both in their individual and home life, and in local organizations for whatever purposes, is a matter of absolute importance to a Settlement before launching into its . . . constructive activities. (Woods 1893: 69, 70)[4]

The settlement residents' most powerful weapon was their cultural capital. Their sociological studies of the conditions they discovered through their settlement work gave them a power base in knowledge at a time when as historian Davis acknowledges "little reliable information on social problems was available" (1967: 96). The research of the settlement sociologists meant that they were the people who could actually describe concrete conditions. They believed that science—understood in this instance as empirical investigation—could both describe and explain conditions and that out of such explanation and description might come solutions. They took seriously the problem of the search for those indicators that would best measure urban poverty and serve as a guide to reform legislation. Underlying that quest is a faith that it is possible to establish norms of social science research on whose validity researchers, policymakers, and the public could agree.

The settlements were involved in launching many major social science research projects. Among the most notable are:

1895 *Hull-House Maps and Papers By the Residents of Hull-House*, research directed by Florence Kelley.

1898 *The City Wilderness: A Settlement Study by Residents and Associates of the South End House* (Boston), principal researcher Robert Woods.

1899 *The Philadelphia Negro* by W.E.B. DuBois with Isabel Eaton, under the sponsorship of the College Settlement of Philadelphia and the University of Pennsylvania.

1902 *Americans in Process: A Settlement Study by Residents and Associates of the South End House—North and West Ends Boston*, principal researcher Robert Woods.

1904 *Out of Work: A Study of Unemployment* by Frances Kellor, working out of the Henry Street Settlement (New York City).

1905 *Five Hundred and Seventy-Four Deserters and Their Families: A Descriptive Study of Their Characteristics and Circumstances* by Lillian Brandt, Greenwich House Settlement (New York City) and *The Survey.*

1909–1914 *The Pittsburgh Survey* in 6 volumes, directed by Paul Kellogg, Kingsley House (Pittsburgh), and the Russell Sage Foundation.

1909 *Women and the Trades, Pittsburgh 1907–1908* by Elizabeth Butler.

1910 *Homestead: The Households of a Milltown* by Margaret Bynington.

1910 *Work Accidents and the Law* by Crystal Eastman.

1910 *The Steelworkers* by John Andrews Fitch.

1910 *Our Slavic Fellow Citizens* by Emily Green Balch of Denison House (Boston).

1911 *Half a Man: The Status of the Negro in New York* by Mary White Ovington, Greenwich House.

1914 *The Pittsburgh District Civic Frontage* by Paul Kellogg.

1914 *Wage-Earning Pittsburgh* by Paul Kellogg.

1917 *The Immigrant and the Community* by Grace Abbott, Hull-House.

1923 *The Zone of Emergence: Observations of the Lower Middle and Upper Working Class Communities of Boston 1905–1914* by Robert Woods and Albert J. Kennedy, South End House.

1936 *The Tenements of Chicago, 1908–1935* by Edith Abbott, Hull-House.

The above are representative book titles. It is important to stress that settlement sociology produced literally thousands of smaller studies published in the form of government reports, reports to the settlement, and journal or magazine articles. One panorama of this volume of work is given in the 1911 *Handbook of Settlements.* Some of this research, as we have said, was published in the *American Journal of Sociology,* the *Annals of the American Academy of Political and Social Science, The Journal of Political Economy, Quarterly Journal of Economics,* and, after 1920, *Social Forces*—to name just a few academic journals; but a review of the research also reveals several lost social science journals—*Charities, Charities and The Commons, Municipal Affairs, The Southern Workman,* and *The Survey.*

In arriving at a standard for accuracy, settlement sociologists were influenced by two developing traditions of empiricism. One was the tradition represented by Carroll Wright at the American Social Science Association and as first chief of the U.S. Bureau of Labor Statistics. Wright's particular interest seems to have been in developing the range of variables—especially of social conditions—that could be collected and tabulated by statisticians. These statistics were used by social reformers as "hard" evidence to advance the Progressive agenda. The second influence was that of British pioneers in empirical research, most particularly Charles Booth and Beatrice and Sidney Webb, who were interested in the general problem of how to use facts to generate policy-relevant theory. Charles Booth's master work *Life and Labour of the People of London* (1891) was well-known in United States social science circles. One finds references to Booth and Webb in the writings of most of the settlement sociologists (e.g., Edith Abbott, Addams, *Hull-House Maps and Papers,* DuBois, Eaton, Kelley, Taylor, and Woods). Settlement sociologists were more ready to incorporate these empiricist trends in social science than were most academic sociologists.

Settlement sociologists were enormously inventive in their data-gathering strategies; indeed, they pioneered for American sociology many of the strategies now taken for granted by academic sociologists: the survey, the interview, the questionnaire, personal budget keeping, participant-observation, key informants, and secondary data analysis (which included the census, legislation, memoirs and diaries, wage and cost of living records, court reports, social worker reports, tax rolls, nursery rhymes, industrial accident reports). They were also pioneering in their methods of presenting data—photographs, detailed colored maps of neighborhoods, tables, bar charts, graphs, statistical analyses, narrative accounts, and extended quotation from subjects.

One exemplar of this vast pioneering work is Crystal Eastman's volume in the Pittsburgh Survey, *Work-Accidents and the Law* (1910), which had its original publication in *The Survey.* Eastman's study is representative in terms of its author's career, its inventiveness in finding social indicators, and its place in linking research to policy. Eastman had graduated with an M.A. in sociology from Columbia University, had had further research training while a resident of Greenwich House, completed New York law school in 1907, and joined Paul Kellogg, another Greenwich House alum, on the Pittsburgh Survey staff. In her research into the causes and costs of industrial accidents, Eastman explains how she overcame the absence of state government records of industrial accidents by turning to local coroners' records on fatal accidents, and then goes on to describe her meticulous use of these records:

> We got permission to use these and made a record of every industrial fatality reported to the coroner during the twelve months from July 1906 to July 1907, taking down on a separate card for each case, the name and address of the man killed, his age, occupation and conjugal condition, the name of his employer, the circumstances of the accident, the names of important witnesses, and the verdict. The plan was to learn from the evidence in the coroner's record, how each accident happened, and to learn from visiting the family what happened after the accident, i.e., how great a financial loss was suffered by the family of the workman killed, how much of this was made up by compensation received from the employer, and how the family was affected in its economic life by the accident. When we have done this with the fatalities, we followed the same course with the records of three months' industrial injuries which we secured from the hospitals. (Eastman, 1910: 789)

Imposing order on her data, Eastman did an assessment of responsibility as far as the data permitted. She found that in 30 percent of the cases no one was responsible, in 30 percent the worker was responsible, in 30 percent the employer, and in 10 percent the responsibility was shared. Eastman insisted that research like hers should be used to generate solution, to social problems: "Investigation just for the sake of investigation does not appeal to me. Social investigators . . . should have not only evidence that there is an evil but a rough plan for remedying it in mind before they commence an investigation" (1910: 788). In the case of industrial accidents, Eastman articulated a clear social analytic principle for arguing that the law needed to be changed:

> If [industry] were carried on solely with safety as the first concern of all, there would be few accidents, but carried on as it is today in America, there are many accidents. . . . Every work-accident leaves a problem of poverty behind. . . . I am an enthusiastic advocate of this compensation law [because] it established the principle that the risks of trade, borne through all these years by the workmen alone, should in all wisdom and justice be shared by the employer. (Eastman, 1910: 789-794)

In *The Settlement Horizon* (1922), Woods and Kennedy claim the enactment of the Workmen's Compensation Law as a result in part of settlement action:

> The process by which workmen's compensation laws were secured is almost as suggestive as the result. For the first time a piece of radical industrial legislation was projected and agreed to in advance by employers, trade union leaders, and representatives of the general public. This method settlements had prefigured. The attitude and atmosphere which they had created were an influence toward making such relations possible; many who throughout the country strove most earnestly toward mutual agreement in framing the several bills had been in close relations with settlements. (Woods and Kennedy, 1922: 196-197)

The study of industrial accidents climaxing in the passage of the various state workmen's compensation laws shows the linkage between research and activism that was the hallmark of settlement sociology.

Social Theory

This extensive body of social science research, which produced many of the policies and understandings that still guide progressive politics, was informed by a distinctive body of social theory. In many instances, the theory is implied in research and practical policy publications by settlement workers. But many settlement sociologists wrote reflectively about the settlement project and its social science implications, creating a body of formally articulated theoretical work. Our review of the journal and monograph literature produced by the settlements shows six key formulators of settlement social theory: Addams, Barnett, Kelley, Simkhovich, Taylor, and Woods. Preeminent among these—both as recognized in her own day and for later students—was Addams, although Woods's writing also shows a serious engagement with social theory. What follows here as an explication of settlement sociology's theory draws primarily on Addams and Woods, but is modified by our sense of what settlement workers as a whole seem to have understood.

Settlement sociology saw as the essential feature of sociology that it is "a system or theory of social relations" (Brandt, 1910: 722). The central problematic, then, became a relational one—"the need to reconstitute connection." This wording of the problematic, which is ours, suggests several key ideas of settlement sociology: that the social world is historical and material; that social change is a permanent fact of social life; that the individual must be a fundamental explanatory unit in social analysis; that ethics are an integral feature of social life; that an ethically sound society is one in which members experienced social connection, and that contemporary society is marred by social disconnection.

When they spoke about "society," settlement sociologists meant particular social relations located in time and place; at the most general that time and place was the Western developed nations, most especially the United States at the end of the nineteenth and the beginning of the twentieth century. This society—their world to work with—was in the throes of massive and disruptive change. Understanding the world around them as the result of change, they took the fact of change as a permanent feature of social life and of the role of the settlement. The predominant and most troubling feature of this change was that it produced what we are calling "disconnection"—which they variously named "social disorganization," "maladjustment," "belatedness," and "the social problem." By "discon-nection" we mean the condition in which people relate to each other as objects, as means or barriers to some selected end. Because the other is not experienced as a full subjectivity, one experiences no mutuality of concern and, thus, the sense of one's self as a social being is diminished in the relationship. Disconnection may be the result of indifference or of the desire for domination. By "connection" we mean the experience of full sociality in relationship—interactively and imaginatively each person takes a full account of the other; ethically each has the sense of being in right relation with the other, each is able to identify with and act for common interests, each subjectively feels completed in relationship.

Settlement sociologists recognize at least three types of disconnec-tion—relational, societal, and subjective; they see these types of discon-nection ultimately involving the phenomenon of ethics which they take to be an appropriate and necessary subject for sociology. Relational disconnection exists when individuals live without any sense of common-ality of interest with either people of their own kind and/or with people different from themselves. Societal disconnection allows geographic areas and interest groups in society to work against each other. Settle-ment sociologists are struck by the contradiction that characterizes their society: that people are being brought together in greater numbers than ever before for the purposes of industrial production, but that such com-ing together is failing to produce social connection. Addams describes this situation:

> The social organism has broken down through large districts of our great cities. Many of the people living there are very poor, the majority of them without leisure or energy for anything but the gain of subsistence. They move often from one wretched lodging to another. They live for the moment side by side, many of them without knowledge of each other, without fellowship, without local tradition or public spirit, without social organization of any kind. Practically nothing is done to remedy this. The people who might do it, who have the social tact and training, the large houses, and the traditions and custom of hospitality, live in other parts of the city. The club-houses, libraries, galleries and semi-public conveniences for social life are also blocks away. We find working-men organized into armies of producers because men of executive ability and business sagacity have found it to their interests thus to organize them. But these working-men are not organized socially; although living in crowded tenement-houses, they are living without a corresponding social contact. (Addams 1893: 4)

The shared assumption guiding both settlement sociology theory and settlement practice was that its project was the reconstruction of "social contact."

Addams argues that this relational and societal disconnection produces a subjective disconnection which may be most reflected upon by the younger members of the educated class: "This young life so sincere in its emotion and good phrases and yet so undirected, seems to me as pitiful as the other great mass of destitute lives. One is supplementary to the other, and some method of communication can surely be devised" (Addams, 1893: 16). Her personal account of this subjective crisis is archetypal of what many settlement workers experienced. In the autobiography *Twenty Years at Hull-House* (1910), a best seller in its own day which has never been out of print, she recalls her encounter with poverty in London's East End and her sense of the inadequacy of her response. She remembers the horror of seeing from the top of an omnibus poor people bidding frantically for spoiled cheap food: "I have never since," she writes, "been able to see a number of hands held upward, even . . . when they belong to a class of chubby children who wave them in eager response to a teacher's query, without a certain revival of this memory, a clutching at the heart reminiscent of the despair and resentment which seized me then" (1910: 68). But she is as profoundly disturbed at the inadequacy of her response: in that moment of crisis her mind had shifted to a short story she had read in college by Thomas DeQuincey. She concludes that she, like others of the first generation of college women, "had taken [her] learning too quickly, . . . had lost that simple and almost automatic response to the human appeal, that old healthful reaction resulting in activity . . . " (1910b: 71). She had earlier generalized from this personal experience to the experience of "our so-called educated young people who . . . feel a fatal want of harmony between their theory and their lives, a lack of co-ordination between thought and action. . . ." Their theory tells them that "all men are united by needs and sympathies far more permanent and radical than anything that temporarily divides them and sets them in opposition to each other" (Addams, 1893: 6, 15). She sees the impulse to form the settlement arising out of a subjective disconnection felt by young educated people like herself confronting this "great social maladjustment."

As they sought to analyze and ameliorate these multiple disconnections, the settlement sociologists moved to one of their most distinctive theoretical arguments: that all these forms of disconnection—subjective, relational, societal—are linked to each other and to a more fundamental disconnection, a failure at the ethical level of individual and collective experience. They assert that the purpose of sociology is not simply to describe the ethics that a people may hold, but to help people understand the ethics that are appropriate to them in the situations in which they find themselves. Addams (e.g., 1893,

1895, 1896, 1902, 1907) in particular makes a cornerstone of her thought about the need to bring ethics into alignment with the new social forms created by the "socialization of production." The ethical failure of the current day is to limit one's responsiveness to other people to a small circle of persons like oneself; to be educated with the injunctions that one should "love one's neighbor as oneself " and then to restrict that sense of neighbor to one's own family or one's own class. As the new industrial order creates elaborate and extensive new forms of interdependency, the ethical order has to adjust and expand the sense of the community and the neighbor, of the persons about whom individuals are expected to care. Settlement sociologists saw this creation of a new ethics not only as spiritually necessary but as a practical necessity for the life of the community and the individual. This re-constitution of social connection along new lines, as a spiritual and practical necessity of social life, is the justification or *raison d'etre* for the settlements.

A second major and distinctive theme in settlement social theory is its solution to these various problems of disconnection—the neighborly relation. The neighborly relation is predicated on the belief that in certain fundamental ways people are alike. The settlement sociologists seem to formulate this sense of "alikeness" by acts of self-reflection. They imagine as the social actor an agentic embodied subjectivity who has desire, interests, emotions, and a capacity for ethical relation. Woods writes,

> There is, of course, in every person a large, impenetrable element of temperament, understood often least of all by this person himself, the resultant of age-long heredity; yet a considerable proportion of what usually goes for temperament in every life is found to be not unintelligible to the dynamic participant [that is, a neighbor or friend] in that life. (Woods, 1970 [1907]: 106)

Addams writes,

> I have never tried so earnestly to set forth the gist of the Settlement movement, to make clear its reciprocity as I have to [my neighbors]. At first we were often asked why we came to live there when we could afford to live somewhere else. I remember one man who used to shake his head and say it was "the strangest thing he had met in his experience," but who was finally convinced that it was not strange but natural. I trust that now it seems natural to all of us that the Settlement should be there. If it is natural to feed the hungry and care for the sick, it is certainly natural to give pleasure to the young and to minister to the deep-seated craving for social intercourse that all men feel. (Addams, 1893: 25)

Settlement social theory is particularly concerned with how the neighborly relation is constructed—especially in a situation which can seem so artificial as that of the settlement residents trying to relate as neighbors across enormous divisions of class and cultural background. Woods addresses this issue in a 1914 article in the *American Journal of Sociology*, in which he analyzes the neighborhood as a unit which permits the development of a particular relational intimacy:

> [O]ne of the most striking facts about the neighborhood is that, though it is not essentially an intimate circle, it is at bottom always a hospitable one, always ready to receive new recruits. The first impact of a new arrival may be chilling, but in due time the newcomer begins almost automatically to go through the degrees of this greatest and freest of human free-masonries. As Mark Twain has suggested, when a man sits down beside you in the railroad car, your first feeling is one of intrusion; but after a little something happens to make your being in the same seat a matter of common interest, and the feeling of recoil dissolves into a continuous friendly glow.
>
> It is surely one of the most remarkable of all social facts that, coming down from untold ages there should be this instinctive understanding that the man who establishes his home besides yours, by that very act begins to qualify as an ally of yours and begins to have a claim upon your sense of comradeship. (Woods, 1970 [1914]: 152)

Woods sees as part of the problem of social science that its practitioners, by virtue of their class background, have had little life experience of the neighborhood:

> Nearly all highly educated persons are snatched out of neighborhood experience at an early age, and few of us every really have it again. Thus our opportunity for experimental, pragmatic study of typical human relations is lost—lost so far that in most cases we forget that we are suffering loss. . . .[O]ur positive interchange is almost exclusively confined to the one sixth of the population of our cities and towns which make the professional and commercial classes—that is, the wide-ranging, unneighborly classes—we are inclined to think of the neighborhood as offering little more challenge to scientific inquiry than our almost faded-out neighbor remembrances would suggest. (Woods, 1970 [1914]: 152-153)

Woods sees in neighborly relation the basis for a new and much-needed methodology of social science: "Social science, if it is to be truly scientific, dealing with human beings, must use the most delicate human apparatus in the way of personal acquaintance and sympathy, in order to gain accurate and delicate results. . ." (Woods, 1970 [1893]: 35-36). The settlement worker learns the life of the neighborhood as "one friend comes to know about another friend"—bit by bit, picking up details as events occur in the person's life and the person wishes to make disclosure, being drawn into the feelings as well as the material facts of a situation. Making this same point and also arguing the settlement's duty to be activist on the part of its neighbors, Addams writes that the settlement:

> by virtue of its very locality . . . has put itself into a position to see, as no one but a neighbor can see, the stress and need of those who bear the brunt of the social injury.

. . If the settlement, then, is convinced that in industrial affairs lack of organization tends to the helplessness of the isolated worker, and is a menace to the entire community, then, it is bound to pledge itself to industrial organization . . . . And at this point the settlement enters into what is more technically known as the labor movement. (Addams, 1895: 183-184)

One of Woods's papers analyzing the role of the settlement sociologist is called "The University Settlements as Laboratories in Social Science." But among many settlement workers, there was a concern that "settlements as sociological laboratories" might become destructive of the neighborly relation. The women in particular emphasized the neighborly relation as an ethical brake on research. Addams did not like to think of settlements as "sociological laboratories" for that reason. Crystal Eastman (1910) had the same reservations; she felt she should not do research for its own sake but only as part of the quest for a solution to a problem. In her introductory comments to *Hull-House Maps and Papers*, resident Agnes Sinclair Holbrook was firm that:

Insistent probing into the lives of the poor . . . and the personal impertinence of many of the questions asked, would be unendurable and unpardonable were it not for the conviction that the public conscience when roused must demand better surroundings for the most . . . long-suffering citizens of the commonwealth. Merely to state symptoms and go no farther would be idle; but to state symptoms in order to ascertain the nature of the disease, and apply, what may be its cure, is not only scientific, but in the highest sense humanitarian. (Holbrook, 1895: 13-14)

Settlement sociology contained, as Holbrook's comments suggest, a significant self-reflective element. Typical of this sociological reflexivity is William Horace Noyes's presentation at the Conference of American Settlements (May 16, 1899), later published in *The Commons*. Drawing on Thorstein Veblen, Noyes warned against settlements becoming institutionalized—a concern of many of the settlement leaders from the beginning.[*] Noyes holds that "Good institutions—i.e., institutions that have proved themselves useful—like good habits lend themselves easily to the conservative forces of society" (1970 [1899]: 62). These institutions become "marks of class distinction." He argues that the settlement as "a mission of culture" may be an instrument in class conflict or class maintenance because "this culture is itself very largely an institution by which the leisure class—or the wealthy class, which is pretty much the same thing—maintain their reputability in the community, for it is only those with wealth and leisure who are able to attain a high degree of culture" (Noyes, 1970 [1899]: 64). He concludes with a call for the settlements to devote more of their effort to "the real cause of class distinction, viz., the economic" (Noyes, 1970 [1899]: 64).

This reflexivity is echoed by early settlement founder Vida Scudder in her concerns that settlements not become so institutionalized that they cease to serve their important function as "hot centres of new thought; they have swung free of the established order; in a very real sense they have been alien and antagonistic to it" (Scudder, 1970 [1900]: 72). Scudder calls for the settlements to remain true to the ethical impulse that gave rise to them: "that the conditions of life forced by our civilization upon vast numbers of the working classes, especially upon the poor in our great cities, are undemocratic, un-Christian, unrighteous; that only the surrender of life itself, probably of many lives of more than one generation can change them; but that in the name of American democracy, changed they must be" (Scudder, 1970 [1900]: 72). In settlement sociology, we thus have an authentically American tradition of critical and reflexive sociology concerned both with issues of material inequality and the ethical framing of human social life.

Conclusion

In the much reviewed *Visions of the Sociological Tradition* (1995), Donald Levine has written in a thoughtful passage on "The American Tradition":

> The challenge posed by the pragmatic synthesis for a science of society was three-fold. Sociology needed to develop a conception of social phenomena that featured the subjective mental processes of actors yet understood those subjective processes both as effects and causes of societal processes. It needed to develop a conception of social dynamics that depicted states of disorder as natural occurrences providing opportunities for adaptive innovation. Above all it needed to help create publics that could exert some kind of informed moral control over current problems and future directions. These tasks were addressed with extraordinary creativity by Charles Horton Cooley, William I. Thomas, and Robert Ezra Park. (Levine, 1995: 251, 252, 263)

Although Professor Levine does not treat of the settlement sociologists, his description serves as an external confirmation of our argument that settlement sociology is a very significant creator of this American tradition. As we have shown, settlement sociology built its theory and its practice on a set of foundational assumptions about the human actor as embodied, willful, purposive, and motivated not only by cognitive interests, but by emotions of sociability and kindness, by an ethical need to be in right relation with others, and by socially situated understandings of reality. Society was, for settlement sociologists, both the relationships among such actors, and the formative context of those actors' development and actions.

To settlement sociologists, change was an inherent quality of social life; as we have shown, they felt that change and disorder could be sociologically explained in terms of tensions between the ethical and productive dimensions in society. They saw around them the "disorder" that change could produce but they also saw "adaptive innovation" and defined themselves as agents of that process. They defined their projects of social research and analysis as a means for informing and mobilizing the American public to demand progressive change. Settlement sociologists organized to address the problem that Levine identifies as part of the pragmatist challenge and which continues to haunt American sociologists: how to make sociological insights available and meaningful to the general public. As Sprague asks in "(Re)Making Sociology: Breaking the Bonds of our Discipline": "If our primary goal is to support informed public discourse, . . . [s]ervice becomes the essence of the profession—a word that comes from the Latin word that means to declare one's beliefs openly. . . . Years ago a student asked me why there was a *Psychology Today* but no *Sociology Today*, no vehicle for systematically getting sociological insights into the popular media" (1998: 27). Over a hundred years ago, *The Survey* was a "Sociology Today." [9]

In all these ways, then, settlement sociologists laid the foundations for the pragmatic and reformist tradition in American sociology. Indeed, we might argue that "the extraordinary creativity" of Cooley, Thomas, and Park emerged out of a context in which the practices and understandings of settlement sociology were a familiar part of the intellectual landscape.

Notes

1. Although overlooked by sociologists, the settlement movement has been explored by historians. Especially interesting for sociologists are Allen F. Davis, *Spearheads for Reform: The Social Settlements and the Progressive Movement 1890–1914* (1967); Mina Carson, *Settlement Folk: Social Thought and the American Settlement Movement* (1990); Judith A. Trolander, *Professionalism and Social Change: From the Settlement House Movement to Neighborhood Centers, 1886 to the Present* (1987).
2. Debates about figures usually involve whether to count organizations with a strong religious affiliation and non-residential "centers."
3. This count does not include those settlements reported in *The Handbook* that listed only "volunteers" without any breakout nor does it include paid employees or students doing settlement work as part of a degree. Including these would, of course, increase the numbers shown.
4. The vocabulary of "social statics" and "social dynamics," of course, locates Woods in the sociological discourse community and the analytic tradition begun by Auguste Comte.

5.   See Shulamit Reinharz (1991: 176-177) for a fine analysis of Eastman's work as an example of what she calls "Feminist Action Research."
6.   Woods is a problematic figure who seems to have been on the conservative end of the Progressive political spectrum to which most settlement workers subscribed. Woods was interested in the whole idea of doing social research, did social research and wrote reflectively and theoretically on the issues of concern to settlement sociologists. But he leaned towards a "scientistic" view of the settlement perspective on its neighborhoods, may have over-romanticized the concept of the neighborhood, and was less open to arguments about racial and ethnic equality than most leading settlement figures and especially less so than Addams (Davis 1967; Carson 1990).
7.   This phrase is used by Lillian Brandt, a member of the editorial staff of *The Survey* and a worker at the Greenwich Settlement, in a book review. We use it precisely because it is not a central part of Brandt's argument but is presented as a taken-for-granted understanding.
8.   Thorstein Veblen (1861–1930) was a pioneering and critical social theorist, best remembered for *The Theory of the Leisure Class* (1899). Noyes is referring to Veblen's conception of institutions as habits of thought that reflect the ideas and interests of the ruling classes.
9.   The issue of accessibility to a general public has been a recurrent theme in sociological discourse, with champions as diverse as Alfred McClung Lee, Pitirim Sorokin, C. Wright Mills, and Herbert Gans, and most recently, of course, feminist sociologists like Sprague.

References

Addams, Jane. 1893. The Subjective Necessity for Social Settlements. In *Philanthropy and Social Progress,* edited by Henry G. Adams, 1-26. New York: Thomas Y. Crowell.

———. 1895. The Settlement as a Factor in the Labor Movement. *Hull-House Maps and Papers by the Residents of Hull-House, A Social Settlement.* Boston: Crowell. 183-204.

———. 1896. A Belated Industry. *American Journal of Sociology* 1: 536-550.

———. 1902/1907. *Democracy and Social Ethics.* New York: Macmillan.

———. 1907. *Newer Ideals of Peace.* New York: Macmillan.

———. 1910. *Twenty Years at Hull-House.* New York: Macmillan.

Alchon, Guy. 1998. The 'Self-Applauding Sincerity' of Overreaching Theory, Biography as Ethical Practice, and the Case of Mary van Kleeck. In *Gender and American Social Science: The Formative Years,* edited by Helene Silverberg. 293-326. Princeton, N.J.: Princeton University Press.

Aptheker, Herbert. 1973. Introduction. In *The Philadelphia Negro* by W.E.B. DuBois 1973 [1899], 5-31. Millwood, N.Y.: Kraus-Thomson Organization, Limited.

Barnett, Samuel. 1906/1950/1971. University Settlements. In *The Development of Settlement Work,* edited by Lorena M. Pacey, 78-86. Freeport, N.Y.: Books for Libraries.

Brandt, Lillian. 1910. Review of *Medical Sociology* by J.P. Warbasse. *The Survey* (February 12): 722.

Carson, Mina. 1990. *Settlement Folk: Social Thought and the American Settlement Movement, 1885–1930.* Chicago: The University of Chicago Press.

Davis, Allen F. 1967. *Spearheads of Reform: The Social Settlements and the Progressive Movement, 1890–1914.* New York: Oxford University Press.

———. *American Heroine.* 1973. New York: Oxford University Press.

Deegan, Mary Jo. 1988. *Jane Addams and the Men of the Chicago School, 1892–1918.* New Brunswick, N.J.: Transaction Books.

———, ed. 1991. *Women in Sociology: A Bio-Bibliographical Sourcebook.* Westport, CT: Greenwood Press.

Eastman, Crystal. 1910. Work-Accidents and Employers' Liability. *The Survey* (September 3): 788-794.

Fitzpatrick, Ellen. 1990. *Endless Crusade: Women Social Scientists and Progressive Reform.* New York: Oxford University Press.

Henderson, Charles R. 1899. *Social Settlements.* New York: Lentilhon and Company.

Holbrooke, Agnes Sinclair. 1895. Map Notes and Comments. In *Hull-House Maps and Papers, By Residents of Hull-House,* 3-23. Boston: Crowell.

Käsler, Dirk. 1981. "Methodological Problems of a Sociological History of Early German Sociology." Paper presented at the Department of Education. 5 November. University of Chicago.

Levine, Donald. 1995. *Visions of the Sociological Tradition.* Chicago: University of Chicago Press.

Noyes, William Horace. 1970 [1899]. Institutional Peril of the Settlements. In *The Development of Settlement Work,* edited by Lorena M. Pacey, 60-68. Freeport, N.Y.: Books for Libraries.

Reinharz, Shulamit. 1992. *Feminist Methods in Social Research.* New York: Oxford University Press.

Scudder, Vida. 1970 [1900]. Settlement Past and Future. In *The Development of Settlement Work,* edited by Lorena M. Pacey, 69-73. Freeport, N.Y.: Books for Libraries.

Simkhovitch, Mary Kingsbury. 1938. *Neighborhood: My Story of Greenwich House.* New York: W. W. Norton.

Small, Albion. 1895. The Era of Sociology. *American Journal of Sociology* 1: 1-15.

Sprague, Joey. 1998. (Re)Making Sociology: Breaking the Bonds of Our Discipline. *Contemporary Sociology* 27: 24-28.

Taylor, Graham. 1930. *Pioneering on Social Frontiers.* Chicago: University of Chicago Press.

Trolander, Judith. 1987. *Professionalism and Social Change: From the Settlement House Movement to Neighborhood Centers, 1886 to the Present.* New York: Columbia University Press.

Woods, Robert A. 1893. The University Settlement Idea. In *Philanthropy and Social Progress,* edited by Henry G. Adams, 57-97. New York: Thomas Y. Crowell.

———. 1970 [1893]. University Settlements as Laboratories in Social Science. In *The Neighborhood in Nation-Building,* edited by Robert A. Woods, 30-46. New York: Arno Press and The New York Times.

———. 1970 [1914]. The Neighborhood in Social Reconstruction. In *The Neighborhood in Nation-Building,* edited by Robert A. Woods, 147-163. New York: Arno Press and The New York Times.

Woods, Robert A. and Albert A. Kennedy. 1970 [1922]. *The Settlement Horizon.* New York: Arno Press.

Woods, Robert A. and Albert A. Kennedy, eds. 1911. *The Handbook of Settlements.* New York: The Russell Sage Foundation.

2

"From the Platform":
Public Sociology in the Speeches of
Edward A. Ross

Sean McMahon

Introduction: Calls for Public Sociology

For more than a century, scholars have debated the public aspect of academic sociology. In his ASA address of early 2004, Michael Burawoy advocated a more viable and visible discipline (Burawoy, 2005). Burawoy implored sociologists to step out of academia, at least periodically, to comment on important issues facing the American public. Sensing a crisis under the Bush administration and the Iraq war, Burawoy noted the power of one sociologist to assemble data and present an argument for or against a specific policy. Massed together, then, sociologists could make themselves heard on any number of critical issues.

In June 2004, the journal *Social Forces* hosted a roundtable discussion on Burawoy's pronouncement. The journal featured strong criticisms of Burawoy's ideas. Neilsen (2004: 1619) felt that Burawoy "greatly overestimate[d] the uniformity of the moral and political agenda of sociologists." Brady (2004: 1629-38) entitled his essay "Why Public Sociology May Fail," and argued that Burawoy's pronouncement lacked the specific and quantifiable practices of perhaps the last major call for public sociology—that of Herbert Gans.

Brady looked back to Herbert Gans's 1989 ASA address, which similarly implored sociologists to emerge from the academy. Yet Gans argued for more media visibility and the inclusion of public intellectuals and criticism in the work of sociologists. Unlike Burawoy's call for public visibility, Gans proposed internal incentives and measures for success (Brady, 2004; Gans, 1989).

These calls for public sociology reveal similarities to the interwar era (that is, the period between World War I and World War II). The discipline of sociology had, and continues to have, an identity crisis (Horowitz, 1993). Sociologists produce strong research but remain unsure of their relevance to the public. If 1989 saw the last calling for a public discipline before Burawoy's most recent announcement, scholars could look back further still to one of the founders of the discipline who was passionately involved in bringing sociology to the public. Edward Alsworth Ross (1866-1951) published over two hundred articles and thirty books throughout his long career; he also gave many public speeches which have never been systematically analyzed. His speeches cover a wide variety of themes. [1] This chapter will trace Ross's own concept of the discipline of sociology through three decades of public speeches. A sampling of his speeches will compare Ross's calls for action and consensus against those of Burawoy.

Ross as Public Speaker

"Why," Ross asked in his 1936 autobiography, "should a speaker with little grace, charm, fire, or art, be in such demand?" Indeed, he was in high demand in the mid-1930s as sociology enjoyed a period of unprecedented legitimacy in America. "Sociology can invest trite things with a fresh interest. Then I let out TNT truth—in earfuls!" (Ross, 1936: 298-99). Ross was a popular speaker for three reasons. First, he had a reputation as a provocative speaker. Second, his writings extended beyond the academy to the public in textbooks as well as numerous popular magazine articles. Finally, sociology itself achieved great popularity in the 1930s (Burawoy, 2005a: 2). His speeches provide a record of how the sociologist sold his discipline as well as his speeches to the public.

The audiences for Ross's speeches ranged from fellow sociologists or other academics at conferences to civic groups and women's organizations. Since the 1890s, Ross had participated in traditional academic discourse through journals and books. However, during his early years as a professor, he also emerged as a noted public figure at Stanford University where he was fired in 1901 for speaking out against immigrant labor (McMahon, 1999:13-26; Mohr, 1970). Eventually he was hired at the University of Wisconsin in 1906, and he remained there for thirty years. Even after his retirement, he thrived in the diverse open environment of Madison and traveled to speaking engagements across the

را اس ص زفت با مردم قلّات سخنرانی . آج . همری ارگا شک بوردکا . صکفت حا
رادیو نفر مردم رو بهتر کند ؟

country. Ross spoke to local groups and imparted knowledge to them in hopes of elevating their social awareness and levels of action. So he engaged in what Burawoy (2005: 7-8) called "organic public sociology." The "dialogue [and] process of mutual education" so vital to Burawoy's 2004 call for public sociology had, as one of its strongest proponents, an early champion of free speech.

Mirroring the later critiques of Gans and Brady, Ross noted the rigors of public communication. His first class, taught in the 1880s in Iowa as a young part-time instructor, was to a group of blind students. "Sometimes I was brought to a dead stop," Ross recalled. "No 'speculation' in those sightless eyes." Although peer review and anonymous critiques certainly provided feedback, Ross responded well to a live audience. He thrived on what he called his "platform work" and set himself on a personal mission to educate the public. "I hate to see the public get its political education via radio instead of the platform." Like today's mainstream media or the Internet, the mass communication of the 1930s contained biases and sometimes misinformed the public. Ross strongly distrusted the press and its control over public opinion. "Fakery would be obvious if they had to submit to the ordeal of the public platform!"[2]

The "public platform" fascinated Ross, but he had to appeal to a broad audience and instill in them a desire to learn. One of the earliest dated speeches in the Ross Papers is a revealing primer on Ross's marketing schemes for his public speeches. His 1921-22 offerings included the "startling" truth about post-revolutionary Russia and a speech on "the social question," which was more appropriate "for thoughtful groups." Finally, he offered a speech on the inequality of women. "It is more popular and entertaining than the others," he explained.[3] By offering a wide range of highbrow and lowbrow topics, Ross could both challenge and entertain various audiences. Thus, Ross promoted himself and his discipline in the accessible, yet intellectually stimulating environment of the public platform.

The Image of Sociology in Ross's Speeches

Burawoy's "public sociology" has as a given assumption that sociology exists as a legitimate discipline. Meanwhile Ross, as one of the discipline's founders, spoke to his listeners as a veteran of a hard-fought campaign. "In 1891 there were three sociology courses in the U.S.," he noted in an undated speech on sociological trends. "Now there are one thousand teachers." Originally trained as an economist, Ross switched in the 1890s to the newer and more exciting field of sociology. Decades later, Ross still found a purity of purpose in a discipline that had "never compromised itself." He praised the virtues of sociology—including honesty and disinteredness—and concluded with a "good outlook" for social problems.[4] He spoke with a positivistic perspective that was quite common in early sociological writings. Yet the discipline around him increasingly focused on research and hard data in response to social questions.

To maintain his legitimacy in a dynamic discipline, Ross often framed his speeches with an empirical viewpoint. "Born 'spell-binder' I am not," he noted in his "Platform" speech. "I must keep to the austere role of the man of science."[5] His "Social Outlook" speech, given in the mid-1920s, offered "encouraging views" on social issues such as the status of African-Americans or religious freedom. He assured his audience that sociologists actively researched topics of current interest. Their statistical surveys might not have interested outsiders so Ross infused current issues with his own personal flavor. "The proportion of women who give signs of frustration and bafflement," concluded Ross, "appears to be much smaller than in my boyhood."[6] Clearly, some of his data proved less than empirical, and his own personal observations sometimes yielded questionable truths.

As a public speaker, Ross projected an approachable personality within a rigorous academic discipline. For Ross, the gathering of data in an organized manner with a purpose of public efficacy—regardless of the type of data or the utility of its conclusions—translated into a tangible theme that the public could consume. Dorothy Ross (1991: 388) noted that in an era of rapid change "only a hard, technological science seemed capable of controlling [such a] fast-moving society." As practitioners of a cutting-edge science, sociologists by the 1920s had distanced themselves between "the lagging body of public policy and public understanding, and increasingly they looked to science to close the distance." Yet, as she noted later in her work (1991: 428-32) scientism exerted a significant influence on the discipline by the late 1920s. Its adherents, especially at Chicago, hoped to eliminate all emotion from sociological research. So Ross, as a founder of sociology, had to balance "hard" research and credibility with a folksy image that would entertain and enlighten audience members. He deliberately injected emotion and feeling into his speeches to counteract the cold intellectual reputation that sociology had in the eyes of the post World War I American public.

Ross's speeches to the general public fused personality with social discourse. When speaking to his peers, however, Ross was more explicit.

"How Sociology Grew," a speech from the 1940s offered "by a 'ground-floor' man who taught his first course in it fifty years ago," functioned as a primer to new students in the field. "Sociology is 'full of promise' to be sure," Ross explained, "but [it] hasn't as yet 'delivered' much." Like his own speeches, the writings of younger sociologists had to strike a balance between formality and public accessibility. "Make the style easy, colloquial, intimate," Ross explained, "but never vulgar or undignified." Sociologists had to communicate as intellectuals engaged in a dialogue with themselves and with the public but they could never stoop to the point of being totally lowbrow. Nor could they set out unrealistic goals. He warned scholars not to make sociology "over-confident, overseeing, or arrogant."[7]

Earlier, Ross had mentioned broad research on women and African-Americans, yet he had offered no specific reform ideas in his speeches. By the mid-1930s, however, sociologists were asked to address current issues and also to seek answers to social problems. Turmoil at home and abroad called for specific answers from a discipline that was well-established in academia. As sociologists were asked to solve increasingly complex questions, Ross called for restraint—but he still asked that the public call be answered. Burawoy also described a division of sociological labor (2005a: 6-7). Sociologists who chose to move beyond academia into the area of public action practiced what he called "policy sociology." Especially in his later years, Ross was a public sociologist who extolled the virtues of policy sociology.

The reformation of the American business system was a theme of several speeches from the Depression era. Ross, a vocal Progressive critic of the railroads, turned more conservative after his 1917-19 journey to Russia. "From my acquaintance with what the Russian Revolution cost," Ross offered in his autobiography "a cast-iron resolution: There must never be a violent revolution in our country" (Ross, 1936:170). His writings of the 1920s were friendlier towards business but, like many Americans, he turned bitter during the Depression.[8] In a powerful speech entitled "Declaration of Faith," Ross pointed to the consumer economic system which had "gone 'haywire' . . . so that the plain duty of . . . sociologists is to search out and relentlessly expose the masters and gougings, the idiocies and crimes which the captains of capitalism would like to conceal."[9] Ross portrayed a culture battle between outside forces and a small but committed band of scholars who often exposed uncomfortable truths. "Fear not, little flock!" he exclaimed in 1936 in an attempt to keep the discipline unified. Despite sociology's growth from "twelve to 1200," big businesses sought to "trample" it by cutting off funds and stifling research.[10]

Ross borrowed the imagery of the Russian Revolution, which he had experienced as an observer, and combined this with the tensions of the mid-1930s to create dramatic speeches. Sociologists, he explained in 1935, had the ability to examine society critically and impartially and "find at just what places the shoe is pinching." They could then freeze a moment in time and "gauge the comparative strength of crystallized or organized social forces." By experimenting with social policies, sociologists could determine what worked for the most people. In a 1936 speech, Ross identified himself as a pragmatist and aligned himself squarely with President Franklin Roosevelt. He rejected Marxist historicism or predestination that things were bound to happen. A combination of disinterested observation, a gathering of data, and a timely word to the public could avert disaster. "Confidently emit the warning," he explained in his conclusion, sounding almost as a clinician rendering a diagnosis. "You are in danger of a serious revolutionary outbreak."[11]

Burawoy (2005a: 15) also noted that American sociology had a unity of purpose and maintained social stability. "Sociology finds itself upholding civil society and the public sphere against the corrosive effects of market resurgence and state authoritarianism." He expressed confidence that, even in a time of crisis, scholars would find their voice. As Ross spoke to his "flock," Burawoy reached out to nonbelievers. "We have to demonstrate our public worth," he exclaimed (2004: 24). In Burawoy's time, as in Ross's, public sociologists had to balance an intellectual reputation with an awareness of current events.

In "Recollections of a Pioneer in Sociology," given in April 1941, Ross reflected on his own past and on the future of sociology. After fifty years in academia, Ross opined that in 1941 sociology was "50-60% of what it will be in 2000 A.D." He anticipated a steady rise towards a "glorious future." The fresh perspectives offered by sociologists first were grounded in research and scholarship and then engaged a receptive public. He concluded that sociology continued to flourish because it had "swept into the rubbish heap" all the "outworn traditions, false dogmas and unsound notions" of the past.[12]

For Ross, sociology had attained solid ground but still had not reached its full potential. His vision of "policy sociology" still was normative and not as active as that of Burawoy. Both Ross and Burawoy implored their peers not to rest on their laurels. Crises loomed in the public sphere, which also presented opportunities for sociology to prove itself.

Crisis and Consensus

In a speech from late in his career, Ross reflected back on his 1920 book *Principles of Sociology* (Ross, 1920). He was pleased to note that the book had withstood both the test of time as well as the quantification movement of the 1920s at the University of Chicago, which created opportunities for grant dollars, corporate funding, and academic prestige (Bulmer, 1984). But Ross was wary of this trend and offered in his speeches a purer type of sociology. "I offer no panacea," Ross plainly said in his "Principles" speech, "nor do I bid men to look for a time when social problems will be vexed." Quantification and large class sizes offered great promise for social engineering, especially as America moved out of the Depression. Yet Ross had simpler aspirations. If sociology could fix "one-fifth the avoidable problems of society," he told his audience that he would be satisfied.

Although pleased at the reputation of his 1920 work, Ross continued his speech with the understanding that soon it would no longer be relevant. His pioneering work helped move sociology from the Gilded-Age study of institutions, done most notably by Herbert Spencer, to the study of social processes, by which "one gets at the actual life of society." Ross's book analyzed thirty-seven different processes, but the increasing pace of life created still more progressions, thus rendering his book obsolete. An increasingly modernizing society soon would have little use for sociology. Perhaps to stir his audience, the enthusiast for the discipline concluded with a warning that "[no] more than one adult in five or six [will] pay any serious attention" to sociology.[13] So here the veteran lamented the impending demise of a discipline which he helped to found. The intended effect was to shock his audience and to convince them that a crisis was at hand.

In another speech, Ross answered a question that some in his audience may have asked: how could someone give one speech that praised sociology and its relevance followed by another speech that warned of its limited influence? He eschewed any "label" that people sought to affix to him. "Sociologists have queer, original ways of their own of looking at things," he admitted. "The only way of learning what they stand for it to listen to them." And, to keep his audience interested and anticipating his next speech, Ross varied his points of views on most topics. Someone hearing his speech would not know until they heard the actual speech how Ross might come down on a particular policy or public trend. "Thus I keep myself a puzzle and an object of curiosity and constantly the public comes back for more."[14]

Ross sought to keep sociology fresh and edgy in order to generate audiences for his own speeches. In a larger sense, he encouraged diverse academic viewpoints although if every sociologist were as difficult to pinpoint as Ross it would be hard to get a majority opinion on practically any singular issue. More recently, Burawoy encouraged a consensus as a challenge to politically charged times. Yet, as his critics (Light, 2005; Neilsen, 2004; Brady, 2004) noted, such an assumption lacked the vision of a truly diverse discipline. Ross himself likely would have rejected Burawoy's concept of consensus because this meant stagnation and irrelevance, which the still-emerging discipline could not afford in the prewar (pre-World War II) years. For Burawoy, comparing the majority of anti-war sociologists in the late 1960s with those during the Iraq war showed that "the political gap between sociologists and the public has widened" (2004: 24). Ross spoke from the platform during an age of consensus against totalitarianism, yet he tried to catalyze stagnant listeners. Several decades apart, both public sociologists share a vision of a discipline with great potential.

At the 1932 American Sociology Society banquet in Chicago, Ross was in rare form. In a broad introductory survey of the discipline, he noted that sociology had emerged out of the "self-justifying stage." He had played a central role in the normative phase by breaking from the determinism of Spencer and the limitations of economics or political science. "Our concern now is to 'deliver better goods,' i.e., to shed on social questions of the day a light even more clear and illuminating." Repeating a theme from some of his other speeches, and previewing what both Burawoy and his critics later would note, Ross lamented the untapped potential of sociology. It had yet to prove itself.

On this night, the critic of quantification who saw his own reputation wane in the crunch of numbers now praised new scholarly trends. "The new passion for measuring social or moral phenomena is encouraging." The speaker who had once used as "data" his own personal observations of womens' "signs of frustration" included himself in the outmoded methods of sociology. "You can hardly conceive what loose statements were put into circulation before the era of quantitative methods." He had found his 1920 book to be still relevant but soon it would outlive its usefulness; similarly, he took jabs at himself from the platform as president of the ASS. His mercurial image engaged audiences and showed a discipline in transition.

In another reversal, Ross moved on to a throwback idea that he had championed—and he noted it as a signal of consensus. "The Wardian idea that more and more will society undertake to shape its own destiny has completely triumphed among sociologists." The "Telic" idea, championed by Ross's close friend Lester Frank Ward, helped shape the social psychology school which eventually was moved entirely over to the field of psychology (Rafferty, 2003; McMahon, 1999:68-75). Here Ross cheered the creation of a common mind-set; if sociologists could agree on self-improvement then they could move on to establish a truly influential discipline.

Yet Ross warned that sociology could not retreat collectively into its journals and monographs in "cloistered detachment." As a precursor of Burawoy, Ross encouraged his peers to be more visible. "Sociology exists to serve men," he concluded. If asked to offer commentary on a subject of popular discussion, they should do so. Sociologists should neither "woo the spotlight" nor "leap gaily into the rough-and-tumble of popular controversy." Again, the same man who marketed himself as a popular speaker, and as a survivor of three grueling academic hearings on free speech—one of which cost him his job in 1901—returned to the center. Ross urged simplicity; an objective answer supported by factual data.

He left his academic audience with one final thought. Over the last century, sociologists have dealt with crises that galvanized the academic community, or even the public at large, and required immediate action. For Burawoy, that event was the Iraq war and the Bush presidency. For Herbert Gans in the late 1980s, it was the dismal state of academic sociology. Ross took issue with immigrant labor and invited controversy in 1896 as a supporter of William Jennings Bryan. Over the next four decades he had taken on many issues but he also had laid out a course of action for his peers. So, in 1932, he spoke from experience when he said that the confines of academia must be left behind to pursue immediate action. "There may come a time in the career of every sociologist when it is his solemn duty to *raise hell*."[15]

Ross had experienced this call to action many times throughout his career. He acted as a catalyst to the discipline in its founding and on into the mid-twentieth century. Similarly, Michael Burawoy has issued a call in the new millennium. The call for a public sociology always attracts controversy. Above all it should inspire both individual and collective reflection on the part of sociologists.

Notes

1.   The Edward A. Ross Papers are maintained at the State Historical Society in Madison, Wisconsin. Ross's speeches constitute some of reel 31, all of reel 32 and much of reel 33 in the microfilm edition of the papers. An indispensable guide to the microfilm is Harold Miller and Lynn Buckley Aber (eds.), *Wisconsin Progressives: The Edward A. Ross Papers, Guide to a Microfilm Edition* (1986). Many of Ross's speeches are not dated. In this paper each speech will be cited by its reel number and frame number (e.g., a speech contained on reel 32, frame 96 would be cited as EARP/M 32:96).
2.   "On the Platform," ND. EARP/M 32: 731-38.
3.   EARP/M 32: 587
4.   "Introductory Lecture in General Sociology," ND, EARP/M 32: 539-554.
5.   "Platform," 32: 732.
6.   EARP/M 33: 110-126; see also "Sociologist's Outlook," ND, 33: 197-210.
7.   "How Sociology Grew," ND, EARP/M 32: 482-83.
8.   Please see McMahon (1999) chapters 1 and 6 *passim*.
9.   "Declaration of Faith," ND. EARP/M 32: 202.
10. "45 Years of It," 29 December 1936. EARP/M 32: 309.
11. "Some Contributions of Sociology to the Guidance of Society," 1935, 1936 (*dates given in microfilm guide*). EARP/M 33: 220-221, 224.
12. "Recollections of a Pioneer in Sociology," 4 April 1941. EARP/M 32: 967-974.
13. "Principles of Sociology." ND. EARP/M 32: 879-886.
14. "Private Maxims." ND. EARP/M 32: 886-899.
15. "Remarks at the ASS Dinner" dated December 1932. EARP/M 32: 1008-1014. In his "Principles of Sociology" speech (see note above), Ross noted that a reporter from the Chicago *Tribune* had attended the banquet to hear Ross, a controversial speaker, on the podium. The reporter soon grew bored and told his companion that there had been "no news" at the banquet. Just as he got up to leave, the reporter heard Ross's exclamation to "raise hell." After the speech, the reporter returned to the *Tribune* offices from which he immediately sent the story across the AP wire. The story ran the next day, but only after the offensive word was sanitized as "h-ll."

References

Agger, Ben. 2000. *From Social Facts to Literary Acts*. Lanham, MD: Rowman and Littlefield.

Brady, David. 2004. "Why Public Sociology Will Fail." *Social Forces* 82: 1629-38.

Bulmer, Martin. 1984. *The Chicago School of Sociology: Institutionalization, Diversity, and the Rise of Sociological Research*. Chicago: University of Chicago Press.

Burawoy, Michael. 2004. "To Advance, Sociology Must Not Retreat." *The Chronicle Review* 50: 24.

_____. 2005a. "The Return of the Repressed: Recovering the Public Face of U.S. Sociology, One Hundred Years On." *Annals of the American Academy of Political and Social Sciences* 600: 68-85.

_____. 2005. "For Public Sociology." *American Sociology Review* 70: 4-28.

Gans, Herbert. 1989. "Sociology in America: The Discipline and the Public." *American Sociological Review* 54: 1-16.

Gattone, Charles F. 2006. *The Social Scientist as Public Intellectual*. Lanham, MD: Rowman & Littlefield.

Horowitz, Irving Louis. 1993. *The Decomposition of Sociology*. New York: Oxford University Press.

Light, Donald W. 2005. "Contributing to Scholarship and Theory through Public Sociology." *Social Forces* 83: 1647-53.

McMahon, Sean. 1999. *Social Control and Public Intellect: The Legacy of Edward A. Ross*. New Brunswick, NJ: Transaction Publishers.

Miller, Harold and Lynn Buckley Aber, eds. 1986. *The Edward A. Ross Papers: Guide to a Microfilm Edition*. Madison: State Historical Society of Wisconsin.

Mohr, James. 1970. "Academic Turmoil and Public Opinion: The Ross Case at Stanford." *Pacific Historical Review* 39: 39-61.

Nielsen, Francis. 2004. "The Vacant 'We': Remarks on Public Sociology." *Social Forces* 82: 1619-27.

Rafferty, Edward C. 2003. *Apostle of Human Progress: Lester Frank Ward and American Political Thought, 1841-1913*. Lanham, MD: Rowman & Littlefield.

Ross, Dorothy. 1991. *The Origins of American Social Science*. Cambridge University Press.

Ross, Edward Alsworth. "Papers." Madison, WI: State Historical Society of Wisconsin.

_____. 1920. *The Principles of Sociology*. New York: Century.

_____. 1936. *Seventy Years of It: An Autobiography*. New York: Appleton-Century.

3

An Epistle on the Origin and Early History of the Association for Humanist Sociology

Chet Ballard

ثدراطی کہ منجربہ بنیاکؐگذاری AHS ثددانی طالہ برزگشتہ و . مصاحبہیا، رنسا، واعصا .

This paper describes the preconditions leading to the founding of the Association for Humanist Sociology (AHS) in 1976, with accounts and descriptions of its founding and early years. Existing records, interviews, and correspondence with key informants, including past-presidents, longtime members, and former members, were utilized in preparing this report on the origin and earliest days of the Association for Humanist Sociology.

Prelude: The Humanist Movement in Sociology

The origin of the AHS has its roots in the struggle to return sociology to its original mission, that is, to produce knowledge that would be put to use to improve the human condition. While not all of the early sociologists shared this vision, the sociology of Karl Marx, Robert Park, Jane Addams, and Thorstein Veblen, among others, is testimony to the humanist values that once characterized the conventional practice of sociology (Lee, 1978). As participants in one of the "newer" social sciences, the aforementioned sociologists believed that sociological knowledge should not be the domain of élites and it should not be produced in exclusionary structures controlled by the privileged in academia. Throughout the last century, the rise and organizational maturation of sociology's premier professional society, the American Sociological Association (ASA), has been subject to troubling organizational patterns of social behavior commonly found in large organizations, namely bureaucratization, massification, elitism, corporate co-optation, and institutional discrimination (Lee, 1977). Two sociologists whose careers spanned the 1940s to the 1980s, Alfred McClung Lee (Drew University) and his life partner, Elizabeth

Briant Lee (University of Pittsburgh), battled problematic organizational behaviors from within the ASA, and later from outside, and in so doing made a lasting contribution not only to humanist sociology but to sociology in our time.

Al and Betty Lee championed the cause of sociologists whose training and academic credentials were not from the most prestigious sociology departments and whose research was not sponsored by the nation's top corporate and governmental sources. Within the ASA, Al and Betty spoke up for the marginalized sociologists and applied practitioners whose ideas were at odds with the ASA. Their experience with the ASA throughout the 1940s led them to conclude that the leadership of the ASA would not accept change in a more humanistic direction. The ASA executive committee's relationship with top business and governmental sponsors was too cozy and the Lees were convinced that those in charge of the ASA would not initiate meaningful changes in how sociology had come to be practiced. The time had come for the creation of a professional society that would practice a brand of sociology that would be responsive to society's social ills—a sociology that would return to its original focus of addressing the real world problems of everyday people.

The 1951 founding of the Society for the Study of Social Problems (SSSP) by the Lees was a direct response to the problems they had encountered in the ASA. "We thought then and we still believe that helping to create more open channels of professional investigations, organization, and communication for the experimentally minded, for the young, for the excluded, and for the dissident and creative was the greatest need facing our own students and our profession" (Lee and Lee, 1976: 6). For these reasons, the Lees founded the SSSP. "The existing social scientific societies are parts of the problems sociologists should be probing in their effort to make human society livable and hopefully more self-fulfilling for a great many more people" (Lee, 1977: 4).

Frustrated with their efforts to reshape the ASA's executive committee practices and annual meeting program structure, the Lees founded the SSSP within the ASA framework, and later, in 1976, they would join with others in founding the AHS, a professional sociological association that was intentionally built outside the structure of the ASA. These words from Al Lee's speech at the founding conference of the AHS in 1976 speak clearly to the reasons that led to the birth of the AHS:

The sociologies of Karl Marx and Friedrich Engels, or Sigmund Freud, or the older W. G. Sumner, the anti-plutocrat P. A. Sorokin, of C. Wright Mills, of W. E. B. DuBois, and of Willard Waller—not to mention the many outstanding humanist sociologists now alive—represent no "underground" movement in sociology. Neglected though they may be by ASA establishment figures, trivialized though they many times may be by their so-called interpreters in our textbooks, and whether or not you agree with them at all or in detail, they are great lights of our discipline. (Lee 1977: 6)

The Turbulent 1960s and 1970s

The Civil Rights Movement, the Vietnam War, the Women's Rights Movement, the Generation Gap, Kent State, urban riots, Attica State Prison, President Nixon and Watergate, the Pentagon Papers, Manson, the assassinations of JFK, Martin Luther King, and Bobby Kennedy, the Black Panthers, student protests—all were momentous events that rocked the institutional foundation of our society and energized the field of sociology. It seemed as if the nation was set aflame from within. The era produced sociologists who were concerned about the condition of humanity as a whole and many took to the streets, marching side by side with student activists and community organizers promoting social change. The gnawing recognition that something was wrong had already turned to violence, some brought directly into our living rooms each night through bloody televised reporting from the war in Indochina, the struggles of Freedom Riders in the Old South, and the shocking killings of the nation's top political figures. By the time that Alvin Gouldner (1970) wrote *The Coming Crisis in Western Sociology* and Irving Horowitz (1972) reported on Project Camelot, the winds of change were already blowing. Radical sociology was challenging the establishment practice of sociology and igniting a generation of student sociologists to take to the streets. But the idealism of the 1960s was fast being replaced by a cynical skepticism as the love and peace generation moved away from protest and resistance and into the corporate structure of the budding technocracy. By the mid-1970s there was reluctant recognition of how resistant to change society's major institutions really were and how powerful corporate interests had grown in shaping popular culture, higher education, and the discipline of sociology.

Sociology during this era was, according to Friedrichs (1970), recovering its prophetic mode, returning to a value-committed, action orientation in the spirit of Park, Becker, and Sorokin. "Alfred McClung Lee's Multivalent Man (1966) was the first of what one might expect to be a wave of introductory texts in the recaptured mode" (Friedrichs, 1970). Instead of a single, establishment-endorsed sociology, there was little doubt that a multiparadigmatic sociology was emerging parallel with the great social movements of the time. For example, Watson (1976) presented a working definition of Black sociology and offered four different types of race-related sociologies. Inspired by the human potential movement, he states, "As humanists, Black sociologists must be sensitive to the broad implications of their work and strive to improve the quality of life for all human groups" (p. 121). Radical sociology, feminist sociology, ethnomethodology, and a variety of newer theoretical approaches were about to redefine the study of society by addressing the crises from within, and the vexing issues of race, class, and gender.

Holistic and humanist perspectives were emerging across the social sciences, beginning with the human potential movement in psychology that stressed choice, awareness, and freedom (Glass, 2001: 81), produced the Association for Humanistic Psychology (1962), the Society for Humanistic Anthropology (1974), the Association for Humanist Sociology (1976), the Clinical Sociological Association, now known as the Sociological Practice Association (1978), and the Society for Applied Sociology (1983). All were established as alternatives to the mainstream theories and traditions that were emblematic of the practice of establishment ideologies in psychology, anthropology, and sociology. These newer groups shared a view of humans as creative actors who shape the world around them and who have the capacity to construct social orders that promote collective human welfare and a social science that is reflexive, proactive, and value-committed. Central figures in the humanist movement across sociology and psychology included C. Wright Mills, Alvin Gouldner, Robert Nisbet, Peter Berger, Al and Betty Lee, Carl Rogers, Amitai Etzioni, Charles Hampden-Turner, Herbert Blumer, Severyn Bruyn, John R. Seeley, Abraham Maslow, and Erich Fromm, to name just a few.

The humanist sociologist's highest commitment is not to a professional group or specific professional clique, but to a concern for humanity. Returning this concern for humanity to contemporary sociology was a defining feature of the work of these key figures in the humanist tradition in contemporary sociology.

Founding the AHS:
Five Precipitating Factors and Consequential Events

Looking back, there were five factors or events that served as precipitating conditions and events that led to the founding of the AHS:

- The revolt against the ASA that the SSSP's founding foreshadowed, resulting in challenges from radical and conflict sociology within the discipline, thereby enhancing the humanist perspective;

- Larger, societal social movements that centered on civil rights, women's rights, anti-war, and anti-establishment that recast social life in 1960s and early 1970s, created a generation of radicalized sociology students and faculty who challenged the foundations of establishment sociology (Deutsch and Howard 1970);
- Al Lee's stunning write-in election as President of the ASA in 1975;
- The writings of John F. Glass and others throughout the 1970s that articulated the meaning of a humanist movement in sociology, gave it visibility, and sparked interest in the perspective among sociologists; and
- Charles P. Flynn's devotion, high energy, and intensity given to the cause of humanist sociology that hastened the founding of the AHS by months or years.

The Humanistic Challenge: Glass and Lee

As a graduate student at UCLA in the 1960s, John F. Glass began informally writing about a value-committed humanistic sociology. In September 1970, he chaired a panel at the Humanistic Psychology Association meetings in Miami Beach entitled "Prospects for a Humanistic Sociology" with panelists Steven Deutsch and Charles Hampden-Turner, both part of the dissension in the social sciences. *In Humanistic Society: Today's Challenge to Sociology* (1972), co-edited by John F. Glass and John R. Staude, Alfred McClung Lee, Herbert Blumer, John R. Seeley, Alvin Gouldner, Peter Berger, Amitai Etzioni, Dennis Wrong, Robert Nisbet, and other respected humanist voices in sociology and psychology made a strong case for a transformed sociology based on humanist values. In the preface (1972: xi-xii) Glass and Staude state:

> a humanistic approach in sociology is conceived in various ways: to Maurice Stein and many radical sociologists, a humanistic sociology, in contrast to a conservative and consensual sociology, views society as an historically evolving enterprise that can only be understood through the struggle to liberate human potentialities. To Peter Berger, sociology can become a humanizing endeavor if sociologists do not become apologists for the existing system....Alvin Gouldner goes further....He calls for a moral sociology that negates the detachment of the scientist from the world he studies.... To still others taking an existential approach, a humanistic sociology captures the subjective nature of man frequently lost in methodologies borrowed from the physical sciences which view man merely as an object.

The book appeared shortly before Al Lee's *Toward Humanist Sociology*, published in 1973.

At the 1971 annual meeting of the ASA, a small group of sociologists led by John F. Glass and Philip Roos initiated discussions about the possibility of forming a humanist sociology section within the ASA (see Appendix A to read correspondence) with a goal of building a membership, publishing a newsletter, and eventually establishing a journal. But the ASA was not interested in establishing such a section.

Later in 1971, John F. Glass published two articles (Glass, 1971a; 1971b) in which implications of a humanist sociological perspective were delineated. One of these, "Toward a Sociology of Being: The Humanistic Potential," had been rejected by the ASA journal, *The American Sociologist*, as having "too little substance" with the recommendation to try one of the more "humanistically" oriented journals such as *The Public Interest* or *Transaction* (letter to Glass from Harold W. Pfautz, Editor, Aug. 13, 1971). The article was subsequently published in *Sociological Analysis* (1971a). In it, Glass states:

> A central task of humanistic sociology would be to ask which institutions and social arrangements, supported by which values and norms, promote the capacity and ability of groups and individuals to make free and responsible choices in light of their needs to grow, to explore new possibilities, and to survive in more than a mere existence style. The humanistically inclined sociologist might ask what are the social correlates of trust, interdependency, autonomy, and other individual characteristics in terms of groups, associations, and other social structures from the family to the giant corporation. (1971a: 195)

At about the same time, an article by Glass, titled "Toward a Humanistic Sociology" (1970), that had appeared in the Association for Humanistic Psychology publication *Newsletter* drew a spirited response from Al Lee, also published in the newsletter. Glass wondered why a humanist movement that was sweeping through psychology had yet to develop in sociology. He noted that in the "new sociology," particularly the Marxian-inspired writings of C. Wright Mills, there are seeds of a humanist movement in sociology. Over the next year, Glass and Lee would exchange correspondence that focused on the essential nature of the humanist tradition in sociology. Their exchange of positions appeared in *Newsletter*, portions of which are reproduced below:

Lee (October, 1970):

> I would like to take issue with my fellow sociologist, John F. Glass over his challenging article, "Toward a Humanistic Sociology," in our April 1970 number.
>   On the one hand, Glass admits that sociology has had a long tradition of humanistic participants. On the other, he proceeds to "poor mouth" by calling humanistic social scientists a kind of oppressed minority and by speaking of the beginnings of a more humanistic sociology in "the last few years."
>   Before proceeding further, I had better note that I associate humanistic sociology with these terms: person-centered, empathic, naturalistic, and existential. In my

own humanistic sociological writing, I have long sought to exemplify also the terms: democratic and non-elitist (non-manipulative).

If one is interested in studying sociology for the purpose of learning more about the nature of human society and of interpersonal relationships within it, one very soon learns and is constantly reminded by the literature that the humanistic sociologists have made practically all of the major contributions to the field.

Graduate students who have read and carefully pondered the actual writings of C. H. Cooley, R. E. Park, W. I. Thomas, W. G. Sumner, H. E. Barnes, Willard Waller, and Herbert Blumer can face the scientistic games of the neo-positivists with security and amusement. Even though the mandarins of an overly precise and complicated methodology—dedicated many times to the manipulative service of elites— appear to have power in the intellectual world because they do have a substantial appeal to business men who control grants and fees, their actual contributions to sociological knowledge have been trivial. In my graduate seminars in sociological theory, I am always hard put to it to point to any really significant contributions made by others than the humanistic sociologists.

Glass (January, 1971):

Alfred McClung Lee's response raises some important points. I heartily agree with Professor Lee that humanistic sociologists have made major contributions to the field. However, with the exception of Herbert Blumer and himself, the ones he mentioned are all dead, and the current movement in humanistic psychology has far outdistanced any comparable resurgence of a humanistic perspective in sociology.

It seems as if the current generation of sociologists has forgotten their humanistic forebears, We're trained in an overly scientific and often outrightly anti-humanistic way, —and never learned about Cooley, Park, Thomas, and company. I am painfully aware of my own "deficiencies" of knowledge in this older tradition. And yet I also see truly new-possibilities for the resurgence of a humanistic sociology: facilitated by the recent work of humanistic psychologists such as Abe Maslow, who alone presented enough sociological hypotheses in his book *Eupsychian Management* to keep a whole generation of sociologists busy for a life time.

Lee (April, 1971):

How accurate John F. Glass unfortunately is. So many of our sociological humanists of stature are dead! But our ranks are not thinned down just to Herb Blumer and myself. My colleague in Brooklyn College and the Graduate Center of The City University, George Simpson, has been a doughty warrior against neopositivism and dehumanization.

A group of my former students, under the leadership of Glenn Jacobs of the Rock County Campus, University of Wisconsin, have published an exciting collection of essays, *The Participant Observer* (George Braziller, 1970).

Robert Bierstedt of New York University continues to publish his humanistic articles and books. Bob is involved in the ACLU national board, and in many ways carries on something of his late father-in-law, Robert M. MacIver.

John Kosa's book, *The Home of the Learned Man* (College and University Press, 1968), contains essays by himself and other immigrant sociologists that are certainly humanistic. Curious enough, Kosa is a sociologist at Harvard—under the shadow of the great dehumanistic guru, Talcott Parsons.

> In spite of these and many other examples I could give, Glass is quite right that the leadership for a humanistic social science has been recently much more in the hands of such psychologists as my late and great friend, Abe Maslow, and others in AHP and also in the hands of cultural anthropologists and social historians.

Both Glass and Lee were able to identify what humanist sociology should be and both made major contributions by providing a generation of sociologists with words with which to describe their own attempts to create a sociology that was liberating, activist, and emergent. Lee would champion the development of humanist sociology through development of a new professional society apart from the ASA, and Glass would co-found a new clinical sociology organization (Glass, 2001). Lee was the first president of the AHS in 1977 and Glass the first president of the Clinical Sociology Association (CSA), later renamed the Sociological Practice Association (SPA). Lee was at the founding meeting of the CSA in 1978, became an active member, and published two noteworthy articles (Lee, 1979/ 1984) portraying clinical sociology in a humanist context.

By 1976, Al and Betty Lee, dissatisfied with what SSSP had become, published a reflexive article, titled "The Society for the Study of Social Problems: Parental Recollections and Hopes," in which they itemized only three points of praise, but seven points of criticism that enumerated what they believed to be shortcomings of the SSSP (Lee and Lee, 1976). Between 1951 and 1976, the SSSP grew in size and status within the ASA and as it developed it increasingly came to look and feel like its parent organization. Betty recalled: "We felt we needed to start the AHS, because while those in the SSSP studied social problems they increasingly did so by writing stiff articles for publication. You need to do more and try to figure out ways of alleviating the situation" (Galliher and Galliher, 1995: 124).

Lee's (1978) cogent thesis in *Sociology for Whom?* explains further why the AHS was created. For years, common people could not recognize themselves in sociologists' explanations and interpretations of "reality." "He (the common person) feels, quite often rightly, that he could tell the expert 'a thing or two' about the way people really live and die" (Atkinson, 1972: 1). The scientism that had consumed mainstream sociology since the Depression years needed to be transcended because it had alienated sociology from its essential subject matter—people. The SSSP's influence in making the whole profession of sociology more open, inclusive, and democratic laid the groundwork for a revolt against the ASA that grew louder in the 1970s. But the SSSP, well integrated into the institutionalized structure of the ASA by this point, would not

be the requisite venue for launching a humanist sociology uprising that
the Lees, Glass, Flynn, and others were working to create. "(H)umanist
sociology is staging a great comeback for which the Association for
Humanist Sociology provides a useful medium and focal point" (Lee,
1978: 219).

At about the same time that the Lees were preparing the SSSP article
that would appear in *Social Problems* in 1976, Al was elected president
of the ASA, the result of an insurgent write-in campaign (See Appendix
B for a look at the original petition that resulted in Lee's name on the
ASA ballot). A quarter century later, his election is as astounding as it
was then. He defeated two ASA handpicked candidates, Hubert Blalock
and Al Short. Before winning, he had to withstand a runoff election with
Blalock. "(T)he final runoff vote drew the largest percentage of voting
members (63%) ever recorded in an ASA election. He shares with Pitirim
Sorokin the distinction of being the only ASA president nominated by
petition" (Glass, 1975: 2). Al Lee's presidency would not reform the
ASA, but it heartened the dispossessed and marginal sociologists whose
ideas the ASA had thwarted or snubbed. His turbulent year as president
was marked by contention and he found his efforts at reform blocked at
every turn. It is probable that his experience as ASA president fortified his
resolve to organize a new sociological society. One of those marginalized
sociologists, Charles P. Flynn, was energized by the revolt taking shape
in sociology, joining the Lees to bring the AHS into existence.

Chuck Flynn (Miami University of Ohio) was an idealist and romantic. Strongly influenced by the human potential movement and a
product of UC-Berkeley in the troubled 1960s, he was the prototypical
young, radicalized, marginal sociologist who was anti-establishment,
anti-war, and disillusioned with establishment sociology. Those who
knew him best remember Chuck as having a remarkable presence. He
was a live energy source, full of emotion and vigor that when teamed
with the Lee's visibility and legitimacy in the discipline, generated the
necessary and sufficient momentum that launched the AHS. The Lees
knew from their SSSP experience that the creation of a new sociological
professional society would be a huge undertaking, and the AHS would
require even more effort because it would require working outside the
ASA's structure and resources. Flynn was the person for the job. In 1975,
at the ASA/SSSP annual meetings in San Francisco, Chuck was one of
the twenty or so people Al invited for lunch and conversation about how
to get a "humanist sociology association" off the ground. Even before
this event in San Francisco, Chuck had been talking with progressives

and activists about the possibility of starting a sociological society that would be everything the ASA wasn't—open, representative, liberating. Al, Betty, and Chuck left San Francisco in 1975 with a plan.

Al and Betty, but especially Al, proved to be relentless recruiters for the new AHS. He reached out to marginal sociologists, graduate students, practitioners, and anyone else with whom he crossed paths in those days, issuing each a personal invitation to participate in AHS' first annual meeting. Meanwhile, Chuck started writing letters to people he thought would be interested in the new group, inviting them to the first annual meeting. He also placed announcements about the founding of AHS and its first conference in ASA's Footnotes and other sociology newsletters. Chuck took the message of the AHS everywhere he could, including organizing informal AHS information tables at regional sociological meetings.

When and Where Did the AHS Begin?

Organizational Meeting and the First Issue of the Newsletter

The founding organizational meeting was held at the ASA annual meeting in New York in 1976. That summer, the first issue of the *Humanist Sociology Newsletter* appeared, edited by Charles P. Flynn. A list of "Concerns and Working Principles for the Association of Humanistic Sociology" was published in that first newsletter and is reproduced here.

I. Over-compartmentalization of the Discipline

The range of subject matter for the exploration of social and cultural phenomena have been severely limited by the demarcation of the discipline into a number of specialized areas: theory, methodology, and many "sociologies of _____." In order to expand the range of social-cultural phenomena dealt with and publishable in scholarly journals, these over-specialized categories should be rendered more flexible and open.

II. Limitations of Empirical Approach

While not opposed to empiricism per se, humanistic sociology aims at widening the range of subject matter to include phenomena not readily quantifiable or measurable. Definitely reject the dictum that "if you can't measure it, it doesn't exist." Moral and ethical implications regarded as legitimate concerns for sociology.

III. Determinism

Accepts symbolic interactionistic assumption that behavior is not entirely determined, but is in part the result of choice and voluntary value-orientations. Questions the possibility of ever deriving laws of social behavior in any real sense comparable to laws governing inanimate matter. Sees social-cultural phenomena as qualitatively distinct from the subject matter of the "hard" sciences.

IV. Disciplinary Chauvinism
Recognizes the value of insights and other material from other social sciences and the humanities. Does not rigidly evaluate something on the basis of whether or not it is "sociological," but nonetheless clearly understands the limitations of generalizability of historical, literary, and philosophical data. Values eclectic and syncretic approaches.

V. Value Neutrality Question
The sociologist as human being necessarily internalizes world views which condition his orientations toward sociocultural reality. "Objectivity" in a total sense is thus ultimately not attainable, since all sociological knowledge is relative to the mode by which it is apprehended, rather than "absolute" knowledge. Sociologist should recognize this and spell it out honestly (cf. Gouldner's *Reflexive Sociology*)

VI. Paradigmatic Pluralism and Opposition to Orthodoxy
Values imaginative approaches to sociological analysis. Rejects claim of any particular theoretical paradigm or method as exclusively valid. Employs those paradigms and theories that are most useful for gaining understanding of particular subject matters. (*The Humanist Sociology Newsletter*, 1976: 5)

On a late October afternoon in 1976 at Chuck Flynn's house in Oxford, Ohio, a small group of sociologists gathered for what would be the first annual meeting of the Association for Humanist Sociology. Chuck Flynn, Al and Betty Lee, Stuart Hills (St. Lawrence University), Victoria Rader (George Mason University), Ann Davis (Miami University of Ohio), Sal Restivo (Rennsaler Polytechnic Institute) and a handful of others gathered for the first official AHS convention. Some of the sessions were held literally in Chuck's living room while others were held on the campus of Miami University. Al Lee delivered an address to the group titled "A Different Type of Sociological Society" (1977) to commemorate the founding of the AHS. Lee explained the intellectual and organizational preconditions existing in professional sociology that made the founding of AHS an inevitability. With these closing words from his address, Lee identified expectations for the new and different type of sociological association: "Let us hope that we are launching an Association of Humanist Sociology which will have some such idealism, which will bring a lot of us together in non-competitive comradeship, and which will help keep more sociological research and teaching on the great humanist high road" (1977: 10).

The founding of the the AHS brought together a vibrant mix of sociologists representing seemingly disparate ideologies. The AHS was energized by an interest in conflict sociology that was sweeping across the discipline at that time, but the AHS membership was more diverse than that and extended beyond the radical and Marxist ideological groups. Those attracted to the AHS included Marxists, anarchists, symbolic interactionists, therapists, experimental teaching advocates, clinicians, spiritualists, and grassroots organizers.

Humanity and Society

With the initial issue of *Humanity and Society* published in mid-1977, the AHS sought to distinguish itself from mainstream sociology by publishing scholarship that promoted the values and ideas of humanist sociology. While a professional society consisting of a journal, newsletter, and annual meeting is conventional fare within academe, the AHS sought to be different in substance and form, establishing a uniquely humanist experience of sociology in its meetings and publications. The statement of purpose introducing the journal makes the point that an activist, value-committed, and humanist vision of society was coming of age:

> *Humanity and Society* seeks to provide a forum for sociologists concerned with the value-related aspects of sociological theory and research, and to extend the boundaries of humanistic sociology by exploring connects between sociology and other disciplines. Since the major goal is communication, articles and reviews will be evaluated on their readability as well as the quality of thought they contain and the depth of insight they provide.
>
> Articles must be preceded by a Reflexive Statement which briefly states the author's value perspectives with respect to the subject matter dealt with. (excerpted from statement of purpose, *Humanity and Society* 1977: i)

In the first issue of *Humanity and Society*, Charles P. Flynn, Editor, introduced the journal, saying:

> We are pleased to present this first issue of a journal which we hope will provide what many sociologists feel has long been needed: a means for the dissemination of ideas and perspectives focusing upon the value implications and humanistic aspects of the discipline. *Humanity and Society* will publish articles and review books which emphasize the examination of underlying value implications and moral dimensions of sociological theory and research. We will also present explorations of possible connections between sociological perspectives and approaches, and the modes of inquiry of other disciplines such as history and philosophy, so that sociologists might be encouraged to look at familiar sociological issues in new ways. In all this, we seek to be as pluralistic as possible, and thus welcome articles and reviews written from any theoretical or methodological perspective. The unique Reflexive Statement that

precedes each article allows the reader to understand where 'theauthor is coming from' with respect to the value orientations and theoretical or ideological perspectives he/she adopts toward the subject matter of the article.

The articles and review essays of each issue will be grouped together according to their congruency of subject material, with the intent of providing a basis for an intellectually stimulating reading experience and communication of interrelated ideas. The position and institutional affiliations of authors are given in the Table of Contents so as to encourage readers to communicate with authors whose articles, essays, or reviews are found particularly interesting (1977: ii).

Actually, in the first issue of *Humanity and Society*, the Table of Contents did not list the position or institutional affiliation of authors, defaulting to the standard practice in sociological journals of listing the title of the article and author's name in the contents page, and then the author's name and institutional affiliation with the article. It is a curious sidenote that in the very first issue of *The Humanist Sociologist the Newsletter*, Chuck Flynn, the first editor of the AHS's journal, called for submissions to the initial issue of *"Society and Humanity"* (note the juxtaposition of words). By publication of the second issue of the newsletter in Summer 1977, the journal was referred to as *Humanity and Society*. The membership form enclosed in the second newsletter promised a copy of Al Lee's *Toward Humanist Sociology* to all new members.

The AHS: The Early Years

Table 1 presents basic information about the organization's earliest years, 1976– 1981.

By the time the second annual meeting was held in November 1977 on the campus of Hofstra University, in Hempstead, NY, the network of AHS members and friends was small but growing, and the meeting program included fifteen sessions. Al Lee completed his term as president and Betty Lee assumed the presidency as the Hofstra meeting drew to an end. The organization's Constitution and By-Laws were discussed and a decision made to send these documents to the full membership for approval. Having the meeting in New York helped solidify a base of humanist sociology support that was growing in New England.

Structuring Humanist Sociology:
The AHS's Constitution and By-Laws

To be the different sociological association that Al Lee envisioned in his address at the inaugural AHS conference, an organizational structure

Table 1
The AHS: The Early Years, 1976–1981

Year	President	Meeting Site	Program Theme
1976		Miami University, Oxford, OH	
1977	Alfred McClung Lee	Hofstra University, Long Island, Hempstead, NY	
1978	Betty Lee	Indiana University at South Bend/Quality Inn, South Bend, IN	
1979	William P. Kuvlesky	Sheraton Inn/University of Pittsburgh at Johnstown	Meliorating Social Oppression: Minorities and Negative Status Categories
1980	Thomas Ford Hoult	Stouffer's Inn, Louisville, KY	Humanism for What?— The Political-Economic Implications of The Humanist Perspective in Sociology
1981	David Gil	The Netherland Hilton, Cincinnati, OH	Humanist Scholarship and Emancipatory Political Practice

would have to be created that embodied the core values of humanist sociology. "The attempt has been to build a structure for [AHS] which maximizes the policy making participation of the full membership, as legislative body, rather than the Board" (*The Humanist Sociology Newsletter*, 3:1, p. 3). Article II of the AHS Constitution describes the fundamental mission of the new professional society:

> Article II: Objectives. [The AHS] shall provide a forum for sociologists concerned with the value-related aspects of sociological theory, research, and professional life. It shall seek to extend the boundaries of humanist sociology through exploring connections among sociology and other disciplines. [The AHS] will emphasize the underlying value implications and moral and ethical dimensions of sociological inquiry. [The AHS] considers it an ethical responsibility of social scientists to contribute actively through their scholarly practice to improvements in the quality of human life, rather than to increase understanding of social reality as an end in itself.

The structure of the AHS, as outlined in its Constitution and By-Laws, sought to formalize decision-making about important issues by giving final approval power to the membership by referendum rather than to its Board. The membership officer and the nominations committee were charged with making a concerted effort to find individuals to fill positions in the organization who represented minority interests, and who would not be identified through self-nominations. A few specific excerpted sections of the Constitution and By-Laws that illustrate the AHS's commitment to a structure reflecting openness, representativeness, and status equality are presented in Appendix C.

The First Elected AHS Officers

Between the second annual meeting in New York (1977) and the third annual meeting in Indiana (1978), results of the first election of AHS officers, all running unopposed, were printed in the May 1978 issue of *Humanity and Society*. Betty Lee was elected President; William P. Kuvlesky, President-Elect; Drew Humphries, Vice-President; David Gil, Vice-President-Elect; Daniel Claster, Treasurer; and Vickie Rader, Secretary (and Newsletter Editor) (see Appendix D for a complete list of the AHS's elected officers and appointees in 1978). Officers hailed primarily from institutions concentrated in the Northeast and Midwest, but there were also a couple of representatives from the Southwest and West. Women and minority racial and ethnic group members were represented, excepting African Americans. The officers' institutions vary from small private to large state schools, but most of sociology's most prestigious schools are absent from this list, as are corporate affiliates.

Annual Meeting Growth

The first annual meeting had less than thirty participants and the second meeting, though larger, was still small by comparison with meetings that followed. The third annual meeting was hosted by the University of Indiana, South Bend, and sessions were held on campus and at the Quality Inn. There were twenty sessions listed in the Third Annual Conference Program, twenty individuals were listed on the inside program cover as officers and/or editorial staff of the AHS and its journal, and eighty people were listed as either session organizers, presenters, discussants, or plenary speakers. Clearly, the annual meeting was growing in size and attracting new members from applied and academic settings, matching the size of AHS conferences today.

William P. Kuvlesky (Texas A&M University) served as AHS's third president and presided over the fourth annual conference held in 1979 in Johnstown, Pennsylvania. The program theme, "Meliorating Social Oppression: Minorities and Negative Status Categories," reflected Kuvlesky's research interests in humanist sociology and studies of Mexican-American families, minority youth, and pejorative treatment of minority status groups. Nearly all of the sessions were held at the Sheraton Inn,

Johnstown, though a couple of special events were held at the University of Pittsburgh-Johnstown campus, a brief bus ride away from the hotel. Jon Darling was largely responsible for both the local arrangements and the meeting program.

The fifth annual conference was held in October 1980 at the Stouffer Inn in Louisville, Kentucky. Thomas Ford Hoult (Arizona State University), AHS's fourth president, selected "Humanism for What?—The Political-Economic Implications of the Humanist Perspective in Sociology" as the meeting's program theme. The meeting would prove to be a memorable one. Hoult's plenary address was polemic and contentious as recalled by several of the members interviewed for this project. He commented on an issue that had the potential to split the AHS apart. One group in the membership believed the AHS should exhibit scientific-based scholarship, and arguments made in annual meeting presentations and in the association's journal should reflect the logic and rigor of science. Hoult charged that another group, consisting of members whose interests spanned new age spiritualism, experimental teaching, gay and lesbian welfare, and other areas less amenable to science, was threatening the reputation and longer-term viability of the AHS in contemporary sociology. He argued that should the latter group come to dominate the AHS—and he forecast that this would likely happen—the organization would be permanently damaged. Hoult ended his affiliation with the AHS after his term as president, convinced that humanist sociology would descend to a collection of touchy-feely, self-absorbed spiritualists and charlatans whose disregard for science would leave the AHS intellectually bankrupt. He received loud criticism for holding the meetings in a Stouffer's Inn. Members expressed dissatisfaction with the sterile, glass and steel corporate meeting environment.

The sixth annual meeting was held in Cincinnati, Ohio at the Netherland Hilton Hotel. David Gil (Brandeis University) delivered a presidential address on emancipatory political structures and despite the fact that the meetings were held entirely in a corporate hotel setting for the second year in a row, there was far less criticism of the site. This was due in large part to the fact that the Netherland Hilton had recently undergone restoration of its art-deco motif, providing a more intimate setting for the annual meeting.

The early years of the association were charted by a volatile mixture of people who strongly argued different agendas and were held loosely together by belief in a progressive political agenda, a deep distrust of establishment sociology, and a willingness to participate in an open

dialogue across traditional status boundaries. (For a look at brief pro-
files of some of the leading figures in the earliest years of the AHS, see
Appendix E.)

Unusual in its day, the annual conference brought together a seemingly
odd collection of Marxists, feminists, anarchists, applied practitioners,
grassroots organizers, experimental teachers, new age spiritualists,
clinical sociologists, humanist psychologists, humanist anthropolo-
gists, radical social workers, civil libertarians, alienated government
bureaucrats, and other marginalized types who were seeking identity,
validation, meaning, and fun. The AHS's third annual meeting, held
jointly on the campus of Indiana University-South Bend and the Quality Inn, was the first time that the number of sessions, participants, and
attendees matched the size of contemporary AHS annual conferences at
approximately 225 people.

The structure and environment of the early AHS annual meetings dis-
couraged formal paper reading. Instead there were short oral presentations
followed by discussion that integrated the themes and issues covered in
the presentations. Reflexive statements were encouraged and became the
norm as an introduction to the brief oral presentations. Rather than list
the title of the presentations first in the program, the AHS chose to list
the name of the person first, and students were not segregated in special
student sessions or competitions.

Were There More Founders?

There is broad consensus inside the AHS that Al, Betty, and Chuck
were the original founders of the AHS. However, some AHS members at
various points in time have credited two others with founder status—Ann
Davis and Stuart Hills. Ann Davis (Miami University of Ohio), Chuck
Flynn's colleague and friend, complemented nicely his raw energy with
her polished organizational skills. It has been often said that Chuck had
the big ideas and Ann had the savvy to put big ideas into practice. Ann
was elected AHS president in 1984, but died prior to taking office.

Stu Hills had met the Lees in the SSSP and he strongly supported
their efforts to make sociology more accessible to people. Stu's extensive
network of colleagues in the burgeoning content areas of social deviance and criminal justice were important to the growth of the AHS in
its early years. He was a strong recruiter for the AHS and served as its
ninth President in 1985.

John F. Glass may arguably be classified as a founder as well. From
1968 on (while on the faculty of California State University, Northridge,

and, later, the California School of Professional Psychology) he was clearly a central voice in humanist sociology discussions, working to build a network of humanist sociologists and to organize as an interest group in the larger discipline of sociology. Although his core interest became clinical sociology (Glass, 2001), his writings and voice were influential in the development of humanist sociology and the AHS. As an active member of the Humanistic Psychology Association beginning in 1963, he gave definition to humanistic sociology by stressing an analogy between the relationship of AHP to mainstream psychology and the possibilities of a similar movement in sociology. He is retired and lives in Los Angeles, where he continues writing and is active in political and community affairs.

Humanity and Society:
A Brief Review of Article Titles Published in 1978

The AHS published its first issue of *Humanity and Society* in the summer of 1977 and that was the only issue published in its inaugural year. The following year, *Humanity and Society* met a full publication schedule, producing four issues (February, May, August, and November). If the AHS and its proponents were indeed constructing a new (or renewed) humanist perspective distinct from mainstream sociology, then a cursory review of article titles should reflect the core humanist concerns that the founders articulated. Substantive themes expected in articles published in *Humanity and Society* included: human liberation, unity and coalition building, analyses of oppression and inequality, studies of specific minority and disadvantaged minority groups, and social change. A few article titles from the first full volume of *Humanity and Society* that affirm such core humanist values are presented here (for a complete listing of titles from Vol. 2, 1977, see Appendix F).

Volume 2:1 (February)
- Power and Symbol in the Chicano Movement
- Gemeinschaft, Essence and Unity: Towards a New Humanist Sociology

Volume 2:2 (May)
- Sociology and Choice
- A Utopian Vision of the Frankfurt School
- Work Management in Organizations: Paradigms and Possibilities
- Comment: A Deviant Approach to Deviance

Volume 2:3 (August)
- Self-Interest and Social Equality
- Illusions of Unity

Volume 2:4 (November)
- The Human Story in Anthropology
- Man and Humanism: An Essay on Language, Gender and Power
- In the Footprints of a Giant: The Heuristic Philosophy of
     Michael Polanyi and Humanistic Scholarship in Sociology
- A Humanistic Perspective on Science and Society

It is clear from even the most casual examination of the article titles that the new journal provided an outlet for dissemination and discussion of humanist sociology's core concerns.

Issues and Themes from the Early Years: Connecting the Early AHS to the Present AHS

The Annual Meeting as Personal Renewal

The feeling that everyone is welcome and everyone's voice is worth hearing remains a lasting legacy of the AHS from its earliest days. The AHS annual meetings tend to be a place where the personal and professional dimensions of sociology are joined in a comfortable and comforting setting. Sessions are characterized by open dialogue and status differences are minimized. The rigid, formal, and impersonal tone of the ASA annual conference is shunned in favor of a community-like structure. There was a feel to the AHS conferences early on that persists today where people are talking to people without much of the status baggage and game-playing that goes on in other areas of the profession.

Identity Crisis I: Relationship with the American Sociological Association

A split occurred early on between those AHS members who fed on Al Lee's disdain for the ASA and those who believed it wise for the AHS to maintain a working relationship with the ASA. The former group preferred keeping a healthy distance from the ASA, while the latter believed it important to have the AHS visible inside the ASA. The AHS today co-sponsors a session at the annual ASA meeting, but there is still wide skepticism inside the AHS about the value of working collaboratively with the ASA.

Identity Crisis II: Humanist Sociology and Science

One group of AHS members valued humanist sociology for its ability to be practical, ideological, and activist, while maintaining standards of science in its theory, research, and practice. Another group valued humanist sociology for its ability to be practical, ideological, and activist, but held far less regard for the utility of science in sociological practice, questioning whether science was germane to the kinds of self-exploration, creative teaching, and quest for meaning that defined them as humanists and sociologists. This fracture within the AHS membership reveals itself most clearly today in members' comments about the quality of the journal and concerns over editorial policy.

Structure versus Anti-Structure

Even in its first years of operation, the AHS faced a core dilemma. On the one hand, members wanted the organization and its annual meeting to be open, flexible, emergent, and spontaneous, appealing to the anarchistic tendencies of AHS members. But on the other hand members (even the same members) wanted the organization and annual meeting to be well planned, crisply structured and fiscally sound. Too much of either—structure or anti-structure—tends to result in dissent and pointed criticism of AHS leadership.

Conclusions

First, humanist sociology is its own sub-area of the discipline as evidenced by development of the autonomous Association for Humanist Sociology, its membership, journal, and annual meeting. The birth of the AHS was a logical outcome of the growth of the humanist movement in the social sciences, not only in psychology. From the mid-1960s through the 1970s, there were a number of books critical of the discipline, calling for the centrality of values and people in social theory and research, describing qualitative and other humanistic research methods, and calling for a sociology relevant to the issues of the day. Such works as Abraham Maslow's *Toward a Psychology of Being* (1968), C. Wright Mills' *The Sociological Imagination* (1959), Floyd Matson's *The Broken Image* (1964), and Severyn Bruyn's *The Human Perspective in Sociology* (1966), to name just a few, laid the foundations for a humanist approach to sociology fundamentally different from most of mainstream sociology.

Second, the founding of the AHS signaled a new day in the period of dissent and struggle among sociologists to find professional identity and meaning inside and outside of institutionalized sociology and, most notably, the ASA. Advancing the cause of those who wanted sociology to be more practical, more accessible, and more meaningful, the AHS provided a professional home for many marginalized and radicalized sociologists practicing within and outside of academe. The AHS created a professional space in the sociological landscape of the time for academics, activists, practitioners, and students to meet and interact with like-minded others interested in humanist sociology.

Third, the AHS provided humanist sociologists with a career-building mechanism (i.e., presentations at annual meetings, a journal for publication of humanist sociology scholarship, opportunities to hold office in the organizational structure, and a means of communicating formally with others sharing humanist sociology interests). The AHS represented an alternate reward and identity structure for those separating themselves from mainstream sociology.

Finally, the early days of the AHS benefited broadly from the notoriety and legitimacy of the Lees. Al's reputation alone was sufficient to attract many followers to the AHS. The early years of the AHS are imprinted with the spirit and attitude that Al and Betty brought to the new organization. بدم لو ابن 6 مانت خودش برای رهوانى انكد دلبل یه AHS

References

Lee ها معروف بودند.

Arcaro, Tom. 1996. "What is Humanist Sociology, Anyway?" *Humanity and Society*, 20 (2): 5-13.

Association for Humanist Sociology. 1978. *Third Annual Conference Program*. October 20-22.

Atkinson, Dick. 1971. *Orthodox Consensus and Radical Alternative: A Study in Sociological Theory*. New York: Basic Books.

Ballard, Chet. 1981. "A Metasociological Examination of Humanist Sociology: The Prospects for a Paradigm." *Humanity and Society* 4 (1): 10-28.

Bruyn, Severyn T. 1966. *The Human Perspective in Sociology*. Englewood Cliffs, NJ: Prentice Hall.

Collins, Randall. 1994. *Four Sociological Traditions*. New York: Oxford Press.

Cuzzort, Raymond P. 1989. *Using Sociological Thought*. Mountain View, CA: Mayfield Publishing.

Deutsch, Steven E. and John Howard. 1970. *Where It's At: Radical Perspectives in Sociology*. New York: Harper and Row.

Friedrichs, Robert W. 1970. *A Sociology of Sociology*. New York: The Free Press.

Galliher, James M. and John. F. Galliher. 1996. "The Lives, Times, and Contributions of Al and Betty Lee." *Humanity and Society* 20 (2): 14-24.

Glass, John F. 1970. "Toward a Humanistic Sociology." *Newsletter*, Association for Humanistic Psychology 6 (4): 1-2.

———. 1971a. "Toward a Sociology of Being: The Humanistic Potential." *Sociological Analysis* 32 (4): 191-198.

———. 1971b. "The Humanistic Challenge to Sociology." *Journal of Humanistic Psychology* 11: 170-183. Reprinted in John F. Glass and John R. Staude (1972).

———. 1975. "Portrait of a President." *Newsletter*, Association for Humanistic Psychology, December.

———. 1979. "Renewing an Old Profession: Clinical Sociology." *American Behavioral Scientist* 23 (3): 513-529.

———. 2001. "The Founding of the Clinical Sociology Association: A Personal Narrative." *Sociological Practice: A Journal of Clinical and Applied Sociology* 3 (1): 75-85.

Glass, John F. and John R. Staude. 1972. *Humanistic Society: Today's Challenge to Sociology*. Pacific Palisades, CA: Goodyear Publishing.

Gouldner, Alvin W. 1970. *The Coming Crisis of Western Sociology*. New York: Basic Books.

Gray, David J. 1979. "American Sociology: Plight and Promise." *The American Sociologist* 14 (1): 35-42.

Horowitz, Irving L. 1965. "The Life and Death of Project Camelot." *Transaction* 3 (November-December): 3-7, 44-47.

Lee, Elizabeth Briant and Alfred McClung Lee. 1976. "The Society for the Study of Social Problems: Parental Recollections and Hopes." *Social Problems* 24: 4-14.

Lemert, Charles. 1995. *Sociology After the Crisis*. Boulder, CO: Westview Press.

Maslow, Abraham. 1968. *Toward a Psychology of Being*. 2nd ed. New York: Van Nostrand.

Matson, Floyd. 1964. *The Broken Image*. New York: George Braziller.

McClung Lee, Alfred. 1966. *Multivalent Man*. New York: George Braziller.

———. 1970. Correspondence in *Newsletter*, Association for Humanistic Psychology. October.

———. 1971. Correspondence in *Newsletter*, Association for Humanistic Psychology. April.

———. 1973. *Toward Humanist Sociology*. Englewood Cliffs, NJ: Prentice-Hall.

———. 1976. "Valedictory: A Report on the Year 1975-76." *ASA Footnotes* 4 (6): 1, 9-10.

———. 1977. "A Different Kind of Sociological Society." *Humanity and Society* 1 (1): 1-11.

———. 1978. *Sociology for Whom?* New York: Oxford University Press.

———. 1984. "Overcoming Barriers to Clinical Sociology" *Clinical Sociology Review* 2: 42-50.

Mills, C. Wright. 1959. *The Sociological Imagination*. New York: Oxford University Press.

Rader, Victoria, ed. 1978. *The Humanist Sociologist*. 1978. Victoria Rader, Ed. 3 (1): 1-5.

Ritzer, George A. 1975. "A Multiple Paradigm Science." *The American Sociologist* 10 (3): 156-167.

Watson, Wilbur H. 1976. "The Idea of Black Sociology: Its Cultural and Political Significance." *The American Sociologist* 11 (2): 115-123.

Young, T. R. 1971. "The Politics of Sociology: Gouldner, Goffman, and Garfinkel." *The American Sociologist* 6 (4): 276-281.

Personal Interviews

The author acknowledges and thanks the following sociologists who were interviewed for this project: Thomas Arcaro, Henry Brownstein, Jon Darling, Lynda Ann Ewen, Walda Katz Fishman, Jan Fritz, David Gil, John F. Glass, Glenn Goodwin, Beth Hess, Stuart Hills, Billy Horton, William P. Kuvlesky, John Leggett, Victoria Rader, Joseph Scimecca, and Jerold Starr. The authors also acknowledge the assistance of Carla Howery, American Sociological Association Deputy Executive Director, who provided information regarding Al Lee's election as ASA president used in this paper.

Appendix A: Correspondence—Glass and Roos and ASA

3245 Broadway
Boulder Colo 80302
19 Sept 71

N. J. Demerath III
Executive Officer
American Sociological Association
1722 N. St. N.W.
Washington, D.C. 20036

Jay:

At the meetings held in Denver a few weeks ago, John Glass scheduled a roundtable on humanistic sociology. We had what I considered a useful discussion about the problems of what humanistic sociology might be, anyway, in contrast to sociology as customarily practiced.

At the end of the discussion, I brought up the question of a more continuing concern for humanistic sociology. I had in mind a newsletter which might evolve into a journal in time. Since then, it has occurred to me that humanistic sociology might become more clearly defined through making it a section, as, in the recent meetings, the section on sociology of sex roles began to take on that more formal status.

It is for these reasons that I am writing you this note. Since I am presently unemployed, my ability to appropriate free secretarial and mailing services is severely restricted. Both John Glass and John Staude are at California State Colleges, where these services are also in short supply. I wonder whether the Executive Office can furnish postage and secretarial assistance for a newsletter, as well as scheduling an organizational meeting for the 1972 meetings. (Unfortunately, I do not believe that I will be able to attend the 1972 meetings as I will probably be in the process of moving to a new job then. However, I will continue to volunteer my services as secretary/co-ordinator until such time as someone else can take over the job.) If the Executive Office can do these things, perhaps it will be possible, when billing for dues and membership for 1973—that is, a little more than a year from now—to be able to include a section membership offering from which the newsletter could begin to expand into a journal.

At the roundtable on Tuesday, 31 August, all present agreed that some further organizational moves would be a good idea, although specifics beyond a newsletter were not discussed for lack of time. Their names and addresses are enclosed on a separate sheet; also a number of persons who, through either acquaintanceship or some other reason (such as being on the program) should be on the initial mailing list.

Your comments will be appreciated,

cc: John Glass   (signed)
    Valley State   Phillip D. Roos

3245 Broadway
Boulder Colo 80302
15 Nov 71

Professor William J. Goode
Chairman, 1972 Program Committee
Department of Sociology
Columbia University New York, NY 10027

Dear Prof. Goode:

At the 1971 meetings of the ASA, a few persons began to talk about the possibility of starting a section within the Association of Humanistic Sociology (Author's Note: the letter's author most probably meant to say that humanistic sociology might be a section within the ASA).

I expect to be unable to attend the 1972 meetings. However, I hope there will be others in attendance who can continue to carry through the steps toward developing the section that were begun in August 1971 and which will be worked on in the coming months.

I assume that program sessions will be scheduled, as they have been in the past, in existential phenomenology, applied sociology, and radical sociology—the three broad areas which we are inclined to suspect would be incorporated in the Humanistic Sociology section.

It might also be useful if a session was scheduled for Section day, as was done in 1971 for sociology of sex roles.

Sincerely,
cc: John Glass   (signed)
    John Staude   Phillip D. Roos

3245 Broadway
Boulder Colo 80302
15 Nov 71

Mrs. Alice F. Myers
Administrative Assistant
American Sociological Association
1722 N. St., NW
Washington, D.C. 20036

Dear Mrs. Myers:

Thank you for your letter of 5 November concerning the organization of a section on Humanistic Sociology.

At the present time it does not appear that we will be able to draft a statement of purpose and gather 50 signatures before the February meeting of the Council. Would you please let us know when the next following meeting of the Council will occur?

In looking over the current By-Laws which you sent, I notice that the "Statement of Purpose" in most of them is extremely short—a sentence or two. We were thinking of something slightly longer—perhaps a page single-spaced. Would this be acceptable?

I further notice that most of the sections have a Committee on Publications but only the section in Education has a journal. We have been considering starting a publication, perhaps first as a newsletter, but eventually growing to a journal. We realize that the ASA cannot take financial responsibility for this. However, this is one of the major reasons for starting the section and we were thinking that John Staude or I would be the first editor, as convenient. The journal/newsletter would, at least at first, simply be mimeographed and sent to section members I imagine. Please let me have your thoughts on this.

Sincerely,
(signed)
cc: John Glass, San Fernando State
    John Staude, Sonoma State

Phillip D. Roos

Appendix B: Petition to ASA to Place Al Lee's Name on Ballot

Editor's Note: For reasons of space, biographical information on Alfred McClung Lee and a listing of forty-six sponsors from universities and colleges around the country have not been reproduced here.

By referendum, the membership of the American Sociological Association has greatly democratized the selection of its officers by making the nomination process responsive to the wishes and needs of rank-and-file members.

As a result, Alfred McC. Lee was nominated by petition to be President-Elect of the Association because his supporters know that he will bring the new leadership and new ideas the organization needs.

Long before it was fashionable to question the authority of the establishment, Al Lee was actively challenging the supporters of the status quo. When the ASA refused to encourage professional sociologists to study critical issues of the day, Al Lee was instrumental in organizing the Society for the Study of Social Problems with its journal, *Social Problems*, devoted to critical developments and issues. He was often one of the few persons within the ASA working to make the organization aware of its responsibilities toward rank-and-file members, toward minority group members, toward women, and toward making the organization responsive to the major issues confronting American society.

Al Lee's program for the American Sociological Association is:

1. To widen sociological discussions by encouraging the expression and participation of the wide spectrum of sociological perspectives that exist.
2. To work for greater participation of regional associations and rank-and-file members in the on-going activities of the ASA.
3. To encourage a greater variety of media to disseminate sociological ideas—symposia, workshops, specialized periodicals, conferences.
4. To promote sociology and thereby broaden occupational opportunities for sociologists.
5. To bring minority groups and women more prominently into the activities of the ASA.
6. To obtain funding for many small research grants-in-aid of $1,000 or less to be distributed by a committee of the ASA.
7. To help assure continued curricula supervision by sociologists of sociological specialties.
8. To encourage and stimulate membership and participation in the International Sociological Association.
9. To provide and disseminate an open ASA budget so that all members

will know where the money comes from and how it is spent.

10. To develop ASA sponsorship for innovative social policies of breadth and action programs of foresight.

We urge you to vote for Alfred Lee.

Thank you.

Appendix C:
Excerpts from the Original AHS Constitution and By-Laws

Article III. Membership. There shall be only two classes of full, voting membership: member and student member. Special dues rates shall be provided by the Board for unemployed and retired members.

Article IV. Section 6: All meetings of the Board of Directors shall be open to Association members as spectators.

Article VI: Membership Interest Groups. The Association shall encourage and facilitate the development of diverse Interest Groups within the membership to encourage activities aimed at furthering the humanist sociological perspective.

Section 2: Once formed Interest Groups are to operate as affiliated but relatively autonomous units of the Association.

Article VII. Section 3: The Nominations Committee shall be charged with making a special effort to seek out members of groups that have ordinarily been discriminated against to run for office, and to present a slate reflecting such efforts. Appointed offices shall be filled with similar attention to representation.

Appendix D:
First Elected and Appointed Officers of the AHS, 1978

President—Elizabeth Briant Lee, Short Hills, NJ
Vice-President—Drew Humphries, Rutgers—The State University
Secretary [and Editor of *The Humanist Sociology Newsletter*]—

Victoria Rader, George Mason University
Treasurer—Daniel Claster, Brooklyn College of the CUNY.
Editor [of *Humanity and Society*]—Charles P. Flynn,
    Miami University of Ohio
Past President—Alfred McClung Lee, Brooklyn College of the CUNY
President-Elect—William P. Kuvlesky, Texas A&M University
Vice-President-Elect—David Gil, Brandeis University
Facilitator of Interest Groups—Richard Sterne, University of Akron

Regional Representatives on the Board of Directors:
Eastern—John Howard, SUNY College at Purchase
Southern—David Simon, University of Northern Florida
North Central—Jaber Gubrium, Marquette University
Southwest—Julius Rivera, University of Texas, El Paso
Pacific—Leo Chall, *Sociological Abstracts*, San Diego, CA
International—Alex Carey, Australia, temporarily at Massachusetts
    Institute of Technology

Nominating Committee:
Peter K. Manning, Michigan State University
Glenn Jacobs, University of Massachusetts
Stuart Hills, St. Lawrence University
George Vickers, New York, NY
Brenda Forster, Elmhurst College

Appendix E:
Brief Profiles of a Few Key, Early-AHS Figures

Natalie Allon (Philadelphia School of Textiles and Arts) had been elected to the position of AHS vice-president-elect prior to the fifth annual meeting held in Louisville, KY. Shocking news was delivered to the conference attendees that Natalie had been in a very serious automobile accident in Louisville on her way to the hotel. For Natalie Allon, a bright, committed young humanist sociologist, attending the fifth annual AHS conference would change her life forever, but in a horrific manner. Following her automobile accident, she remained in a hospital in Louisville for quite a long time after the conference, eventually returning to Philadelphia where she continues today to require extensive healthcare assistance. She has not been able to resume the life she led prior to the accident.

Jon Darling (University of Pittsburgh—Johnstown) became a member when he met Chuck at one of his informal AHS information booths at the Eastern Sociological Society annual meeting in 1976. Jon joined Chuck, Vickie Rader, and Richard LeFevre (University of Akron) at the Lees' home in Short Hills, New Jersey, in the summer of 1977 to draft the AHS Constitution and by-laws. Jon was the seventh president of the AHS in 1983. His presidency brought structure and order to AHS business, but the price was high. Jon's efforts to be orderly were publicly criticized by some of the membership and he drifted away from AHS feeling a bit let down by the group. He is a teacher and practitioner at the University of Pittsburgh-Johnstown.

Lynda Ann Ewen (West Virginia Technical Institute) championed the causes of community organizing and feminism within the AHS in both its early years and today. She had a knack of connecting the personal with the professional, and continues to be a strong recruiter for the AHS, introducing many progressive students to the AHS. She is an active organizer, teacher, and scholar.

Jan Marie Fritz (University of Cincinnati) was active in the AHS during its early years, contributing to *Humanity and Society* and working on membership issues. She was influential in the founding of the CSA and has become a leading environmental justice scholar and policy activist.

David Gil (Brandeis University) was recruited to the AHS by Al Lee. Impressed by Al's work inside the ASA and the SSSP, David was attracted to the AHS because its structure was open to all and its mixture of Marxists, anarchists, feminists, activists, students, and teachers made the AHS an intriguing place for humanist conversations and debates. Whenever a debate tended to become too personal or overblown, David was there, with quiet dignity, to remind those involved in the debate that we are dependent on each other for our emancipation—that hate is self-destructive. David, a Holocaust survivor, joined Al in committing the AHS to take public stands in support of academics who were being fired or punished for their progressive social and political views. He was the fifth AHS president in 1981. He remains an active teacher at Brandeis University.

William P. Kuvlesky (Texas A&M University) was among the Marxian-inspired radicals and progressives working to change the ASA when he met Al Lee. He was among those invited to lunch by Al in San Francisco to discuss the framework for a new humanist sociological society. He drove his graduate students Chet Ballard (Valdosta State University) and Richard Wells (University of Wisconsin-Oshkosh) as well as a few of his campus colleagues halfway across the country to participate in the early AHS annual meetings. He served as the third AHS president in 1979. He is retired and enjoying his grandchildren in College Station, Texas.

John Leggett (Rutgers University) made a noisy impact on the early AHS annual meetings (and recent ones, too) by bringing labor activists and union concerns into AHS programming. John was an important link between the labor activism of the 1960s and the new social contract of the 1990s. He also made significant contributions to *Humanity and Society* and served as the twenty-first president of the AHS.

Vickie Rader (George Mason University) received one of Chuck Flynn's AHS recruitment letters in 1975. Chuck knew Vickie from their graduate school days at the University of California-Berkeley. He figured Vickie would be interested in the new sociological organization and was right. Vickie was appointed AHS secretary and was also given the task of editing the official newsletter, *The Humanist Sociologist*. She was editor of the newsletter from 1976–1980 and served as the AHS's eighth president in 1984. She is teaching and pursuing humanist causes at George Mason University in Virginia.

Jerry Starr (Citizens for Independent Public Broadcasting and West Virginia University) met the Lees at an AHS information table in 1976 and he later invited Al to speak to a humanist reading group on his campus. He became an important editorial policy voice in the AHS and used his considerable talents to bring important issues to the attention of AHS members. He has been described as putting C. Wright Mills's ideas into practice. He served as the tenth president of AHS in 1986. As Executive Director of Citizens for Independent Public Broadcasting, he has become a public lecturer and author.

Appendix F: Titles of Articles Published in *Humanity and Society*, Vol. 2, 1-4, 1977

Volume 2:1 (February)
  Power and Symbol in The Chicano Movement
  Gemeinschaft, Essence and Unity: Towards a New Humanist
      Sociology
  Interaction, Drama, and Freedom: The Social Theories of
      Erving Goffman and Victor Turner
  Cash Connection: Looking in on the Small Time Fence-Hustler

Volume 2:2 (May)

Sociology and Choice

A Utopian Vision of the Frankfurt School

Work Management in Organizations: Paradigms and Possibilities

Toward a Sociology of Griping Comment: A Deviant Approach
to Deviance

Volume 2:3 (August)

Self-Interest and Social Equality Illusions of Unity

A Social Welfare Approach to the Value Issue in Social Problems
Theory

Prolegomenon to a Sociology of Evil

Volume 2:4 (November)

The Human Story in Anthropology

Man and Humanism: An Essay on Language, Gender and Power

In the Footprints of a Giant: The Heuristic Philosophy of Michael
Polanyi and Humanistic Scholarship in Sociology

Energy and Sociology

A Humanistic Perspective on Science and Society

4

Working with the Labor Movement:
A Personal Journey in
Organic Public Sociology

Edna Bonacich

Michael Burawoy has done an immense service to our discipline by opening up the discussion of public sociology.[1] By acknowledging a long tradition within our discipline, and recognizing its important contribution to the field, he is providing legitimacy to many of us who have been toiling in this area for years. We knew that many of our students were attracted to sociology because it promised the opportunity not only to understand our complex social world better, but to try to do something to change it. Yet we also knew that many in our discipline and departments felt compelled to crush this impulse, and to drive students into a narrow professionalism. "If you want to be an activist," they would say, "you don't belong in graduate school."

Some of us fought against this claim. We would tell students that, once they got past these gatekeepers, they could do as they pleased. We would try to stand up for an expansive view of the discipline, that allowed room for those of us who didn't want a sociology that saw itself as "pure science," and left unexamined both its roots in, and its effects on the social world. We wanted to change the world, and we wanted room for our students to pursue the same goal. But we also felt like a threatened minority that had to watch its back and be careful whom it talked to. And there have been casualties among our ranks. Now Michael Burawoy has brought the ideas and ideals we have tried to stand for out into the daylight. Yes, we *do* have a right to exist! Yes, we *are* a legitimate part of our discipline. We no longer have to hide, or expend endless energy trying to defend ourselves.

73

In this essay I plan to discuss my own journeys in public sociology. I want to examine five aspects: what brought me to this approach, what I have tried to do in terms of research, some of my efforts to teach public sociology, some of the difficulties one confronts, and why I think it contributes to the discipline. This is a very personal story. Perhaps I have chosen this approach because I am of an age (65) where looking back, interpreting, and trying to make sense of one's life becomes attractive. But I have also chosen it because the story has been hidden under the pressures that have come from a narrower definition of the discipline. With the emergence of public sociology, I feel a new freedom to show myself fearlessly. I hope that this exercise will be more than just an autobiography, that it may help younger people who are exploring similar paths.

Before describing my own journey, I want to consider the niche I find myself in, namely "organic public sociology." Burawoy draws a distinction between traditional and organic public sociology. The traditional type involves addressing broader publics, in the form of books, lectures, newspaper commentaries, etc. According to Burawoy (2005: 7-8): "The publics being addressed are generally invisible in that they cannot be seen, thin in that they do not constitute a movement or organization, and they are usually mainstream." The role of the sociologist is to spur debate. In contrast, with organic public sociology "the sociologist works in close connection with a visible, thick, active, local and often counter-public.... Between the organic public sociologist and a public is a dialogue, a process of mutual education." This latter describes precisely what I try to do with labor unions.

Where Did the Impulse to Work with Labor Come From?

I am Jewish in background. My father was a rabbi. We did not live on the Lower East Side of New York, and neither of my parents worked in sweatshops or joined the ILG—the International Ladies Garment Workers Union (though my father's Eastern European parents were working class and settled in Brooklyn). Nevertheless, the values of that community permeated our domestic culture to some extent. At least we learned a little anti-racism.

Then in 1950, when I was ten years old, my family moved to South Africa—at the height of Apartheid. This was a life-transforming experience in terms of witnessing first-hand the world's most racist regime. It also opened up another kind of opportunity. Like all the Jewish kids in South Africa, I was recruited to join a Zionist youth movement. The movement I joined, Habonim (the Builders), was oriented towards building kibbutzim (collective farms) in Israel. It was socialist—believing in the centrality and dignity of labor, fiercely equalitarian in terms of gender, and (given the South African context) very critical of the racist regime. The movement was rebellious, counter-cultural, and idealistic. We read some Marxism. We believed it was possible to build a better society, based on collectivist principles, and we tried to live these ideas in practice as much as possible. After graduating from high school, I spent a year in Israel on an Institute for Youth Leaders from Abroad. I was a member of a delegation from my movement in South Africa, and we decided to live collectively, pool our money, and make group decisions. This led to lots of fights, but also proved that it can be done. Half the time was spent living and working on a couple of kibbutzim. In that year I also began to see some of the massive problems with Zionism, and its unjust treatment of the Arab population. I left Israel disillusioned about Zionism, but the socialist ideals stuck.

After college, where I became somewhat involved in anti-Apartheid efforts, I returned to the United States to go to graduate school, where I got married and had two children and have remained here ever since. I was naturally drawn to issues of race and class. My first published work of significance was on the "split labor market." I wanted to understand how racism could divide the working class, and how the working class became complicit in racism, even though it was against its long-term interests. When I got a job at the University of California, Riverside or UCR (where I have been forever) I joined the union, and tried a bit to work on the issue of tiers of workers who are pitted against each other by taking up the issue of lecturers and their "super-exploitation."

Serving as president of my local (American Federation of Teachers, or AFT Local 1966), a tiny organization in a non-union workplace when public employees in California were not allowed to engage in collective bargaining,[2] I ran into Ralph Cuaron, a custodian who was president of the AFSCME (American Federation of State, County, and Municipal Employees) local on campus. Ralph had been a Communist and trade union activist in Los Angeles and, as a working-class Chicano, knew a lot about racism as well. Ralph had little formal education, but was one of the smartest people I ever met. I became Ralph's student, and he taught me a ton about teaching, philosophy, and trade unionism. We formed a coalition of campus unions, and tried to bridge the colossal status gaps between faculty and staff. During our tenure the State of California passed the Higher Education Employee Relations Act (HEERA) legitimizing collective bargaining for us. This attracted unions like AFSCME to become suddenly interested in our activities. They decided the existing locals were "too left," and tried to do us in. This was not a new experience for Ralph, who led the fight to try to stop this takeover, even as we fought for strong union representation. I remember sitting on the floor through the night at statewide meetings of the UC AFSCME locals as we passionately argued about how to counter the domination of the international and still have a successful organizing drive.[3] These learning experiences lay the ground for my moving to work with the ILG (International Ladies Garment Workers Union) when the opportunity arose.

What I Have Tried to Do in Terms of Research

In general, I have tried to conduct research that can be of value to the labor movement. I have not been employed by a union and have a principled resistance to taking money from them, since I certainly earn enough as a professor. Ideally I like to work with the Organizing Department, helping them to devise campaigns, and trying to do research that is relevant to the campaign. Of course, some unions, like the SEIU (Service Employees International Union) and HERE (Hotel Employees and Restaurant Employees, now merged with UNITE, the Union of Needletrades Industrial and Textile Employees, into UNITE HERE) have their own, highly skilled research staffs, who are experts in campaign research. I cannot compete with their knowledge and experience. What I try to do is develop the "big picture"—how the industry works, what are the social forces surrounding it—and to suggest how they might be used.

My first experience was in the garment industry, with the ILG. I became interested in the industry by a circuitous route. I was hanging out at the UCLA Asian American Studies Center, where a friend, Lucie Cheng, was director, and we decided to do a collaborative study on "the new Asian immigration" in Los Angeles. We brought a team together and divided up the topic. I knew that Asian immigrants were active in the apparel industry, especially as contractors, and wanted to find out more, so I decided to take this topic. This proved so interesting that Lucie, some others, and I developed a project on the apparel industry in the Pacific Rim.

Out of that, I decided to study the Los Angeles garment industry in some depth. All of this research ended up in books, and a few articles (Ong, Bonacich, and Cheng, 1994; Bonacich et al., 1994; Bonacich and Appelbaum, 2000; Bonacich, 2000).

The basic theme of this work was the exploitation of racialized labor—either immigrant or global. I wanted to understand how the structure of the apparel industry, with its pyramid of power: retailers dominating manufacturers, who dominate contractors, who dominate subcontractors, who exploit factory-workers and home-workers (or what the union called the "pulpo," or octopus) led to the emergence of sweatshops even in the United States and Western Europe, let alone in the poorer "developing" countries. I also was intrigued by the role of the contractors, a form of ethnically identifiable middleman that fit into the concept of "middleman minorities." The apparel industry let me study both of my major sociological themes: split labor markets, and middleman minorities.

The garment industry also allowed me to study how a networked production system, with dispersed, hidden, and mobile, arm's length production arrangements, makes union organizing so difficult. If you successfully organize a contracting shop it simply goes out of business, whether on the local or the global level. The garment industry was one of the first to use contracting out as a way of weakening labor—this is the industry where the concept of "sweatshops" was first developed. But now, almost all of the consumer goods industries have adopted this pattern of production (global contracting)—the world is more and more coming to look like the garment industry. I have come to believe that finding a way to gain power against retailer-centered production networks is the key to gaining power for the international working class, and this is the reason for my current study of the ports of Los Angeles and Long Beach, as I shall explain below.

Parenthetically, the Asian American Studies Center at UCLA, and Ethnic Studies departments in general, represent efforts to institutionalize a form of public sociology (though they are inter-disciplinary and extend beyond sociology). They try to exemplify the principle that the university should serve the community, including the excluded and oppressed. They are highly critical of an institution that has a history of white male, Eurocentric domination, with a particular political and cultural slant, yet claiming to be "universal." During the time of Lucie's tenure, the AASC, inspired by the Chinese revolution, tried to create a garment cooperative in downtown LA, rewrite Japanese-American history from a Japanese-American perspective, and many other worthwhile projects.

In the course of studying the LA apparel industry, I decided that I wanted to find a way to link the research to union organizing. I contacted the director of organizing at the ILG, David Young, and tried to explain to him how I might be helpful. It took quite a bit of effort to get David to trust me but eventually he did and we have been friends ever since. We eventually got to the point where we were meeting weekly to discuss the following questions: What are the characteristics of the LA garment industry? What would it take to organize it? What research is necessary to achieve this goal? We talked about all aspects of the industry. I mainly listened and took notes, then wrote them up adding my own thoughts.

We eventually came up with a lengthy document, which we boiled down into a proposal to the union. Jeff Hermanson, who was the organizing director for the International in New York, supported our effort, but we could not get the union leadership to adopt it. Eventually we developed a more modest proposal to organize a single company, Guess Jeans, which was the largest garment manufacturer in LA. I helped David and others develop a plan to organize Guess and we began to implement it. Unfortunately, in the middle of this the ILG merged with the Amalgamated Clothing and Textile Workers Union (ACTWU) to form UNITE, and the campaign ceased to be supported, for complicated internal political reasons. David and Jeff, two of the most talented organizers I have ever met, left the union.

What did David get out of our dialogue, and what did I get? I think this question has a bearing on the value of organic public sociology. Very briefly, most labor leaders are caught up in the hurly burly of dealing with daily crises. They rarely have the opportunity to step back and assess the big picture. My weekly meetings with David gave him a chance to do that, which (I hope) helped him to think strategically. He could bounce ideas off a reasonably intelligent and well-informed listener. In turn, I learned a heap about social struggle, strategy, and union politics. I learned about the labor movement from the inside, rather than studying it as an object.

I was extremely fortunate that David happened to be the Organizing Director of the ILG at the time. I have tried working with other union leaders, but none of the relationships were as effective as this one. Why? I think it is because David is himself an intellectual who likes to understand the "big picture." For example, he studied Sun Tzu's *The Art of War* with deep attention, trying to find its applicability to union struggles. I was also lucky that the ILG had no local research department at all, so there was a hole for me to fit into.

At some point I began attending Organizing Department meetings. These were conducted entirely in Spanish, of which I knew not a word. I went on a crash course to learn it, taking regular language classes, getting a tutor, reading books and newspapers, and imbibing Spanish-language TV and radio. I do not want to claim that I can speak or understand well, but learned enough to get by. This allowed for me to be able to participate in the newly created Garment Workers' Justice Center. I will not tell the whole story of that here, but briefly, the union ran a Center for non-union workers, and I helped to develop an education program for their weekly meetings. This allowed me to get to know some garment workers personally, if superficially—another invaluable contribution to my academic work.

During the Guess campaign, I helped to form a women's support group called Common Threads. My chief co-conspirator was Karen Brodkin, UCLA anthropologist. This became a wild and creative group that did some street theater, developed some anti-Guess art, met with workers, and eventually faced a lawsuit from Guess. It was fun and educational, as well as political. I learned first-hand how ready a multi-million dollar corporation can be to try to silence even the tiniest criticism. Luckily, Guess withdrew its suit, because Common Threads was able to embarrass the company publicly about it.

I also participated in the formation of a Jewish Coalition against Sweatshops, which eventually transformed itself into a Jewish Commission against Sweatshops. This group was built upon the contradiction that a number of major apparel capitalists were Jewish, including the owners of Guess, but so were many of the people who formed the garment industry unions and the unions still had many Jews in positions of power. The Coalition brought together some rabbis and progressive community organizations, based on a concern that Jewish values were being undermined by sweatshop production. The Commission eventually held hearings and wrote a report (authored by Richard Appelbaum) that denounced the local industry. I was kicked off it because Guess's lawyer insisted that I was too pro-union. He was right, of course, but, unlike him, I did not see the union as evil so that having a pro-union voice on the Commission did not seem to me to be a form of bias. Ah well....

When UNITE formed and many of the ILG organizers left, I stuck around for a while, but never found a niche. Meanwhile some community forces formed a coalition to work on garment worker issues in the face of what was now perceived as UNITE neglect. Out of that grew the LA Garment Workers Center. I played a small role in the conception and development of that, and serve on its board.

The global garment industry has also generated an international anti-sweatshop movement, and I participated in that in a small way too. A student movement, USAS (United Students Against Sweatshops), formed and pressured universities to make sure that their licensed apparel (typically with university logos on it) not be made in sweatshops, either

here or abroad. This in turn led to the creation of university Codes of
Conduct regarding apparel production, moves to get licensees to disclose
the location of their factories, efforts to move towards a living wage, etc.
Out of USAS grew the Worker Rights Consortium (WRC), a tripartite
organization of students from USAS, university administrators, and an
advisory group of "experts" which I joined. The WRC now investigates
reports of problems in factories producing collegiate apparel, and puts
pressure on licensees to intervene. Some victories have come out of it.
USAS has a new campaign now, trying to ensure that all collegiate-wear
is manufactured in unionized factories that pay a living wage.

The garment industry work was my most focused "public sociology"
project. It could have been a lifelong endeavor, and is for some individuals, but at some point I felt I needed to move on. I had published
everything I wanted to say about the industry and, as a "professional"
sociologist, needed another project. This is one of the contradictions of
public sociology. Social activism has a different time frame from academia. Activism has both a very short and a very long time range—it
requires quickly changing decisions, and people are often in it for the
long haul, because the problems do not disappear. Academics have more
of a middle-range time frame. We work hard on a topic, we develop a
model, we give talks, we publish, and we are done. It is hard to keep
working on something when you have finished your project.

Since apparel, I have been engaged in a number of other union/political
projects. I will not go into them in detail, but will just give the flavor of what
they have been about. One line has been, after a hiatus connected with the
demise of the ILG and Guess campaign, to continue to work with David
Young and to follow him through his union experiences. He worked for
the Carpenters during a period in which I had no contact with him, but we
hooked up again when he got a job as an organizer at LIUNA (Laborers
International Union of North America), another construction union. There I
participated in a team effort to try to determine which sector of the industry
should be organized and how we should go about it. We decided to focus
on the residential sector, which the union had lost over the years. One of
my concerns was to try to counter the union's fierce "developmentalist"
bias, and to seek coalitions with slow growth environmentalists, as well
as low-cost housing, and homeless advocates. I think this has been my
contribution to the labor movement, if I have made one—to push for a
socially "progressive" unionism that links with other social movements,
and that tries to stand for the broad interests of the "working class," and
not just for the advantage of union members and organizations.

Unfortunately, as is too often the case, LIUNA was not as interested in a large scale organizing project as it professed. For lots of complex internal political reasons, including a history of autonomy of the locals, it was impossible to move our project forward, and I dropped out. David stayed on and managed to win some small contracts, but was never permitted to pursue a bigger vision, and he eventually quit and moved to a completely different kind of union: the Writers Guild of America (WGA), one of the entertainment industry unions. David invited me to participate in developing a strategy, and I am currently attending a weekly discussion and planning meeting.

At first I had doubts about working with the WGA. I was used to working with low-wage, immigrant workers, not "privileged," mainly white, Hollywood creative artists. I wondered whether this work had any social significance. But in hanging out on the periphery of this work, I have come to realize that the entertainment guilds sit on a very important set of issues: the role of the powerful media in our society. The corporate opponent consists of giant media conglomerates like Viacom, News Corp (Fox) and Disney, each of which owns and controls multiple media outlets. Taking on these giants is no small or insignificant task.

The current organizing project at the Guild concerns reality TV writers, a group of unacknowledged creators who work under harsh conditions for low pay. The campaign has hired an excellent team of researchers and organizers, so my role is minor indeed. But I believe I did play a small role in raising a central social issue, namely, the pernicious degree of advertising penetration, especially in the Reality genre, but also in other areas of the media. As part of the campaign, we contend that "product integration" (making a sponsor's advertised item an integral part of the plot in a deeper way than occurs with mere product placement) is reaching dangerous levels, and that creative writers are being asked to participate in producing essentially advertising copy. We are calling for the right of the creative community to have some say over this process, including developing a Code of Conduct setting limits on product integration. This issue brings us close to the problem of the corporate domination of every facet of society (including the university, where I sit on the Academic Freedom committee and hope to counter the dangerous growth of corporate interference in research.)

My main research/political project right now is about global logistics, the rise of the giant discount retailers like Wal-Mart, and the ports of Los Angeles and Long Beach as key nodes in global production and distribution. The fact that this port complex is one of the biggest in the world, and the major gateway into the United States for the importing of manufactured goods from Asia (especially China), affords the labor movement a strategic opportunity for international organizing. It opens up the possibility of joining production workers in Asia (for example) with distribution workers in the United States as a means of gaining power against giant networked companies (like Wal-Mart) that have created global sweatshops and can move their production around in a "race to the bottom." I decided to study the ports and their surrounding logistics systems to get a picture of how it all works. I also wanted to get a better picture of the state of workers and unions in this complex, to see whether such international, coalition work is possible, and how it might be developed.

I have been working on this project for the last four to five years, and am finishing up a book on it, co-authored with Jake B. Wilson. This is the academic side of the project. We found that, indeed, logistics labor has been shafted. With the major exception of the International Longshore and Warehouse Union (ILWU), logistics workers, including seafarers, port truckers, railroad workers, and warehouse workers, have suffered from a decline in working standards and a weakening of their unions. The mighty ILWU still retains a strong position, but it has come under serious attack, and it is unclear whether it will be able to maintain its strength. But all of these logistics workers/unions occupy a strategic site in global production/ distribution that could literally shut the system down. There is definitely untapped power here that could be used to achieve serious social change, not only for logistics workers, but of global capitalism as a whole.

In an attempt to hook up with a union, I decided that the group to work with was the most oppressed workers in the system—the port truckers. As it happened the International Brotherhood of Teamsters (IBT) had recently started a campaign to organize them, and I contacted Gary Smith, the local organizer, and started meeting with him. I attended some meetings of the truckers, and gave a talk to them on the analysis I was developing of the ports system. They were all Latino, and we spent some time talking about the racial implications of the way truckers are treated, both by the industry and by some other unions.

Gary is a great guy and talented organizer, but he did not have significant power in the union, so there was not much I could do to help him. At one point he, Goetz Wolff (research director at the LA County Federation of Labor at the time) and I made a presentation to the local Teamsters regarding the possibilities of organizing warehouse workers in the Inland Empire (Riverside and San Bernardino Counties), where a huge, port-related, warehouse and distribution center complex has grown up. For a while, we met together with organizers from the ILWU and IBT, in a kind of tripartite effort. Goetz and I would try to provide research assistance, while the unions would develop and implement the campaign. But this never really got off the ground.

The political aspect of the ports project remains in limbo. I have given talks, including at an AFL-CIO Solidarity Center event, and have various feelers out about it. There have been some efforts to develop a Wal-Mart campaign, and if one is developed that incorporates their pro-duction/procurement/distribution empire, then our work may prove to be relevant. Jake and I have published a couple of relevant articles in the *New Labor Forum* (Bonacich, 2003; Bonacich and Wilson, 2005). I do not know how the split in the labor movement will affect the Wal-Mart efforts, but assume they will continue.

In general, in all of this effort, I see my underlying goal as the deepen-ing of democracy. As Burawoy states, democracy is threatened by the domination of corporations and states. The decline of the labor movement reflects an attack by these forces on the rights to full representation and participation by working people in shaping the direction of our society. Unions, with all their difficulties, are vital institutions of civil society that fight for the voices of workers to be heard. They take on the power of corporations in direct confrontation. Labor struggles involve great risk and even greater courage. Workers take on the most powerful forces in our society. It is a glorious endeavor, even if messy in practice, and I want my work to contribute to it in some way.

Teaching Public Sociology

I usually try to put the concept of public sociology in the classroom, especially in undergraduate classes, by having a class project of some sort. I have been deeply influenced by Paulo Freire's *Pedagogy of the Oppressed*, and try to use its principles as much as possible. Freire advocates a dialogic approach to education, in which both teacher and students learn from each other. Since UCR has a substantial working class student body, and is the most racially diverse of the UCs, it affords lots of opportunities for co-learning, as in working together on social change that students find to be relevant to their lives. Ideally, I want the students to learn, in part, by doing—by taking some form of action in society to try to create change for the better.

I am fortunate to teach half the time in ethnic studies, which lends itself to this kind of teaching. For example, I teach a course on Research

Methods in Ethnic Studies, and use it to have the class decide on a common research project that we can all work on together—one that will be of relevance to the ethnic communities of Riverside. At the end of the quarter, we compile the results of our research, try to make a presentation to the community, and make our findings available.

To decide on a "class project" I start by dividing the class into small groups to discuss what they want to work on (there are usually 35-50 students in the class). We then hear from each group and develop a list of possibilities that I write up on the board. We discuss the pros and cons of each one, and combine them where possible. Then we vote on which one we want. I play a role in encouraging topics that are multi-faceted, with clear research as well as action implications.

Once we have agreed upon a broad topic, we divide it up into sub-topics, and students decide which of them they want to work on. They form teams that work together on the sub-topic for the rest of the quarter. Each individual is required to write a report, but each team also summarizes their findings, and at the end of the quarter we create a committee that writes a final class report, summarizing our research, and making recommendations about what should be done. Sometimes one of the teams focuses on "alternatives" and examines efforts that have successfully dealt with the social problem under investigation.

I try to inject a "Marxist" understanding into our research and discussions. What are the underlying power relations? What are the major economic interests? How does the capitalist system shape social policy? How are people and communities, especially racialized groups, hurt by these policies? What community organizations have formed to combat them, and how can we help them? We invite guest speakers from the community to share their vision with us. We also sometimes invite representatives from the "powerful" so that we can question them. I feel there is an important lesson in democracy to be learned here: we have the *right* to challenge the powerful and hold them accountable for their harmful actions.

This particular class has studied a number of topics. One concerned the geographical expansion of our university (UCR) into a poor, ethnic neighborhood. We uncovered a link between the university, local police, and corporate interests in trying to get rid of the homeless and local small businesses. Another looked at the Riverside school system, how segregated it was, how various groups of students of color are performing, and what might be done to improve their achievement. The School Board got wind of our efforts, complained to the Chancellor, and sent representatives to our public forum. Another year we focused on a poor, Chicano community called Casa Blanca, which was having problems with police abuse. Last year we studied the issue of political under-representation of communities of color in Riverside, including such topics as disenfranchisement, election rules, control of the media, and corporate influence over City Hall.

Sometimes in sociology classes I am able to have the students do group projects, with a view to "lessening inequality" or "countering racism." The students approach these projects with youthful creativity and enthusiasm. For some, it is the first time they have ever engaged in political action, like participating in a demonstration. They see the police reaction first hand, and are amazed and invigorated. I see these efforts as exercises in democracy. Students learn that they have a right to participate in their society's decision-making, that they have a right to protest, and that they can participate in and create social movements.

I am careful not to force anyone to engage in any political action that makes them uncomfortable. Groups choose for themselves what they will do. And if someone disagrees with their group, they are always free to opt out and do something else. Still, I think that getting off campus and trying to *do* something in the community, is a valuable lesson that could affect them for the rest of their lives.

Three of the graduate students with whom I have worked most closely, Ralph Armbruster Sandoval, Jill Esbenshade, and Carol Bank Muñoz, have become public sociologists as well as teachers. Ralph is in the Chicano Studies department at UC Santa Barbara, and has won the Distinguished Teaching Award for his ability to involve students in the learning process in a profound way that affects their lives. Jill teaches Sociology at San Diego State University, and has been active in anti-sweatshop work for years. Carol is an assistant professor at Brooklyn College, where she is active in the campus union, and studies and teaches about immigrant workers. They are all courageous young people who live by what they believe.

Difficulties and Challenges in Doing Public Sociology

A number of serious challenges arise in this approach to the discipline. I will discuss four of them: access, betrayal, human subjects, and career issues. I will then attempt to give some "advice" about how to do it for those who want to pursue organic public sociology, but are not sure how to get started.

Access

I have already given some sense of the difficulty of getting to work with unions. Some already have research teams and do not need outside assistance. Or if they do, they want to be able to specify exactly what it should be. They typically want impeccable academic research to prove their point. The academic researcher provides credibility for the union's point of view. The union contracts the research out to a professional, and sometimes pays for it. There is no question that this kind of research can be very useful, and I applaud those who do it. This kind of research sometimes straddles the line between public and policy sociology, as the work may address policy issues that are supported by the unions.

This is not the role that I play. For one thing, I am not good at that kind of research. But also I do not like being told what to do. I value the freedom to study whatever I want to study, and to take an independent stance. So, as I said above, I do not take money from unions, and I am not subject to their determining what I do. This is tricky because, undoubtedly, some people see me as someone who cannot be controlled and therefore cannot be completely trusted. One way to avoid being distrusted is to be trustworthy. I do not study the unions themselves. I study their industries. I study the powerful, and share what knowledge I acquire with the unions. When I work with a union, I try to keep its dirty laundry to myself and do not write about it.

My approach is certainly not the only, or necessarily the best way for public sociologists to work with unions. For example, some sociologists and academics study the labor movement, providing invaluable feedback to the unions. A prime example is Kate Bronfenbrenner, who has conducted research about what makes unions successful at organizing, thereby suggesting possible ways of changing and improving. Ruth Milkman has conducted a census of California unions, as well as helping to build a strong Labor Center at UCLA. And there are many others, many of whom are associated with the ASA Section on Labor and Labor Movements, who have found innovative ways of working with and for the labor movement.

For me, given that what I have to offer is not always readily apparent, access has depended on developing relationships, especially with people in organizing departments. This has sometimes meant attending lots of meetings and being willing to help with the mundane but essential activities of setting up rooms, leafleting, walking the picket line, etc. I have tried to dispel the notion that I have "higher status" and that my education deserves any special respect. It certainly does not. As I learned from Ralph Cuaron, wisdom is not necessarily acquired from a university education. And people without formal education have a wealth of knowledge gained from their own experience and studies. On this issue I am a firm follower of Paulo Freire.

But none of these efforts guarantee access. All one can do is try, be persistent, and do work that the union may find useful.

Betrayal

Here is an ethical dilemma. My research typically involves interviewing people in positions of power. They are far from the most powerful. Most are likely to be members of the managerial-professional stratum who are paid a salary but hardly command a fortune. They are servants of the capitalist class. They serve as its functionaries. But the reality is that most of them are firm believers in the system as it is, and would be appalled if they knew how "radical" I am.

When I interview people like this, I hide my true intentions. I want to learn about their industry from them. Typically they are gracious and helpful. They are experienced in dealing with the public, and are happy to help an academic researcher. I believe I am a good interviewer. I get into the person's space and become authentically sympathetic to their point of view. They sometimes open up to me, and I acquire valuable information. And the truth is, I tend to like most people, enjoy talking with them, and get something out of learning their worldview. I feel that most of the middle-management people that I talk with are decent, sincere, sensitive, well-meaning people.

So the harsh question arises: am I betraying them in this research? In a sense I am. I am using their information to build the weapons of their enemies. I am a Robin Hood researcher, stealing information from the privileged to give to the poor. But it is not a completely comfortable role. I rationalize it as follows: Unions are good for society in that they create greater social equality. Unless they are already in unionized industries—and even that might not be enough in an era of union decline—corporations and their staff will be fiercely anti-union because a union would weaken their competitive position. Yet collectively, they would (in my opinion) all benefit from the existence of floors of decency for their employees below which no one should be allowed to sink. They benefit morally, they benefit from the extension of a market of consumers that can afford their products, and they benefit from a more equal, hence less crime-ridden, society. In general, I strongly believe that social equality is much better for everyone, because, when everyone can flourish, we all gain more from each other. So even if, as individuals, they may feel that the union is their bitter enemy, at a social level they ought to have some interest in seeing it flourish

Human Subjects

In the University of California, the Human Subjects Committee is now called the Institutional Review Board or IRB. As you can imagine, my approach to research is not one that is likely to please the IRB. While I cannot say that organic public sociology is the primary thing they want to blot out, it would certainly raise some serious concerns. I personally think that the main mission of the IRB is to protect the university from being sued, but it is veiled with the language of "looking after" the well-being of research subjects. Indeed, it is best suited to biomedical research, where experimental subjects could be put in serious jeopardy, and is poorly adapted to ethnographic-style research, where the investigator cannot provide a blueprint for the research until she is actually in the field.

I must confess up-front that I simply do not deal with the IRB. I do not go after big grants, which is one way you get caught in their net. And if I get a small grant, I use it to hire Research Assistants and to cover the "respectable" aspect of the project. I know that I am violating university regulations, but I believe there is a clear, pro-business aspect to this policy. Somehow, it is perfectly okay for a university researcher to work with and on behalf of a business corporation. While I have not tested this proposition, my strong suspicion is that the same does not hold true for working with or for a union. The class struggle is not treated even-handedly. At UC, for example, huge sums are spent on funding business schools, yet one small labor institute (the Institute for Labor and Employment) has faced intense opposition, mainly from the governor, from the minute it was started, with the intention of snuffing it.

But I am aware that I have the advantage of old age and a long career behind me. In not cooperating with the IRB, I do not risk much. For younger public sociologists this has got to be a more serious challenge. What can you do about it? It seems to me there are two possibilities: confront the IRB's biases head on, or disguise your political intentions under the language of scientific research. The reality is that organic public sociology is not something that establishment research universities embrace. But, in the name of academic freedom, I strongly believe that we have a right to do it. Burawoy's efforts to give it recognition are in the spirit of carving a legitimate spot for it, not only in the discipline, but in the university as a whole.

Career Issues

Will your career be harmed by involvement in social action? The messages most young scholars receive from their older colleagues are likely to urge caution and conservatism. "Focus on publishing in the major journals. Don't waste your time on activism. You need to do what it takes to get tenure, first and foremost. Maybe you can do some activism on the side later, when you have some security." A similar message is given to politically involved undergrads and graduate students.

I personally find this kind of pressure infuriating. It is linked to the philosophy of individualistic upward mobility, rather than concern for the public good. I do not see a contradiction between being socially engaged and doing good sociology (as I discuss below). My advice, for what it is worth, is to be as true as possible to your own beliefs. Don't try to shape yourself to someone else's model of success. Rather, do what you believe is the right thing. That way you will give it your best effort, your deepest thought, your most creative ideas. Your sociological work will be better because you believe in it. Alienated academic labor is no better than any other form of alienated labor. It sours the soul. It shrinks the heart.

I am aware that some people have lost their jobs because of their pursuit of organic public sociology. I feel that, for myself, I have never been particularly careful. I always felt that people would respect you if you stood up for what you believe in. I certainly have tried to keep writing and publishing, and did not expect the academy to reward me for my political work. I think that, in general, if you do good work and are productive as a scholar, you are protected against retaliation for your political activities. Academic freedom is a very important value and protection.

Some Advice on How to Do It

These are tentative reflections, based on one person's experience. Everyone needs to find their own way. It is important to be authentic in your goals and your behavior. There is no blueprint. Nevertheless, here are some of the principles I have learned:

- You can approach your topic from either end, i.e., you can decide on a research topic, and look for its political implications, or you can decide on a political project and look for its research implications. In the case of the garment industry I moved from research to politics, while the ports project moved from a belief in the strategic importance of the ports to a research project.

- As I have said, gaining access can be difficult. One approach is to hang around with the group you want to work with, help with small things, and offer to help with bigger ones. The biggest error is likely to be an assumption that you have a lot to offer, and that the people who have been struggling on the ground for years do not know what they are doing. Arrogance is an unfortunate tendency among academics, and it certainly will not open doors. It is important to realize that you have a lot to learn, rather than much to teach. Try to maintain a stance of humility and respect.

- Be prepared to spend time on activities that are not directly relevant to your research. You want to become part of the organization as much as possible, and that can entail hanging out, doing the kinds of things that staff do, serving on community boards, and making yourself generally useful. You should use the skills learned in academia, where possible: writing, knowing how to run a meeting, keeping good notes, identifying useful materials, etc.

- Share your findings, not only with the leadership but also with the rank and file (by volunteering to hold educational events, for example). This is predicated on the idea that you are not studying the organization, but the world in which they are embedded. Also, share your write-ups with the leadership. You might even co-author pieces with them.

Does Organic Public Sociology Contribute to the Discipline?

Speaking only for myself, I believe that my political involvements have made me a better sociologist. One benefit is close to those of ethnography. By getting inside your subject, you get to understand it in a very different way from what you learn by running regression analyses on the computer based on abstracted data acquired at a distance. This is not the place to present a critique of "abstracted empiricism." I have philosophical objections to that entire approach to knowledge. The point is that a good deal of insight is to be gained from being part of the lived experience of the people you are studying. Like an ethnographer, one must ponder the meanings of things to participants, and try to make sense of the social world they are involved in. The process is more of an art than a science, and the result is more interpretative than conclusive. It also enables one to incorporate the vital moral element inherent in all social relations in one's work.

These things are true of any ethnographic research, so what does the political element add? I believe that participating in social/political conflict reveals the fault lines of society in an especially vivid way. You learn how power is wielded. You feel the overbearing hand of institutional authority. And you also learn that there are ways to counter it, and to fight back. These understandings can also enrich your work. Moreover, you also get to witness the complexities of the alliances: how your opponents may be mixed and conflicted in their positions (for example, Jewish garment manufacturers), and how your allies can sometimes be self-righteous and self-promoting. But overall, engagement in social conflict and social struggle is a wonderful way to see how society works, in living color.

My major interests in the field concern race and class, and particularly, the racialization of labor. I approach the study of society from a Marxist perspective, and believe that capitalism is a system that is inherently exploitative. I also believe that race (also gender, but I do not focus on it as much) is a major tool of super-exploitation that is used not only by capitalists to suck surplus labor out of workers of color, but is also a basis for some workers and unions to create niches of privilege for themselves in opposition to people of color. This vicious triangle gets enacted in a myriad of ways.

By working with the labor movement, I get to witness some of these dynamics first hand. What does it mean to be an oppressed, Mexican immigrant garment worker in Los Angeles? What is the human side of this experience? More importantly, how do people maintain their dignity under these circumstances? What does it take for people to develop the courage to stand up with their fellows to protect themselves? How does the union answer their needs, and where does it fail them? How can you *win* a social struggle against a very powerful and wealthy opponent? How is social change created? And once a gain is made, how are people changed by it? If these are not topics of importance to our discipline, I do not know what are.

I keep coming back to the concept of "witnessing." By being in the middle of it all, you get to see it up close, to *live* the experience, to try to understand it from the inside. I feel this produces a different kind of knowledge, one that is closer to the way society, in all its complex conflicts, works.

Now I can imagine the objections: How can you be objective when you are involved? Doesn't this distort your perspective? Shouldn't a sociologist stand outside the fray, and consider all sides of a question? I would not argue that there is no room for some people to study subjects from the outside, though I do think that "objectivity" is a questionable concept. We are, willy-nilly, part of the society we study. We have a social location both in our personal histories and in our current situations. As sociologists we know that these experiences color the way we see the world. Can anyone free themselves from these things? Does it matter if one grew up Black or white, male or female? Don't academics occupy a particular class position that shapes their social attitudes and values at least to some extent? Society is a contested arena. There is no truly objective vantage point. But that does not mean one should not try to tell the truth, as best you understand it. This is what I try to do.

This brings me to the question: how does the kind of public sociology that I do relate to the other three types identified by Burawoy? The connection with critical sociology should be clear. My work draws heavily on the critical tradition in sociology, especially Marxism, but also on the tradition that criticizes racism, following W.E.B. DuBois and many others. I see my work as deeply rooted in the critical tradition, which informs my choice of research projects, my method of research, and my interpretation of findings. All of my work is focused on questions of social inequality, and how to fight against it.

Another way to put this is to say that my work is informed by values, especially the values of diminishing inequality and increasing democracy. I want to promote full equality, and not just equality of opportunity, since the latter inevitably creates hierarchies of various kinds. I am still the person who believes in the values represented by the early kibbutz movement: the dignity of labor, the right of everyone to participate in the intellectual, artistic, and political life of their community, and the right of everyone to the same basic material well-being. This is not to say that leadership has no place, and that special contributions should not receive recognition. But leadership and effort need not be rewarded in terms of better housing, food, healthcare, and education for one's children. There are other, more equalitarian ways of honoring people.

In sum, I do not attempt to take a "value neutral" stance with regard to research. I believe every researcher brings values to their work whether they acknowledge it or not. By combining values and social action, I see myself as working at the intersection of critical and public sociology, trying to develop the social critique through theory and research, and to use that research towards moving from critique to involvement in trying to make it a reality.

Policy sociology is more problematic for me to link with. Some of policy sociology, as I understand it, is directed towards the state. Since I tend to view the state *in this country* as closely linked with private capital, it is hard for me to want to give them any advice. This is not to say that I do not admire and respect some of the excellent sociological work that has been done to get state policy to change. And, indeed, I have been linked with projects that have tried to impact the state. For example, the garment industry work has implications for state inspections (and their lack), legislation such as "joint liability" (or the legal responsibility of manufacturers for their contractors' malfeasance), and state certification programs that claim factories are sweat-free (which may end up as a public relations ploy).

One can define Policy Sociology more broadly as research that is done for a client (a practice that I generally try to avoid), or as research that is conducted to foster a particular social goal. Using this latter meaning, I think my work can be said to be influenced by this tradition a bit, as well. I am certainly pursuing a policy goal of trying to help unions win collective bargaining agreements, and more generally, of strengthening the power of labor as we weaken the power of corporate capital. These goals are central to my work as a sociologist. My ports project, for example, is aimed at getting a seat for labor at the table in the construction of globalization. As it stands now, globalization is largely being propelled by private corporations and states, while workers and unions (as well as other important social actors) are excluded from the planning. I believe that a series of demands need to be placed on global corporations from a working class perspective, so that world development is not exploitative of either the peoples or the ecology of the planet.

Finally, as I think I have already indicated, contributing to professional sociology is definitely a central thread of my work. I try to develop "theory" that expands the field. I try to do empirical work that contributes to our theoretical understanding. I believe that theory and action *must* be connected, in both directions. Mindless activism may serve an expressive function, but it does not bring about needed social change. Similarly, theory, without action, can end up as a hollow intellectual game. I want the theory that I develop to be rooted in the real world, and to be useful to practitioners, but I also want it to be part of the discipline's debates, especially on the intersection of race and class.

Notes

1. Thanks to Ralph Armbruster Sandoval, Carol Bank Muñoz, Michael Burawoy, Vince Jeffries, and Rochelle McAdam for their careful reading and excellent feedback on an earlier draft of this paper.
2. It may seem puzzling that unions existed in the University of California before the passage of a law that legitimated collective bargaining, but the right to freedom of assembly protects such organizations. The AFT met regularly, discussed campus issues, passed resolutions regarding public events, and generally provided a community for the leftist faculty.

3.   For those who are interested, the result was that AFSCME won the election and stripped the locals of their power. The result was a much weakened union, which took decades to bounce back and develop some membership involvement, at least at UCR.

References

Bonacich, E. 2000. "Intense Challenges, Tentative Possibilities: Organizing Immigrant Garment Workers in Los Angeles." Pp. 130-149 in *Immigrants and Union Organizing in California*, edited by R. Milkman. Ithaca, NY: Cornell University Press.

_____. 2003. "Pulling the Plug: Labor and the Global Supply Chain." *New Labor Forum* 12(Summer): 41-48.

_____, and Appelbaum, R. 2000. *Behind the Label: Inequality in the Los Angeles Garment Industry*. Berkeley, CA: University of California Press.

_____, Cheng, L., Chinchilla, N., Hamilton, N., and Ong, P.1994. *Global Production: The Apparel Industry in the Pacific Rim*. Philadelphia, PA: Temple University Press.

_____, and Wilson, J.B. 2005. "Hoisted by Its Own Petard: Organizing Wal-Mart's Logistics Workers." *New Labor Forum* 14(Summer): 67-75.

Burawoy, M. 2005. "For Public Sociology." *American Sociological Review*, 70: 4-28.

Ong, P., Bonacich, E. and Cheng, L. 1994. *The New Asian Immigration in Los Angeles and Global Restructuring*, Philadelphia, PA: Temple University Press.

5

Social Gerontology as Public Sociology in Action

Norella M. Putney, Dawn E. Alley, and Vern L. Bengtson

Burawoy (2005) argues that sociology needs to re-establish a public sociology oriented toward society's problems and the practice of its unique knowledge if it is to again be taken seriously by the public, policymakers, and others. Yet, it is unclear how best to achieve these goals. We argue that the relatively young field of social gerontology provides a useful model of successful public sociology in action. As a multidisciplinary field engaged in basic and applied research and practice, social gerontology's major aim is to improve the lives of older people and to ameliorate problems associated with age and aging. Thus social gerontology has routinely reached beyond the academy to engage with its publics. We review the field's historical and theoretical development and present four examples of public sociology in action. Several factors have contributed to social gerontology's success in achieving the goals of public sociology: (1) Working in multidisciplinary teams which promote collaboration and respect for diverse perspectives. (2) Its ability to advocate "professionally" for its publics without favoring one group at the expense of another. (3) The unique affinity of its theories and practices with its disciplinary values. (4) The constructive effects of its ongoing questioning of values and ethics. Working in a multidisciplinary field with multiple publics, social gerontologists have been able to blend professional, critical, policy, and public sociologies to a considerable degree while contributing toward improvements in well-being.

Public sociology has recently emerged as a topic of significant debate within the broader field of sociology. At its core, public sociology involves reaching a public audience and working to improve the public's well-being (Brady, 2004). Its aim is "to enrich public debate about moral and political issues by infusing them with sociological theory and research" (Burawoy, 2004: 1603). Yet it is unclear how best to achieve these goals, or even whether these are appropriate goals for sociologists. Little published work has discussed whether or how public sociology can be practically achieved. We propose that the field of social gerontology can offer insights as to how a social science discipline can enact its "public" dimension— engagement with various publics both inside and outside the discipline for the mutual benefit of its constituent interests.

Burawoy (2005) proposes that public sociology brings sociology into a conversation with publics, motivated by a concern that sociology may be isolated from public discourse and public action. Social gerontology, on the other hand, has been in continuous conversation with its publics since its beginnings: the elderly and their families, practitioners, policy-makers, government agencies, employers as the providers of pensions, gerontology students, and many others. Gerontologists almost by defi-nition are involved in public sociology. Many act in the public arena as advocates for elders.

In this paper we argue that the field of social gerontology provides a useful model of successful public sociology in action. First we present our understanding of what is meant by public sociology, as described by its major proponent (Burawoy, 2004; 2005) and some of its skep-tics (Brady, 2004; Nielsen, 2004; Tittle, 2004). We then introduce the relatively young field of social gerontology. We describe its historical and theoretical development and comment on the theoretical debates as well as the underlying values that have animated its basic and applied research agendas. Next we provide four examples of social gerontology as public sociology in action. We then identify several factors that have made social gerontology successful in achieving the goals of public sociology. Finally, we summarize the ways in which social gerontology can inform the development of public sociology.

The Pursuit of Public Sociology

Pointing to a growing divide between sociology and the world it seeks to understand, Burawoy (2005) argues that sociology is in danger of losing its connection to civil society and thus losing sight of its primary purpose. The discipline needs to re-establish a public sociology oriented toward society's problems and the practice of its unique knowledge if it is again to be taken seriously by the public, policymakers, the mass media, and others. To this end, Burawoy conceptualizes a division of sociological labor representing a matrix of four kinds of knowledge that are nevertheless interdependent: professional, critical, policy, and public. To regain its relevance and vitality, professional sociology, in particular, needs to pay heed to the emancipatory values of its critical side.

Debate has centered largely around whether or not public sociology is desirable or, at its extreme, unethical and an abuse of professional authority. Proponents of public sociology argue that sociological work should be relevant to the public, that sociologists are accountable to the public, particularly at state-funded universities, and that public sociology is a natural and necessary counterpart to professional sociology (Burawoy, 2004). Opponents of public sociology argue that working to better society assumes both a consistency of values across sociologists and a consistency of findings in sociology that do not exist, and that the pursuit of public sociology undermines professional or scientific sociology (Nielsen, 2004; Tittle, 2004). If a public sociology as proposed by Burawoy (2005) is desirable, how can a sociology of this kind be developed? The relatively young field of social gerontology provides an example of how this can occur.

The Multidisciplinary Field of Social Gerontology

The Goals of Social Gerontology   هدف بهبود زندگی و رفع مشکلات پیری است.

Social gerontology is a multidisciplinary field grounded in the sociology of age but informed by psychologists, policy and public health researchers, medical and social work practitioners, demographers, and economists, among others. A central aim of social gerontology since its inception as a discipline has been to understand and improve the lives of older adults, and to ameliorate the "problems" of aging (Achenbaum, 1995). Thus social gerontologists are interested in the impact of socioeconomic, political, and cultural forces and conditions on the processes of aging, and in the statuses and well-being of older people. Social gerontology explores the ways in which the older population and the diversity of the aging experience affect and are affected by social structures (Hooyman and Kiyak, 2005). Research in social gerontology addresses many domains of social life and behavior, including family relationships, health and disability, and older adults' social participation. Social gerontologists are also interested in social inequality by age—the unequal treatment of older people and in the deleterious effects of ageism. The recognition of diversity and inequality has been crucial to the development of the field, and these factors are incorporated in theory and practice.

Social gerontology is oriented around the "so what?" question: a concern for applying findings to improve the lives of older persons and their families. Social gerontologists often look to public policy as a way of making these improvements. Indeed, much of gerontological research is aimed at influencing public policy for the benefit of publics. Because it is involved in basic as well as applied research, the field has devoted and

عکس العمل سیاستها در افراد ناتوان، برای بهبود شرایط زندگی مردم

enthusiastic audiences. Its activities range from traditional quantitative and qualitative sociological research to direct community-based research and service, to advocacy for the elderly before agencies and lawmakers. Thus social gerontologists have been doing much of what Burawoy suggests is public sociology long before it was labeled as such.

In social gerontology, distinctions between professional, critical, policy, and public domains are blurred, even as ideal types, particularly between policy and public. Perhaps this is because of social gerontology's multidisciplinary origins and its common vision of ameliorating the problems of old age. Often, the same scholars are responsible for conducting basic research and communicating that research to various publics. In social gerontology public priorities are more than just "moments" (Burawoy, 2005); they crosscut the domains of labor. This may be because each domain, to the extent domains are distinguishable at all, sees itself as accountable to the well-being of older people and their families.

The Problem of Aging

Social gerontologists—whether as scientists, practitioners, or policymakers— concern themselves with three sets of issues as they attempt to analyze and understand the phenomena of aging. The first set concerns *the aged*: the population of those categorized as elderly in terms of their length of life lived or expected life span. Most gerontological research in recent decades has focused on the functional problems of aged populations, seen as medical disability or barriers to independent living. How can we better address the needs of elderly people? How can they live healthier and more fulfilling lives? How can we identify and mitigate the pernicious effects of ageism? A second set of issues focuses on *aging as a developmental process*. Here the principal interest is in the conditions and problems that accumulate during the lifespan and cannot be understood separate from developmental experiences and processes across a lifetime.

A third set of issues involves the study of *age* as a dimension of structure and behavior. Social gerontologists are interested in how social organizations are created and changed in response to age-related patterns of birth, socialization, role transitions and retirement or death. The phenomena to be explained relate to how institutions such as labor markets, retirement and pension systems, healthcare organizations, and political institutions take into account or deal with "age." Rapid population aging and higher old age dependency ratios will create major challenges for states and economies over the next half-century. Less obvious but equally important is the profound effect that population aging will have on social institutions such as families. A major question concerns the provision of care for the growing numbers of very old people. Is it primarily the responsibility of families? Of individual's themselves? Or the responsibility of government? Through their research, social gerontologists concern themselves with these challenging societal issues. While these three sets of research issues are quite different in focus and inquiry, they are nonetheless interrelated in research and practice.

The Young Science of Gerontology

Gerontology emerged as a distinct field of study in the United States only a half-century ago, following World War II, when scientists from biology, psychology, and human development founded the Gerontological Society of America. Since its beginnings gerontology's scholarly and scientific interests have been broadly defined, because old age was considered "a problem" that was unprecedented in scope and complexity (Achenbaum, 1987). To understand and explain the multi-faceted phenomena and processes of aging required the scientific insights of biology and biomedicine, psychology and the social sciences. Over time the field expanded beyond these core disciplines to include anthropology, demography, economics, epidemiology, history, the humanities and arts, political science, and social work, as well as the many professions that serve older persons.

As it developed, gerontology endeavored to define itself as a "science" (Achenbaum, 1995). Today science is the reigning paradigm for conducting research and developing theoretically based, cumulative knowledge in the field. Science and theory guide recommendations for policy and interventions. Thus, theory is necessary not only in the conduct of basic research concerning phenomena of aging, but also in application—in practice—in order to design effective interventions to assist older adults and effectively deal with the countless problems associated with aging and old age.

Theoretical Development in Social Gerontology

We shift to a discussion of theories in social gerontology not only because they reflect the progression of ideas in our field over time, but also because current theoretical perspectives show a loose correspondence with Burawoy's (2005) professional and critical types of sociologies.

While most social gerontological research is scientific and quantitative, interpretive and critical approaches and qualitative and narrative methods have become more common in recent years. Arguing that science and positivistic approaches are limited for understanding aspects of aging, social gerontologists with critical and social constructionist perspectives suggest that there are nonscientific ways to examine, interpret, and develop knowledge about aging. Further, critical theorists argue that such knowledge should be emancipatory. To be sure, social gerontologists have engaged in heated debates over the virtues of science in developing and applying knowledge and whether human behavior can be understood at all in terms of laws, causality, and prediction—not unlike the debates in sociology. In our field, researchers in the interpretive tradition focus on describing and understanding how social interactions proceed and on the subjective meanings of age and aging phenomena (Gubrium and Holstein, 1999). This perspective posits that knowledge of the social world derives from the meanings individuals attach to their social situations. In addition, individuals are seen as active agents who can change the nature of their social environments, thus casting doubt on the possibility of finding any general scientific explanations of human social organization (Turner, 2003).

Like the aging process itself, theoretical development is embedded in institutional and historical contexts. Achenbaum (1995) observes how the development of gerontological theories paralleled the historical construction of gerontology around new scientific methods and medical practices that would be used to address the "problems" associated with declining health and growing old. Not surprisingly, the biomedicalization of aging is still a guiding research paradigm, while using science to help ameliorate of the problems of older people remains a central goal.

As social gerontology developed in the post-World War II period, it drew theoretical insights from the prevailing theoretical paradigm of the time, structural functionalism, as well as symbolic interactionism. The most explicitly developed of these theories, disengagement theory (Cumming and Henry, 1961), explained human aging as an inevitable process of individuals disengaging and adaptively withdrawing from social structures in anticipation of the person's inevitable death, a functional process ultimately beneficial for individuals and the social system. Disengagement theory created a firestorm of criticism. The theory had attempted to explain both macro- and micro-level changes with one "grand theory," but when tested empirically its validity and generalizability claims were not supported. While many older people appear to be "disengaging" or withdrawing from their social connections and activities, many are not. Activity theory (Lemon, Bengtson, and Peterson, 1972) represented an alternative explanation of aging. Its legacy, reflected in the concept "successful aging," has reappeared in a bestselling book (Rowe and Kahn, 1998) but has been criticized for its excessive individualism and discounting of social diversity and inequalities (Schmeechle and Bengtson, 1999). Modernization theory as applied to aging (Cowgill and Holmes, 1974), and subculture theory (Rose, 1965) also emerged during this formative period. One outcome of the profound criticism of disengagement theory was to curtail further attempts to develop a general theory of aging. Interestingly, modernization theory has recently resurfaced, although more limited in scope (Aboderin, 2004).

In the 1970s a second generation of theories of aging emerged, many based upon older more general sociological or rational choice theories: continuity theory (Atchley, 1993) and social breakdown/ competence theory (Kuypers and Bengtson, 1973), both coming from symbolic interactionism; and exchange theory (Dowd, 1975), a rational choice perspective. Two macro-level perspectives included age stratification theory (Riley, Johnston, and Foner, 1972), drawing from structural functionalism, and the political economy of aging (Estes et al., 1984), a conflict perspective. Since the late 1980s many of these theories have been refined and reformulated, and a third generation of theoretical perspectives emerged (Hendricks, 1992).

Contemporary Theoretical Perspectives in Social Gerontology

A brief review of the major theories used in the social gerontology reveals the pluralism and diversity of today's thinking about the "why" and "how" of phenomena of age and aging. Some of these theoretical perspectives appear more closely related to Burawoy's (2005) category of "professional" sociology while others are more aligned with "critical" sociology. We have not included theories from the social psychology and psychology of aging, some of which are used in combination with the theories listed below when testing competing hypotheses.

1) Life Course Perspective. This perspective is the field's most widely cited theoretical framework. It generally corresponds to the professional domain of social gerontological labor. While there is debate as to whether the life course is a "theory" or an orienting perspective, it represents a convergence of thinking in sociology and psychology about processes at both macro- and micro-social levels of analysis and for both populations and individuals over time. Researchers using this perspective are attempting to explain: (1) the dynamic, contextual, and processual nature of aging; (2) age-related transitions and life trajectories; (3) how aging is related to and shaped by social contexts, cultural meanings, and social structural location; and (4) how time, historical period and cohort shape the aging process for individuals as well as for social groups (Bengtson and Allen, 1993; Elder, 1992; Elder and Johnson, 2002). This approach is multidisciplinary, drawing content and methods from sociology, psychology, anthropology, and history. The life course approach is also explicitly dynamic rather than static, attempting to focus on the life cycle in its entirety while allowing for deviations in trajectories. Typically seen as a "mainstream" perspective, the life course perspective is often used by critical theorists in their research designs but who then cross typological boundaries to evaluate findings critically (Dannefer, 2003).

Social Exchange Theory. Social exchange theory also falls into the professional social gerontology quadrant. Frequently used in the study of intergenerational relations and support, this micro-level theory attempts to explain exchange behavior between individuals of different ages as a result of the shift in roles, skills, and resources that accompany advancing age. Developed and extended by Dowd (1975), social exchange theory draws from sociological formulations by Homans (1961) and Blau (1964) and work in economics that assumes a rational choice model of decision-making behavior. It explicitly incorporates the concept of power differences. A primary assumption is that various actors (such as an elderly parent and an adult child) each bring resources to an interaction or exchange and that such exchanges are governed by norms of reciprocity, an obligation to repay the receipt of valued assets, services or sentiments. Repayment may be deferred for decades, as when a parent's investment in his or her adolescent child is repaid by that child in midlife when the parent is old and frail (Silverstein et al., 2002).

Age and Society Paradigm (Age Stratification Perspective). One of the oldest traditions of macro-level theorizing in social gerontology (Riley, Foner, and Waring, 1988), this perspective's intellectual roots can be traced to structural functionalism, particularly the works of sociologists Sorokin (1947), Mannheim (1922/1952), and Parsons (1942). It too aligns more closely with professional social gerontology. There are three components to this "paradigm": studying the movement of age cohorts across time in order to identify similarities and differences between them; exploring the interdependence of age cohorts and social structures; and examining the asynchroniaty between structural and individual change over time. A major concept is that of structural lag (Riley, Kahn, and Foner, 1994), which occurs when social structures cannot keep pace with the changes in population dynamics and individual lives. Women's experience of work/family stress because of the unavailability of adequate childcare programs is an example of structural lag. Using this theoretical perspective, Riley and Loscocco (1994) argue that a more age-integrated society—where activities of work, family caretaking, education, and leisure are not strictly segmented by age—can compensate for structural lag.

Critical Perspectives of Aging. Critical perspectives in contemporary social gerontology include several theoretical perspectives: the political economy of aging, feminist gerontology, theories of diversity, humanistic gerontology, and strands of social constructionism. Most social gerontologists using one of these critical perspectives are in fact engaged in critical scholarship—following Burawoy's scheme (2005), although a critical theorist may also do professional social gerontology.

Critical Gerontology. Coming primarily out of the Frankfurt School of Critical Theory (Horkheimer and Adorno, 1944; Habermas, 1971), and post-structuralism (Foucault, 1977), critical theories of aging share a common focus on criticizing "the process of power" (Baars, 1991). Critical gerontology has developed two distinct patterns in social gerontology, one which focuses on humanistic dimensions of aging, and the other on structural components. Moody (1993) proposes a humanistic critical gerontology that has four goals: (1) to theorize subjective and interpretive dimensions of aging; (2) to focus on praxis (involvement in practical change) instead of technical advancement; (3) to link academics and practitioners through praxis; and (4) to produce "emancipatory knowledge." A second strand emphasizes that critical gerontology should create positive models of aging, focusing on the strengths and diversity of age in addition to critiquing positivist knowledge (Bengtson, Burgess, and Parrott, 1997).

Political Economy of Aging Perspective. Drawing from Marxism (Marx, 1867/ 1967), conflict theory (Simmel, 1908/1950) and critical theory (Habermas, 1971), the political economy of aging perspective seeks to explain how the interaction of economic and political forces determines the unequal allocation of resources, thereby shaping the experience of aging that results in older persons' loss of power, autonomy, and influence. Variations in the treatment and status of the elderly can be understood by examining public policies, economic trends, and social structural factors (Estes, 2001). Life experiences are seen as being patterned not only by age, but also by class, gender, and race and ethnicity. These structural factors, often institutionalized or reinforced by economic and public policy, constrain the opportunities, choices and experiences of later life. The political economy of aging perspective is also concerned with how ageism is constructed and reproduced through social practices and policies, and how it negatively affects the well-being of older people (Bytheway, 1994).

8. *Feminist Theories of Aging.* Feminist gerontology gives priority to gender as an organizing principle for social life across the life course that significantly affects the experience of aging (Calasanti, 2004; McMullen, 1995). At the macro-level of analyses, feminist theories of aging combine with political economy to examine differential access to the key material, health, and caring resources which substantially alter the experience of aging for women and men (Arber and Ginn, 1995). For example, from a feminist perspective, family caregiving can be understood as an experience of obligation, structured by the gender-based division of domestic labor and the devaluing of unpaid work (Stroller, 1993). At the micro-level, a feminist gerontology perspective holds that gender should be examined in the context of social meanings and everyday experiences, reflecting the influence of social constructionism.

9. *Social Constructionist Perspectives.* Social constructionism is the second most frequently cited theoretical approach in the major social gerontology journals (Bengtson, Burgess, and Parrott, 1997). Contemporary constructionist researchers in social gerontology may be engaged in professional labor, but more frequently in critical labor. These perspectives come from a long tradition of micro-level analysis in the social sciences: symbolic interactionism (Mead, 1934), phenomenology (Berger and Luckmann, 1966), and ethnomethodology (Garfinkel, 1967). Using hermeneutic or interpretive methods, social constructionism focuses on individual agency and social behavior within social institutions—such as the family, or retirement centers—and particularly on the subjective meanings of age and the aging experience in everyday life. Researchers working in this tradition emphasize their interest in understanding, if not explaining, individual processes of aging as influenced by social definitions and social structures. Examples include Gubrium's (1993) study of the subjective meanings of quality of care and quality of life for residents of nursing homes, which explored how each resident constructs meanings from her or his own experiences. These meanings emerge from analyses of life narratives and participant observation.

This diversity of perspectives alerts social gerontologists to be concerned with the connections between scientific inquiry and the social milieu at particular points in time that influence how a subject matter is conceived. In recent years, interpretive and critical social gerontologists have called attention to these connections (Hendricks and Achenbaum, 1999), cautioning researchers to be more reflective on their own values or biases as they interpret findings, develop interventions, and make policy recommendations.

Epistemological Debates and Gerontological Values

Critical perspectives in social gerontology (including political economy of aging, feminist gerontology, and many variants of social constructionism) challenge the mainstream scientific approach as a principal source of knowledge. The understanding of meanings and the analysis of power and domination in social relations and structures are seen as important as "objective knowledge" in the understanding of social phenomena (Bengtson, Burgess, and Parrott, 1997; Moody, 2001). Critical theory assumes that values cannot be separated from "facts" and that all research is value-laden. While acknowledging researchers' values, science assumes that objective knowledge not encumbered by values is both possible and desirable. Thus critical perspectives and the quest for emancipatory knowledge in social gerontology operate under different assumptions than positivism and science about the subject and the purpose of aging research. At the same time, there is a growing recognition that the insights provided by these nonscientific approaches about the experience of aging, what it means to grow old and be old, and about issues of social justice for the aged, have filled gaps in the knowledge base obtained through the positivist paradigm, and we feel they have enriched the field of social gerontology. An example is the contribution of Barbara Myerhoff's (1976) classic ethnographic study of Jewish elders, *Number Our Days*. Social gerontology continues to see epistemological debates surrounding different kinds of knowledge and the use of theory. However, we suggest that one way to address such differences is to regard these perspectives as providing complementary lenses that can broaden our understanding of the multiple facets of aging.

These differences in epistemology have not created hard battle lines in our field, however, in part because there is implicit agreement by most on the important goals of social gerontology, and also because the field is still young; its pioneers, some of whom are still alive, remind the field of its original vision and purpose. Coming out of its history and culture, gerontology's foundational values—to help older people and alleviate their problems—derive not so much from critical awareness as from adherence to progressive ideals and the use of science to improve conditions for humankind and alleviate suffering. Nevertheless, as the critical culture of social gerontology has evolved, these values have been complemented and explicated.

Because social gerontology developed simultaneously as an active area of scientific research, policy, and practice, researchers are often called upon to act as public social gerontologists; they must be able not only to explain the relevance of their results for improving the lives of older persons, but also to *use* their knowledge to design effective policies that will improve the lives of older people and their families. The latter mandate is epitomized by the words of Maggie Kuhn, founder of the Gray Panthers' movement and a tireless advocate for older people, in an address before the Gerontological Society of America: "We have enough research! We have enough theories! What we need are more programs to help senior citizens in need!" (Kuhn, 1983).

Examples of Public Sociology in Social Gerontology

In the following section we present four examples of "public sociology" in the field of social gerontology.

Research on Grandparents Raising Grandchildren

The issue of grandparents raising grandchildren provides one example of social gerontology's public sociology in action. Here, research on the growing number of grandparent caregivers initiated a public dialogue among older persons, service providers and interest groups, and policy researchers, eventually leading to a federal program and a range of community support programs. This process began when demographic analysis at the early 1990s showed a surprising 44 percent increase in the number of children living with grandparents or other relatives over the prior decade (Saluter, 1992). A group of social gerontologists with backgrounds in sociology, public health, and social work began to explore qualitatively the characteristics of these grandparent caregivers and the reasons for this trend (Minkler, Roe, and Price, 1992). Guided by feminist and critical sensibilities, advocacy objectives were incorporated into the research design (Roe, Minkler, and Barnwell, 1994). The researchers involved grandparent subjects in all phases of the study as well as a community advisory group composed of local health and social worker professionals and individuals working with grandparents of young children. The goal was to maximize respondent benefit from the experience of participating in the study. The researchers shared their findings with their grandparent participants and elicited their suggestions in the development of policy recommendations (Roe, Minkler, and Barnwell, 1994).

The researchers found that more than one in ten grandparents had cared for a grandchild for at least six months, and most were engaged in an even longer-term commitment. Although grandparent caregiving occurs among all gender, class, and ethnic groups, single women, African Americans, and low-income persons are more likely to become custodial grandparents (Fuller-Thompson, Minkler, and Driver, 1997). Additional research has found that substance abuse, teen pregnancy, AIDS, and incarceration all contributed to this problem (Dressel and Barnhill, 1994; Jendrek, 1994; Minkler and Roe, 1993). It became clear that grandparent caregivers faced unique challenges with negative consequences for both grandparents and grandchildren, resulting in unmet needs for social services (Burton, 1992; Dowdell, 1995; Minkler et al., 1993; Roe et al., 1996).

Research on grandparent caregivers attracted the attention of aging service professionals, leading to the involvement of the Federal Administration on Aging and several aging interest groups, including AARP and Generations United. Cooperation between researcher, practitioner, and advocacy communities resulted in a variety of community, state, and federal programs, most notably provision for grandparent caregivers through the 2000 amendments to the Older Americans Act under the National Family Caregiver Support program.

Centers for Applied Gerontology

The Edward R. Roybal Centers for Research on Applied Gerontology is a second example of public sociology in social gerontology. Authorized by Congress in 1993 and sponsored by the National Institute on Aging, the Roybal Centers' mandate is to move social and behavioral research findings out of the laboratory and into programs, practices, and policies to benefit the lives of middle- and older-aged people and their families (National Institutes of Health, 1997; Pillemer et al., 2003). The Roybal Centers reflect a growing interest by federal agencies in translational research: translating basic behavioral research findings into research interventions to improve real-world practices (National Institute of Mental Health, 2000). There are currently ten Roybal Centers for Research on Applied Gerontology (National Institute on Aging, 2004). Located at major universities and research institutions, each Center focuses on a different thematic area (such as mobility and driving, enhancement of late-life functioning, social support and involvement in meaningful roles, exercise adherence, compliance with medical orders, and use of technology).

Reflecting the aims of a public sociology, the Roybal Centers interact with multiple publics. Protocols for each Center call for broad-based expertise involving collaboration across disciplines as well as between researchers, practice professionals, and older people and their families. Several projects feature collaboration between scientists and organizations involved with older people, such as healthcare agencies, community-based services, state and local government agencies, the AARP, and others. Findings from some of the research are being tested at several large organizations that have an interest in more effective ways to meet the needs of older people, as employees and as consumers (National Institute on Aging, 1993).

Participatory Action Research. A third example of public sociology is participatory social gerontology. Biggs (2005) reports that gerontological researchers in the United Kingdom are more frequently turning to older participants in their studies as a way to examine the lived experiences of elders in an environment of growing concerns over the distribution of government resources and equity between age groups. This is part of a larger effort toward more participatory research in program development and evaluation that gives more control and ownership to those being investigated (Evans and Carmichael, 2002). In the United Kingdom there is increasing recognition of the importance of involving elders and other service users in service planning and policy development (Department for Work and Pensions, 2004). Older people are acknowledged to have direct insight into the effects of services, and this insight can provide policymakers with evidence that is not biased by professional interests (Biggs, 2005). Involving older people in research and service planning can uncover stereotypic assumptions. For instance, the Older People's Steering Group (2004) found that many policy and practice assumptions are still based on seeing older people as a burden or as patients whose rights are annulled by their need for health and social services. Equally unacceptable is to conceptualize "successful aging" (a term currently in vogue in both the United Kingdom and the United States) as a continued ability to compete with younger people in physically demanding activities. The group recommends that older people should have the strongest voice in deciding what makes a good quality service, and whether it is being delivered.

Feminist Gerontology. As a final example of public social gerontology, Ruth Ray (2004) presents the case for a feminist gerontology that is more self-reflexive, urging feminist gerontologists to become more self-conscious about their age identities and the images of aging that underlie their own work. Feminist gerontologists are concerned with the extent to which the standpoint of the researcher—in terms of age, health, place in the life cycle, race, gender, class—affects what is being studied and how the findings are interpreted and reported. For example, in caregiver research that may involve collaborating with caregivers to create the meaning of care, feminist researchers needs to be aware of their own ideas and fears about the care recipient's illness, such as Alzheimer's disease, lest the care recipient be seen as a victim whose identity is defined only by his or her disease and the problems it causes for others (Ray, 1996).

Feminist gerontologists are also concerned with the role of the elderly as research subjects and the extent to which their lived experiences and understandings are incorporated into the development of knowledge in social gerontology. In another instance of engaging in public sociology, feminist gerontologists would feel obliged to question whether academic research and practices might contribute to older people's adaptation to conditions that really should be changed. And finally, Ray (2004) suggests that feminist gerontologists need to address the general public in their writing and work toward improving the image of old women in the larger culture—that is, to engage in organic public sociology.

Why Social Gerontology Is an Exemplar of Public Sociology

There are several reasons for social gerontology's success in doing public sociology: (1) its experience with working in multidisciplinary teams, (2) its ability to advocate "professionally" for its publics without favoring one group at the expense of another, (3) the unique affinity of its scientific theories and practices with its disciplinary values, and (4) the constructive effects of its continuous questioning of values and ethics.

First, researchers in social gerontology often work in multidisciplinary teams, which might include sociologists, psychologists, social workers, biomedical practitioners, epidemiologists, and others. As Burawoy (2005) notes, the development of public knowledge often comes about through multidisciplinary collaboration, particularly, "participatory action research" that brings communities together with academics from complementary disciplines, where a community defines the issue. Such collaboration between researchers, practitioners and those they serve has marked gerontology since its inception. Working with researchers and practitioners in other disciplines has several advantages. Practitioners may help sociologists determine which problems are "worth solving," creating a didactic connection between research and practice. Also, the experience of communicating across disciplinary boundaries has given social gerontologists tools that may assist them in working with various publics. In addition, working in multidisciplinary teams affords an efficient division of labor in terms of engaging with various publics. Other fields that have traditionally placed a large emphasis on creating change and improving social welfare, such as public health, social work, or public administration, may be in a better position to draw the attention of the public or relevant interest groups and to advance practical applications of sociological findings.

Second, while social gerontology advocates for the well being of older people, in general it refrains from overt political or activist confrontation that can offend its diverse publics. Because older people vote in large numbers and are backed by strong and stable political organizations that actively promote their interests (Binstock and Quadagno, 2001), other activists or lobbying organizations, such as AARP, take on many of these advocating tasks, calling upon social gerontologists for their expert knowledge. Social gerontology recognizes that social science researchers can approach problems and raise issues from various theoretical or epistemological perspectives in a professional manner. When it does support a specific group, such as caregiving grandparents, it typically attempts to do so without denigrating another group or public. Indeed, because the best social gerontological research is likely to consider the motives and interests of all groups (e.g., concerns of healthcare providers and workers in addition to the concerns of older people), researchers are not put in the position of "taking sides."

Social gerontologists do report their research findings to nonacademic audiences. As an example, in a recent issue of *Contexts,* Lisa Berkman (2004) reports a widening gap between the health of the rich and of the poor. Berkman is not working to organize the working poor, nor is she advocating that we develop any specific health care program. However, she is drawing attention to a serious issue and generating debate by suggesting that health in the United States will continue to lag behind other industrialized nations until we address health care coverage for low-income Americans.

Because all of us will eventually be old, social gerontology has focused on issues that affect individuals across the lifespan. Social gerontologists are not only advocates for the elderly, but advocates for all generations, which can lead to successful aging across the lifespan.

Furthermore, the emphasis on diversity and inequality across the lifespan has led social gerontologists to focus on the needs of multiple age, race, ethnic, and income groups.

Third, research in social gerontology can be, and usually is, guided by both scientific theory and values. To suggest that professional sociology is guided exclusively by theory and public sociology exclusively by morals—even as ideal types—in fact emphasizes an unrealistic boundary between professional and public sociology. In reality, as critical sociologists have pointed out, even professional sociologists are likely to include some values and/or morals in their choice of research questions and interpretation of results. Certainly most social gerontologists are concerned about the well being of older people and trying to solve the many problems associated with aging. Sociologists interested in aging, or in any subject area, bring a lifetime of experiences to their work, as well as values, even when that work is driven by scientific explanation. Based on our experience in social gerontology, we believe good public sociology can balance the claims of objectivity and values and examine research findings in light of moral dilemmas without compromising veracity.

If it is public sociology that keeps sociological passion alive, as Burawoy (2005) believes, than it is social gerontology's commitment to help older people and solve the mysteries of age and aging that energizes and inspires, whether the domain is professional, critical, policy, or public. Professional social gerontology does not require a public social gerontology to infuse it with values and passion.

Fourth, researchers in social gerontology have engaged in continuous debates over values and ethics, sometimes heated, yet this has also stimulated ideas and new directions for research. Many of these debates have focused on quality of life and end of life dilemmas, often because these issues raise the specter of limited medical and public resources and economic burden. One of the major debates in our field concerns relations between age groups and the fair distribution of public resources—that is, issues about generational equity. What do we owe the generations that came before us and what do we owe those that will follow us? Is there, or should there be, a balance between what we give and what we receive? This debate has been enriched by dialogue between researchers (Preston, 1984; McKerlie, 2001), interest groups (Americans for Generational Equity, Generations United), the press (Kristof, 1996; Samuelson, 2005), and the public. Thus the critical evaluation of ethical and moral issues has been salient in our field. It is unlikely that we will ever reach a consensus on this ethical and moral dilemma, but the presence of public discussion reminds researchers to be judicious in their policy recommendations and to be aware that benefits to one age group may come at a cost to others.

It is unrealistic to think that as public sociologists we can operate from a common values base, as Burawoy (2005) has suggested. It is easy enough to say we oppose the "erosion of civil liberties, the violation of human rights, the degradation of the environment, the impoverishment of the working class, the spread of disease, the exclusion of ever greater numbers from the means of their existence, and deepening inequalities" (Burawoy et al. 2004: 125). However, as Nielsen (2004) has observed, the decisions involved in making changes and creating improvements in people's lives are far often more complicated and difficult. To use an example from this paper, should the goal of research on grandparent caregivers be to help the caregivers or the children they care for? How should limited resources be distributed? These are not easy questions, and answers can only be found through discussion and negotiation with the multiple publics and stakeholders.

Conclusion

We have argued that social gerontology represents a model of public sociology in action. Social gerontology is a young field with a short history, yet its focus on increasing the well-being of older persons has guided its development in a way that has helped it achieve the goals of public sociology. However, there are several differences between social gerontology and sociology, as it has been described by Burawoy (2005). First, social gerontology is inherently multidisciplinary, built on sociology but borrowing from psychology, social work, biomedicine, demography, and public health as well as other fields. Second, research in social gerontology has blended professional, critical, policy, and public sociologies to a considerable degree so that they often work as an organic whole. The template of four sociologies with four distinct publics, even as ideal types, does not neatly overlay the division of labor and epistemological perspectives of social gerontology.

Third, social gerontologists, perhaps because of their experience with applied scholarship and practice or their strong policy orientation with its focus on the art of the possible, are less likely to be moral crusaders. This may be because the broader field of gerontology, including social gerontology, is overwhelmingly scientific, which tends to dampen a critical activism or expressions of moral outrage. It may also be a mat-

مگر پیر شناسی خیلی علمی است و جار اجلاسی ساره ۰ یا عموم درا نباط مولی هذه تحرک
مرام د کتن گری نت ۰

ter of style. Working in a multidisciplinary field with multiple publics, social gerontologists have learned to negotiate, to be diplomatic. At the same time, researchers in social gerontology have engaged in debates about values, ethics, and morals, necessary for generating new ideas and forming a consensus and foundation for any successful effort that seeks to improve well-being.

As a multidisciplinary field engaged in basic as well as applied research, social gerontology routinely reaches beyond the academy to engage with, and sometimes create, its publics: older people and their families, students, practitioners, interest groups representing the elderly such as AARP, community-based programs, healthcare organizations, government agencies, schools and churches, and others. This is a continuous interactive process. Social gerontologists engage in public sociology (op-ed pieces, speaking to community organizations, testifying before Congress), although most do not directly agitate for change or challenge existing structures.

In many ways, these differences between social gerontology and sociology have allowed social gerontologists to be successful in the two primary goals of public sociology: engaging multiple publics and working toward improvements in wellbeing. In an aging world, social gerontology is a dynamic and increasingly important multidisciplinary scholarly and applied field. We believe it has a great deal to offer sociologists as a model of public sociology in action.

References

Aboderin, I. 2004. "Decline in Material Family Support for Older People in Urban Ghana, Africa: Understanding Processes and Causes of Change." *Journal of Gerontology: Social Sciences* 59B: S128-S137.

Achenbaum, W.A. 1987. "Can Gerontology Become a Science? *Journal of Aging Studies* 1: 3-15.

_____. 1995. *Crossing Frontiers: Gerontology Emerges as a Science.* New York: Columbia University Press.

Arber, S., and Ginn, J. 1995. *Connecting Gender and Aging: A Sociological Approach.* Philadelphia, PA: Open University Press.

Atchley, R.C. 1989. "A Continuity Theory of Normal Aging." *The Gerontologist* 29: 183-190.

Baars, J. 1991. "The Challenge of Critical Theory: The Problem of Social Construction." *The Journal of Aging Studies* 5: 219-243.

Bengtson, V.L., and Allen, K.R. 1993. "The Life Course Perspective Applied to Families over Time." In P. Boss, W. Doherty, R. LaRossa, W. Schumm, and S. Steinmetz (Eds.), *Sourcebook of FamilyTheories and Methods: A Contextual Approach* (pp. 452-475). Boston, MA: Allyn and Bacon.

Bengtson, V.L., Burgess, E.O., and Parrott, T.M. 1997. "Theory, Explanation, and a Third Generation of Theoretical Development in Social Gerontology." *Journal of Gerontology* 52B: S72-S88.

Berger, P.L., and Luckmann, T. 1966. *The Social Construction of Reality*. New York: Doubleday.

Biggs, S. 2005. "Beyond Appearances: Perspectives on Identity in Later Life and Some Implications for Method." *Journal of Gerontology: Social Sciences 60B*: S118-S128.

Binstock, R.H., and Quadagno, J. 2001. "Aging and Politics." In R.H. Binstock and L.K. George (Eds.), *Handbook of Aging and the Social Sciences* (pp. 333-351). San Diego, CA: Academic Press.

Birkman, L.F. 2004. "The Health Divide." *Contexts* 3: 38-43.

Blau, P.M. 1964. *Exchange and Power in Social Life*. New York: Wiley.

Brady, D. 2004. "Why Public Sociology May Fail." *Social Forces* 82: 1629-1638.

Burawoy, M. 2004. "Public Sociologies: Contradictions, Dilemmas, and Possibilities." *Social Forces* 82: 1603-1618.

_____. 2005. 2004. "Presidential Address: For Public Sociology." *American Sociological Review* 70: 4-28.

_____, Gamson, W., Ryan, D., Pfohl, S., Vaughan, D., Derber, C., and Schor, J. 2004. "Public Sociologies: A Symposium from Boston College." *Social Problems* 51: 103-130.

Burton, L. 1992. "Black Grandmothers Rearing Children of Drug-Addicted Parents: Stressors, Outcomes, and Social Service Needs." *The Gerontologist* 32: 744-751.

Bytheway, B. 1994. *Ageism*. Buckingham, UK: Open University Press.

Calasanti, T. 2004. "Feminist Gerontology and Old Men." *Journal of Gerontology: Social Sciences,* 59B: S305-S314.

Cowgill, D.A., and Holmes, L.D. 1974. "Aging and Modernization. A Revision of Theory." In J. Gubrium (Ed.), *Laterlife: Community and Environmental Policies* (pp. 305-323). New York: Basic Books.

Cumming, E., and Henry, W. 1961. *Growing Old: The Process of Disengagement*. New York: Basic Books.

Dannefer, D. 2003. "Cumulative Advantage/Disadvantage and the Life Course: Cross-Fertilizing Age and Social Science Theory." *Journal of Gerontology: Social Sciences* 58B: S327-337.

Department of Work and Pensions. 2004. *Linkage: Developing Networks of Services for Older People*. Retrieved August 2005 from: http://www.dwp.gov.uk/publications/dwp/2004/linkage/link_age.pdf

Dowd, J.J. 1975. "Aging as Exchange: A Preface to Theory." *Journal of Gerontology* 30: 584-594.

Dowdell, E.B. 1995. "Caregiver Burden: Grandparents Raising Their High-Risk Children." *Journal of Psychosocial Nursing* 33(3): 27-30.

Dressel, P., and Barnhill, S. 1994. "Reframing Gerontological Thought and Practice: The Case of Grandmothers with Daughters in Prison." *The Gerontologist* 34: 685-690.

Elder, G.H., Jr. 1992. "Models of the Life Course." *Contemporary Sociology: A Journal of Reviews* 21: 632-635.

_____ and Johnson, M.K. 2002. "The Life Course and Aging: Challenges, Lessons, and New Directions." In R.A. Settersten, Jr. (Ed.), *Invitation to the Life Course: Toward New Understandings of Later Life* (pp. 49-81). Amityville, New York: Baywood.

Estes, C.L. 2001. "Political Economy of Aging: A Theoretical Framework." In C.L. Estes and Associates. *Social Policy and Aging: A Critical Perspective*. Thousand Oaks, CA: Sage.

_____, Gerard, L.E., Jones, J.S., and Swan, J.H. 1984. *Political Economy, Health, and Aging*. Boston, MA: Little, Brown.

Evans, C., and Carmichael, A. 2002. *Users Best Value—A Guide to Good Practice in User Involvement in Best Value Reviews*. York, UK: Joseph Rowntree Foundation.

Foucault, M. 1977. *Discipline and Punish: The Birth of a Prison*. Trans. A. Sheridan. New York: Vintage/ Random House.

Fuller-Thomson, E., Minkler, M., and Driver, D. 1997. "A Profile of Grandparents Raising Grandchildren in the United States." *The Gerontologist* 37: 406-411.

Garfinkel, H. 1967. *Studies in Ethnomethodology*. Englewood. NJ: Prentice-Hall.

Gubrium, J.F. 1993. *Speaking of Life: Horizons of Meaning for Nursing Home Residents*. New York:Aldine de Gruyter.

_____, and Holstein, J.A. 1999. "Constructionist Perspectives on Aging." In V.L. Bengtson and K.W. Schaie (Eds.), *Handbook of Theories of Aging* (pp. 287-305). New York: Springer.

Habermas, J. 1971. *Knowledge and Human Interests*. Trans. J.J. Shapiro. Boston, MA: Beacon Press.

Hendricks, J. 1992. "Generations and the Generation of Theory in Social Gerontology." *International Journal of Aging and Human Development* 35: 31-47.

_____ and Achenbaum, A. (1999). "Historical Development of Theories of Aging." In V.L. Bengtson and K.W. Schaie (Eds.), *Handbook of Theories of Aging* (pp. 21-39). New York: Springer.

Homans, G.C. 1961. *Social Behavior: Its Elementary Forms*. New York: Harcourt Brace Jovanovich.

Hooyman, N.R., and Kiyak, H.A. 2005. *Social Gerontology: A Multidisciplinary Perspective*. Boston, MA: Allyn and Bacon.

Horkheimer, M. and Adorno, T.W. 1944. "The Culture Industry: Enlightenment as Mass Deception." In M. Horkheimer and T.W. Adorno (Eds.). *Dialectic of Enlightenment*. Trans. J. Cumming.

Jendrek, M.P. 1994. "Grandparents Who Parent Their Grandchildren: Circumstances and Decisions." *The Gerontologist* 34: 206-216

Kristof, N.D. 1996. "Aging World, New Wrinkles." *New York Times,* September 22, pp. 4-1.

Kuhn, M. 1983. Remarks to symposium at the Gerontological Society of America annual meeting, November 21.

Kuypers, J.A., and Bengtson, V.L. 1973. "Social Breakdown and Competence: A Model of Normal Aging." *Human Development* 16: 181-201.

Lemon, B.W., Bengtson, V.L., and Peterson, J.A. 1972. "An Exploration of the Activity Theory of Aging." *Journal of Gerontology* 27: 511-523.

McKerlie, D. 2001. "Justice between the Young and Old." *Philosophy and Public Affairs* 30: 152-177.

McMullen, J. 1995. "Theorizing Age and Gender Relations." In S. Arber and J. Ginn (Eds.), *Connecting Gender and Aging: A Sociological Approach*. Philadelphia, PA: Open University Press.

Mannheim, K. 1952. "The Problems of Generations." In D. Kecskemeti (Ed.), *Essays on the Sociology of Knowledge* (pp. 276-322). London: Routledge and Kegan Paul. (Original work published 1922).

Marx, K. 1967. *Capital Vol. 1: A Critique of Political Economy*. New York: International Publishers. (Original work published 1867).

Mead, G.H. 1934. *Mind, Self, and Society*. Chicago, IL: University of Chicago Press.

Minkler, M., Driver, D., Roe, K., and Bedeian, K. 1993. "Community Interventions to Support Grandparent Caregivers." *The Gerontologist* 33: 807-811.

Minkler, M., and Roe, K.M. 1993. *Grandmothers as Caregivers: Raising Children of the Crack Cocaine Epidemic*. Newbury Park, CA: Sage.

Minkler, M., Roe, K.M., and Price M. 1992. "The Physical and Emotional Health of Grandmothers Raising Grandchildren in the Crack Cocaine Epidemic." *The Gerontologist* 32: 752-761.

Moody, H.R. 1993. "Overview: What Is Critical Gerontology and Why Is It Important?" In T.R. Cole, W.A. Achenbaum, P.L. Jakobi, and R. Kastenbaum (Eds.), *Voices and Visions: Toward a Critical Gerontology*. New York: Springer.

————. 2001. "The Humanities and Aging: A Millennial Perspective." *The Gerontologist* 41: 411-415.

Myerhoff, B. 1979. *Number Our Days*. New York: Dutton.

National Institute of Mental Health 2000. *Translating Behavioral Science into Action. Report of the National Advisory Mental Health Council Behavioral Science Workgroup*. Washington, DC: National Institutes of Health.

National Institute on Aging. 1993. "Aging Institute Funds Six New Centers to Apply Social and Behavioral Research." Retrieved August 2005 from: http://www.nia.nih.gov/NewsAndEvents/PressReleases/ PR19931102AingInstitute.htm

National Institute on Aging. 2004. "Six New Roybal centers for applied gerontology established by National Institute on Aging." Retrieved August 2005 from: http://www.nia.hih.gov/NewsAndEvents?PressReleases/ PR20041026RoybalCenters.htm

National Institutes of Health. 1997. "Edward R. Roybal Centers for Research on Aging," *NIH Guide,* 26(14). Retrieved August 2005 from: http://grants.nih.bov/grants/guide/rfa-files/RFA-AG-97-005.html

Nielsen, F. 2004. "The Vacant 'We': Remarks on Public Sociology." *Social Forces* 82: 1619-1627.

Older People's Steering Group. 2004. *Older People Shaping Policy and Practice*. York, UK:Joseph Rowntree Foundation.

Parsons, T. 1942. "Age and Sex in the Social Structure of the United States." *American Sociological Review* 7: 604-616.

Pillemer, K., Czaja, S., Schulz, R., and Stahl, S.M. 2003. "Finding the Best Ways to Help: Opportunities and Challenges of Intervention Research on Aging." *The Gerontologist* 43, *Special Issue I* (Challenges of Traditional Research on Aging: The Experience of the Roybal Canters), 5-8.

Preston, S. 1984. "Children and the Elderly: Divergent Paths for America's Dependents." *Demography* 21: 435-457.

Ray, R.E. 1996. "A Postmodern Perspective on Feminist Gerontology." *The Gerontologist* 36: 674-680.

————. 2004. "Toward the Croning of Feminist Gerontology." *Journal of Aging Studies* 18: 109-121.

Riley, M.W., Foner, A., and Waring, J. 1988. "Sociology of Age." In N.J. Smelser (Ed.), *Handbook of Sociology* (pp. 243-290). Beverly Hills, CA: Sage.

Riley, M. W., Johnson, M., and Foner, A. 1972. *Aging and Society. Vol III: A Sociology of Age Stratification*. New York: Russell Sage Foundation.

Riley, M.W., Kahn, R.L., and Foner, E. 1994. *Age and Structural Lag: Society's Failure to Provide Meaningful Opportunities in Work, Family, and Leisure*. New York: John Wiley.

Riley, M.W., and Loscocco, K.A. 1994. "The Changing Structure of Work Opportunities: Toward an Age-Integrated Society." In R.P. Abeles, H.C. Gift, and M.G. Ory (Eds.), *Aging and Quality of Life*. New York: Springer.

Roe, K.M., Minkler, M., and Barnwell, R-S. 1994. "The Assumption of Caregiving: Grandmothers Raising the Children of the Crack Cocaine Epidemic." *Qualitative Health Research* 4: 281-303.

Roe, K.M., Minkler, M., Thompson, G., and Saunders, F.F. 1996. "Health of Grandmothers Raising Children of the Crack Cocaine Epidemic." *Medical Care 34*: 1072-1084.

Rose, A. 1964. "A Current Theoretical Issue in Social Gerontology." *The Gerontologist, 4*, 46-50.

Rowe, J.D., and Kahn, R.L. 1998. *Successful Aging.* New York: Pantheon Books.

Saluter, A.F. 1992. "Marital Status and Living Arrangements: March 1991." *Current Population Reports* (Series P-20 No. 461). Washington, D.C.: U.S. Government Printing Office.

Samuelson, R. 2005. "It's More than Social Security." *The Washington Post,* January 14, p. A-19.

Schmeeckle, M., and Bengtson, V.L. 1999. "Successful Aging. Conclusions from a Longitudinal Study: Cross National Perspectives." Review of J. W. Rowe and R. L. Kahn, *Successful Aging. Contemporary Gerontology,* 5(3): 87-90.

Silverstein, M., Conroy, S. J., Wang, H., Giarrusso, R., and Bengtson, V. L. 2002. "Reciprocity in Parent-Child Relations over the Adult Life Course." *Journal of Gerontology: Social Sciences*, 57B: S3-S13.

Simmel, G. 1950. *Conflict:The Web of Group-Affiliations.* Translated by K.H. Wolff (and) Reinhard Bendix. Glencoe, IL: Free Press. (Original work published 1908).

Sorokin, P. A. 1947. *Society, Culture, and Personality.* New York: Harper and Brothers.

Stroller, E.P. 1993. "Gender and the Organization of Lay Health Care: A Socialist-Feminist Perspective." *Journal of Aging Studies* 7: 151-170.

Tittle, C.R. 2004. "The Arrogance of Public Sociology." *Social Forces* 82: 1639-1643.

Turner, J.H. 2003. *The Structure of Sociological Theory.* Belmont, CA: Wadsworth/ Thomson Learning.

6

Reflections on Public Sociology:
Public Relations, Disciplinary Identity, and
the Strong Program in
Professional Sociology[1]

David Boyns and Jesse Fletcher

Public sociology is an attempt to redress the issues of public engagement and disciplinary identity that have beset the discipline over the past several decades. While public sociology seeks to rectify the public invisibility of sociology, this paper investigates the limitations of it program. Several points of critique are offered. First, public sociology's affiliations with Marxism serve to potentially entrench existing divisions within the discipline. Second, public sociology's advancement of an agenda geared toward a "sociology *for* publics" instead of a "sociology *of* publics" imposes limitations on the development of a public interface. Third, the lack of a methodological agenda for public sociology raises concerns of how sociology can compete within a contested climate of public opinion. Fourth, issues of disciplinary coherence are not necessarily resolved by public sociology, and are potentially exacerbated by the invocation of public sociology as a new disciplinary identity. Fifth, the incoherence of professional sociology is obviated, and a misleading affiliation is made between scientific knowledge and the hegemonic structure of the profession. Finally, the idealism of public sociology's putative defense of civil society is explored as a utopian gesture akin to that of Habermas' attempt to revive the public sphere. The development of a strong program in professional sociology is briefly offered as a means to repair the disciplinary problems that are illustrated by emergence of the project of public sociology.

Introduction: Sociology and Its Public Face

Michael Burawoy is right—if sociology is to thrive, it needs a stronger public presence. Sociology has an unconvincing presentation of self, and is wracked by a marked inability to establish and manage a coherent and public face. In many respects, sociology is all but invisible to the public

119

eye, dominantly overshadowed by its social science brethren—psychology, economics, and political science. The emergence of public sociology has once again elevated the problem of sociology's public (in)visibility to an issue central to the discipline. However, the debates that it has engendered have raised the important concern of whether or not sociology is ready to go "public." The dubious reception of public sociology by sociologists themselves highlights an issue that must be confronted in the discussion about "going public." In short, sociology does not simply have a problem of public relations; sociology itself has an identity crisis.

That sociology has a problem of public relations should be of little surprise to most sociologists. The recent attempts to disembowel sociology departments at American universities (Wood, 1998, 1999) only serve to underscore the tenuous legitimacy held by sociology in the academic and public consciousness. We are typically and frequently confronted with the question, "Sociology? (pause) Huh. (pause) What's that? What exactly do you study? Is it something like psychology?" While for sociologists this question is rather easy to manage, the public misconceptions about sociology are somewhat troubling. Frequently, sociology is conflated by the layperson (and even by some academics) with psychology, social philosophy, social work, criminology, social activism, urban studies, public administration, journalism, and perhaps, most disquieting of all, with socialism.

The concern endemic to this problem of public relations is that as a discipline we do not, ourselves, seem to know who we are. Are we scientists or activists, ideologists or empiricists, symbolic interactionists or functionalists, positivists or postmodernists, philosophers or theorists, teachers or researchers, qualitative or quantitative, micro or macro? The trouble is that in an eclectic way we are a *bricolage* of all of these elements. Sociology tackles a broad range of issues, from manifold perspectives, using multiple methodologies. In many respects, sociology has good reason to celebrate this eclecticism as it provides rich and broad insights into the social world. However, amidst its polymorphism and multivocality, it is easy to lose the disciplinary coherence of sociology. It is as if sociology's manifold nature causes it to be stretched too thinly, forming a segmented series of subdisciplines that have broken into factions and fragments competing not only for hegemonic status in the discipline but also for public attention. It is no wonder that students of sociology are often confused about what they do.

This paper is centrally concerned with the legitimation crisis endemic to sociology and stems from questions about the possibilities of sociology's public engagement and the coherency of its disciplinary identity. Burawoy's public sociology attempts to provide answers to these questions and should be commended for its efforts; but in many ways it falls short of a successful resolution to sociology's identity struggles and much needed public interface. In the following sections, we take up the issues of sociology's problem of public relations and its identity crisis. First, we examine sociology's problem of public relations by exploring the development of public sociology with respect to the questions of publics, public opinion formation, and the contemporary public intellectual. Next, we explore sociology's identity crisis and its relationship to public sociology. Here, issues of multivocality, disciplinary coherence, and the hegemonic structure of its institutionalization come to the foreground. Of particular concern are the misrepresentations of scientific knowledge within sociology and their contributions to hegemonic structure of the sociological discipline. We suggest that Burawoy's endeavor to legitimize sociology through a greater public engagement is a necessary project, but much too idealistic. In place of energies devoted to the development of a public sociology, we contend that efforts should first be directed toward increasing the coherence of sociology's disciplinary knowledge and the development of a strong program for professional sociology.

Sociology and Its Problem of Public Relations

The emergence of Burawoy's public sociology raises a single, over-arching question: Why is there a perceived need for an institutionalized public sociology within the discipline? Burawoy's answer is tied to an issue raised by Turner and Turner (1990) in their historical examination of the institutionalization of sociology. While there has been more than one period in sociology's history where it was viewed as an important and necessary science in the public sphere, sociology's contemporary level of influence is suffering. Today, there is a detachment of sociology from the public consciousness, a fact that is one of the primary catalysts for the emergence of public sociology. The appearance of public sociology is no doubt timely, as it has created momentum toward investigating the prospect that sociology should have "something to say" to the larger public. As Burawoy (2004) states, public sociology is ostensibly inspired by Mills' (1959) sociological imagination, the ability to transform private troubles into issues of public concern, initiating conversations with these publics, and strengthening the relevancy of the discipline. Like Seidman's (1994) push towards a postmodern social theory, grounded in an invigoration of sociology through local discussion and moral advocacy,

Burawoy's public sociology implies that without open, moral dialogue with laymen, sociology will wallow in irrelevancy.

It is clear that sociology has a problem with its public relations. The public at large has a very limited conception of what kind of discipline sociology is, who the notable sociologists are, or what kind of insights sociologists has about the social world. In short, sociology has a very limited public visibility and has earned little respectability within extra-academic populations. Burawoy's public sociology seeks to rectify this situation, but falls short in many respects.

Conceiving Public Sociology

Public sociology is a renewed attempt to establish a greater social visibility and relevance for the discipline of sociology. Burawoy (2005c) argues that one of the chief sources of sociology's failure to engender social contributions and achieve societal prominence is its lack of public standing and interface. He contends that the inability of sociology to develop a public significance is deeply problematic for the profession and a mark of its growing self-insulation and irrelevance. The efforts directed toward the development of a public sociology are Burawoy's attempt to salvage the waning public face of sociology and bring a common focus to the discipline.

Burawoy (2005c) paints the picture of sociology as a left-leaning professional community, naturally politicized, that has vested interests in communicating and disseminating its views and insights to the wider public. He outlines a renovated vision of sociology that embodies four "faces"—professional, critical, policy, and public—and advances an agenda for a sociology organized around a greater public involvement. In Burawoy's model, public sociology is the face that ostensibly will directly intersect with the extra-academic social world, serving to both inform and influence the greater public. It will not only carry the trove of sociological knowledge to the wider society but will also be directed toward the establishment of meaningful public conversations toward the advancement of the social good.

Burawoy suggests that public sociology has two distinct but complementary manifestations: traditional and organic public sociologies. On the one hand, traditional public sociology is based upon an accidental or providential engagement with the public. Sociologists who fall into this course of public sociology do not necessarily set out to address the public but, instead, develop insights during the course of their professional activities that come to acquire significant public notability. The efforts of Robert Bellah et al. (1985), Diane Vaughan (1996, 2004), and David Riesman (1950) stand out as exemplars of traditional public sociology. On the other hand, organic public sociology is premised upon an intentional and conscious public engagement where sociologists work closely with individuals and groups in the public sphere, sharing insights and working together toward the solution of problems. William Gamson's (2003) efforts with the Media Research Action Project and Bonacich and Appelbaum's (2000) labor market study are illustrations of organic public sociology. Burawoy suggests that most contemporary public sociology is of an organic nature and that, while it is often informed by traditional approaches, it is the form of public sociology that will provide the discipline with the greatest public currency.

Although public sociology is the central focus of Burawoy's discussion, he both interrelates and juxtaposes this form of sociology with the three other types. As Burawoy sees it, professional sociology, is that which is dominantly practiced within the discipline, organized around theoretically driven empirical research programs and emphasizing scientifically oriented investigations. The conversations and debates that sociologists have with one another in academic journals, classrooms, conference rooms, and behind closed doors are the hallmarks of what Burawoy describes as professional sociology. In his approach, professional sociology is the *sine qua non* of sociology itself (Burawoy, 2005c: 10) providing the foundation for all other dimensions of sociological practice. Critical sociology, on the other hand, is that component of sociology that is self-reflexive, providing the basis of sociology's self-examination and critique, establishing its moral compass, and acting as the self-monitoring mechanism of the discipline. Finally, there is policy sociology, which is performed as sociologists are hired out on a contractual basis in order to practice their craft. In short, policy sociology is sociological work done under the auspices of an agreement, oriented toward the pragmatic investigation of specific clients' requests. Combined, these four forms of sociology comprise Burawoy's model of the discipline as it stands today. In his view, each should work with the others in a cybernetic, interdependent, and dialectic fashion, together providing the support and coherency to the discipline as a whole. Burawoy's model of sociology is presented in Table 1.

While this four-dimensional model of sociology is a clear and simple portrait of the discipline, Burawoy suggests that this typology is an ideal type that is vastly oversimplified relative to the empirical reality of contemporary sociological practice. On his own account, Burawoy

Table 1
Burawoy's Model of Public Sociology

	Academic Audience	Extra-academic Audience
Instrumental Knowledge	Professional Sociology	Policy Sociology
Reflexive Knowledge	Critical Sociology	Public Sociology

contends that all four dimensions of sociology are, in fact, "organically" interrelated, informing and supporting one another (Burawoy, 2005c: 15). However, Burawoy also suggests that the discriminations between these four types of sociology blur fractally into one another. Each form of sociology embodies elements of all the others. Professional sociology is often critical; critical sociology is found in policy sociology; policy sociology is embedded in the professional path; all three are aspects of the public; and so on with many other combinations (Burawoy, 2005c). In fact, public sociology is not only a *type* of sociology, but also a dimension of any one of the other forms of sociology. With all of these interdependencies, one wonders why this project has been labeled "public sociology" in the first place.

One of the troubling features of Burawoy's model of sociology, when understood as a typology of forms of sociological practice, is that it lends itself to such easy reification around one face as a dominant focus of the discussion. While Burawoy's clear intent is to develop a greater public presence for sociology—making appropriate the label *"public sociology"*—it is certainly not clear why public sociology itself needs to be established as a distinct form of sociology. If, as Burawoy (2005c) suggests, professional sociology already carries a public dimension, why not develop the public face of professional sociology instead of establishing public sociology as a distinctive form of sociological practice? After all, the public dimension of professional sociology is, in essence, what he means by "traditional" public sociology. If the discipline truly embodies the multidimensionality that Burawoy describes, why choose "public" sociology as the moniker for a new professional identity? Why not choose one of the other three faces of sociology—professional, critical, or policy? Such a move is certainly feasible, and similar attempts have been offered.[22]

The move to establish public sociology with a fair amount of disciplinary distinction and autonomy raises important concerns that do not find adequate resolution in Burawoy's model. Does sociology need a *public* sociology (i.e., Burawoy's organic public sociology) or a public dimension to *professional* sociology (i.e., that which is seemingly described by what Burawoy calls "traditional public sociology")? Is there an important difference between them, which should frame the agenda for sociology's public engagement, and why? A more nuanced answer to these questions needs to be found and requires a further explication of Burawoy's proposal for public sociology and its putative role in sociological practice.

Public Sociology or Sociological Marxism?

The emergence of public sociology by a sociologist of an overtly Marxist orientation raises the question of the ideological orientation of "public sociology." As others have suggested (Nielsen, 2004), Burawoy's affiliations with Marxism elevate the concern of whether or not public sociology is simply an attempt to redress the late twentieth-century failings of Marxism, to place old "red" wine in new bottles, creating a new niche for sociologists inspired by left-leaning politics. Is public sociology a magicians' "smoke and mirrors," misdirection trick to disguise the reinvigoration of Marxist sociology? While Burawoy is clear on the point that public sociology has no "intrinsic normative valence" (Burawoy, 2005c: 8), the leftward tilt of public sociology is a salient concern. As one reads Burawoy's vision of public sociology, it seems impossible not to be reminded of his "Sociological Marxism" (see Burawoy, 1989, 1990; Burawoy and Wright, 2002) where he advances a vision of the flagging Marxist enterprise that, much like public sociology, is both normative *and* scientific. In some readings, one must work hard to overlook the contradictions in that alliance. Public sociology and its affiliations with sociological Marxism serve to create a similar paradox in Burawoy's work.

In his most comprehensive statement of public sociology (his "manifesto" of public sociology), Burawoy (2005c) paints the picture of the potential for an admittedly leftist, sociological community to utilize politically normative standards in order to advance sociological knowledge to the foreground of a public consciousness. This is simultaneously the point of both his support of public sociology and sociological Marxism; the two seem to be ideologically and structurally parallel. In the same way that the *Communist Manifesto* can be seen as one of the earliest calls to a public sociology, so too can the writings on public sociology be seen as a revival of Burawoy's sociological Marxism. It is no coincidence that Burawoy's "manifesto" of public sociology is written in 11 theses, directly invoking Marx's famous 11 "Theses on Feuerbach." In fact, Burawoy's eleventh thesis on public sociology parallels that inscribed by Marx in his celebrated call to praxis. Whereas Marx invoked a call for social philosophy not to simply theorize about the social world but, instead, to change it; Burawoy does much the same for sociologists. He writes:

> If the standpoint of economics is the market and its expansion, and the standpoint of political science is the state and the guarantee of political stability, then the standpoint of sociology is civil society and the defense of the social. In times of market tyranny and state despotism, sociology—and in particular its public face—defends the interests of humanity (Burawoy, 2005c: 24).

In this final thesis on public sociology, Burawoy contends that the objective of sociology (and not just *public* sociology) is "partisan," oriented toward the "defense of the social" and the reinvigoration of civil society. While this is a noble goal for sociology (no doubt a noble goal for humanity), it is clearly driven by an ideological orientation that is not uniformly shared by those who are personally invested in the discipline. Burawoy's (2005b) essay "The Critical Turn to Public Sociology" only exacerbates this situation by invoking the last two of Marx's theses as an epigraph[4] and then directly linking public sociology to the development of "socialist utopias." Such an explicit connection serves to prescribe a potentially problematic normative agenda for public sociology, further segmenting the discipline along ideological lines and reinforcing questions of the collusion between public sociology and Marxism.

The affiliation of public sociology with Marxism, incidental as it may seem, is a liability for the project of public sociology and for sociology in general. Such an alliance not only threatens to segment further an already divided sociological discipline along ideological lines, but more importantly, it jeopardizes the acceptance of sociological insights within publics dramatically unreceptive to Marxism. The costs for American sociology are of particular concern, as the reception of Marxism has a history of stolid and passionate skepticism among the general public; moreover, it is a central point of division within the profession itself. In short, the Marxist connotations of Burawoy's project of public sociology are problematic both in their means of attempting to revitalize an increasingly specialized and divided discipline, and in their normative and teleological bent towards the historically unpopular ideals of Marxism.

Toward a Sociology of (for) Publics

Regardless of the true ideological face of public sociology, there are key conceptual problems that also frame the project. While the central concept in the development of public sociology is the "public," Burawoy is surprisingly vague in his definition of the term, using it in a broad range of contexts—from local community groups, to organizational structures, to marginalized populations, to the nebulous "civil society"—without developing any one guiding conception. Despite his insufficient definitions of "public," Burawoy does offer a number of examples. Students, he suggests, are sociologists' "first" and most immediate public, followed by secondary and tertiary publics in professional associations, community groups and the broader public sphere (Burawoy, 2005c: 7-9). Burawoy argues that these publics have the common characteristic of unification and constitution by shared discourse, remarking that even populations shaped by sociological definitions come to form publics (2005c: 8).

While, the idea of "creating" a public is ripe with possibilities, this notion creates a paradox. Should public sociology be oriented toward a "sociology *of* publics," as Burawoy (2005c: 8) suggests, or toward a "sociology *for* publics"? As it exists, the sociological endeavor is putatively a "sociology of publics" investigating the history and organization of individuals in society. Burawoy's public sociology (and here we disagree with his characterization) advocates more of a "sociology *for* publics" establishing forms of knowledge that can be utilized by individuals in society, and at times constituting those individuals as publics. In short, public sociology appears to be an attempt to convert a sociological discipline oriented toward a "sociology of publics" into one organized around a "sociology for publics," and perhaps blurring the distinction between the two.

It is not difficult to imagine Karl Marx as the first true "public sociologist," and the first to make noticeably fuzzy the distinction between a sociology "of" and "for" publics. Clearly, Marx wished to make his sociological impact felt in the world that surrounded him, developing a systematic set of sociological insights with the intention of both informing workers about the exploitative nature of capitalism and unraveling its scientific laws. Marx's work is often separated between that of the young, activist Marx of the *Economic and Philosophical Manuscripts* and the *Communist Manifesto*, and the older more scientific Marx of *Capital* (Fromm, 1961). The efforts of the young Marx, in the advocacy of worker solidarity and improved working conditions, are most clearly directed toward a "sociology for publics" (and of the development of workers as a public-for-itself); while the works of the older Marx, in analyzing the theoretical principles of the capitalist political economy, are more directed toward a "sociology of publics" (and an analysis of workers as a public-in-itself). Thus, Marx's early sociology can be seen as an attempt to transform a "public-in-itself" into a "public-for-itself" through the production of discourse, a project motivated by Marx's intention of creating a collective awareness and a common identification among workers.

Bearing a kinship with Marx's project, Burawoy envisions public sociology not only as a process through which publics can be studied "in-themselves" but, moreover, as a means through which they can be constituted "for-themselves" by the insights of sociologists. While it is too much of a caricature to type-cast Burawoy's conceptualization of public sociology as obviating the concerns of a "sociology of publics" entirely in favor of a "sociology for publics"—as his project clearly contains both elements—it is obvious that he places the emphasis of public sociology on the latter. Consider Burawoy's examination of the constitution of women as a public. He writes:

> part of our business as sociologists is to define human categories—people with AIDS, women with breast cancer, women, gays—and if we do so with their collaboration we create publics. The category woman became the basis of a public—an active, thick, visible, national nay international counter-public— because intellectuals, sociologists among them, defined women as marginalized, left out, oppressed, and silenced, that is, defined them in ways they recognized. (2005c: 8)

While Burawoy highlights other examples in his discussion of public sociology, this description is highly reminiscent of Marx's move to develop a "sociology-for-publics" and create the proletariat as a "public-for-itself."

The development of a public sociology has to distinguish clearly between its analytic role as a "sociology of publics" and its constitutive role as a "sociology for publics." Realistically, sociology can both investigate publics (the putative goal of professional sociology) and invigorate them as an active component of civil society (the apparent objective of organic public sociology). However, this duplicity of sociological roles is a significant source of confusion for the discipline of sociology. Burawoy's project does not resolve this dualism but in fact reproduces it in the question of whether or not an increased public presence to sociology should be earned under the auspicious of "public sociology" or through a more developed public component to professional sociology.

As Burawoy's project of public sociology reveals, simultaneously analyzing and constituting civil society is tricky business (to which many of those engaged in contract-based policy sociology will attest) because of inevitable conflicts of interest. A public sociology bent on shaping or constituting civil society walks a dangerous line, as it may not only provoke an ideology of social engineering, but may be undeservedly and unwarrantedly prescriptive. With this in mind, the distinction between professional sociology and public sociology seems decidedly premature.

Public Sociology and the Problems of Public Engagement

Whatever one believes about the roles of sociology in respectively analyzing and constituting publics, there are considerable issues that must be examined in articulating a public face to sociology. Sociologists have long explored images of publics—from Weber's "inarticulate mass" and Marx's metaphor of peasants in a potato-sack, to the Frankfurt School's "mass society" and Habermas' "public sphere"—as well as the obstacles endemic to the development of a sociologically informed and active public. While Burawoy (2005a) recognizes the history of these debates, there is still a concern about the methods of public engagement that are left unaddressed by public sociology. In short, and as Brady (2004) suggests, there is no "concrete proposal for practice" delineated in the public sociology enterprise.

Because Burawoy's formulation of public sociology is only, as he recognizes, in "primitive" form (2005c: 8), it is not surprising that its "action plan" is underdeveloped. However, his articulation of public sociology does not address in a meaningful way those dynamics of contemporary public opinion formation that will likely create significant obstacles for sociology's public engagement. In a way that echoes Habermas (1989), Burawoy (2005c) does point out that the contemporary public sphere has been threatened, destroyed by market forces, colonized by the influence of the mass media, and thwarted by bureaucratic rationalization. However, and in a way that again parallels Habermas, Burawoy contends that these obstacles can be overcome if sociologists actively seek out publics and attempt to build dialogical relationships with them. On the face of it, this is a methodology for public sociology that is much too idealistic and one that will inevitably have to confront the sociological threats to the public sphere that he assumes conversation will resolve.

Let's take as an example the contemporary sociological world of public opinion in the United States. Today, not only do sociologists have to compete for public attention with social sciences that have much greater public currency and cultural resonance—i.e., psychology, economics, and political science—but we must also contend with advertisers, broadcasters, marketers, spin-doctors, special effects experts and many others whose skills of public engagement grandly outshine our own. C.W. Mills (1956), who certainly advocated a greater public presence to sociology, was well aware of this problem, and was much more pessimistic, and perhaps more realistic than is Burawoy, about the possibilities of public engagement. If we follow Mills' analysis of the manipulative power inherent in public opinion formation, it becomes apparent that the public today can no longer be understood as a simple social fact—a mass organized around a "herd consciousness"—but rather as a contested terrain dominated by powers of influence that have extensive resources and considerable expertise. The contemporary public is continually invoked, addressed, spun, and disenchanted by the powers of political influence and the arbiters of the mass media. However, in this message-saturated climate, the public has also become increasingly skeptical of such power plays. How public sociology will be able to differentiate the intentions behind its own efforts from those of a sophisticated power elite requires more than a moment of thoughtful consideration.

The climate of public opinion formation imposes significant constraints upon the emergence of public sociology and in particular the development of sociologists as public intellectuals. Sociologists have long known that intellectuals play a significant role in the advancement of public debate, focusing public attention, and enriching the ideas that circulate in the public sphere (Parsons, 1969; Shils, 1958, 1982). The strong interrelationship of intellectuals and civil society has always been the classic role of the *intelligentsia* (Gouldner, 1985). However, in the contemporary climate of public opinion, there have increasingly been significant questions raised about the diminished role of the public intellectual in society (Bender, 1997; Jacoby, 1987; Posner, 2002). Michaels (2000) argues that the contemporary public intellectual is too frequently conflated with media celebrity, reducing their overall impact and the seriousness of their message. Public intellectuals have been heavily criticized for their pretentiousness, status-seeking, intellectual dilution of complex ideas, and self-aggrandizement (Posner, 2002). The collapse of the prominence of the public intellectual has been perhaps best announced by the *New York Times* which, in a recent review of intellectual ideas, listed the "public intellectual" as one of the most overrated (*New York Times*, 2003). Burawoy (2005c: 15) recognizes these issues, but reduces the decline of the public intellectual to a disciplinary tug-of-war between "pop sociology" and professional hegemony.

Academics who write for popular audiences have always been marginalized with respect to the hegemonic legitimacy structure of their discipline. Burawoy's attempt to balance this situation is through the elevation of the general stature of public engagement within the profession, by leveling the disciplinary "playingfield" between the legitimacy of professional and public dimensions of sociology; but, there is no attempt to address the public skepticism of intellectual activity. Consideration must be give to the fact that the emergence of public sociology has come at a time of significant popular concern over the demise of the public intellectual. If the milieu of the contemporary mass media is any reflection of the current state of "the public" then clearly, as Michael (2000) suggests, these are politically and culturally anxious times for intellectuals, public sociologists among them.

In short, given that sociology must compete with the skilled architects of mass mediated discourse, questions must be raised, not only about whom public sociology will serve, but also about how a publicly oriented sociology will interface with the general public. When the contemporary cultural climate of public discourse is fully considered, it will become obvious that public sociologists will likely have to take a serious lesson from educational, political and religious practitioners, who have grappled with the issues of successful public engagement for decades.

Reflections on Sociological Identity

Many of the problems surrounding sociology's public invisibility likely stem from its disciplinary incoherence. The multivocality of contemporary sociology has broken the discipline into a loose assemblage of fragments, making it difficult for its practitioners to establish a coherent sense of identity. Given the currently complex and segmented disposition of the profession, one wonders what will be presented to a public audience by public sociology. While Burawoy is correct in his diagnosis of the public failures of contemporary sociology, it is questionable whether or not the development of public sociology is actually a solution to sociology's public invisibility or simply another symptom of the problem. We suggest that the latter is likely to be the case and that the development of Burawoy's public sociology as a panacea for sociology's disciplinary ills is a misdirected and premature offering. The movement toward public sociology seems to be premised upon the idea that collective efforts toward public engagement will serve to ameliorate sociology's crisis of incoherence, thus facilitating the development of a more cohesive professional agenda. We contend, however, that issues of disciplinary identity and internal coherence must first be resolved before any public presence to sociology will be significantly attained. It is not so much that a public sociology should simply strive to have a more salient public involvement; it must also have something to say to publics.

Burawoy argues that sociology already accumulated a vast storehouse of knowledge that is ripe for public use (Burawoy, 2005c: 5), and that the advancement of public sociology is intrinsically based upon the coherence of disciplinary knowledge that sociology has accumulated for almost two centuries. It is true that sociology has acquired a great deal of knowledge about human behavior and the social world. However, most sociologists would probably have a good deal of trouble delineating what it is that sociology knows *as a discipline*; furthermore, it is far from certain that when acting as a collective body the members of the profession would identify a common set of ideas as an intellectual foundation. Even the classical cannon of sociological theory has become a ripe point of controversy for the discipline (see the Connell, 1997 and Collins, 1997 debate for an example). Concerns over the state of knowledge in the profession strike directly at the issue of what the discipline of sociology is, what it has to say, how it might say it, and what contributions it might make to public life.

Public Sociology and the Problem of Disciplinary Identity

Burawoy argues that public sociology can be useful in providing a coherent identity for sociology through its greater efforts at cultivating public engagement. To illustrate his vision, Burawoy (2005c: 25) invokes the image of tributaries flowing into a common stream, where a myriad of public sociologies combine to create a common sociological current. This lofty image of a sociological future is ideal, but it is also contradicted by Burawoy's less than idealistic description of the contemporary state of the discipline—one characterized by internal multidimensionality and power struggles, where the hegemonic dominance of professional sociology reigns over the critical policy and public dimensions. For Burawoy, the public irrelevancy of sociology does not stem simply from the disciplinary incoherence and power plays endemic to the discipline. Instead, sociology's public irrelevance is also derived from its squelching of moral commitments, and the discipline's decreased interest in cultivating an ethos directed toward the formation and advancement of civil society (Burawoy, 2005c: 14).

Burawoy seeks to rectify this situation with the development of public sociology. In his eleventh thesis on public sociology, he suggests that economics, political science and sociology (geography, history and anthropology are excluded from this analysis and, strangely, psychology is completely ignored) all address "partisan" aspects of the social sciences, investigating realms of social life that are of particular concern. Economics, he argues, reflects the standpoint of the market and seeks to ensure its expansion, while the standpoint of political science is the state and the assurance of political stability. Sociology reflects the standpoint of the civil society and embodies the goals of protecting the social and defending the "interests of humanity" (Burawoy, 2005c: 24); and, it is clearly public sociology that will have the primary objective of carrying out this defense.

These putative goals for sociology are tall orders and certainly present a sociological agenda that is clearly partisan not only with respect to other social sciences, but within sociology itself. As we have suggested, it is extremely doubtful that practicing sociologists, who carry a multiplicity of orientations and agendas, will accept the "partisan" goal of protecting and defending the social as the teleology of their sociological practice. Although most sociologists would probably support the moral direction of this pursuit, Burawoy threatens to entrench further an already divided profession by advocating this agenda as an overarching disciplinary identity for sociology. It is clear that Burawoy's eleventh thesis is not just a statement of advocacy for a publicly engaged sociology; it is also a statement of identity for sociological practitioners.

The question over the proper "standpoint" and identity for sociology raises deep-seated concerns and sends resounding echoes of C.P. Snow's (1959) pronouncement of the emergence of "two cultures" in intellectual life. With some prescience, Snow contends that intellectual discussions are increasingly splitting into two distinct traditions separated by an impassible gulf, with scientific inquiry on the one side and humanistic concerns on the other. Twentieth-century sociology has been characterized by this same duplicity, and public sociology has exacerbated the distinction. The professional embodiment of Snow's two irreconcilable cultures has already made the disciplinary identity of sociology deeply problematic. Today, it is common to hear of departments divisively separated over major themes internal to sociology (e.g., science vs. activism, quantitative vs. qualitative, structure vs. agency, value-neutrality vs. ideological advocacy, etc.). The discord over the American Sociological Association's vote to condemn the United States military involvement in

Iraq has only served to entrench these divisions further. Disappointingly, there is little new to these debates, and few collective attempts at disciplinary resolution. In many ways, public sociology has served to intensify these disputes and enflame deeply scarred disciplinary wounds.

In recent decades, however, these debates have taken on a new dimension. Largely driven by the popularity of postmodernism and cultural studies, sociology has witnessed what Ward (1995) has called "the revenge of the humanities" whereby the efforts of the sociological enterprise have been confounded and appropriated by the logic of literacy criticism. Inspired by the metastasis of postmodernism throughout both the humanities and social sciences it has become increasingly common to find interdisciplinary appropriations of humanities discourse within the social sciences and a reversal of this process within the humanities. It is an ironic, and often bewildering, experience for social scientists to read descriptions of literary "theory" and "methodology." The simulation of the language of the scientific method in literary criticism has certainly served to increase the legitimacy of literary discussions, but the social sciences have not fared as well in the exchange. On the one hand, literary theories and methods certainly borrow legitimacy from the conceptual currency of the social sciences and elevate their own prestige. On the other hand, the interpenetration of cultural studies and textual analysis with sociology has deflated the general legitimacy and efficacy of sociological discourse. This is not to say that the humanities cannot have theories and methods; they can and should label them as they choose. This is also not to imply that cultural studies are an irrelevant avenue of social investigation; they are not. The problem is that sociology has come to embody increasingly a conflation of literary and social science approaches, where the methods of textual analysis have been applied to the study of social life. As a result, the disciplinary schisms that divide sociology have expanded, making it all the more difficult for the profession to establish a coherent identity. As Seidman (2003) suggests, sociological knowledge is now surely "contested knowledge," as uncertainties have escalated about the kind of discipline sociology should be.

The conflation of the social sciences and the humanities is perhaps a primary illustration of the postmodern moment in contemporary sociology. The decentered and multivocal nature of the discipline has localized sociological knowledge in a way that would make Lyotard (1984) and Derrida (1978) proud. However, the contemporary polyvalence of sociology raises some crucial issues for the discipline; namely, who, or what, sets the standards for intellectual discourse, *and* who, or what sets the standards for public sociology. On the one hand, it cannot be a case that anything passes for sociology. On the other hand, not everything will serve as effective public sociology. In many ways, the current postmodern moment to sociology is a threat to both the traditional practice of sociology and Burawoy's notion of public sociology.

Burawoy's public sociology is an answer and, alternatively, a response to the postmodern condition in sociology. The failure of sociology to establish and maintain disciplinary coherence matched with its inability to establish a commonly shared, professional identity has left it defenseless in the wake of postmodern fragmentation. While some celebrate our disciplinary patchwork, as does Burawoy, the tangled web of sociological interests poses a series of dilemmas for both the development of its public face and for the ultimate fate of the profession. If we cannot agree upon our disciplinary identity and, more importantly, upon the state of our cumulative knowledge, then who will listen to us, and why should they? What serious and long-lasting public contributions can we make if we have little sense of cumulative, sociological knowledge upon which we can establish a common ground? Burawoy does suggest that the goals of professional sociology should be based upon the establishment of theoretically based research programs around specific areas of investigation (2005c: 16-17). However, our sociological research programs are less than coherent and are internally segmented. The advancement of a public face to sociology is intrinsically tied to collective agreements about what we know and who we are as a discipline based upon that knowledge.

Burawoy recognizes the dependence of public sociology on professional activities and is correct in his contention that professional sociology is, and should be, the *sine qua non* of sociology. It is difficult to disagree with the premise that our professional efforts should be the means by which sociological knowledge accumulates and upon which public sociology is premised. However, given that the discipline lacks a cohesive paradigmatic structure, and that it is dominated by a multivocality of perspectives and orientations, both the discipline *and* public sociology are left without any true intellectual foundation. Without a foundational compass, who, or what, will monitor sociology and its public efforts? What will prevent the hegemonic institutionalization of *public* sociology within the profession?

Burawoy suggests that the standards for intellectual discussion in sociology should be established through a dialectical relationship between professional and critical sociology (Burawoy, 2005c: 10). He argues that there is a clear sociological division of labor within the discipline, where the objective of professional sociology is to develop the instrumental knowledge that drives the discipline, and the role of critical sociology is to be the conscience of professional sociology and provide it with a moral and evaluative direction. However, Burawoy gives these two dimensions of his sociology model an equivalence that is disorienting. The professional and critical faces of sociology cannot be equal partners in the dialogue. Somewhere a standard must be set for what counts as sociology and as sociological knowledge. An intellectual foundation for the discipline, and for public sociology, cannot be based simply upon a dialogue between the critical and professional components of sociology, but requires a system through which the results of the dialogue are evaluated. We contend that the most effective foundation upon which both sociology and public sociology can be based, as well as the results of the dialectical engagement of professional and critical sociologies, is the scientific process.

Public Sociology and Scientific Reflexivity

It may be cliché today, and perhaps a bit unfashionable, to invoke science as both the foundation for sociology's disciplinary identity and as a method for developing a cumulative storehouse of sociological knowledge. In fact, it summons a longstanding debate in sociology about the respective roles of scientific and critical knowledge. Burawoy addresses this debate in his development of public sociology, but in a rather caricatured manner, and he clearly takes sides. On the one side, he places the "declinists" (e.g., Bell, 1996; Berger, 2002; Collins, 1989; Horowitz, 1993; Turner, 1989, 1998) who advocate the scientific method in sociology and bemoan the theoretical fragmentation and disintegration of the discipline, believing it to be overrun by the growth of identity politics and political correctness. On the other side, are those who contest the hegemony of science as a basis of sociological legitimacy and, instead, support a strong political, moral and normative agenda for the discipline. By his own account, Burawoy sides with the latter, arguing that the current hegemonic order of the discipline drowns out critical voices and creates a Bourdieuian "field of power" where those who are inclined toward public sociology eventually either capitulate to hegemony or experience marginalization (Burawoy, 2005: 18-19).

Burawoy is undoubtedly correct in his depiction of the hegemonic structure of the discipline, and argues that the primary cost to sociology has been the deterioration of the reflexive and critical capacity of the profession (2005c: 14-15). In the contemporary sociological field, a rigid and hegemonic institutionalization of the profession does exist that smacks of elitism and smothers marginalized perspectives—where quantitative overshadows qualitative, formal theory trumps "soft" sociology, and publication in one or two top-flight journals brings disciplinary prestige. Wilner's (1985) analysis of the narrowness and public irrelevance of *American Sociological Review* is perhaps the one of the most poignant demonstrations of sociology's institutional hegemony; as is Burris' (2004) examination of nested hiring practices among elite departments. Of course, as sociologists we have the sufficient, disciplinary knowledge to facilitate self-criticism about our own institutional hegemony and to make reparations. But, sadly, we rarely exercise that wisdom to its fullest extent.

In his description of the organization of the discipline, all too often, Burawoy finds the fault of sociology's institutional narrowness in the hegemony of scientific pursuits. Although he describes it as the foundation for the discipline, Burawoy depicts the current structure of professional sociology to be constricting of marginalized voices, and the valorization of science is a major factor in this condition. Clearly there are undeniable associations between science and hegemony within our discipline. However, the hegemonic organization of sociology is first and foremost a problem of the means by which science has been institutionalized in the profession and not of the scientific practice in and of itself. Sociology has undoubtedly been constituted as a "field of power," as Burawoy suggests; however, this is not a result of the use of science by sociologists. It is, instead, a consequence of a parochial institutionalization of science within the discipline and a failure to utilize and understand science effectively. At its base, science is an intrinsically reflexive and critical practice that can serve to shatter longstanding assumptions and reorganize taken-for-granted knowledge, even that developed by science itself. In many ways, science is an ideal method for the critical reflexivity that Burawoy advocates for the discipline.

Burawoy's understanding of science is clearly not simplistic, as his works on scientific Marxism demonstrate (Burawoy, 1989, 1990). However, his criticism of the hegemony of science in sociology is certainly narrow, and tends to reflect a critique of the institutionalization of science within the discipline and not of the scientific practice itself. As Burawoy recognizes (2005c: 10), both the philosophy and sociology of science have long explored the limits of the scientific practice and the different ways in which science has been institutionalized; but he does not expand this point. These investigations have not simply denounced the "truth" claims of science. They have also examined the limitations inherent to the ways in which science has been institutionalized and practiced. It is true that the claims of scientifically oriented sociology to produce "truth" have recently been considered a failure by many well-respected sociologists (Lemert, 1995; Seidman, 1994; Wallerstein et al., 1996). It is also true that the institutionalization of science and the production of scientific knowledge have been roundly critiqued in many social investigations (Bourdieu, 1993; Foucault, 1970; Garfinkel, 1967; Harding, 1986, 1991; Horkheimer and Adorno, 1993; Latour and Woolgar, 1979; Luhmann, 1994). Far from a call to the abandonment of science, however, these studies demonstrate that the sociological discipline understands a great deal about science, the limitations of its institutionalization, and the means by which the merits of scientific knowledge and practice can be reflexively assessed.

As an example, take the work of Niklas Luhmann (1994), who argues that scientific knowledge is quintessentially a modern enterprise and that it has too frequently been conflated with hegemonic discourse. He suggests that science and its methodologies are systematic means for simplifying (even rationalizing) both theoretical and empirical understandings, reducing them to surrogates for objectivity in order to establish baselines for knowledge, and to communicate to wider audiences. The label of "true" or "scientific" simply serves to move science past struggles over validity so that it does not need continually to reinvent its claims and can instead rely upon mechanisms that simulate consensus even in the reality of its absence. On Luhmann's account, the way that science deals in the currency of truth works to limit conflict and expedite the resolution of validity claims. Thus, the ability to attach the label of "truth" to scientific work is in many ways a function of the way that science is institutionalized, and not simply a hegemonic dominance of scientific "truth" over both the empirical facts of reality and the means of acquiring legitimate knowledge.

The critiques of science, like that espoused by Luhmann, raise the issue of what Whitehead (1967) has called the "fallacy of misplaced concreteness," where conceptual understandings of reality are misrecognized as concrete instances of the truth. Strangely, Burawoy's description of the use of science in sociology is consistent with this same fallacy. Within sociology, science and scientific knowledge have been significantly undermined by discipline-wide fallacies over the misunderstandings of scientific claims to truth. In many ways, the idea of the scientific pursuit of "truth" as concrete reflections of objective reality is a well-worn idea and has been met with significant criticism. The collective works of Popper (1959), Lakatos (1978) and Kuhn (1962)—all of whom Burawoy cites (2005c: 10)—have emphasized a philosophy of scientific practice organized around a questioning of scientific "truth." Of particular relevance is the work of Popper, who initiated a model of science that is driven by falsification as opposed to verification. While it may be convincingly argued that scientific sociology has advanced our knowledge of the social world, it is a fallacy to claim that the outcome of these investigations has resulted in the "truth."

Despite the mispresentations of the objectivity of its knowledge, science is the most "tried and true" system for evaluating validity claims about the physical and social world; and, it is the only system of knowledge that can be subject to empirical falsification. In short, scientific knowledge can be wrong, and science itself can be used to make this kind of evaluation. However, Burawoy (2005c: 16) suggests that scientific knowledge is not the only means by which sociology makes claims to validity. Driven by scientific norms, professional sociology provides theoretical and empirical knowledge based upon the correspondence of theory to real-world observations; critical sociology stipulates foundational knowledge organized around a moral vision and normative claims to truth; policy sociology offers concrete knowledge based upon effective and pragmatic problem solving; finally, public sociology supplies communicative knowledge that pivots upon public relevance and consensual understandings. Burawoy claims that each of these forms of knowledge makes necessary contributions to sociology, but it is the communicative knowledge that is most relevant for facilitating public engagement. We disagree. While each of these forms of knowledge provides insight into the social world, only the scientific knowledge of professional sociology is based upon a system that is intrinsically organized around falsification. In addition, science and the pragmatic problem solving it engenders is the most likely avenue through which a convincing set of insights about the social world can be offered to a public that is already skeptical and indifferent to sociology's public contribution.

If sociology is to have a greater public presence it should seek to establish a disciplinary identity that is based upon a form of knowledge that can be convincingly presented to those naturally unresponsive to sociological insights. We can expect a public already indifferent to sociology (and embracing of other social sciences like economics and psychology) to be skeptical of moral and normative claims without an empirical basis of support. Science already has strong public legitimacy and it seems appropriate that sociology should channel its efforts to make the most of this affinity. Instead of a sociology organized around public engagement, it seems much more appropriate for the discipline to develop a strong program in professional sociology, bringing clarity to its scientific insights and assessing its potential to make social contributions. If professional sociology is to be the foundation of a public sociology, as Burawoy recommends, it is essential that some coherence be first established around sociology's body of scientific knowledge. A stronger move toward the development of theory-driven research programs will certainly help in the pursuit of disciplinary coherence and facilitate the advancement of the cumulative knowledge of the discipline. Such an investment will not only serve to crystallize sociology's disciplinary knowledge, but it will also help to provide a more coherent identity to the profession.

Out of Utopia ... Again: The Utopian Identity of Public Sociology

We have argued that one of the problems endemic to contemporary sociology is its identity crisis. The project of public sociology is not simply an attempt to facilitate a greater public engagement for sociology; it also strives to provide sociology with a common identity around a broader communicative engagement with the public. Burawoy's articulation of a more public sociology, however, is strongly utopian, not only in its ideals, but also in its conceptualization. Resonant with his advocacy of socialist utopias (Burawoy and Wright, 2002), Burawoy argues that public sociology can be used not only to increase the public use of sociological ideas, but also to advance the ideals of "real utopias" (Burawoy, 2005b). We conclude our discussion of Burawoy's public sociology with an investigation of his utopian agenda and the limitations of its promise for the development of a greater public presence for sociology.

In his essay "Out of Utopia," Dahrendorf (1958) warns sociologists about the fallacies of utopian thinking within sociology. Although the primary target of his critique is the ideological conservativism of Parsonsian functionalism, Dahrendorf extends his caution to all of sociological thought and suggests that a scientific sociology, "problem-conscious at every stage of its development is very unlikely to find itself in the prison of utopian thought" (1958: 124). Dahrendorf's prescription for sociology is based upon a program of continual reflexivity of sociological insights and perspectives, with particular admonitions given to the blinding effects of ideological associations.

As we have suggested, Burawoy's public sociology is strikingly ideological in its Marxist affiliations. On his own account, Burawoy's four-box conceptualization of public sociology is also surprisingly reminiscent of

Parson's AGIL-model of the social system that dominated sociology during the medial years of the twentieth century (Burawoy, 2005c: 11). While Burawoy's own Marxist position bears a certain polarity to that reflected in the conservativism of Parsonsian functionalism, his model of public sociology is also strikingly utopian. However, instead of directly reflecting the idealistic conservativism of Parsons' functional theory, Burawoy's utopian thought runs parallel to that of Jurgen Habermas and this theory of communicative action (Habermas, 1985, 1987). Like Parsons, Habermas' work also has been considerably criticized for its idealistic and utopian framework, especially his normative idealism of the public sphere (for examples see Calhoun, 1992; Kellner, 2000; McCarthy, 1978). Burawoy's conceptualization of public sociology is reminiscent of Habermas' theory of communicative action, and seems to reflect a very similar idealism.

Like Burawoy's four faces of sociology, Habermas' work speaks to four dimensions of social life. Habermas identifies four types of rationality (i.e., instrumental, moral-practical, aesthetic-expressive, and communicative), their integral connections to four "worlds" that describe the layers of sociological reality (i.e., objective, social, subjective, and the lifeworld), and the respective moments of reason to which they are connected (i.e. science, law, art, and communication). These four dimensions of social life directly parallel the faces of sociology described by Burawoy in his description of the sociological discipline (see Table 1 above). Habermas' theory also illustrates a utopian emphasis on the establishment of communicative action in the public sphere in much the same way that Burawoy seeks to direct the efforts of public sociology toward the reinvigoration of civil society. A comparison of Habermas' theory of communicative action and Burawoy's model of public sociology is presented in Table 2.

Table 2
Comparison of the Models of Habermas and Burawoy

		Habermas		Burawoy
Rationality	**World**	**Questions Addressed**	**Moment of Reason**	**Face of Sociology**
Instrumental	*Objective*	Truth/ Knowledge	*Science*	*Professional*
Moral-Practical	*Social*	Justice/Morality	*Law*	*Critical*
Aesthetic-Expressive	*Subjective*	Aesthetics/Taste	*Art*	*Policy*
Communicative	*Lifeworld*	Social Relations	*Communication*	*Public*

As illustrated in this table, for Habermas, instrumental rationality is based on action bent towards strategic ends, and directed toward the objective world. This form of rationality raises questions of truth and knowledge that are resolved by science as a social institution. Moral-practical rationality on the other hand, corresponds to the social world and is concerned with the norms, mores and common values that actively bind society together, and serve to address issues of justice and morality that are ensconced in the institution of law. Habermas' third type of rationality is aesthetic-expressive, which is connected most intimately with the subjective world where individuals evaluate their inner experiences, thoughts, feelings, desires, and self-presentations and form structures of taste and aesthetic judgment. The institution of art is a manifestation of this form of rationality. Finally, communicative rationality is the essence of the lifeworld, where individuals develop social relations, establish common interpretive schemas, create collective value orientations, and come to consensual agreement through dialogue.

As Table 2 illustrates, there are clear parallels between Burawoy's typology of public sociology and Habermas' conceptual framework. Here, one can see that the structure of the two theories is nearly identical. Professional sociology, ostensibly objective in nature, is concerned with the instrumental forms of rationality and their subsequent concern with truth, knowledge, and science. Critical sociology is the moral base of the discipline, creating the norms and mores of sociology, acting as the conscience or informal law of the land. In policy sociology, sociologists represent the discipline according to their own subjective standards; each decides which projects to take, and which aren't sociologically sound. It is neither a purely objective nor moral moment in the sociological discipline, but rather is one that is up to the tastes and subjectivities of each individual sociologist. Lastly, public sociology is championed as the communicative form of sociology, addressing issues of social relations, and invigorating the lifeworld toward the constitution of civil society. While Burawoy stipulates that each of his faces of sociology should be informed by professional sociology, as the *sine qua non* of sociology, Habermas, also claims that even though the other forms of rationality emphasize one world over the others, each must *also* take into account the objective world in order to be successful. Thus, in both conceptual frameworks, the investigation of the objective world holds a place of particular importance and prestige.

It should be clear that the theoretical models of Burawoy and Habermas both emphasize communication as solution to dissensus and discord over knowledge. Both suggest that, under ideal conditions, the interface of instrumental knowledge and everyday, public life can serve to enrich and empower civil society. Toward these ends, Habermas emphasizes "narration" as a specialized form of communicative and constitutional speech. For Habermas, narrative speech represents a communicative translation of instrumental ideas such that they are accessible to the lifeworld, can be used to enrich and shape taken-for-granted understandings, and perhaps play a central role in identity formation for both individuals and groups. Burawoy's project of public sociology parallels this Habermasian approach in that it endeavors to reframe sociological understandings such that they can be made more accessible and useful to the public sphere, and facilitate the identity formation of publics "for-themselves."

The arguments of both Burawoy and Habermas are premised upon the assumption that communicative action within the public sphere can be instrumental in the advancement of civil society, and that knowledge of the objective world is central to this process. While the enrichment of civil society is a dignified goal, Burawoy's approach to public sociology illustrates the same idealism that has beleaguered Habermas' theoretical approach. A sociological project that is primarily directed toward the development of civil society confronts a teleological utopianism that underlies many of the endeavors that are centrally premised on normative ideologies. Burawoy's public sociology reflects this same idealism, possibly as an extension of his Marxist project of "utopian socialism." Communicative action is only idealistic dialogue without proper grounding in a reflexive, and falsifiable, system by which knowledge can be assessed and agreement can be determined. We think that a strong program in professional sociology is crucial in developing such a reflexive system and should be established before a more public sociology advances further. Otherwise, Burawoy's public project for sociology may simply reproduce the utopian efforts of Habermas' theory of the public sphere.

Conclusion: Toward a Strong Program in Professional Sociology

Michael Burawoy's project of public sociology undoubtedly seeks to advance the interests of both the discipline of sociology and of the greater public. We agree that efforts toward both of these ends are essential, but disagree that public sociology has gotten off on the right foot. Public sociology is a premature sociological venture that first requires significant reflection upon and consolidation of sociological knowledge. Burawoy argues that the sociological professional has accumulated a vast trove of knowledge that is ripe for use in our efforts at public engagement, and this is probably true. However, the discipline demonstrates very little consensus over the state of this knowledge, what exactly is known, and the best means by which sociological knowledge can be gained. In short, sociology does not have a systemic inventory of its professional storehouse of knowledge.

It is true that the sociological discipline is multifaceted and multivocal, rich with ideas, perspectives and insights. While some may celebrate the virtues of this diversity, the lack of sociological coherence may be detriment to the discipline and to its public face. This is not to say that the homogenization of sociology should be the goal, but some degree of uniformity and agreement *within* the discipline and *about* the discipline is long overdue. We have argued that public sociology is, in part, premature because sociologists do not agree on what is known; we have also suggested that public sociology lacks a vision for public engagement that will find general acceptance within the professional community. Without a sense of collective coherence, any disciplinary voice that endeavors to speak for sociology will only serve to segment the profession further. The discipline is probably too fragmented at heart for it to be otherwise. Already, fragmentation has been a principal consequence of public sociology.

It is clear that sociology needs to develop a stronger and more coherent public presentation of self; but we should be careful in doing so. Our demeanor must reflect the respect that we have for our public audience, and a greater reflexivity about our sociological knowledge. A public indifferent to sociology is not likely to be won over with ideology and speculation. In essence, we believe that establishing a strong program in professional sociology, based upon the inherent reflexivity of science, presents the most promising avenue for the strengthening of the discipline and the facilitation of our public engagement. Burawoy may be right—by attempting to become public "narrators" within society, sociologists may establish a disciplinary identity and find their collective and public voice. However, in exploring the avenues of our public engagement, the ultimate lesson of public sociology may not primarily involve our interface with civil society. Instead, public sociology may first and foremost serve to increase the reflexivity of the discipline and teach the profession about itself.

Notes

1. The authors would like to thank Vincent Jeffries and Larry Nichols for their efforts in assembling this special issue on Public Sociology and for their insightful editorial suggestions on this paper.
2. See Turner's (1998), for one example. Turner advocates the development of a sociological discipline that mirrors that of engineering. He outlines what might be called a mixture of Burawoy's professional and policy sociologies.
3. In fact, Burawoy frequently mentions the leftward nature of sociology, and mentions the "left" frequently with positive connotations. While the "right" are rarely criticized in Burawoy's descriptions of public sociology, they are hardly ever mentioned.
4. "The standpoint of the old materialism is civil society; the standpoint of the new is human society, or social humanity" and "The philosophers have only interpreted the world, in various ways; the point is to change it."

References

Bell, W. 1996. "The Sociology of the Future and the Future of Sociology." *Sociological Perspectives* 39, 1: 39-57.

Bellah, R., R. Madsen, W.M. Sullivan, A. Swidler, and S. Tipton. 1985. *Habits of the Heart: Individualism and Commitment in American Life*. Berkeley, CA: University of California Press.

Bender, T. 1997. *Intellect and Public Life: Essays on the Social History of Academic Intellectuals in the United States*. Baltimore: The Johns Hopkins University Press.

Berger, P. 1963. *Invitation to Sociology: A Humanistic Perspective*. Garden City, NY: Doubleday Books.

_____. 2002. "Whatever Happened to Sociology." *First Things* 126: 27–29.

Bonacich, E., and R. Appelbaum. 2000. *Behind the Label: Inequality in the Los Angeles Apparel Industry*. Berkeley: University of California Press.

Bourdieu, P. 1993. *Sociology in Question*. London: SAGE Publications.

Brady. D. 2004. "Why Public Sociology May Fail." *Social Forces* 82, 4: 1-10.

Burawoy, M. 1989. "Two Methods in Search of Science: Skocpol versus Trotsky." *Theory and Society* 18, 6: 759-805.

_____. 1990. "Marxism as Science: Historical Challenges and Theoretical Growth," *American Sociological Review* 55: 775-793.

_____. 2005a. "The Return of the Repressed: Recovering the Public Face of U.S. Sociology, One Hundred Years On." *The Annals of the American Academy of Political and Social Science*, July: 1-18.

_____. 2005b. "The Critical Turn to Public Sociology." *Critical Sociology* 31, 3: 313-326.

_____. 2005c. "For Public Sociology." *American Sociological Review*, 70, 1: 4-28.

_____, and E.O. Wright. 2002. "Sociological Marxism," in *The Handbook of Sociological Theory*, edited by Jonathan H. Turner. New York: Kluwer Academic/Plenum Publishers.

Burris, V. 2004. "The Academic Caste System: Prestige Hierarchies in Ph.D. Exchange Networks." *American Sociological Review* 69: 239–264.

Calhoun, C. 1992. "Introduction: Habermas and the Public Sphere." Pp. 1-48, in Craig Calhoun (ed.) *Habermas and the Public Sphere*. Cambridge, MA: MIT Press.

Collins, R. 1989. "Sociology: Proscience or Antiscience?" *American Sociological Review* 54, 1: 124-139.

_____. 1997. "A Sociological Guilt Trip: Comment on Connell." *The American Journal of Sociology* 102, 6: 1558-1564.

Connell, R.W. 1997. "Why Is Classical Theory Classical?" *The American Journal of Sociology*, 102, 6: 1511-1557.

Dahrendorf, R. 1958. "Out of Utopia: Toward a Reorientation of Sociological Analysis." *American Journal of Sociology* 64: 115-127.

Derrida, J. 1978. *Writing and Difference*. Chicago: University of Chicago Press.

Foucault, M. 1970 [1966]. *The Order of Things: An Archaeology of the Human Sciences*. New York: Vintage Books.

Fromm, E. 1961. *Marx's Concept of Man*. New York: Frederick Ungar.

Gamson, W. 2004. "Life on the Interface." *Social Problems* 51,1: 106–110.

Garfinkel, H. 1967. *Studies in Ethnomethodology*. Englewood Cliffs, NJ: Prentice Hall.

Gouldner, A. 1985. *Against Marxism: The Origins of Marxism and the Sociology of Intellectuals*. New York: Oxford University Press.

Habermas, J. 1984. *The Theory of Communicative Action. Volume 1, Reason and the Rationalization of Society*. Boston: Beacon Press.

_____. 1987. *The Theory of Communiciative Action. Volume 2, Lifeworld and System: A Critique of Functionalist Reason*. Boston, MA: Beacon Press.

_____. 1989. *Structural Transformation of the Public Sphere*. Cambridge, MA: MIT Press.

Harding, S. 1986. *The Science Question in Feminism*. Ithaca: Cornell University Press.

_____. 1991. *Whose Science? Whose Knowledge? Thinking from Women's Lives*. New York: Cornell University Press.

Horkheimer, M., and T.W. Adorno. 1993 [1947]. *Dialectic of Enlightenment*. New York: Continuum Publishing Company.

Horowitz, I.L. 1993. *The Decomposition of Sociology*. New York: Oxford University Press.

Jacoby, R. 1987. *The Last Intellectuals: American Culture in the Age of Academe*. New York: Noonday Press.

Kellner, D. 2000. "Habermas, the Public Sphere, and Democracy: A Critical Intervention," in *Perspectives on Habermas*, edited by Lewis Hahn. Illinois: Open Court Press.

Kuhn, T. 1962. *The Structure of Scientific Revolutions*. Chicago, IL: University of Chicago Press.

Lakatos, I. 1978. *The Methodology of Scientific Research Programmes*. Cambridge, England: Cambridge University Press.

Latour, B., and S. Woolgar. 1979. *Laboratory Life: The Social Construction of Scientific Facts*. Beverly Hills, CA: SAGE Publications.

Lemert, C. 1995. *Sociology after the Crisis*. Boulder, CO: Westview Press.

Lyotard, J.-F. 1984. *The Postmodern Condition: A Report on Knowledge*. Minneapolis, MN: University of Minneapolis Press.

Luhmann, N. 1994. "The Modernity of Science." *New German Critique* 61: 9-23.

McCarthy, T. 1978. *The Critical Theory of Jurgen Habermas*. Cambridge, MA: MIT Press.

Michael, J. 2000. *Anxious Intellects: Academic Professionals, Public Intellectuals, and Enlightenment Values*. London: Duke University Press.

Mills, C.W. 1956a. *The Power Elite*. New York: Oxford University Press.

_____. 1956b. *The Sociological Imagination*. New York: Oxford University Press.

New York Times. 2003. "Judging 2003's Ideas: The Most Overrated and Underrated." *New York Times*, December 27.

Nielson, F. 2003. "The Vacant "We": Remarks on Public Sociology." *Social Forces* 82, 4: 1-9.

Parsons, T. 1969. "'The Intellectuals': A Social Role Category," in *On Intellectuals*, edited by Philip Rieff. New York: Doubleday and Company.

Popper, K. 1959. *The Logic of Scientific Discovery*. New York: Basic Books.

Posner, R.A. 2002. *Public Intellectuals: A Study of Decline*. Cambridge, MA: Harvard University Press.

Riesman, D., Glazer, N., and R. Denney 1950. *The Lonely Crowd: A Study of the Changing American Character*. New Haven, CT: Yale University Press.

Seidman, S. 1994. "The End of Sociological Theory," in Steven Seidman (ed.), *The Postmodern Turn: New Perspectives on Social Theory*. Cambridge: Cambridge University Press.

_____. 2003. *Contested Knowledge: Social Theory Today*. Oxford: Blackwell Publishers Ltd.

Shils, E. 1958. "Intellectuals and the Powers." *Comparative Studies in Society and History* 1, 1: 5-22.

_____. 1982. *The Constitution of Society*. Chicago: University of Chicago Press.

Turner, J.H. 1989. "The Disintegration of American Sociology." *Sociological Perspectives* 32, 4: 419-433.

_____. 1998. "Must Sociological Theory and Sociological Practice Be So Far Apart?: A Polemical Answer." *Sociological Perspectives* 41, 2: 243-259.

Turner, S.P., and J.H. Turner. 1990. *The Impossible Science: An Institutional Analysis of American Sociology*. Newbury Park, CA: Sage.

Vaughan, D. 1996. *The Challenger Launch Decision: Risky Technology, Culture, and Deviance at NASA*. Chicago, IL: The University of Chicago Press.

_____. 2004. "Public Sociologist by Accident." *Social Problems* 51: 115–118.

Wallerstein, I., et al. 1996. *Open the Social Sciences: Report of the Gulbenkian Commission on the Restructuring of the Social Sciences*. Stanford: Stanford University Press.

Ward, S. 1995. "The Revenge of the Humanities: Reality, Rhetoric, and the Politics of Postmodernism." *Sociological Perspectives* 38, 2: 109-128.

Whitehead, A.N. 1967. *Science and the Modern World*. New York: The Free Press.

Wilner, P. 1985. "The Main Drift of Sociology between 1936 and 1982." *The History of Sociology* 5, 2: 120.

Wood, J.L. 1998. "The Academy under Siege: An Outline of Problems and Strategies." *Sociological Perspectives* 41, 4: 833-847.

_____.1999. "C.P. Snow Revisited: The Two Cultures of Faculty and Administration." *Faculty Coalition for Public Higher Education Occasional Monograph Series* (November 1999): 3.

7

Pitirim A. Sorokin's Integralism
and Public Sociology

Vincent Jeffries

Major features of the thought of Pitirim A. Sorokin are related to Michael Burawoy's four forms of sociology. The article develops the theme that Sorokin's system of sociology makes major contributions to identifying standards of excellence for professional, critical, policy, and public sociology and for their interrelationships. Sorokin's integral ontology and epistemology are described and identified as sources of the distinctive characteristics of his system of thought.

The year 2004 was characterized by considerable interest in the idea of public sociology. Through the impetus provided by Michael Burawoy, it was the theme of the annual meeting of the American Sociological Association (2004), the subject of university and academic addresses and papers (Burawoy, 2003a; 2003b; 2004f; Burawoy and VanAntwerpen, 2001), of symposia (Zimmer et al., 2004; Burawoy et al., 2004; Acker, 2005; Aronowitz, 2005; Baiocchi, 2005; Brewer, 2005; Ghamari-Tabrizi, 2005; Katz-Fishman and Scott, 2005; Urry, 2005), book chapters (Burawoy, 2005a; 2005c), and of articles in professional journals (Burawoy, 2004a; 2004b; 2004c; 2004d; 2004e; 2005b; 2005d; 2005e). A formal "Task Force on Institutionalizing Public Sociologies" was established within the American Sociological Association in 2004 (Hossfeld and Nyden, 2005).

In a recent paper Burawoy and VanAntwerpen (2001) describe the nature of public sociology as follows:

Public sociology is less a *vision of* than it is an *orientation toward* the practice of sociology. It is a sociology that is oriented toward major problems of the day, one that attempts to address them with the tools of social science, and in a manner often informed by historical and comparative perspectives. It is a sociology that seeks as its audience not just other sociologists, but wider communities of discourse, from policy makers to subaltern counter-publics. In its robustly reflexive mode, sociology manifests itself as a public sociology designed to promote public reflection on significant social issues. (2001: 2)

A comment on Burawoy's (2004c) proposal of public sociology by David Brady (2004) specifies its fundamental emphases:

public sociology essentially involves two ideas: reaching a public audience and serving to improve the public's well-being.... The first matter ... involves gaining a broader and larger reception for sociological research and theories.... The second matter ... involves seeking to contribute to the betterment of society and the lives of its members. (2004: 1629-1630)

In addition to public sociology, Burawoy (2004a, 2004c, 2005b) posits three other forms: professional, critical, and policy. Professional sociology provides theoretical and empirical knowledge, critical sociology formulates foundational value perspectives, and policy sociology applies concrete knowledge to problems in society. Each form has weaknesses, or "pathologies," that develop when it becomes too autonomous. These negative tendencies can be counteracted by positive features of the alternative forms.

These four ideal types of sociology represent a "division of labor" in which there is "reciprocal interdependence" between the forms such that "the flourishing of each depends on the flourishing of all" (Burawoy, 2004c: 1611). In this total system of sociology there is, ideally, "an organic solidarity in which each type of sociology derives energy, meaning, and imagination from its connection to the others" (Burawoy, 2005b: 15). Each form can thus be viewed as a component of the total scientific system of sociology.

This article addresses the question of how a creative public sociology that will make positive contributions to society can be developed. Pitirim A. Sorokin's system of sociology, including his idea of integralism, is taken as a starting point for the analysis. Sorokin is the most published and most translated scholar in the history of sociology (Martindale, 1975: 105-106). His thought is diverse and comprehensive, and has made major contributions in many areas of sociology (Jeffries, 2002a; Johnston, 1995).

Burawoy's (2005b) analysis of the forms of sociology can be regarded as initiating an extensive dialogue to evaluate the criteria of excellence for the science of sociology. His model dictates that each form must be considered separately, in terms of its most important characteristics, and systemically, in terms of its potential influence on the other interdependent forms, and on the overall level of excellence of sociology as a science.

This article is intended to demonstrate that Sorokin's ideas provide foundational contributions to the development of each form of sociology, and to a greater understanding of their role in the total system of sociology. Further, his ideas can provide counter tendencies to the potential pathologies of each form, and can neutralize some of the criticisms directed toward public sociology. His system of thought thus constitutes an exemplar for the scientific system of sociology, including public sociology.

Professional Sociology

Professional sociology is the *sine qua non* of the other three forms (Burawoy, 2004c: 1611). This form furnishes the theoretical frameworks and research techniques that provide scientifically based knowledge and understanding. It is exemplified in the theoretical traditions and scientific research programs characteristic of the history of the discipline. Professional sociology is accountable to the academic audience of peers to which it is primarily addressed, and is legitimated by scientific norms. Pathologies of professional sociology include insularity, irrelevance, placing method ahead of substance, and unnecessary abstraction (Burawoy, 2004a; 2004c; 2005c).

The system of sociology contained in Sorokin's writings is based on a comprehensive program of professional sociology. His ideas make three particular contributions to this form: a basic orientation to the nature and organization of the discipline, a close correspondence of theoretical development and empirical research, and the ontology and epistemology of integralism.

The Nature of Sociology

Sorokin's sociology rests on the assumption that there are three "inseparable" components of the subject matter—personality, as thinking and acting individuals; society, the totality of interacting individuals and social relationships; and culture, composed of meanings, values, and norms and the vehicles through which they are manifested (Sorokin, 1947: 63-64; 1966: 635-649). Since "none of the members of this indivisible trinity (personality, society, culture) can exist without the other two" (Sorokin, 1947: 63-64), each must ultimately "be referred to the triadic manifold, or matrix in which it exists" (Sorokin, 1947: 47) to produce optimum knowledge and understanding. This basic conceptual and analytic frame of reference leads to a definition of sociology as "a generalizing science of sociocultural phenomena viewed in their generic forms, types, and manifold interconnections" (Sorokin, 1947: 16). General sociology includes the structural, which studies culture, society, and personality as systems, and the dynamic, which studies process and change in these systems. This same basic delineation of the subject matter is applicable to "special sociologies" that focus on a particular class of sociocultural phenomena, such as family, religion, economics, or crime (Sorokin, 1947: 16-17).

Sorokin's formulation of the frame of reference of sociology and its application in various special sociologies provides a foundation for professional sociology that is broad in its scope and powerful in its analytic potential. Unlike more restrictive perspectives that typically minimize one, or even two, of the culture, society, personality triumvirate, Sorokin's delineation of the nature of sociology fully encompasses the essential features of the objective reality that is its subject matter. This comprehensive view of the science of sociology is open to study and elaboration through a variety of theories, methodological techniques, and subject matters. The topics of public sociology that can be derived from this source can be addressed as a general orientation or in the universe of special sociologies, such as cultural sociology, sociology of education, criminology, or any other area. This orientation includes the study of civil society emphasized by Burawoy (2004b), while broadening the potential scope and focus of public sociology to a wide variety of socio-cultural phenomena and substantive areas.

Scientific Research Programs

A second contribution of Sorokin's system of sociology is a strong emphasis on both theoretical development and empirical research. Particularly important and illustrative in this regard in Sorokin's professional sociology are the following: his comparative, historical, and statistical analysis of culture that underlies his theories of cultural types, integration, and change (Sorokin, 1937a; 1937b; 1941a; 1947; 1957a); his analysis and typology of social relationships (1937c); his theoretical and statistical analysis of the historical fluctuation of war and revolution (1925, 1937c, 1950d, [1941]1998a, [1942]1998b); his analysis of mobility and stratification (Sorokin, 1947; 1959), including the relation between power and morality (Sorokin and Lunden, 1959); his analysis of social theories (1928, 1950c, 1966) and of methodology (1956b); and his pioneering theoretical formulations and empirical work in the study of altruistic love (1950a, 1950b, 1954a, 1954b). In these areas Sorokin

provides an exemplar for professional sociology with innovative theoretical and conceptual formulations systematically related to the analysis of
various types of empirical data.

Sorokin's professional sociology illustrates a model of science in
which theory and research are closely connected. The ultimate aim
of scientific endeavor in this context is to explain basic structures and
processes (Turner, 1998). Lakatos' (1978) exposition of the nature of
scientific research programs exemplifies this emphasis on rigorous
scientific development, and provides a model for building a firm foundation of scientific knowledge and understanding within professional
sociology. In his analysis Burawoy (1989, 1990, 2004c: 1609, 2005b:
10) consistently maintains that developing vigorous scientific research
programs in diverse areas is a necessary foundation for a creative and
socially significant public sociology. ✓ empirical. ایراد یک سری مطالعه موضوعی

Integralism ——→   منهب دارد توش . مذهب حواس و ماورای حواس، ایراد دارد، استدلالی و بجو سی ریاضی بار

A third contribution of Sorokin's system of sociology to public sociology is his idea of integralism. It is the basis of various aspects of
Sorokin's thought (Ford, 1963; 1996; Johnston, 1995; 1996: 166-220;
1998), including his ontology and epistemology. The foundational idea
of integralism is that the <u>reality that is the subject matter of the social</u>
<u>sciences contains empirical-sensory, rational-mindful, and superrational-</u>
<u>supersensory</u> components (Sorokin, 1941a: 741-746; 1956a; 1957b). This
assumption opens the spiritual and transcendental realm to consideration
and analysis. Since reality contains these three elements, this ontology
necessitates a corresponding epistemology suitable for obtaining knowledge regarding all its aspects.

The system of truth and knowledge of a culture involves its scientific,
philosophical, and religious thought. Sorokin's integral model is based on
a system of truth and knowledge that has appeared in different societies
and periods of history over the last 2,500 years (Sorokin, 1937b: 1-180;
1957a: 225-283). In this period of time in Western civilization some
variety of integralism has occurred approximately as often as alternative
epistemological systems that are based primarily on either empiricism or
on faith (Sorokin, 1937b: 54-55). Integralism historically has been eclectic in terms of religious and philosophical orientation (Nichols, 2001).
It is represented in the "idealistic rationalism" of particular branches of
such diverse systems of thought as Taoism, Buddhism, Hinduism, classical Greek philosophy, and Christianity (Sorokin, 1963a: 373-374. See
also 1937b: 57-69, 95-103).

154   Public Sociology

The distinguishing characteristic of an integral epistemology is that it combines faith, reason, and the senses into a harmonious system. The truth of faith is regarded as including both intuition and the religious idea of revealed truth (Sorokin, 1964a: 227-229. See also 1956a, 1957b). Sorokin (1941a) describes an integral system of truth and knowledge as follows:

> the *integral truth is not identical with any of the three forms of truth, but embraces all of them.* In this three-dimensional aspect of the truth of faith, of reason, and of the senses, the integral truth is nearer to the absolute truth than any one-sided truth of one of these three forms. Likewise, the reality given by the integral three-dimensional truth, with its source of intuition, reason, and the senses, is a nearer approach to the infinite metalogical reality of the *coincidentia oppositorum* than the purely sensory, or purely rational, or purely intuitional reality, given by one of the systems of truth and reality.The *empirico-sensory aspect of it is given by the truth of the senses; the rational aspect, by the truth of reason; the super-rational aspect by the truth of faith.* (pp. 762-763)

An integral epistemology can produce significant advances in knowledge and understanding in the social sciences (Sorokin, 1961; 1963a: 372-400; [1944]1998c: 284). As stated by Sorokin (1963a):

> A systematic development of such an adequate integral system of cognition is an urgent need of our time. Such a system would include in it not only rational, sensory, and intuitive knowledge of rational-sensory realities but also the cognition of "supra-sensory and suprarational" forms of reality-the knowledge called "no-knowledge" by the Taoist sages, *prajna* and *jnana* by the Hindu and the Buddhist thinkers, and *docta ignorantia* by Nicholas of Cusa. Development of such a genuine integral system of truth and cognition can greatly help mankind in enriching, deepening, and enlarging human knowledge of total reality, in eliminating the mutually conflicting claims of science, religion, philosophy, and ethics through reconciliation and unification of their real knowledge into one integral system of truth, in stimulating man's creativity in all fields of culture and social life, and in the ennoblement and transfiguration of man himself. (1963a: 400)

Scientific endeavor within sociology is a continuum ranging from the metaphysical realm of presuppositions and ideological assumptions, to the middle level of theories and models, to the empirical realm of observation and data gathering (Alexander, 1982: 1-46). The comprehensive scope provided by the tripartite epistemology of integralism involves in its most basic sense the incorporation of ideas derived from religious traditions at all levels of this scientific continuum (Jeffries, 1998).

The Practice of Science

Two general criteria guide and provide impetus to scientific endeavor within professional sociology: scientific importance and value judgments. Both provide unique contributions to the advancement of knowledge and understanding, and to the assessment of the relative importance of past and future topics of study. Thus both contribute to the cumulation necessary for both policy and public sociology.

Determining scientific importance is an ongoing process of assessment emerging from theoretical development and cumulative research findings. In sociology, professional activity is focused on advancing knowledge and understanding regarding basic structures and processes within the frame of reference of culture, society, and personality (Sorokin, 1947: 16-17). This focus on the most fundamental aspects of the subject matter provides for considerable parallel between theories and research findings in general and special sociologies, thus maximizing scientific cumulation (Turner, 2005a).

The second criterion guiding the practice of science is value premises that are derived from conceptions of the good (Myrdal, 1958). The values that are formulated in the metaphysical environment of the scientific continuum influence scientific activity at less abstract levels. They guide problem selection and focus the evaluation of the significance of empirical results within professional sociology. They also contribute to cumulation and generalization by focusing theory and research on a limited range of problems. In these senses value premises guide the ongoing practice of science. The nature of these values and the reasons for their importance can be formulated and considered within the sphere of critical sociology.

← Critical Sociology

Critical sociology raises questions and initiates dialogue within the academic community about basic assumptions and values, and about the moral foundations and concerns of sociology (Burawoy, 2004a; 2004c). It is the "conscience" of professional sociology (Burawoy, 2004c: 1609). It also disciplines policy sociology and initiates value commitments in public sociology. In executing these activities, critical sociology has on occasion drawn ideas from outside the discipline to formulate perspectives regarding these questions (Burawoy, 2004a: 105). The legitimacy of critical sociology is based on its ability to "supply moral visions" (Burawoy, 2005b: 16). These contributions of critical sociology will be lessened if it becomes overly sectarian or dogmatic.

Sorokin's critical sociology encompasses two areas. The first is his evaluation of the state of professional sociology, the second his formulation of the alternative of integralism, particularly with reference to its value premises.

The State of Sociology

The scientific accomplishments of professional sociology and its level of contributions to the general society were regarded by Sorokin as minimal ([1941]1998a, 1956b). Because the sociology of the first part of the twentieth century focused on a natural science model, it "did not create referential principles adequate for a study of sociocultural phenomena nor develop methods fit for such a study" (Sorokin, [1941] 1998a: 94). Although a "vast" amount of information was collected, because of the neglect of reason and the rejection of intuition as sources of truth, these facts were not systematically gathered in a manner to produce knowledge. As a result, "only a few generalizations and correct formulas of uniformities in sociocultural processes were discovered" (Sorokin, [1941]1998a: 95). This failure of professional sociology led inevitably to failure in the policy and public realms, where "they were unable to eliminate any important social evils or to contribute to social welfare. They were incapable of offering any systematic plan of sociocultural reconstruction" (Sorokin, [1941]1998a: 98).

This lack of creativity in sociology can only be alleviated by a shift to an integral epistemology, referential principles that recognize the logical and meaningful nature of sociocultural phenomena, and resultant changes in the nature of the problems that are studied (Sorokin, [1941]1998a: 100-103). To a limited degree, these changes had begun to take place by the latter part of the twentieth century. One example is the general recognition of culture, society, and personality as the basic subject matter of sociology. Others are widespread agreement in sociological analysis on both the importance of the dimension of meaning and the concept of system. Despite these advances, an integral sociology had not been adequately or fully developed at Sorokin's (1965, 1966: 635-649) last evaluations, and still has not today.

The Integral Model

One function of critical sociology is to "dialogue about ends" as it "interrogates the value premises of society as well as our profession" (Burawoy, 2005b: 11). This assessment of values is fundamental in evaluating what problems should be studied in professional sociology and in justifying their relative importance. The content of an integral model of critical sociology at the highest level of value generalization is described by Sorokin as follows (1957b):

Among all the meaningful values of the superorganic world there is the supreme integral value—the veritable *summum bonum*. It is the indivisible unity of Truth,

Goodness, and Beauty. Though each member of this supreme Trinity has a distinct individuality, all three are inseparable from one another.... These greatest values are not only inseparable from one another, but they are transformable into one another.... Each newly discovered truth contributes also to the values of beauty and goodness. Each act of unselfish creative love (goodness) enriches the realms of truth and beauty; and each masterpiece of beauty morally enobles and mentally enlightens the members of the human universe.... For these reasons, the main historical mission of mankind consists in an unbounded creation, accumulation, refinement, and actualization of Truth, Beauty, and Goodness in the nature of man himself, in man's mind and be-havior, in man's superorganic universe and beyond it, and in man's relationships to all human beings, to all living creatures, and to the total cosmos.... Any important achievement in this supreme mission represents a real progress of man and of the human universe (p.184).

These highly general values can be considered separately at a level of generalization below their transformability described above. Each needs to be specified and clarified to be incorporated in the system of ideas and practices that constitute the forms of sociology. Truth and good-ness are the most important for shaping the discipline of sociology. The previous analysis has indicated that the ontology and epistemology of integralism can facilitate increased understanding of the truth regarding the nature, structure, and dynamics of sociocultural phenomena. The general value of goodness can also be expressed in concepts suitable for theoretical development and research application in professional and policy sociology. خوبٌ رو باید از نیه جایی بیارم • سوروکین از ادیان مکگیره

Studying Goodness

An integral concept of goodness can be formulated from fundamental religious ideas which appear to be close to universal in the major world religions. The religious truth of faith provides the core values of critical sociology that discipline and guide professional sociology to the common focus of theory and research that is necessary for scientific cumulation. Sorokin (1948) notes

religion enters into harmonious cooperation with science, logic, and philosophy without sacrificing any of its intuitive truth revealed through the superconscious of its seers, prophets, and charismatic leaders. On the other hand, in its turn it supple-ments science, logic, and philosophy through its system of ultimate reality—values. In this way religion, logic, science unite to form a single harmonious team dedicated to the discovery of the perennial values and to the proper shaping of man's mind and conduct (1948: 158).

In an integral model religious ideas can be used as value premises and concepts within the basic frame of reference delineated by Sorokin (1947: 63-65) of culture, society, and personality. They can be incorporated at various levels of the scientific continuum, ranging from the metaphysical level as value premises in critical sociology, to the theoretical level as basic concepts, to the empirical level as operational definitions applied to data of a particular nature within the practice of professional sociology (Jeffries, 1999).

Particularly important for sociological analysis are ideas from religious traditions pertaining to topics such as human nature, the characteristics of goodness and of perfection, the ends of human existence, and moral and ethical precepts. Ideas of this nature from religious traditions can be used to define goodness for study at two different levels of sociological analysis: the sociocultural and the individual personality.

Goodness at the Sociocultural Level

In regard to social interaction and intergroup relations, religious moral and ethical systems universally emphasize ideas such as doing good and avoiding evil, the Golden Rule of behaving toward others as one would have others behave toward oneself, and attitudes and behavior that are directed to benefiting the other in some manner. This orientation of doing good to the other has also frequently been referred to as love: benevolent or agape love in traditional terms, altruistic, compassionate, or unlimited love in more recent usage (Post, 2003). Concepts such as "solidarity" and "familistic" signify the manifestation of this love in terms of forms of interaction and social relationships, respectively (Sorokin, 1954a: 13). Though often differing in specifics, the world religions are similar in the essential nature of such ideas regarding the good in a context of interaction and intergroup relations (Hick, 1989; Hunt, Crotty, and Crotty, 1991; Post, 2003; Sorokin, 1948: 154-158; 1954a: 111-112; 1998c).

Sorokin's (1947: 93-144) theory of solidarity and antagonism provides a basis for scientific research programs in this area, ranging on the micro- macro continuum from interpersonal to international relations. The importance of the sociological problem of solidarity and antagonism to professional, policy, and public sociology is noted by Sorokin:

> The paramount theoretical and practical importance of the factors of solidarity and antagonism is obvious. Had we known what caused either solidarity or antagonism, and with such knowledge been able to increase the familistic and eliminate the antagonistic from interpersonal and intergroup relationships, had we but known this, all the main social tragedies—war, bloody revolution, crime, coercion and compulsion, misery and unhappiness, the contrasts of poverty and luxury, domination and enslavement—would have been eliminated or reduced to a minimum. (1947: 119)

Solidary interaction is a situation in which "the aspirations (meanings, values) and overt actions of the interacting parties concur and are mutually helpful for the realization of their objectives" (Sorokin, 1947: 93). In contrast, in antagonistic interaction the meanings—values and actions "of the parties are opposite and mutually hinder one another" (Sorokin, 1947: 93). These forms of interaction also appear in more complex systems of social relationships, in which the "familistic" is predominately solidary and the "compulsory" is predominately antagonistic (Sorokin, 1947: 99-110. See also 1937c; 1941b: 167-240).

Internal solidarity has often been a factor in enabling some groups to establish compulsory relations of domination over others. Within an integral framework that derives concepts from religious traditions, such as the Golden Rule or the unconditional love of agape, the concept of solidarity must be formulated in terms of potentially universal application. In this sense, the concept of solidarity is limited to interaction directed toward ends that are not known to violate the good of the human person, or basic rights of a personal, social, economic, or political nature. It thus includes the idea of justice, in which each receives his or her right or due (Pieper, 1966: 43-53).

Sorokin (1947: 119-131) explains solidarity and antagonism by cultural factors characteristic of the interacting parties: the nature of norms and values, whether they are concordant or discordant, and the degree to which they are expressed in behavior. Moral norms that are characteristic of religions, such as love and the Golden Rule, are a basic variable in Sorokin's (1947: 130-131) theory of the cultural sources of solidarity. Values and norms such as the aforementioned that are considered universal and are consistently practiced are primary factors in solidarity, particularly if this is true of each of the interacting parties. In contrast, sources of antagonism are values and norms that emphasize rivalry, egoism, or competition for limited resources, that are regularly practiced, and that are discordant among the interacting parties.

Extensions and elaborations of Sorokin's basic theory of solidarity and antagonism occur in his analysis of topics such as the problematics of sensate culture (Sorokin, 1937c: 161-180; 1941a: 737-779; 1941b), the relation between culture types and systems of social relationships (Sorokin, 1937c: 123-138), the relation between power and morality (Sorokin and Lunden, 1959), and war (Sorokin, 1937c: 370-380; [1942]1998b; [1944]1998c).

Goodness in Individual Personality

The desirability of individual development toward greater personal goodness is espoused by all major religions (Hick, 1989: 36-55). Such individual goodness is typically defined as a movement from self-centeredness to centeredness on God or the Ultimate Reality. This transformation entails a process of movement toward salvation/liberation involving progressively greater moral goodness on the part of the individual (1989: 299-315). This focus provides for studying goodness at the level of analysis of the individual personality. Two related concepts can be used to analyze the nature of goodness at this micro level: virtue and altruistic love.

The development in recent years in psychology of a major tradition called "positive psychology" has given a central theoretical and research focus to the concept of virtue (Vitz, 2005). Virtues are traditionally regarded as habits that are good, and thus that produce good works. They represent the perfection of the powers that move the individual toward what is good within human nature (Aquinas, 1981: 819-827; Pieper, 1966).

In a recent major work in the tradition of positive psychology, Peterson and Seligman (2004: 3-52) emphasize the historical and cultural universality of the concept of virtue. They maintain that six broad categories of virtues emerge as universally regarded personal manifestations of the good in the thinking of moral philosophers and religious thinkers representing the major world religions: wisdom, courage, humanity, justice, temperance, and transcendence. In this formulation, these universal virtues are manifested through character strengths, the psychological processes through which the virtues are activated. Character strengths in turn are linked to situational themes. These are habits linked to specific situations. For example, the virtue of humanity that involves "tending and befriending others" (Peterson and Seligman, 2004: 29) is expressed in character strengths such as love or kindness, which in turn can be expressed in situational themes such as empathy, inclusiveness, or positivity. The greatest cultural variation exists at the level of themes, is found less often for character traits, and is regarded as absent in the case of the universal virtues (Peterson and Seligman, 2004: 14).

More traditional formulations of the virtues, such as those of Aristotle (1941: 927-1112) and Aquinas (1981: 817-894, 1263-1879), parallel this list despite variations in terminology, emphasis, and organization

(Peterson and Seligman, 2004: 46-48). The virtues can also be equated with the idea of benevolent or altruistic love since the virtues specify the attitudes and behavior necessary to benefit the other in a consistent manner (Jeffries, 1998).

Sorokin equated the idea of personal goodness with the manifestation of altruistic love (Sorokin, 1954a, 1964b: 160-208). This love is manifested in self-sacrifice, the giving of aid, the performance of duty, generosity, friendliness, unselfish service, and similar forms of behavior (Sorokin, 1954a: 47-79). Love of this nature is related to conceptions of the good in religious traditions. Sorokin (1954a: 79) notes: "There is no need to argue that *love is the heart and soul of ethical goodness itself and of all great religions*. Their central command has always been love of God and of neighbor."

Altruistic love has five dimensions (Sorokin, 1954a: 15-35): intensity, the degree of expenditure of energy and effort; extensity, the scope of others to whom love is given; duration, the amount of time during which love is expressed; purity, the degree to which the motivation to love is not self-centered; and adequacy, entailing both the degree to which the subjective intent of love is present and the degree to which the objective consequences of actions benefit the other. Lower levels of these dimensions of altruistic love are ego-centered, in that they are based primarily on enlightened self interest, while higher levels are ego-transcending, in that the end of love dominates the individual's motivation and actions (Sorokin, 1954a: 288-289). This range of attitudes and behavior manifested in altruistic love can be contrasted with behavior not related to altruism by its nature, and egoistic or anti-altruistic behavior, which may include hatred or enmity (Sorokin, 1948: 58-62). Recent writings indicate that Sorokin's formulation of the dimensions of love has potential applicability in scientific research programs on a variety of topics (Jeffries, 1998, 2002b; Post, 2003).

The Power of Love

On the personality level, evidence indicates that love is related to personal vitality and longevity, is a curative factor in some mental and physical disorders, and is a decisive factor in the overall development and well-being of the individual (Sorokin, 1954a: 60-66). On the social level, the practice of altruistic love can transform social relationships, and the entire society and culture, in a positive manner (Sorokin, 1954a: 66-77). Love is a powerful creative force in the realization of ultimate values in all aspects of human life and experience (Sorokin, 1954a):

the power of love generates, inspires, reinforces, and operates in all the individual and collective actions of the realization of truth and knowledge, of goodness and justice, of beauty and freedom, of the *summum bonum* and happiness, throughout the whole creative history of humanity (p. 79).

Critical Impacts Professional

The value perspective of critical integralism leads to two broad areas of theoretical development and empirical research in professional sociology. The first is the goodness of individuals, defined in terms of virtue and benevolent love. The second is social solidarity, the manifestation of goodness in interaction. It ranges from interpersonal, to intergroup, to international relations. This value perspective can be integrated with a variety of theoretical perspectives, research techniques, and substantive concerns, ranging from micro- to meso- to macro-levels of analysis, in both general and special sociologies. Two general theoretical and research problems emerge: how culture and society influence individual goodness, and how individual goodness influences culture and society (Jeffries, 1999).

By concentrating scientific practice through the investigation of the cultural, social, and personality sources of goodness in its various forms, an integral critical sociology adds greatly to the ability of professional sociology to establish the cumulation necessary for valid generalizations and the advance of knowledge and understanding. This strong professional foundation is crucial to a viable policy and public sociology.

Policy Sociology

Policy sociology is the form that "focuses on solutions to specific problems" (Burawoy, 2004c: 1608). It provides instrumental knowledge regarding the means to reach a concrete goal. The legitimacy of policy sociology is based on its effectiveness. The problem is defined by a client or patron. A wide variety of organizations may contract for the services of sociologists. Policy sociology is thus directed primarily to an audience outside of the academic community. Potential pathologies are servility and the use of policy sociology by power holders in a manner in which scientific integrity is diminished (Burawoy, 2004a; 2004c; 2005b).

The Promise of Integralism

Sorokin ([1951]1998d) specifically advocated the development of a policy sociology directed toward realization of the values mandated by critical integralism:

We seemingly know little about how to make friends and build a harmonious universe.

The time has come when this knowledge must be obtained and fully developed. The historical moment has struck for building a new applied science or a new art of amitology—the science and art of cultivation of amity, unselfish love, and mutual help in interindividual and intergroup relationships. A mature amitology is now the paramount need of humanity. Its development tangibly determines the creative future of *Homo sapiens* ([1951] 1998d: 302).

Because the integral model of professional sociology will yield "more valid and more accurate" knowledge and understanding "of the nature of sociocultural phenomena and of the uniformities that can be observed in its static and dynamic forms" (Sorokin, [1941]1998a: 103), it will provide a sound basis for policy sociology and have clear implications for the dialogue of public sociology. Sorokin ([1941]1998a) notes this contribution of the knowledge gathered by an integral professional sociology to these other forms:

The importance of such knowledge for applied social science is obvious. Some important future trends can be roughly predicted: efficient means of correcting social evils can be devised, the creative enrichment of human experience can be inspired; and in all fields of culture there can be created magnificent and lasting values (p. 103).

Integral Theoretical Foundations and Policy Implications

A central element of policy sociology is to provide knowledge that is "practical" or "useful" about how something can be achieved (Burawoy, 2005b: 16). Such knowledge can range from broad theoretical orientations to specific solutions to particular problems. In Sorokin's integralism the most basic theoretical orientation for policy sociology is derived from the fact that culture, society, and personality phenomena "constitute an indivisible trinity bound together by the ties of causal and meaningful interdependence" (Sorokin, 1948: 94). Therefore, policy intervention directed toward positive change must involve all three of these aspects of reality. Thus in regard to establishing and maintaining peace and social solidarity, Sorokin (1948) observes:

If we desire to eliminate war and to establish a harmonious world order, we must pay the fullest price for this value: we must transform in a creatively altruistic direction all human beings, all social institutions, and the entire culture of mankind in all its main compartments, including science, religion, law and ethics, the fine arts, economics, and politics. Otherwise all attempts are doomed to be abortive and to prove harmful rather than beneficial (pp. 95-96).

Sorokin's more specific agenda for policy formulation and intervention derives from the aforementioned principle that cultural, social, and personality factors must all be changed. However, there is a causal priority in generating reconstruction. Since "the total fabric of a given culture is woven of millions of trifling individual deeds" (Sorokin, 1948: 234), positive change rests on the necessary condition that "*every individual as such* can begin to work upon himself" (Sorokin, 1948: 233) in an effort to become more altruistic and creative. Thus individual deliberation and choice, and micro level initiatives beginning with individual behavior, become the necessary condition of effective social and cultural reconstruction. Sorokin (1948) describes the nature and importance of this effort at self-transformation toward greater personal goodness:

> one can carry on this self-education in thousands of specific actions, beginning with minor good deeds and ending with the acts of exceptional unselfishness. If most persons would even slightly improve themselves in this way, the sum total of social life would be ameliorated vastly more than through political campaigns, legislation, wars and revolutions, lockouts and strikes, and pressure reforms (1948: 233-234).

Sorokin's (1954a: 125-455) professional sociology devoted to the study of altruism includes an investigation of self-directed altruistic transformation. Various techniques that the individual can perform on his or her self, such as doing good deeds, individual creative activity, the development of altruistic self-identification, prayer, conscience examination, and rearrangement of group affiliations are analyzed and illustrated with case studies (Sorokin, 1954a: 323-355). Building on foundations from Sorokin, the study of various techniques of altruistic transformation is an important part of the recent movement to develop a scientific field devoted to research on "unlimited love" (Post, 2003: 159-202).

Resting on the necessary condition of individual transformation, Sorokin (1948) develops a general policy agenda for social and cultural reconstruction. This agenda moves from individual behavior to meso- then macro-levels. This continued advance of reconstruction is considered dependent on the contributions of scientific knowledge.

> *The second and third lines of attack consist in a well-planned modification of our culture and social institutions through the concerted actions of individuals united in groups, which, in turn, are merged in larger federations or associations.* At the present time the tasks are twofold: first, *to increase our knowledge and wisdom and to invent better, more efficient techniques for fructifying our culture and institutions and rendering human beings more noble and altruistic;* second, *through this increased knowledge and these perfected techniques to draw up more adequate plans for the total process of transformation, to diffuse and propagate them, and to convince ever-larger sections of humanity of the urgency, feasibility, and adequacy of the proposed reconstruction* (pp. 234-235).

Integralism's Basic Policy Model: Individual Agency

Sociology has traditionally studied phenomena ranging from micro to macro levels, concretely, from the individual to the society or civilization. Work has been directed to developing theories of influence from either of these levels to the other: from micro to macro, and from macro to micro (Ritzer, 1981; Turner and Boyns, 2001). Much of Sorokin's sociological system pertains to the influence of macro factors such as general culture types and systems of social relationships upon more micro level phenomena and on individual personalities. However, his policy integralism places particular emphasis on movement from micro to macro. Therefore, the role of human choice at the most micro level of the individual, and its implications at increasingly macro levels, becomes a major focus of theory and research in professional and policy sociology, and a major criterion of relevance for public sociology.

The underlying theoretical logic of this model of policy sociology and its implications for professional sociology is similar to that developed by W.I. Thomas (1951: 35-38). While the mutual interdependence of personality and sociocultural factors is acknowledged, theoretical development and research on personality and the effect of individual attitudes and actions on transforming the sociocultural world of values in a positive direction is emphasized. In a statement that parallels Sorokin's model, Thomas (1951) notes:

> We must establish by scientific procedure the laws of behavior, and then the past will have its meaning and make its contribution. If we learn the laws of human behavior as we have learned the laws of mathematics, physics, and chemistry, if we establish what are the fundamental human attitudes, how they can be converted into other and more socially desirable attitudes, how the world of values is created and modified by the operation of these attitudes, then we can establish any attitudes and values whatever. (1951: 37-38)

Policy Sociology Initiated by the Sociologist

Sorokin's comprehensive system of thought frequently contains policy formulations in the sense of presenting specific solutions to clearly identified problems. Sorokin began to move from his primarily professionally oriented writing to focusing more on problems in his works on the crisis of contemporary culture and social relations (1941b), on war ([1944]1998c), and on behavior in situations of social calamity (1942: 296-319). In these writings he also proposed solutions to these problems. In his autobiography he notes that while completing the writing of his comprehensive system of sociology (Sorokin, 1947) he became increasingly preoccupied with "the highly critical situation of mankind" (Sorokin, 1963b: 268). He decided that when this writing was finished "I would devote all my free time to the investigation of the means of preventing the imminent annihilation of the human race and of ways out of the deadly crisis" (Sorokin, 1963b: 268). Shortly after he made this decision, in the form of a commitment to study altruistic love scientifically, he was approached by Eli Lilly and offered financial support for his studies. Subsequent grants from Lilly made possible the establishment of the Harvard Research Center in Creative Altruism, with Sorokin as director (Sorokin, 1963b: 275-280).

Although Lilly provided valuable financial support, the direction of the Center for ten years of its existence, and all decisions regarding topics and methods of study, were left entirely in the hands of Sorokin (Johnston, 1995: 166-220; Sorokin, 1963b: 271-292). Thus Sorokin's policy sociology began before any contact with Lilly, and was completely free from control by a client or patron after Lilly became involved. It is therefore free from the pathologies of servility and loss of scientific integrity that can occur in this form (Burawoy, 2004c; 2005b). In his autobiographical statement Sorokin notes that "my independence and freedom of thought" were values that he was unwilling to compromise to obtain financial aid for his scientific work (Sorokin, 1963b: 274-275).

The nature of Sorokin's policy sociology can be more specifically understood in the context of the four forms of sociology. Burawoy (2005b: 11-13) notes that at a more descriptive and empirical level each ideal type form of sociology has within itself "moments" that reflect the dominant concerns of the other types. For example, critical sociology exists within professional sociology in the debates that take place both within and between research programs. This internal complexity can be seen in Sorokin's works. For example, his major work on altruistic love is clearly professional sociology in its content and intended audience, yet it contains a considerable section that deals with policy in terms of the techniques of altruistic transformation (Sorokin, 1954a: 125-489). Similarly, his analysis of power and morality is public sociology in terms of its intended general audience, while containing an extended policy analysis of how lack of morality in the exercise of power can be reduced and controlled (Sorokin and Lunden, 1959: 104-193).

Sorokin's (1948) analysis of reconstruction represents a detailed and comprehensive statement of policy sociology addressed to the general public. The policy intent and character of this work is clearly illustrated in the preface introducing the reader to the book:

> If this plan for personal, social, and cultural transformation is carried through, international and civil wars are likely to be eliminated, interpersonal and intergroup conflicts largely abolished, vast creative forces released, and an unprecedented renaissance of human values ushered in. (Preface)

The entire work is a comprehensive statement of the various means necessary to reach more solidary and peaceful relations in this historical era. After a brief analysis of ineffective means to reach these ends, an increase in altruism is proposed as the only effective solution to the problem of antagonistic and compulsory interpersonal, intergroup, and international relations. The rest of the work consists in a detailed exposition of the instrumental knowledge of how the goal of personal, social, and cultural reconstruction toward greater altruism can be effectively achieved. What must be changed, effective remedies, and the prospects of success are all considered in some detail.

The varied contexts of Sorokin's policy formulations, the fact they were of his own initiation, and their complete independence from the influence of client or patron suggest it is useful to distinguish a form of policy sociology that is initiated by the sociologist. Taking Sorokin's case as a model, sociological knowledge and understanding are applied to finding the solution to some problem. Focus is on the means to accomplish a particular goal, and thus on instrumental knowledge. However, the analysis is not initiated by, or responsible to, a client or patron. Rather, the problem and goal to be attained are formulated by the concerns of the sociologist himself or herself. A systematic program for reaching a goal is presented to an audience that can range from academic to varied publics. Confirmatory research is not required, as it typically is in policy research for a client, and, in some instances, a patron. In this sense the nature of this manifestation of policy sociology, "sociologist initiated," is a variation within the practical tradition of sociology described by Turner and Turner (1990). This policy sociology may be "moments" in writings primarily in another form, or, as in Sorokin's (1948) work on reconstruction, policy may be the central intent and pervade the entire work. Other examples of this manifestation of policy sociology can be seen in Yablonsky's analysis of effective gang interventions (1997: 125-222) and of therapeutic communities (1989), and in Jacobson's (2005) analysis of how to reduce crime and incarceration.

Policy Integralism and Civil Society

Burawoy stresses the link between sociology and civil society (2005b: 24-25), with multiple associations of a wide variety being viewed as necessary to further "the interests of humanity," and to insulate this social arena from possible threats from either the state or a market economy. However, these positive effects of civil society are not viewed as inevitable. A vigorous civil society can also contribute to political or economic domination (2005c: 324). Burawoy (2005c: 325) suggests two "real utopias" that emerge from the values of critical sociology and that can be the focus of the professional and policy forms of sociology: a civil society that facilitates participatory democracy, and a political system of democratic socialism. In relation to both, three basic research questions are posed: the conditions of genesis, of existence, and of long-term maintenance. These goals and questions are regarded as the basis for engagement with publics outside the academic community.

The theoretical and research agenda deriving from critical integralism is different from that proposed by Burawoy's analysis, but is complementary. Sorokin's (1948) policy model provides the assumption that a necessary condition of a civil society that produces positive effects is individual goodness that is then manifested in agency directed toward social and cultural reconstruction. A second focus deriving from Sorokin's (1963a: 482-492) professional sociology that has policy implications is provided by his detailed analysis maintaining the greater explanatory power of culture in comparison to social factors. Emerging from this analysis is the research question of the nature of a culture that will provide for a civil society that furthers human welfare. The creation of this culture that is supportive of reconstruction needs to be understood from micro to macro sources of genesis, beginning with individual deliberation and choice. An understanding of how this can be done is a major focus of policy integralism.

Following the strategy suggested by Burawoy and Wright (2001: 480-484), the perspective of critical integralism can also serve as a basis for formulating utopian models. Sorokin's (1954a) analysis of individuals and communities that are exemplars of altruistic love provides insight regarding one of the varieties of case materials that can be used in this type of analysis. Such models of "real utopias" can serve as a reference for research into how goodness in individual and sociocultural forms can be more fully realized in civil society, and within the state and economic sectors of society as well.

Providing Foundations for Public Sociology

The integral theoretical and research agenda of professional and policy sociology provides a strong foundation for public sociology. It includes an emphasis on producing knowledge and understanding of the role of individuals in personal, social, and cultural reconstruction. This focus leads directly to the importance of the study of meso level organizations and social movements and their role in reconstruction. This agenda also focuses on how a culture that supports reconstruction is created through micro and meso activity. As a result of these directions of theory and research, some of the ideas that sociology will offer for dialogue with the public are applicable to individual decision-making and initiative, and to meso level organizational activity. The focus on goodness at the personal and societal level in integral critical sociology is complementary in providing a value framework that has the potential to interest significant numbers of individuals in various publics in the ideas offered by sociology.

Public Sociology

Public sociology involves dialogue with audiences outside the academic community regarding "matters of political and moral concern" (Burawoy, 2004c: 1607). This sociology can be of two different forms, "traditional" and "organic" (Burawoy, 2004c: 1607-1608). The former is typically directed to a general issue and large and diverse audiences, the latter to the particular interests of specific groups and communities. Public sociology "has no intrinsic normative valence, other than the commitment to dialogue around issues raised in and by sociology" (Burawoy, 2005b: 8), and can thus involve and support differing value orientations. However, the potential contribution of public sociology to the debate of significant problems and issues can be compromised when it becomes too influenced by the values and concerns of the public (2004c).

Sorokin's attempt to enlighten and engage a wider public outside of sociology began with his revolutionary speeches and writings in Russia, where he was active in expressing opposition first against the Czarist government, then later the Communists (Nichols, 1999; Sorokin, 1963b: 55-205). The focus of Sorokin's later efforts to write for the general public regarding the most fundamental and crucial issues of this era derives from the basis of his professional sociology, including his historical and comparative analysis of culture types and sociocultural organization and change (Sorokin, 1937a; 1937b; 1937c; 1941a; 1957a), his analysis of social differentiation and stratification (1947, 1959) and his explorations of the nature, causes, and effects of altruism (1950b; 1954a; 1954b).

Sorokin's extensive analysis of various problematic aspects of this historical era and his vision of a creative response involving the increase of altruistic love provides a broad and comprehensive basis for his public sociology. His public sociology in this general context is expressed in writings on the cultural crisis of our era (1941a), basic trends in social change (1964b), the relation between power and morality (Sorokin and Lunden, 1959), the sexual revolution (1956), the nature and importance of altruism (1950a), and a program of personal, social, and cultural reconstruction (1948). All of these works are exemplars of public sociology in the sense that they were directed toward the general reading public in an attempt to inform, heighten awareness, and inspire social action directed toward reconstruction.

In identifying significant books in public sociology Burawoy (2005b: 7) notes that their importance is indicated by the fact that they became "the vehicle of a public discussion about the nature of U.S. society—the nature of its values, the gap between its promise and its reality, its malaise, its tendencies." Sorokin's ideas are particularly illustrative of this type of portrayal, and its relationship to the potential goal-oriented activity of individuals and groups. Sorokin's public sociology is comprehensive. He describes the problematics of our contemporary era, outlines an alternative, and considers the means of realizing that alternative.

The significance of the current historical moment, and its problematic nature, is dramatically stated by Sorokin (1941b):

> We are living and acting at one of the epoch-making turning points of human history, when *one fundamental form of culture and society—sensate—is declining and a different form is emerging.* The crisis is also extraordinary in the sense that, like its predecessors, it is marked by an extraordinary explosion of wars, revolutions, anarchy, and bloodshed; by social, moral, economic, political, and intellectual chaos; by a resurgence of revolting cruelty and animality, and a temporary destruction of the great and small values of mankind; by misery and suffering on the part of millions.... (1941b: 22)

Sorokin posits that the emerging culture will be idealistic, or integral (These terms are synonymous. Sorokin, 1961: 95-96, 1963: 481; Ford, 1963: 53). The reasons why this type of culture will contribute to the betterment of the everyday lives of humankind are described by Sorokin (1948: 107):

> The major premise of sensate culture must be replaced by the broader, deeper, richer, and more valid premise that the *true reality and value is an infinite manifold possess-*

ing not only sensory but also supersensory, rational, and superrational aspects, all harmoniously reflecting its infinity.... such a premise is incomparably more adequate than the purely sensate premise of our present culture.

A culture built upon such a premise effectively mitigates the ferocity of the struggle for a greater share of material values, because material values occupy in it only a limited place and not the highest one. A large proportion of human aspirations tend to be channeled in the direction of the rational or the superrational perennial values of the kingdom of God, of fuller truth, nobler goodness, and sublimer beauty. The very nature of these values is impersonal and universal, altruistic and ennobling. As these values are infinite and inexhaustible, the quest for them does not lead to egoistic conflicts (p. 107).

The change to this type of culture follows general principles of cultural integration and change derived from Sorokin's professional sociology: the premise pertaining to the nature of reality is foundational (1937a: 3-152; 1957a: 2-52). As a result of this ordering of cultural integration "the replacement of the major premise of sensate culture by the fundamentally different one which I designate as the idealistic premise, is the most fundamental step toward the establishment of a creative, harmonious order" (Sorokin, 1948: 107-108).

This fundamental cultural change is influenced by social science knowledge, and is both cause and effect of a movement toward greater altruistic love (Sorokin and Lunden, 1959):

This new socio-political order aims to be built upon the up-to-date scientific knowledge and accumulated wisdom of humanity; it is animated ... by the spirit of universal friendship, sympathy, and unselfish love with ensuing mutual aid of everyone to everybody. (1959: 147)

Sorokin (1941b) notes the difficulty of the transition to a different culture and system of social relationships, emphasizing his model of policy sociology that gives first priority to self-directed individual change. A call to action on the part of each member of the public is issued:

Our remedy demands a complete change of the contemporary mentality, a fundamental transformation of our system of values, and the profoundest modification of our conduct ... All this cannot be achieved without the incessant, strenuous, active efforts on the part of every individual in that direction. (1941b: 321)

Relevance Is Foundational

Public sociology is legitimated by its relevance (Burawoy, 2005b: 16). Sorokin presents a potentially engaging and powerful public sociology in this regard. Because it is closely linked to his professional, critical, and policy sociology, it rests on a strong foundation. It defines the nature of current problems in a broad scope that can be readily understood by a general audience if presented appropriately. It points to the solution of these problems in a manner that can involve both organic and traditional publics in participation in personal, social, and cultural reconstruction.

Sorokin and Lunden (1959) note the potentially comprehensive and unifying force of a public sociology focused on the study of goodness in the following statement:

> The wonderful radiation of creative love by its living incarnations is acceptable to scientists and philosophers, to religious and moral leaders of different denominations, even to atheists and agnostics. It is the common ground and the common value for scientists, philosophers, religious leaders, irreligious sceptics, and for all, except perhaps the few partisans of hate, enmity, and evil who are still polluting the creative course of human history. (1959: 178)

Conclusion

In the conclusion of his Presidential Address to the American Sociological Association Burawoy (2005b) maintains:

> if we are going to acknowledge and reward public sociology then we must develop criteria to distinguish good from bad public sociology.... We must encourage the very best of public sociology whatever that may mean. Public sociology cannot be second-rate sociology. (2005b: 25)

Sorokin's system of sociology provides a potentially significant contribution to recognizing the criteria of "good" public sociology. Because his integral sociology is systemic and comprehensive it makes major contributions to each of the interdependent forms of sociology delineated by Burawoy (2004a, 2004b, 2004c, 2005b). His public sociology can be viewed as an outcome of the other three forms.

Sorokin's professional model contributes a broad and inclusive conceptual frame of reference and an exemplary display of original theoretical development linked to empirical research. It also contains an innovative ontology and epistemology that incorporates the knowledge and understanding of philosophy and religion in the scientific continuum of a professional sociology based on the idea of integralism. The critical perspective deriving from this integral base in turn provides a focus of theoretical development and empirical investigation for scientific research programs in diverse areas of sociological analysis and practice. This concentration can greatly advance the cumulation of scientific knowledge in professional sociology. The strong program of professional sociology that emerges from Sorokin's model provides a corrective to Tittle's (2004) criticisms that center around the lack of reliable and valid scientific knowledge, and mitigates Nielsen's (2004) concern that advocacy can undermine scientific objectivity. The close relation between theory and research also insulates to some degree against the professional pathologies of irrelevance, unnecessary abstraction, and placing method ahead of substance.

Sorokin's critical sociology contributes the idea of goodness as a core value. It provides ideas of altruistic love, virtue, and solidarity as basic formulations of the good at the individual and sociocultural levels of analysis. It is important to recognize that this general value core of an integral model of critical sociology, that of goodness in its personal and sociocultural manifestations, is essentially apolitical and potentially universally available. The linking of these values to particularistic group interests or political agendas, especially at the personal level, is difficult. Goodness in terms of altruistic love, virtue, and social solidarity is probably as close as possible to a statement of universal values. Thus Sorokin's critical sociology provides at least partial correctives to concerns about how choices of values are to be made (Tittle, 2004), narrowness of values (Nielsen, 2004), unduly close association of Marxism and public sociology (Boyns and Fletcher, 2005), and the political nature and incompatibility of the values of public sociology with a significant portion of the general public (Turner, 2005). The critical sociology pathologies of dogmatism and sectarianism are lessened because of the inclusive nature of the values themselves and their universality as conceptions of the good.

These contributions of Sorokin's integral model of professional and critical sociology in turn greatly enhance the development of a vigorous policy sociology. This policy sociology is explicitly directed towards the means of realizing personal, social, and cultural reconstruction in terms of increased personal goodness and greater social solidarity. Brady (2004) has questioned whether there is a clear program in public sociology that can be practiced by sociologists with diverse interests. Sorokin's model provides for multiple activities of a specific nature that are unified around the development of knowledge and understanding regarding how the core multidimensional value of goodness can be realized. It provides diverse theoretical and research activities for professional and policy sociologists, a multidimensional value core for critical sociologists to explicate, and should yield a series of topics that can be presented to publics with reasonable hope for a response of interest. The universal and engaging nature of the end values of integral policy sociology, combined with the specific goal direction of reconstruction, should provide some insulation against the policy pathologies of servility and manipulation by power holders.

The base provided by these three forms creates a public sociology that can engage both organic and traditional public audiences in dialogue regarding the nature of the good, the means by which it can be realized, and the part each and every individual can play in the enterprise of reconstruction. The clearly defined goals of integral sociology and their comprehensive nature provide an inherently interesting and innovative field of dialogue while providing sufficient foundational ideas and direction to insulate against the pathologies of faddishness and pandering to public concerns. Sorokin's system of integral sociology thus appears as a powerful base for a public sociology that is aptly suited in "conveying sociology to a wide lay audience through sociological interventions that set a new agenda for the discussion of public issues" (Burawoy, 2005e: 4).

References

Acker, J. 2005. "Comments on Burawoy on Public Sociology." *Critical Sociology* 31: 327-331.

Alexander, J.C. 1982. *Theoretical Logic in Sociology: Positivism, Presuppositions, and Current Controversies*. Berkeley, CA: University of California.

American Sociological Association. 2004. *An Invitation to Public Sociology* Washington, D.C.: American Sociological Association.

Aquinas, T. 1981. *Summa Theologica*. Volumes 1-5.Westminister, MD: Christian Classics.

Aristotle. 1941. *The Basic Works of Aristotle*. New York: Random House.

Aronowitz, S. 2005. "Comments on Michael Burawoy's "The Critical Turn to Public Sociology." *Critical Sociology* 31: 333-338.

Baiocchi, G. 2005. "Interrogating Connections: From Public Criticism's to Critical Public's in Burawoy's Public Sociology." *Critical Sociology* 31: 339-351.

Brady, D. 2004. "Why Public Sociology May Fail." *Social Forces* 82(4): 1629-1638.

Brewer, R.M. 2005. "Response to Michael Burawoy's Commentary: "The Critical Turn to Public Sociology." *Critical Sociology* 31: 353-359.

Burawoy, M. 1989. "Two Methods in Search of Science: Skocpol versus Trotsky." *Theory and Society* 18: 759-805.

_____. 1990. "Marxism as Science: Historical Challenges and Theoretical Growth." *American Sociological Review* 55: 775-793.

_____. 2003a. "Public Sociologies in a Global Context" Polson Memorial Lecture. *Third Annual Workshop of the Polson Institute for Global Development*. Ithaca, NY: Cornell University.

_____. 2003b. "South Africanizing U.S. Sociology."*From the Left* 24(3): 1, 12-13.

_____. 2004a. "Introduction." *Social Problems* 51: 103-106.

_____. 2004b. "Manifesto for Public Sociologies." *Social Problems* 51(1): 124-130.

_____. 2004c. "Public Sociologies: Contradictions, Dilemmas, and Possibilities." *Social Forces* 82(4): 1603-1618.

_____. 2004d. "The World Needs Public Sociology." *Sosiologisk tidsskrift* (Journal of Sociology, Norway) No. 3.

_____. 2004e. "Public Sociology: South African Dilemmas in a Global Context." *Society in Transition* 35(1): 11-26.

_____. 2004f. "To Advance, Sociology Must Not Retreat." *Chronicle of Higher Education* August 13.

_____. 2005a. "Provincializing the Social Sciences." Pp. 508-525 in *The Politics of Method in the Human Sciences*, edited by George Steinmetz. Durham, North Carolina: Duke University Press.

_____. 2005b. "For Public Sociology." *American Sociological Review* 70: 4-28.

_____. 2005c. "The Critical Turn to Public Sociology." Pp. 309-322 in *Enriching the Sociological Imagination: How Radical Sociology Changed the Discipline*, edited by Rhonda Levine. Boulder, CO: Paradigm Publishers.

_____. 2005d. "Rejoinder: Toward a Critical Public Sociology." *Critical Sociology* 31: 379-390.

_____. 2005e. "The Return of the Repressed: Recovering the Public Face of U.S. Sociology, One Hundred Years On." *The Annals of the American Academy of Political and Social Science* 600 (July): 1-18.

Burawoy, M., Gamson, W., Ryan, C., Pfohl, S., Vaughn, D., Derber, C. and Schor, J. 2004. "Public Sociologies: A Symposium from Boston College." *Social Problems* 51: 102-130.

Burawoy, M., and Van Antwerpen, J. 2001. "Public Sociology at Berkeley: Past, Present and Future." Unpublished paper.

Burawoy, M., and Wright, E.O. 2001. "Sociological Marxism." Pp. 459-486 in *Handbook of Sociological Theory*, Edited by J.H. Turner. New York: Kluwer Academic/Plenum Publishers.

Ford, J.B. 1963. "Sorokin as Philosopher." Pp. 39-66 in *Pitirim A. Sorokin in Review*, edited by Philip J. Allen. Durham, NC: Duke University.

_____. 1996. "Sorokin's Methodology: Integralism as the Key." Pp. 83-92 in *Sorokin and Civilization: A Centennial Assessment*, edited by J.B. Ford, M.P. Richard, and P.C. Talbutt. New Brunswick, NJ: Transaction Publishers.

Ghamari-Tabrizi, B. 2005. "Can Burawoy Make Everybody Happy? Comments on Public Sociology." *Critical Sociology* 31: 361-369.

Hick, J. 1989. *An Interpretation of Religion*. New Haven, CT: Yale University Press.

Hossfeld, L., and Nyden, P. 2005. "Institutionalizing Public Sociologies." *Footnotes* 33(1): 3.

Hunt, A.B., Crotty, M.E., and Crotty, R.B. 1991. *Ethics of the World Religions*. San Diego, CA: Greenhaven Press.

Jacobson, M. 2005. *Downsizing Prisons*. New York: New York University Press.

Jeffries, V. 1998. "Virtue and the Altruistic Personality." *Sociological Perspectives* 41(1): 151-166.

_____. 1999. "The Integral Paradigm: The Truth of Faith and the Social Sciences." *The American Sociologist* 30(4): 36-55.

_____. 2002a. "Integralism: The Promising Legacy of Pitirim A. Sorokin." Pp. 99-135 in *Lost Sociologists Rediscovered*, edited by M.A. Romano. Lewiston, NY: Edwin Mellon Press.

_____. 2002b. "Virtue and Marital Conflict: A Theoretical Formulation and Research Agenda." *Sociological Perspectives* 43(2): 231-246.

Johnston, B.V. 1995. *Pitirim A. Sorokin: An Intellectual Biography*. Lawrence, KS: University Press of Kansas.

_____. 1996. "Sorokin's Life and Work." Pp. 3-14 in *Sorokin and Civilization: A Centennial Assessment*, edited by J.B. Ford, M.P. Richard, and P.C. Talbutt. New Brunswick, NJ: Transaction Publishers.

_____. 1998. "Pitirim Sorokin's Science of Sociology and Social Reconstruction." Pp. 1-55 in *Pitirim A. Sorokin on the Practice of Sociology*, edited by B.V. Johnston. Chicago, IL: University of Chicago Press.

Katz-Fishman, W., and Scott, J. 2005. "Comments on Burawoy: A View from the Bottom-Up." *Critical Sociology* 31: 371-374.

Lakatos, I. 1978. *The Methodology of Scientific Research Programs* edited by J. Worral and G. Currie. New York: Cambridge University Press.

Martindale, D. 1975. *Prominent Sociologists since World War II*. Columbus, OH: Charles E. Merrill.

Myrdal, G. 1958. *Value in Social Theory*. New York: Harper & Brothers.

Nichols, L.T. 1999. "Science, Politics, and Moral Activism: Sorokin's Integralism Reconsidered." *Journal of the History of the Behavioral Sciences* 35(2): 139-155.

_____. 2001. "Sorokin's Integralism and Catholic Social Science: Concordance and Ambivalence." *The Catholic Social Science Review* 6: 11-24.

Nielsen, F. 2004. "The Vacant 'We': Remarks on Public Sociology." *Social Forces* 82(4): 1619-1627.

Peterson, C., and Seligman, M.E.P. 2004. *Character Strengths and Virtues*. New York: Oxford.

Pieper, J. 1966. *The Four Cardinal Virtues*. Notre Dame, IN: University of Notre Dame Press.

Post, S.G. 2003. *Unlimited Love: Altruism, Compassion, and Service*. Philadelphia, PA: Templeton Foundation Press.

Ritzer, George. 1981. *Toward an Integrated Sociological Paradigm*. Boston, MA: Allyn and Bacon, Inc.

Sorokin, P.A. 1925. *The Sociology of Revolution*. Philadelphia, PA: J.B. Lippincott.

_____. 1928. *Contemporary Sociological Theories*. New York: Harper and Brothers.

_____. 1937a. *Social and Cultural Dynamics*. Volume 1. New York: American Book Company.

_____. 1937b. *Social and Cultural Dynamics*. Volume 2. New York: American Book Company.

_____. 1937c. *Social and Cultural Dynamics*. Volume 3. New York: American Book Company.

_____. 1941a. *Social and Cultural Dynamics*. Volume 4. New York: American Book Company.

_____. 1941b. *The Crisis of Our Age*. New York: E.P. Dutton.

_____. 1942. *Man and Society in Calamity*. New York: E. P. Dutton & Co.

_____. 1947. *Society, Culture, and Personality*. New York: Harper & Brothers.

_____. 1948. *The Reconstruction of Humanity*. Boston, MA: Beacon Press.

_____. 1950a. *Altruistic Love*. Boston, MA: Beacon Press.

_____. ed. 1950b. *Explorations in Altruistic Love and Behavior*. Boston, MA: Beacon Press.

_____. 1950c. *Social Philosophies of an Age of Crisis*. Boston, MA: Beacon Press.

_____. 1950d. *Leaves from a Russian Diary*. Enlarged Edition. Boston, MA: Beacon Press.

_____. 1954a. *The Ways and Power of Love*. Boston, MA: Beacon Press.

_____. ed. 1954b. *Forms and Techniques of Altruistic and Spiritual Growth*. Boston, MA: Beacon Press.

_____. 1956a. "This is My Faith." Pp. 212-227 in *This Is My Faith*. edited by S.G. Cole. New York: Harper & Brothers.

_____. 1956b. *Fads and Foibles in Modern Sociology and Related Sciences*. Chicago, IL: Henry Regnery.

_____. 1956c. *The American Sex Revolution*. Boston, MA: Porter Sargent.

_____. 1957a. *Social and Cultural Dynamics*. One Volume Edition. Boston, MA: Porter Sargent.

_____. 1957b. "Integralism is My Philosophy." Pp. 179189 in *This is My Philosophy*, edited by Whit Burnett. New York: Harper and Brothers.

_____. 1959. *Social and Cultural Mobility*. Glencoe, IL: Free Press.

_____. 1961. "A Quest for an Integral System of Sociology." Pp 71-108 in *Memoire du XIX Congres International de Sociologie*. Volume 3. Mexico: Comite Organisateur du XIX Congres Intertnational de Sociologie.

_____. 1963a. "Reply To My Critics." Pp. 371-496 in *Pitirim A. Sorokin in Review*, edited by P.J. Allen. Durham, NC: Duke University.

_____. 1963b. *A Long Journey*. New Haven, CT: College and University Press.

_____. 1964a. *Sociocultural Causality, Space, Time*. New York: Russell and Russell.

_____. 1964b. *The Basic Trends of Our Times*. New Haven, CT: College and University Press.

_____ 1965. "Sociology of Yesterday, Today, and Tomorrow." *American Sociological Review* 30(6): 833-843.

_____ 1966. *Sociological Theories of Today*. New York: Harper & Row.

_____. [1941]1998a. "Declaration of Independence of the Social Sciences." Pp. 93-103 *Pitirim A. Sorokin: On the Practice of Sociology*, edited by B.V. Johnston. Chicago, IL: University of Chicago Press.

_____. [1942]1998b. "The Cause and Factors of War and Peace." Pp. 265-278 in *Pitirim A. Sorokin: On the Practice of Sociology*, edited by B.V. Johnston. Chicago, IL: University of Chicago Press.

_____. [1944]1998c. "The Conditions and Prospects for a World without War." Pp. 279-291 in *Pitirim A. Sorokin: On the Practice of Sociology*, edited by B.V. Johnston. Chicago, IL: University of Chicago Press.

_____. [1951]1998d."Amitology as an Applied Science of Amity and Unselfish Love." Pp. 302-304 in *Pitirim A. Sorokin: On the Practice of Sociology*, edited by B.V. Johnston. Chicago, IL: University of Chicago Press.

Sorokin, P.A. and Lunden, W.A. 1959. *Power and Morality*. Boston, MA: Porter Sargent.

Thomas, W.I. 1951. "The Need for a Social Science." Pp. 35-38 in *Social Behavior and Personality: Contributions of W.I. Thomas to Theory and Social Research*, edited by E.H. Volkart. New York: Social Science Research Council.

Tittle, C.R. 2004. "The Arrogance of Public Sociology." *Social Forces* 82(4): 1639-1643.

Turner, J.H. 1998. "Must Sociological Theory and Sociological Practice Be So Far Apart?: A Polemical Answer." *Sociological Perspectives* 41: 243-258.

_____. 2005a. "Is a Scientific Theory of the Family Desirable?" Pp. 26-29 in *Sourcebook of Family Theory & Research*, edited by V.L. Bengtson, A.C. Acock, K.R. Allen, P. Dilworth-Anderson, and D.M. Klein. Thousand Oaks, CA: Sage Publications.

_____. 2005b. "Is Public Sociology Such a Good Idea?" *The American Sociologist* 36.

Turner, J.H., and Boyns, D. 2001. "The Return of Grand Theory." Pp. 353-378 in, *Handbook of Sociological Theory* edited by J.H. Turner. New York: Kluwer Academic/Plenum Publishers.

Turner, S.P., and Turner, J.H. 1990. *The Impossible Science* Newbury Park, CA: Sage Publications.

Urry, J. "The Good News and the Bad News." *Critical Sociology* 31: 375-378.

Vitz, P.C. 2005. "Psychology in Recovery." *First Things* 151 (March):17-21.

Yablonsky, L. 1989. *The Therapeutic Community*. New York: Gardner Press, Inc.

_____. 1997. *Gangsters*. New York: New York University Press.

Zimmer, C., Burawoy, M., Nielsen, F., Brady, D., and Tittle, C. 2004 "Commentary and Debate: Introduction to a Debate on Public Sociologies." *Social Forces* 82(4):1601-1643.

8

Global Public Social Science[1]

Christopher Chase-Dunn

Burawoy's classification of the complementary aspects of the discipline of sociology is used to describe an emergent global public social science that will assist transnational social movements in the building of a democratic and collectively rational global commonwealth.

Michael Burawoy's 2004 ASA presidential address (Burawoy, 2005) has raised anew the significant issues about what sociology is and is not, the connections between scholarship and activism, and the responsibilities that sociologists have to larger publics, and to human society. These are the big questions and have been since the emergence of modern social science. The tension between humanism and science is not external to social science. It is internal to it. And Burawoy's most important thesis is that this is a productive and generative contradiction that should be used to produce both better science and a better society. I will employ the distinctions that Burawoy has elaborated in his presidential address between professional, critical, policy, and public sociology to discuss the issues he raises and to describe the emergence of global public social science.

I mainly agree with Burawoy's analysis and strongly support his effort to renew the dialogue within sociology about the symbiotic relationship between science and activism. The value of his approach is starkly demonstrated by those social science disciplines (especially anthropology) that have largely failed in the effort to live under a big umbrella that includes professional, public, critical, and policy social science. The internecine battles between the politically correct activists and the stalwart defenders of scientific purity have left all the parties weaker and the interests of all the contenders have been profoundly undermined by

179

the combat. This is not a path that any sane person would choose to follow. The anger and mistrust that are often generated in conflicts of this
kind live for years in the psyches of the combatants. They erupt again
and again, reinjuring old warriors and harming younger generations of
scholars and students. The big tent of activists, scientists, scholars, and
scholar-activists is a good shelter and good social science has been, and
will be, crafted within it.

Public Sociology Is More Than Sociologist-as-Citizen

Most of the students that come into social science are motivated by
a humanistic desire to improve upon society, often by helping the most
exploited and oppressed peoples. They believe that social science will
be an avenue for designing policies, programs, and activities that will
change society in a progressive direction. These motivations are an
important basis of the ability of our social science disciplines to recruit
hard-working and smart young people. Social science is not a road to
wealth or power. So humanistic motivations are an important part of our
cultural capital and a substantial basis of our ability to recruit those who
will become the next generation of scholars.

One very valuable aspect of Burawoy's approach is the acknowledge-
ment that "professional sociology" is the necessary center and source of
strength for public, critical, and policy sociology. My own scholarly work
is quite interdisciplinary (combining ecology, geography, history, political
science, anthropology, and sociology), but I nevertheless acknowledge
the importance of core disciplinary values and procedures in sociology.
I agree with Burawoy that professional sociology is central to the constitution of the discipline of sociology, and that public sociology, and the
other forms, derive immense cultural, political and scientific value from
their connection with, and interactions with, professional sociology.

This is the main reason why Burawoy's insistence that public sociology
is something distinct from the sociologist in the citizen role is valuable
and useful. The "sociologist-as-citizen" makes claims to expertise that
may, or may not, be acknowledged by larger publics. But public sociology
is a stance within sociology, and it is evaluated by both external publics
and by other sociologists because *it is a legitimate form of sociological
practice* that should be recognized and encouraged by all sociologists,
and because we have a duty to serve the human societies that fund our
science. This means that the sociological methods and theories employed
in public sociology need to meet the standards of the discipline and that
all sociologists bear some responsibility to evaluate the work that is

carried on in the name of the discipline. There are no insuperable and conflictive contradictions between professional scientific sociology and engaged public sociology, though they are not the same thing. The big tent requires that we acknowledge and respect both the scientific and the humanistic roots of our discipline.

Emergent World Society and Public Social Science

I do not agree entirely with Burawoy's characterization of the historical development of social science in the last few decades. His characterization of the rise of radical sociology in the 1960s is mainly used to make the point that mainstream sociology was rather conservative then, and that most sociologists have become (or remained) fairly liberal while much of the rest of American society has moved to the right. I do not disagree with this, but Burawoy's depiction of the struggles and outcomes that occurred in the 1960s misses an important development: the discovery that the United States is part of a larger global social system. There was a split within radical sociology between the Workerists and the Third Worldists. Burawoy (1979, 1985) wrote his great ethnographic studies of shop floor politics, and this was some of the best research and analysis from the Workerist camp. His close ethnographies are comparative, but they are nearly silent on the world historical linkages that produce the very different everyday realities of workers in different countries.

Burawoy's narrative of sociological practice does not really even acknowledge the other path that emerged strongly in the 1960s and 1970s: Third Worldism and the world-systems perspective. The Third Worldists argued that strong challenges to capitalism are not likely to come from the core because the most exploited peoples are in the periphery. Some of them also discovered that the "developed and less developed" national societies are tightly linked into a global stratification structure—the core/periphery hierarchy. These issues are directly relevant for both professional and public sociology. One of the mainstays of professional sociology is the study of socially constructed inequalities. If there is really an institutionalized core/periphery hierarchy (rather than a set of disconnected "advanced" and "underdeveloped" national societies) then the most unequal contemporary socially structured inequalities are global in scope. A sociology that focuses exclusively on inequality within countries is ignoring the most important part of the phenomenon about which it claims expertise.

With regard to public sociology, it is not enough simply to be of service to existing popular movements or groups or to address larger publics. The first job is to analyze which groups are worth serving and which ones are likely to have an important impact in the struggle to make human societies more humane and more equal. This analysis requires an understanding of the processes of modern social change and the directions that historical development is likely to take.

I am a proponent and producer of what has become known as the comparative world-systems perspective. The basic idea is that social change occurs in systems of societies rather than in single isolated societies, and that this has been true since the Paleolithic, though earlier world-systems were small regional affairs (Chase-Dunn and Hall, 1997). From this point of view most of sociology, including all the types designated by Burawoy, is hopelessly presentist and core-centric. Social change is primarily about the historical development of human social institutions. Social change has been a singular world historical process increasingly since the sixteenth century. So telling stories of national societies as if they occurred on separate planets is a major distortion of reality for both social science and for progressive politics.

Contemporary social change can only be comprehended in its world historical context. Focusing solely on the United States, as most sociologists and most other people in the United States do, makes it impossible not only to understand the extremely important world historical events and developments that are occurring elsewhere, but also precludes understanding of what is happening within the United States. Why did politics in the United States take a rightward turn in the 1970s and 1980s? Most sociologists and most Americans do not have a clue.

What are the implications of the above for Burawoy's public sociology project? His search for the relevant publics for public sociology is a good idea, but the relevant publics need to be understood as parts of an emerging global civil society. World sociology needs to analyze non-U.S. realities and the whole emergent global system of which the United States is an important part. This is also true of professional sociology. Both science and politics are distorted by focusing on one's own national society, city, or region as if it is distinct and unconnected with anything else. Humans have always been primarily interested in their own home place. Most sociologists share the spatial and temporal blinders of their neighbors in this regard. To his credit, Burawoy is far more comparative than most. He tells us about workers in socialist countries and about sociology in South Africa. But he does not see sociology in world-historical perspective.

The crucial slip in Burawoy's description of what happened in sociology and what happened in the United States comes in his rendition of the world revolution of 1968. Many sociologists and world citizens discovered the Third World because of the war in Vietnam. Some saw the systemic connections. The Third World is not just a distant place or a set of underdeveloped regions. The social conditions that exist in the core have only been made possible by the strong connections with the periphery, both the exploitation and the resistance to domination.

Waves of Globalization

Understanding contemporary globalization requires that we compare the wave of globalization since World War II with earlier waves, especially the last half of the nineteenth century when international trade as a proportion of the whole world economy was nearly as high as it is now (Chase-Dunn, Kawano, and Brewer, 2000). It is important to distinguish between globalization as large-scale connectedness, which is a structural and empirical question about economic, political, cultural and communications network linkages, and the "globalization project," which is the political ideology of Reaganism-Thatcherism that became hegemonic in the 1980s (McMichael, 2004). One reason why many see the contemporary wave of globalization as a completely new stage of global capitalism is that nationalism and Keynesian national development policies were powerfully institutionalized and centrally propagated from World War II until the 1970s. The Keynesian national development project (the Global New Deal) was itself a world historical response to the "Age of Extremes" (Hobsbawm, 1994) and the deglobalization of the early decades of the twentieth century. It never really created a world of separate national economies, but it did focus strong attention on the problem of national import substitution and the development of the national welfare state. This focus on national policy is what allows many of the contemporary analysts of global capitalism to imagine that the world was really composed of separate national societies before the most recent wave of globalization.

A profit squeeze and accumulation crisis occurred in the 1970s when Japan and Germany caught up with the United States in the production of important core commodities (Brenner, 2002). This occurred in the wake of the world revolution of 1968, which was a global mobilization of radicalized college students who were the politically unincorporated generation produced by the massification of higher education all around the world during the 1950s and 1960s (Arrighi et al., 1989). The reactionary response to the accumulation crisis and the critiques of the radical students was Reaganism-Thatcherism, also called neoliberalism, the Washington Consensus and the globalization project (McMichael, 2004).

Neoliberalism was a political ideology that took hold and became hegemonic beginning in the 1970s. It was a revival of the nineteenth century ideology of "market magic" and an attack on the welfare state and organized labor. It borrowed the anti-statist ideology of the New Left and used new communications and information technologies to globalize capitalist production, undercutting nationally organized trade unions and attacking the entitlements of the welfare state as undeserved and inefficient rents. This "global stage of capitalism" is what has brought globalization into the popular consciousness, but rather than being the first time that the world has experienced strong global processes, it was a response to the problems of capitalist accumulation as they emerged from the prior Global New Deal, which was itself a response to the earlier Age of Extremes and deglobalization. This is what I mean by saying that social change is world-historical.

The pace of global social change accelerated dramatically with the late eighteenth century industrial revolution, culminating in the first wave (1840-1900) of what can properly be called globalization in the sense of Earth-wide integration and connectedness. The United Kingdom of Great Britain was the world leader in industrialization, an exporter of the key technologies (railroads, steamships, and telegraph communications) and the advocate of free trade policies and the gold standard (O'Rourke and Williamson, 2000). As Germany, Belgium, France, and the United States began to catch up with, and surpass, the British in the production of highly profitable goods, Britain turned to high finance as a source of profits and continued to make money on money in the "beautiful" Edwardian Indian summer of the early twentieth century. The centrality of London in the global financial system was a valuable asset that prolonged the hegemony of Great Britain (Silver and Arrighi, 2005). The British also played their other remaining cards—control of a large empire in the periphery and an advantage in military technology—in order to try to have their way in international matters. The Boer War in South Africa, in which they put down the resistance of Dutch farmers at great cost, was a clear example of what has been called "imperial overstretch."

The decline of British hegemony was accompanied by a downturn of trade globalization from 1880 to 1900 and then by a period of interimperial rivalry—two world wars with Germany. The deglobalization of the late nineteenth and the first half of the twentieth century has been called the "Age of Extremes" by historian Eric Hobsbawm (1994). The

Bolshevik Revolution of October 1917 was part of a larger challenge to the social injustices of the global order that included the Mexican Revolution of 1910, the Boxer Rebellion in China, and radical labor and national movements in most of the other countries.

World Wars I and II were long and massively destructive battles in a single struggle over who would perform the role of hegemon. Between the wars was a short wave of economic globalization in the 1920s followed by the stock market crash of 1929 and a global retreat to economic nationalism and protectionism during the depression of the 1930s. Fascism was a virulent form of zealous nationalism that spread widely in the second tier core and the semiperiphery during the Age of Extremes. This was deglobalization.

The point here is that globalization is not just a long-term trend. It is also a cycle. Waves of globalization have been followed by waves of deglobalization in the past, and this is also an entirely a plausible scenario for the future.[2]

The U.S. itself was, in Seymour Martin Lipset's famous title, *The First New Nation*. U.S. hegemony was made possible because the United States could represent itself as the leader of the "free world," a world in which colonial empires were being dismantled. Formal colonialism was being replaced by the ideology of "one nation, one vote" and by the reality of a new form of neo-colonialism constituted by the institutions of direct foreign investment, gunboat diplomacy, covert operations, structural adjustment programs, and low-intensity democracy that kept dependent peripheral countries in Africa, Asia, and Latin America at the bottom of the global food chain.

The United States incorporated a sizeable segment of its own working class into the hegemonic project by providing cheap gas, cheap cars, cheap suburban housing, mass education, military Keynesianism, and a large, racially integrated public employment program called the U.S. Army. Not everyone was incorporated, but enough got theirs so that the rest could hope that they would too.

Mass education created a large throng of not-yet politically incorporated students in all the countries of the world, and this group led the world revolution of 1968, a protest against the capitalist welfare state, the shams of parliamentary democracy, and the fakeries of state communism. In the wake of this political and cultural challenge and the emergence of a spate of "new social movements," core capital experienced a profit squeeze because Germany and Japan caught up with the United States in the production of the most profitable lead technologies, and so prices could no longer be raised to keep profits high (Brenner, 2002).

This spurred a change of strategy by the now-global capitalist class in which the Keynesian national development project that had justified the capitalist welfare state and the developmental programs in the periphery and semiperiphery was scuttled in favor of Reaganism-Thatcherism. Free markets were to replace government intervention. Downsizing, streamlining, attacks on politically guaranteed entitlements, all this was justified by the eighteenth century idea that the market is the most efficient and fairest arbiter of human interactions.

With new technologies of communications, transportation and infomatics businesses were able to relocate to take advantage of cheaper labor costs, lower tax rates, and less environmental protection. This was the globalization project and the new international division of labor (McMichael, 2004). Industry moved from the core to the semiperiphery and the periphery. New lead technologies (the Internet, biotechnology) were touted as the potential basis for a new round of U.S. or core hegemony, but most core profits were generated in the service and financial sectors. It was a repeat of the turn toward financialization that had occurred in the late-nineteenth-century *belle époque* during British hegemonic decline (Silver and Arrighi, 2005). The financial portion of the world economy expanded so rapidly that it dwarfed the real economy of trade and production. In the past this had always led to a crash in which the fictitious capital ("securities") were used as wallpaper, but this time the global capitalist class managed enough solidarity to prevent the crash, at least so far.

To make a long story short, with a few important differences, the world-system is repeating what happened during the decline of British hegemony at the end of the nineteenth century and the beginning decades of the twentieth century. To be sure, the United States is larger than Britain was, it commands military power much more completely than Britain did, and the whole world economy is much larger and more tightly wound than it was one hundred years ago.

But the basic logic of capitalist uneven development and the mismatch between the economic and political structures are quite similar. The hegemon is desperately trying to stay on top. Financial centralization only works for a while. It is the first card that is played, but when the potential for instability and collapse becomes obvious, the powers-that-be pull out their other remaining card: military capability. This produces what has been called the "new imperialism " (Harvey, 2003) and the neo-conservative "Global Gamble" (Gowan, 1999). Oil is running out. If "we" can control global oil the potential challengers (Japan, Germany, China) will have to keep sending goods, accepting our paper money and being polite.

Some see this as pouring gasoline on the smoldering coals of resistance. It appears to contradict blatantly the very ideologies of equality and democracy that the United States promoted during its rise to hegemony. The crisis of neoliberalism is producing new turns in elite political ideology as well as new popular mobilizations. Some former neoliberals (e.g., Jeffrey Sachs, 2005) are now espousing a revamped and globalized Keynesianism, another "New Deal" in which the most marginalized peoples left out of global corporate development will be saved if their governments agree to rather stringent fiscal and policy reforms.

The continuing decline of U.S. hegemony and emerging challenges to the policies of neoliberalism and neoconservativism are likely to lead to a new period of deglobalization. Understanding the dynamics of uneven development and the repeated patterns of the global system in the past can be helpful tools for preventing the return to collapse and crisis that gripped the world during the last Age of Extremes.

In the U.S., demographic changes, immigration, former ethnic minorities becoming majorities in several regions, growing inequalities and slow economic growth are going to result in important political reorganizations that will test the abilities of Americans to get along with one another in a trying time of hegemonic decline.

The contemporary wave of global industrialization based on fossil fuel may have already led to a substantial overshoot in the ability of human society to sustain a livable biosphere. If this is the case we may encounter environmental disasters that require global cooperation in order to restore the balance between human society and the natural systems upon which it depends. Another round of conflict over global hegemony may be forthcoming despite the current monopolization of serious military power by the United States. The "global gamble" by the neoconservatives to prop up the U.S. hegemony by playing the military card to control the world's oil supplies is already fueling movements of resistance in those regions that have been left out of the wonders of globalization.

If this sounds gloomy, I want to point out also that the coming period of contestation is an opportunity to create global democratic cooperative institutions that set up a more sustainable relationship between human society and the natural environment and more humane and just relationships among the peoples of the world. A global democratic and collectively rational commonwealth will probably emerge eventually, unless we manage to extinguish ourselves completely (Wagar, 1999). With intelligent political action based on a world historical understanding of global social change, it is possible that this will emerge sooner rather than later.

A new call is rising from global civil society and from those countries in the semiperiphery that have both the motivation and the means to resist global corporate capitalism. The World Social Forum (Fisher and Ponniah, 2003) is a movement of movements and a forum for organizing a global party (or parties) that will challenge the transnational capitalist class. Another world revolution is in the making. Global public social science needs to explain world historical processes to people and to engage actively with global civil society so that the worst excesses of deglobalization can be (hopefully) avoided and we can move toward a democratic and collectively rational global commonwealth (Wagar, 1999; Boswell and Chase-Dunn, 2000).

I have declared the value of disciplinary sociology above in my discussion of the centrality of professional sociology. But many of the institutional boundaries between contemporary social science disciplines are annoying obstacles to both the scientific and the political understanding of social reality. I do not recommend abolishing the disciplines, but rather that a sizeable number of professional and public sociologists should learn the basics of theories and methods in geography, history, political science, economics, ecology and anthropology. This will allow the disciplinary blinders to be thrown off without wrecking the good parts of the disciplines.

Global Public Social Science

So what is global public social science? And, following Burawoy's typology, what are global professional, critical and policy social science? The short answer is that these all take the emergent Earth-wide human system as an important unit of analysis in its own right, although other entities are also important. Global professional social science studies social realities (culture and institutions, politics, inequalities, transnational relations, globalization processes, etc.) on a global scale using the methodological tools and theoretical perspectives of the social sciences. Examples in economics, geography, political science, history, anthropology and sociology are too numerous to enumerate here. Michael Burawoy's (2000) work on global ethnography is certainly a valuable exemplar.

Global critical social science critiques, deconstructs and reformulates important global social science concepts (such as globalization) as well as global institutions. It also proposes critical ways of categorizing social forces, contradictions, and antagonisms in ways that are intended to be of use for transnational social movements. This is also a voluminous literature. Important recent examples are Michael Hardt and Antonio Negri's (2004) *Multitude*, a valiant effort to rethink political theory for the purposes of building global democracy, and Amory Starr's (2000) *Naming the Enemy*, an analysis of the main dimensions of the antiglobalization movements and a structural conceptualization of global corporate capitalism as the enemy that must be confronted.

Global policy social science would seem to be an unlikely activity, since there is (currently) no true world state that could implement global policies. There are, however, important global institutions that do formulate and try to implement global policies (e.g., the United Nations, the World Bank, etc.). But all people now need to formulate global policies because everyone lives in a global polity, a global economy, and an increasingly globalized set of cultures. Global policies are planful ways of coping with global economic, political and social forces. Global Policy Institutes (by that name or some close variant) now exist in New York, Geneva, Berlin, Honolulu, and at the University of Virginia at Charlottesville, and many public policy institutes and centers all over the world are establishing globally oriented policy research programs.

Global public social science refers to social scientists who use their research skills and analytic abilities to address global civil society and in the service of transnational social movements. Burawoy reminds us that one of our important publics is our undergraduate students. Teaching and writing textbooks for undergraduates is an important part of public sociology. A growing number of universities have established interdisciplinary undergraduate majors in global studies (e.g., University of California-Santa Barbara, http://www.global.ucsb.edu/programs/gs/).

The new Global Studies Association (http://www.net4dem.org/may-global/ index.htm) has had several exciting conferences and it has been attacked by right-wing ideologues as famous as David Horowitz. This red badge of courage may be the highest credential in public social science. Some very useful textbooks and readers for global studies courses are those by McMichael (2004), Hall (2000) and Chase-Dunn and Babones (2006).

Research at the behest of global civil society is another important activity of global public social science. A large corpus of the research and published monographs and journal articles comprising global professional social science serves global civil society and transnational social movements. My recent favorites are Rich Appelbaum and Edna Bonacich's (2000) *Behind the Label*, Stephen Bunker and Paul Ciccantell's (2005) *Globalization and the Race for Resources,* big historian David Christian's (2004) inspiring *Maps of Time*, Jared Diamond's (2004) *Collapse*, Michael Mann's (2003) *Incoherent Empire*, Valentine Moghadam's *Globalizing Women* (2005), J.R. and William McNeill's (2003) *The Human Web*, William I. Robinson's (2004) *A Theory of Global Capitalism*, Beverly Silver's (2004) *Forces of Labor* and Immanuel Wallerstein's (2003) *The Decline of American Power.* These are works of professional sociology that serve global civil society and local groups trying to deal with the forces of globalization by providing research and theories that help people understand what is going on.

But Burawoy's most important precept of public sociology endorses direct interaction with, and participation in, civil society groups, and research that is directed toward helping these groups achieve their goals. Since, as I have pointed out above, everyone now needs to deal with the issues and forces of globalization, practically any project could qualify. But I will focus on the research of those who have studied and participated in transnational social movements. Arguably social movements have been importantly transnational at least since the nineteenth century in the sense that the conceptual frames, collective action repertoires, and communications networks already involved intercontinental interaction, migration, and flows of other important resources (Keck and Sikkink, 1998). But here I will discuss social science research on, and involvement with, the emerging movements that have focused on contemporary globalization. I already mentioned Amory Starr's (2000) excellent contribution to global critical sociology above. Starr's new book (2005), *Global Revolt*, is an inspiring and informative "how-to-do-it" manual for antiglobalization activists based mainly on Starr's intensive participant observation in anti-globalization protest demonstrations.[3]

Jackie Smith's (Smith and Johnston, 2002; Smith, 2004) studies of transnational social movements are based on both careful formal analyses of systematic data and Smith's involvement with, and participation in, the movements she is studying. Bruce Podobnik's (2004) studies of the changing location and frequency of anti-globalization protest events is another important contribution, and the new book that he co-edited with Tom Reifer (Podobnik and Reifer, 2005) contains several works that must be included in a survey of global public sociology. I have already mentioned the important work by Thomas Ponniah and William Fisher (2003) on the World Social Forum.

UCR Project on Transnational Social Movements

At the University of California-Riverside (UCR) the Research Working Group on Transnational Social Movements has undertaken a study of the participants in the World Social Forum that is intended to help the participating groups better understand the contradictions and overlapping issues and agendas among the movements so that they might be better able to cooperate and collaborate with each other in forming a credible and effective political force in world politics. Professor Ellen Reese and I organized the research working group, which is composed of graduate and undergraduate students at UCR, most of whom are majoring in sociology.[4] This participant observation and survey research is sponsored by the UCR Institute for Research on World-Systems (irows.ucr.edu). Ellen and five of our students attended the 2005 World Social Forum in Porto Alegre, Brazil where they obtained over 600 written responses to a survey questionnaire (in Portuguese, Spanish, and English) (irows.ucr. edu/research/tsmstudy/wsfsurvey.htm) that gathers information on the backgrounds of participants and their involvements in different kinds of issues and social movements. We also asked respondents to help us identify possible contradictions among the participating transnational social movements, and to suggest ways in which two well-known contradictions might be overcome (see http://www.irows.ucr.edu/research/tsmstudy.htm).[5]

At the time of this writing we are still in the midst of processing and analyzing the survey results. We will present papers based on our research at the annual meetings of the Society for the Study of Social Problems, the American Sociological Association, the International Studies Association and the World Congress of Sociology in Durban, South Africa. We also will make our results known on the project web site and will present results at future regional and global meetings of the World Social Forum so that participants can benefit from our study.

The issue of representation and legitimacy is a huge one for the participants at the World Social Forum and our study will be able to add to the available knowledge about who attends and what participants believe about representation. Earlier research (Schonleitner, 2003) found that a majority of the attendees are majoring in, or have undergraduate or graduate degrees in, social sciences and our survey confirms this. The activists in the emerging global civil society, who are very concerned about the extent to which poor and disadvantaged groups are able to participate in global politics, are themselves mainly people who have training in the social science disciplines. This simple fact speaks volumes about the complementary relationship between global professional and public social science and also about the real makeup of global civil society.

Gramsci, Gouldner, and many other observers of social change have long noted the important role of intellectuals in both sustaining and challenging the structures of power. That most of the activists in global civil society are trained in the social sciences would come as no surprise. The reaction of popular forces against global corporate capitalism and the ideology of neoliberalism is generating new constellations of ideas and new forms of organization. Elites have long participated in the global polity as statesmen, diplomats, publicists, scientists, religious leaders and etc. What is happening now is the emergence of large transnationalized segments of the popular classes who are using new information technologies to organize globally. The World Social Forum is the most important arena for the organization of global networks and parties that claim to represent the peoples of the Earth (Gill, 2000). The processes of party-network formation are what we are studying, and also what we intend to facilitate. This is both professional and public global social science.

Notes

1. For a clear and thorough definition of public sociology see Jeffries (2005). Thanks to Michael Burawoy, Vincent Jeffries, and Christine Petit for helpful comments on earlier drafts of this essay.
2. At the 2002 World Congress of Sociology in Brisbane there was a session entitled "After Globalization?" One of the presented papers was entitled "After Globalization—More Globalization."
3. The potential and possible contradictions and complementarities between anti-globalization and "globalization from below" movements are discussed in Chase-Dunn (2005)
4. Five University of California-Riverside (UCR) students attended the World Social Forum in Porto Alegre, Brazil January 26-31, 2005 to do participant observation and survey research on transnational social movements. They are Rebecca Giem, Erika Gutierrez, Linda Kim, Christine Petit, and Darragh White. They were accompanied by UCR Sociology Professor Ellen Reese.
5. Question 404 is " How might actual or potential contradictions between the environmental movements and the labor movements be resolved? And Question 405 is "How might actual or potential contradictions between the labor movements in the developed countries and the labor movements of the less developed countries be resolved?"

References

Appelbaum, R., and Bonacich, E. 2000. *Behind the Label*. Berkeley, CA: University of California Press.

Arrighi, G. 1994. *The Long Twentieth Century*. London: Verso.

_____, Hopkins, T.K, and Wallerstein, I. 1989. *Antisystemic Movements*. London: Verso.

Boswell, T., and Chase-Dunn, C. 2000. *The Spiral of Capitalism and Socialism: Toward Global Democracy*. Boulder, CO: Lynne Rienner.

Brenner, R. 2002. *The Boom and the Bubble: The U.S. in the World Economy*. London: Verso.

Burawoy, M. 1979. *Manufacturing Consent*. Chicago, IL: University of Chicago Press.

_____. 1985. *The Politics of Production: Factory Regimes under Capitalism and Socialism*. London: Verso.

_____. 2000. *Global Ethnography*. Berkeley, CA: University of California Press.

_____. 2005. "2004 ASA Presidential Address: For Public Sociology" *American Sociological Review* 70,1: 4-28 (February).

Chase-Dunn, C. 2005. "Social Evolution and the Future of World Society," Pp. 13-38 in M. Herkenrath, et al (eds.) *The Future of World Society*. Zurich: Intelligent.

_____, and Hall, T.D. 1997. *Rise and Demise: Comparing World-Systems*. Boulder, CO: Westview.

_____, Kawano, Y., and Brewer, B.D. 2000 "Trade Globalization since 1795: Waves of Integration in the World-System." *American Sociological Review* 65(1): 77-95 (February).

_____, and Babones, S. 2006. *Global Social Change: Comparative and Historical Perspectives*. Baltimore, MD: Johns Hopkins University Press.

Fisher, W.F., and Ponniah, T. 2003. *Another World Is Possible: Popular Alternatives to Globalization at the World Social Forum*. London: Zed Press.

Gill, S. 2000. "Toward a Post-Modern Prince?: The Battle of Seattle as a Moment in the New Politics of Globalization" *Millennium* 29 (1): 131-140.

Gowan, P. 1999. *The Global Gamble: Washington's Faustian Bid for World Dominance*. London: Verso.

Hall, T.D. 2000. *A World-Systems Reader*. Lanham, MD: Rowman and Littlefield.

Hardt, M., and Negri, A. 2004. *Multitude: War and Democracy in the Age of Empire*. New York: Penguin.

Harvey, D. 2003. *The New Imperialism*. New York: Oxford University Press.

Hobsbawm, E. 1994. *The Age of Extremes: A History of the World, 1914-1991*. New York: Pantheon.

Jeffries, V. 2005. "Pitirim A. Sorokin's Integralism and Public Sociology" *American Sociologist*, Vol 36.

Keck, M.E., and Sikkink. K. 1998. *Activists beyond Borders: Advocacy Networks in International Politics*. Ithaca, NY: Cornell University Press.

Lipset, S.M. 1963. *The First New Nation: The United States in Historical and Comparative Perspective*. New York: Basic Books.

Mann, M. 2003. *Incoherent Empire*. London: Verso. McMichael, P. 2004. *Development and Social Change*. Thousand Oaks, CA: Pine Forge Press.

Moghadam, V. 2005. *Globalizing Women*. Baltimore, MD: Johns Hopkins University Press.

O'Rourke, K.H., and Williamson, J.G. 2000. *Globalization and History*. Cambridge, MA: MIT Press.

Podobnik, B. 2004. "Resistance to Globalization: Cycles and Evolution in the Global-
    ization Protest Movement" Paper presented at the annual meeting of the American
    Sociological Association, San Francisco, August 15.
_____, and Reifer, T.E. 2005. *Transforming Globalization: Challenges and Oppor-
    tunities in the Post 9/ 11 Era.* New York: Brill.
Robinson, W.I. 2004 *A Theory of Global Capitalism.* Baltimore, MD: Johns Hopkins
    University Press.
Sachs, J. 2005. *The End of Poverty: Economic Possibilities of Our Time.* New York:
    Penguin.
Schönleitner, G. 2003. "World Social Forum: Making Another World Possible?" Pp. 127-
    149 in J. Clark (ed.): *Globalizing Civic Engagement: Civil Society and Transnational
    Action.* London: Earthscan.
Silver, B. 2003. *Forces of Labor.* Cambridge: Cambridge University Press.
_____, and Arrighi, G. 2005. "Polanyi's 'Double Movement': The *Belle Époques* of
    British and U.S. Hegemony Compared" In Friedman, J. and Chase-Dunn, C. *Hege-
    monic Declines: Present and Past.* Boulder, CO: Paridigm Press.
Smith, J. 2004. "The World Social Forum and the Challenges of Global Democracy."
    Global Networks 4(4): 413-421.
_____, and Johnston, H. 2002. *Globalization and Resistance: Transnational Dimen-
    sions of Social Movements.* Lanham, MD: Rowman and Littlefield.
Starr, A. 2000. *Naming the Enemy: Anti-corporate Movements Confront Globalization.*
    London: Zed Press.
_____. 2005. *Global Revolt: A Guide to the Global Revolt against Globalization.*
    London: Zed Press.
Wagar, W.W. 1999. *A Short History of the Future.* Chicago, IL: University of Chicago
    Press.
Wallerstein, I. 2003. *The Decline of American Power: The U.S. in a Chaotic World.* New
    York: New Press.

9

The Intellectual Canons
of a Public Sociology:
Pragmatist Foundations, Historical
Extensions, and Humanly Engaged Realities[1]

Robert Prus

Introduction

The term "public sociology" is notably ambiguous, but to date has been used predominantly in two ways—one, with the objective of making sociology better known, more respected, more accessible, and of greater potential use to the public as a stock of information and associated resources; and two, with the intention of using sociology as a forum and resource for promoting various moral or ethical or reform standpoints and agendas.

Michael Burawoy (2005a,b), the 2004 president of the American Sociological Association, has emerged as a prominent champion of moralist motifs and activist agendas but, as clearly indicated in Weber's (1918) "Science as a Vocation," these and related issues pertaining to scholarship and morality are far from new in our discipline (also see Sorokin, 1956; and Horowitz, 1993; along with more recent commentaries by Boyns and Fletcher, 2005; and McLaughlin et al., 2005). Nevertheless, public sociology has emerged as a more prominent, if not also a notably intense, topic of interchange among sociologists during the last few decades.

Still, whereas most of these debates revolve around considerations of the place of various modes of ideology and activism relative to the more scholarly, scientific emphases of mainstream sociology, this chapter provides an occasion to consider what the intellectual criteria of a public

195

sociology might be and what sorts of implications these notions might have for the discipline of sociology more generally.

This statement is not intended to preclude or eliminate other things that sociologists and others might present or describe as "public sociology." However, it offers a set of standards against which the intellectual integrity of various instances of things described as public sociology might be assessed. As well, it provides a clearer sense of direction for the development of a scholarly field of endeavor that addresses human group life in broadly comprehensive and enduringly humanist terms.

Relatedly, this is not an attempt to promote "public sociology" as a phenomenon that somehow is separate from, or antithetical to, sociology more generally. Instead, it is mindful of the very foundations of a discipline, which by its nature (as in talk, thought, and inquiry pertaining to community life and the realms of knowing and acting within) *is* a public phenomenon in the most basic of terms. Likewise, it is in striving to provide materials that inform others about the nature of human group life in more fundamental and thorough terms, rather than promoting certain kinds of moral orders and/or particular life-styles, that sociology achieves its greatest relevance both as a social science and as a service to all realms of a worldly public.

As suggested in the title of this chapter, the present consideration of the intellectual canons of public sociology draws notably on symbolic interactionism (particularly its pragmatist foundations, ethnographic research tradition, and its conceptual attentiveness to generic social process).[2] Still, the present statement also is notably informed by classical Greek and interim scholarship, including some works from Emile Durkheim (especially 1904-1905, 1912, 1913-1914) as well as some more recent considerations of human group life. Accordingly, the canons presented here notably extend the parameters of Chicago-style interactionism associated with George Herbert Mead and Herbert Blumer in conceptual as well as transhistorical terms. Thus, although enabled by the humanist emphasis of pragmatist social thought and an attentiveness to the ethnographic study of human group life as "something in the making," this statement has a much broader sociological relevance than that implied in the more particular contributions of interactionist scholarship. Still, before engaging this task more directly, it is important to acknowledge at least briefly some aspects of what is been termed "public sociology."

A Public Sociology—for Whom?

As many readers likely realize, the matters of social thought (or theory about human group life) and public reform (also moralism, idealism, remedialism, activism, etc.) have been separated and mixed in a variety of ways that can be traced at least as far back as Plato's (420-348BCE) *Republic* and *Laws*, as also have questions pertaining to the roles that scholars might assume in maintaining intellectual foci, sharing their knowledge with others, promoting particular agendas, serving in advisory capacities, and the like. Without dwelling on the problematic quality of the actual wisdom of the many well-intentioned moral agendacists to be found in sociology and elsewhere, one may ask, "how might a more viable public sociology be achieved?"

Whereas some might suggest that the answer resides in "more research," it is to be appreciated that all research requires thought. Thus, even before one counts or observes something, for instance, some notions of categories and instances minimally are required. Research becomes relevant only with respect to purpose and context. No, more research is not sufficient in itself. Something more is required.

Some sociologists might claim that they already know enough and that it is time to emphasize remedial, moral, or activist related objectives. The assumption is that, as especially knowledgeable academics, sociologists are particularly well situated to assume more significant roles in guiding public affairs. Often, this is presented in terms of helping those that one might define as oppressed or underprivileged in some way. Interestingly, while forgoing a scholarly role in more immediate and sustained terms, those adopting moralist viewpoints typically intend to be recognized as scholars and often reference particular studies, the discipline, or the broader scholarly community to buttress their claims to expertise.

Further, whereas some people have very clear notions of scholarship and more readily contrast these with moralist positions of various sorts, a historical review of the development of Western social thought (Durkheim, 1904-1905) reveals that scholarship (like morality) also is far from one thing. Indeed, like many other aspects of human group life, scholarship has been the subject of notably differing emphases over the millennia as well as the target of intense hostility in certain places and times.

So, if like morality, social thought, and associated scholarship, is not one thing, what does this suggest about public sociology? Are morality and scholarship to be blended in some way? Presumably, the promotion of moralist agendas is not to be conflated with scholarship. Still, is scholarship to provide a haven, front, or intellectual veneer for the moral agendas that some academics wish to pursue? Or, is the study of human group life to be subordinated to activist agendas?

Insofar as the emphasis on "what should be" is considered comparable to examinations of "what is," moral viewpoints tend to compromise if not more extensively displace intellectual concerns with knowing. Moralism, activism, idealism, fiction, and desire, thus, begin to assume parity with, if not a priority over, sustained pluralist inquiries into the nature of human group life. Although these other emphases may appeal to various sectors of the community, it will result in a more vacuous, less credible sociology, as well as one that lacks standards for delineating moralism, idealism, and fiction from more sustained research and analysis. Moreover, even if some of those adopting advocacy roles have engaged in instances of more sustained pluralist scholarship, these earlier scholarly emphases frequently become disregarded as others in their midst become caught up in the more emotional and behaviorally engaged features of activist ventures.

Some moral advocates might also claim that there can be no genuine sociology without a central moral core. Although there can be no society without a moral order, it should be recognized that each instance of morality represents a realm of cultural content rather than a generic process unto itself. Morality has a particularistic, albeit also a relativist, quality. Denoting a mode of ideology, morality differs from sociology which has as its focal point the study of the processes by which human group life takes shape. Even if one puts aside the question of "whose morality is to prevail," it should be emphasized that morality is not something to be imposed on sociology. Instead, like religion and other cultural matters, instances of morality are things to be studied and understood as the specific but variable contents of broader sets of social interchange (also see Durkheim, 1912; Weber, 1918).

When one examines the debates surrounding public sociology, one encounters a great deal of controversy pertaining to maintaining sociology as a scholarly discipline versus the pursuit of various ideological and activist positions. Interestingly, although some proponents of public sociology present this venture as the way in which (learned) sociologists would encourage, assist, advise, instruct, and otherwise promote particular moral viewpoints, practices, life-styles, and other arrangements in the community at large, it is not apparent that there is a great deal of concern about developing a sociology that is attentive to the public in a more comprehensive, sustained humanly engaged sense.

If we are to have a public sociology, it should be a realm of scholarship that is notably authentic, encompassing, pluralist, conceptually and substantively informative, and enduring. In the currently popular vernacular, it will not be "modernist" or "postmodernist" sociology, and it will not promote any moral order over any other. *Instead, it will be a sociology for all of the public for all times.* It will be one that is conceptually transhistorical (or transmodern) as well as transcontextual in a most comprehensive sense. While attending astutely and carefully to the situations, interchanges, and events of the present, it should not be a sociology that is caught up in the excitement of the passing moment or a position that adopts any particular moral frame (other than learning about the human condition) as its primary point of reference.

The Intellectual Canons

Intended as a set of reference points for defining a viable public sociology, the canons that follow consider the nature of the human group, things to pursue in a scholarly fashion, and emphases to convey to others as consumers of a public sociology. Quite directly, insofar as it denotes a focused realm of scholarship, a public sociology not only is one in which (1) authenticity is emphasized, but also one that is (2) empirically grounded, and (3) conceptually articulated. Moreover, a scholarly public sociology must be (4) community-based and thereby centrally attentive to human group life as (5) intersubjectively accomplished, (6) relationally engaged, (7) activity minded, and (8) technologically enabled. As well, if it is to have greater intellectual integrity, a public sociology is to be (9) memorably historical and (10) enduringly humanist in its emphasis.

Although given an order for presentational purposes, these cannons are best viewed in more holistic terms. Indeed, whereas each denotes a somewhat different emphasis, none can be comprehended apart from the others. This is because community life exists as a unity and public sociology, if it is to be viable, must not only respect that unity but also must be one with it—even as public sociology (as with other instances of social thought) at the very same time reflects upon that of which it is a part.

Authenticity emphasized

Let me begin by identifying the empirical social world in the case of human beings. This world is the actual group life of human beings. It consists of what they experience and do, individually and collectively, as they engage in their respective forms of living; it covers the large complexes of interlaced activities that grow up as the actions of some spread out to affect the actions of others; and it embodies the large variety of relationships between the participants. . . . The empirical world, in short, is the world of everyday experience . . . Ongoing group life, whether in the past or the present, whether in the case of this or that people, whether in one or another geographical area, is the empirical social world of the social and psychological sciences. (Blumer, 1969: 35)

The first and most essential criterion for a public sociology is that of authenticity—that the representations of human group life that sociologists provide be as genuinely sincere, open, and thoroughly representative of the things people know and do as possible. This requires a sustained focus on the "what and how" of human group life—on *what is*, not what should be. It also implies that any other agendas (e.g., moralism, activism, entertainment) clearly be subordinated to the emphasis on achieving authenticity with respect to the concepts, research, analyses, publications, and other presentations of public sociology.

The quest for authenticity requires that those developing a more scholarly public sociology also respect the nature of human group life. This not only means attending to all realms of community life and all modes of human interchange within, but it also means being highly mindful of the ways that human group life is accomplished in practice. This involves striving for a public sociology that is informed by the sustained examination of the ways that people do things (and relate to one another) in the instances in which these take place.

In no way does this emphasis on activity deny the importance of organizational routines or other arrangements and practices that people may develop over time. Whereas the organizational features of human group life, as with all other instances of technology, culture, and the like, are consequential because of their relevance for human activity, all of these arrangements, practices, and object definitions only maintain an existence because they are invoked, developed, maintained, and modified through instances of human endeavor. Likewise, in no way does this approach ignore the importance of locating human behavior within the broader matters of change and continuity. Still, it is to be recognized that all aspects of community life achieve meaning and maintain viability only as people actively participate in those specific arenas of community life.

The quest for authenticity also requires that we attend to and examine the ways that people experience and enter into all realms of human group life as agents—as minded essences who not only develop interests and capacities to act, assess, and resist, but who also encounter resistances and resources of various sorts in their capacities as knowing, intentioned actors. Further, because of the multiplistic nature of human group life, it is essential that a scholarly public sociology, as much as possible, represent the viewpoints of any and all of those people whose life-worlds and activities are under consideration in any given situation. A genuine public sociology must be pluralist and inclusive in that sense. This not only means carefully and fully attending to all accessible variants (and instances within) of people's activities and interchanges, but also locating these matters within a broader community context, without assuming partisan stances or encouraging particular viewpoints or moralities over others.

Moreover, if we are to pursue a more authentic sociology it will be necessary to examine and establish, as explicitly, directly, and thoroughly as possible, the linkages between the matters under consideration. I contrast this with the generally vague, speculative connections implied in most structuralist approaches, including the seemingly more "scientific" applications of variable analysis. Thus, for instance, it is of little value to claim (even with massive arrays of studies and fairly consistent statistical correlations) that class, age, race, gender, and the like contribute to crime, delinquency, or other social problems without indicating exactly what these things are and how these things are connected in actual instances. If we cannot do that, we have an obligation to acknowledge these limitations. It is not enough to talk about correlations between two or more sets of the vaguely defined essences and then speculate on their linkages.[3] We need to openly and directly address the tenuous quality of claims of these sorts.

Nor is it adequate to acknowledge, as quantitative researchers sometimes do when pushed far enough by their colleagues, that these are merely "quick and dirty indicators" that only suggest general tendencies at most. Likewise, whereas descriptive statistics may be useful in defining aspects of situations and suggesting some general patterns within, it is most important that sociologists (and other social scientists) not confuse correlations with explanations when presenting their work to others.

As scholars, we need to be much more attentive to the ways that things are interconnected by more directly examining and analyzing instances of the phenomena under consideration. Until we establish the linkages much more fully than those implied in structuralist analyses (even amidst highly refined flow charts that identify independent, dependent, and intervening or other qualifying variables) our claims will lack authenticity despite increasing masses of studies and more extended volumes of learned speculation. It is for this reason that there is no substitute for ethnographic inquiry and historical research for examining and comprehending both the developmental flows of human group life and the instances taking place within.

Further, as Durkheim (1912) stresses, because human society can only exist as a unity, it is important that sociologists be highly mindful of these developmental, foundational affinities even as they examine particular instances in extended horizontal detail. This means attending to language and concepts, sensations and natural phenomena, activities and relationships, purposes and accomplishments as ongoing instances of situationally enacted, historically-enabled flows.

In all cases, we need to be mindful of the contexts in which particular matters are embedded and of the relation of particular things to the other things that constitute human group life in both vertical-historical and horizontal-situated terms. Thus, one cannot understand matters defined as deviance, education, politics, or science, for instance, except through a broader awareness of the ways that community life is accomplished in practice—in both historically achieved and situationally enacted terms. Because community life exists only in and through activity (and associated interchange) an authentic analysis of human group life requires a highly sustained attentiveness to ethnographic inquiry and historical materials.

These are matters that we, as sociologists, need to stress not only in presenting materials to the broader public but also among ourselves—in our research, analysis, and instruction. As Durkheim (1912) and Mead (1934) emphasize, reality does not exist outside of the human community. It is *the interactive, humanly engaged context of community life that represents a centering point for all knowing and acting, for all senses of reality.*

Empirically grounded

> No theorizing, however ingenious, and no observance of scientific protocol, however meticulous, are substitutes for developing a familiarity with what is actually going on in the sphere of life under study. (Blumer, 1969: 39)

In stating that a public sociology is to be empirically grounded, I am not proposing that a public sociology be extensively or centrally quantitative in emphasis. Although descriptive statistics can be very helpful in defining certain contexts and patterns of phenomena, quantitative analysis not only is most inadequate as an explanatory process in itself but statistical data generally also are to be approached with caution. This is because measurements not only are categorically imposed on instances, but they also often poorly represent the very things they are purported to portray.

This is especially problematic in dealing with the actual processes and dynamic complexities of human group life, wherein the "observables" necessary for measurement simply cannot capture the enacted reality of the instances in which people—as living, thinking, feeling, interpreting, acting, interacting beings—mindfully adjust to the emergent realms of whatness in which they operate.

Hence, whereas statistics of all sorts are often presented as "objective" instances of empirical or scientific data because they are categorized in standardized ways, it should be recognized that these "claims to information" are especially limited with respect to matters involving human knowing and acting.

While not dispensing with a scientific attitude, the study of human group life requires a conception of science different from that employed in the physical or material science; one which as Blumer (1928, 1969) insists respects the nature of the human group. This means attending to the emergent, linguistically-enabled, actively engaged, agency-based, and intersubjectively achieved nature of human group life.

An empirically grounded approach to a viable public sociology not only would be processually oriented (wherein sociologists attend to the longer and shorter term developmental flows of the phenomena under consideration) but it also would imply a concerted effort to achieve "intimate familiarity" with one's subject matter (Blumer, 1969); it would examine instances of human knowing and acting in close, careful, detailed, and sustained manners. This not only means studying human life-worlds and instances of people's lived experience therein, as these are known and dealt with by the people involved, but also doing so in ways that are minimally affected by researcher agendas, presence, and inquiries.

As public sociologists, we also should not be in the business of making grandiose claims and promising or implying "quick fixes" when these do not exist. Even if we seem less relevant in the short-term, it is incumbent on those doing public sociology to be honest with the public. We can indicate our desire to learn, discuss our resources for doing so, and tell people what our discipline has to offer, but we also have an obligation to stay close to our data and to acknowledge the limitations that we encounter as scholars.

Relatedly, we need to be openly pluralistic in the ways that we study and analyze the matters at hand. If our work is to be empirically grounded in a more genuine or authentic sense, it cannot be motivated or presented in more selective, partisan manners. A more viable empirically-informed public sociology, thus, also requires the courage of character to represent what is there in more pluralist, nonpartisan terms, regardless of any other concerns, agendas, or sympathies that researchers or analysts might have.

Conceptually articulated

> That is what makes conceptual thought so valuable for us. If concepts were only general ideas, they would not enrich knowledge a great deal, for, as we have already pointed out, the general contains nothing more than the particular. But if before all else they are collective representations, they add to that which we can learn by our own personal experience all that wisdom and science which the group has accumulated in the course of centuries. (Emile Durkheim, 1912, *The Elementary Forms of the Religious Life*, Swain translation 1915/1965: 483-484)

If it is to be viable, a public sociology must represent people's lived experiences as they know them to be as well as attend to the actual instances in which human group life takes place. However, a sociology that is to be of broadest possible value to the public also must be centrally conceptual in nature.

Not only do concepts (as Durkheim, 1912 emphasizes) allow people to make sense of *all* of the things that they experience (i.e., all phenomena; including motion, sensations, and other people, as well as themselves or any other objects of reference) but it also is only through concepts that people meaningfully may share (or communicate) any aspects of knowing and acting with others.

For these reasons, it is essential that sociologists not only strive to (a) define their terms of reference as clearly and precisely as possible, but also (b) delineate and specify the interlinkages of the particular concepts under consideration. It is in these ways that scholars not only more adequately inform themselves about the nature of human group life but also make their work more completely accessible to others.

Moreover, despite the somewhat fixed qualities that concepts necessarily assume (if they are to serve as consequential, shareable representations of particular phenomena) concepts are not invariant points of reference. Instead, concepts denote working notions of whatness and, as such, are subject to revision on the basis of people's subsequent experiences with, inquiries into, and assessments of the instances of the matters under consideration.

Whereas concepts are at the base of all knowing and all meaningful activity, all conceptual representations of things are problematic and inevitably partial, as well as the products of the contexts, purposes, applications, and actual endeavors in which people give viability to the representations with which they work. Consequently, even though particular concepts, or composite sets thereof, cannot capture all the features that people might eventually invoke with respect to some phenomenon, it is in the matters selected for emphasis that concepts achieve both their realism and their relevance.

If sociologists are to develop concepts that serve as more viable conduits for knowing, it is important that they strive to minimize distortions (e.g., fiction, idealism, moralism) in their representations of human group life. As well, while not simplifying unduly, it is important that sociologists strive for clarity and consistency as they articulate points of reference that can be more readily shared with others. Even in the midst of pursuing precision, the most valuable concepts also are those that are more readily comprehended by others. Likewise, eloquence and erudition are of greatest service when they enable people to communicate matters in more direct, crystalline, comprehensible terms.

Although some may object to this emphasis on concepts, contending that these more generic or transsituational (transhistorical, transcontextual) representations destroy the unique or idiographic features of particular phenomena, one may observe that to be meaningful even the most idiographic features of instances also must be interpreted from some perspective. Indeed, it is only in establishing some point of reference that particular aspects of the idiographic or unique can in any way be appreciated—even as being unique in some respect.

Further, because they are derived from comparisons or considerations of similarities and differences, concepts inevitably imply categories or qualities of more generic (also transsituational, transhistorical) sorts. Once established, thus, concepts (as notions of whatness) enable people to make sense of the particular instances of things that they subsequently encounter. However, as a result of their limitations, concepts also provide indications of the unknown (including people's senses of the incomplete, the unique, the puzzling, and the confusing).

Still, as with people's concepts more generally, not all sociological concepts are equally viable. To be more valuable as central features of a public sociology, our concepts not only should be generic in a more thoroughgoing sense but they also should reflect process or the developmental flows of human group life and attend fundamentally to the social nature of community life—ergo, generic social processes.

These generic social processes (GSPs) might deal with matters such as acquiring perspectives, achieving identity, doing activity, experienc-

ing relationships, experiencing emotionality, developing communicative
fluency, participating in collective events, establishing associations, ob-
jectifying associations, and encountering outsiders. As much as possible,
our concepts should enable scholars to address the sociological features
of any humanly engaged situation.

Moreover, as representations of empirically grounded phenomena,
our concepts are to be investigated, assessed, and modified, extended or
rejected on an ongoing basis relative to subsequent inquiries into instances
of human group life and the existing stocks of knowledge on community
life that have been accumulated to date.

In addition to the transsituational comparisons that may be feasible
when utilizing data from similar inquiries of more immediate, contemporary sorts, other valuable comparisons may be achieved by examining
similarities and differences in materials developed on somewhat parallel
processes (e.g., experiencing relationships, participating in collective
events) of human group life in other places and times. By attending to
comparisons of these sorts, we may be able to develop transcontextually
and transhistorically informed concepts that have a more enduring value
as reference points for subsequent research and analysis.

Community oriented

> It does not seem extreme to say that those brilliant social philosophers who have
> developed the sociology of conflict might have found adequate material for their
> discussions without having left their own classrooms. Nearly all the classic concepts
> apply to life in the school room, war, feuds, litigation, conflict of ideals, victory,
> conciliation, compromise, conversion, accommodation, and assimilation. (Waller,
> 1932: 351)

Whereas the hallmark of sociology is its attentiveness to human
group life, and it is this emphasis that most fundamentally distinguishes
sociology from the other social sciences, it may be stressed that a viable
public sociology is one that focuses on the nature of community life as
this takes place in the instances in which people do things. Moreover, if
it is to serve a broad, enduring public, the emphasis should be on "what
is" and how this takes place rather than "what should be." A genuine
public sociology must respect the nature of community life in its fullest,
most comprehensive, and historically informed senses.

Not only, thus, would a more viable public sociology attend to the full
range of association (as in cooperation, conflict, friendship, competition,
persuasive endeavor, organizational interchange, and the like, as well
as all matters of transformations thereof) that one encounters in human

group life, but it also would be highly mindful of the ways that people enter into and give shape to the various aspects of community life in conjunction with one another (linkages, affinities, disjunctures, and so forth) in both wittingly intentional and more inadvertent ways.

Hence, while the broader community cannot be understood except in relation to instances of meaningful human activity (and interchange) neither can the individuals acting within be understood except through a more thorough examination of the more encompassing features of community life. Moreover, although it has been common to refer to these latter matters as "structural" or "macro" sociological essences and the viewpoints and activities of people often are referenced as "subjective" or "micro" sociological phenomena, divisions of these sorts are antithetical to a more genuine, more authentic public sociology.

Consistent with Durkheim (1912) it might be said that whereas individuals (as instances of species-humans) have no sense of reality or purpose apart from that generated within the collectivity (and this pertains to all knowing, meaningful activity, and survival) society also cannot exist except through the activities and thoughts of the people within that collectivity.

Thus, although all community life has a transindividual and transhistorical quality as the particular people in any community build on things (language, concepts, practices, organizations, objects, technologies) developed by earlier generations, thereby benefiting from collective memories of behavioral, linguistic, contextual, and emotional sorts, all aspects of community life are dependent on people, as active participants in human group life, for their very existence. Without more immediate instances of these activities (and interchanges) there would be no reality of which to speak.

As part of this process, I will more pointedly be addressing intersubjectivity, relationships, activity, and the adjustive features of human lived experience. However, just as there would be no meaningful human community without these (also highly pervasive) aspects of community life, intersubjectivity, relationships, activity, and the adjustive features of people's experiences cannot be comprehended except within more sustained considerations of (a) the multiplistic nature of community life and people's participation in the various life-worlds or subcultural contexts that constitute the broader community; (b) civil arrangements, governing practices, and intergroup relations; (c) religion and secular morality; (d) deviance and, regulation; and (e) education, philosophy, and science. Even though it is possible to consider these features of community life only in the briefest of terms in the present paper, they represent central features of an authentic public sociology and are to be approached as such.

While addressing community life more generally, it still may be best to begin by acknowledging *the multiple life-worlds* that constitute human communities. Even though all human communities may be viewed as unities (suggested by the interlinkages of the people constituted within) it also should be recognized that even in their most elementary or fundamental forms, human communities are not homogenous entities. Accordingly, it is essential that those embarked on a public sociology be acutely mindful of the importance of differentiating the various life-worlds or subcultures found within. While these life-worlds revolve around more focused realms of activity—as in gathering food, attending to children, engaging in playful endeavors, and dealing with illnesses, for instance, it is these multiple fields of endeavor that constitute the basis of any human community

Thus, even though societies may vary in the multiplicity of life-worlds represented therein as well as the ways that particular subcultural ventures are articulated and the intensity with which these are pursued by the people involved, it is most important that sociologists not overlook the multiplicity of these life-worlds or the relevance that these have to the participants by trying to reduce the complex, dynamic features of human group life to more singular notions of structure, cooperation, conflict, rational choice motivations, and the like.

This emphasis on multiple life-worlds or subcultural realities offers sociologists a particularly valuable set of vantage points. Not only does this allow scholars to examine the many life-worlds that constitute particular societies and develop more sustained analytic comparisons both within and across subcultural life-worlds in the process, but it also provides sociologists with opportunities to examine and better comprehend the sequences or careers of people's involvements in these various life-worlds.

Whereas people more generally can more readily connect their experiences and situations with the experiences (similar and different) of those involved in particular life-worlds, sociologists who embark on more focused inquiries along these lines will have opportunities to take these life-worlds apart, piece by piece, and see more precisely how these subcultural arenas are constituted. The can also see how people enter into particular settings, manage their activities, and relate to one another at various points along the way.

Each of these life-worlds offers occasions in which to learn about people's perspectives, activities, relationships, identities, emotionality, linguistic expressions, and their participation in all manners of collective events as well as people's careers of participation (initial involvements, continuities, disinvolvements, reinvolvements) and the interconnectedness of people's involvements with those of others in those settings.

Furthermore, since even the seemingly most encompassing of categories (e.g., age, gender, class, ethnicity) imply somewhat differentiated fields of activity, these categories also can be envisioned as denoting subcultural life-worlds of sorts. When approached as realms of human knowing and acting, as opposed to abstract constructs, the life-worlds implied in these categories not only become much more amenable to ethnographic inquiry and historical research, but they also are apt to have much greater relevance for comparative analysis and conceptual development.

Rather than treating these categories as structures that determine people's views and behaviors, the emphasis here is on (a) the ways that these aspects of human group life are developed, sustained, adjusted, disregarded, and resurrected over time; (b) the ways that the people involved use these categories as reference points for framing and assessing both their own behaviors and those of others in the community; and (c) the ways that people enter into and engage (learn about, enact, experience, accept, adjust, and resist) these aspects of community life on an ongoing, day-to-day basis.

A community-oriented sociology also would be highly attentive to *the politics of community life*, that is, to (a) the broader sets of civil relations that people develop with one another in the community; (b) the governing arrangements that take place in these settings; and (c) the relations that people within particular communities have with outsiders and the communities that these outsiders represent. Consistent with the earlier material on subcultural life-worlds and people's participation within, these matters of "political science" also need to be approached mindfully of the ways that people enter into these arenas and engage one another in these contexts as they go about their activities.

Relatedly, rather than enshroud community (also, regional, national and international) politics in a vague mysticism of structures, factors, or forces, it is much more instructive to examine the ways that people enter into these realms of activity and develop understandings, arrangements, and procedures for managing the affairs of the community. This also means attending to the ways that people make sense of and adjust to unexpected matters (including challenges from outsiders, natural disasters, and impending threats of various sorts) that are thought to affect the broader community or some significant sectors thereof.

In addition to attending to the arrangements that people develop for dealing with one another within particular communities, both on a more situated basis and over time, it also is important that sociologists develop somewhat parallel sets of inquiries and analyses that focus on the ways in which those representing the community in some way deal with the assortment of the outsiders whose lives and activities intersect with their own. Regardless of whether these involve more isolated or extended sets of encounters, are more casual or formal in character, assume more congenial or hostile qualities, and so forth, it is important to consider the full range of association that insiders develop with the outsiders as well as any shifts or transformations that these associations might undergo as the people involved relate to one another over time and/or in broader or more restricted sets of contexts.

Although some sociologists may be tempted to reduce complex sets of human association and interchanges to structures, factors, variables, and other forces, possibly arguing for the value of "big pictures" and the greater accessibility of certain kinds of statistical data, it is extremely important that sociologists develop highly sustained, close-up ethnographic examinations of all aspects of the political process. This latter undertaking will be more demanding, much slower, and more humbling (i.e., less immediate as well as less grandiose) but, until this is done, we will have little "political sociology" of a more authentic nature to offer colleagues or the public at large.

Even though *religion and morality* are extensively interfused with the political processes just discussed, these fields of activity also represent an array of life-worlds that are separated in other ways from people's participation in civil relations and the more central governing arrangements of the community.

The sociological focus is not on the ultimate truth of any specific religion, ideology, or other set of beliefs but instead envisions each of these contexts as a field for the more sustained study of human knowing and acting. Whether sociologists "believe that the gods exist or not" (also see Cicero) or place their personal faith in certain ideological standpoints is not what is important to the development of a genuine public sociology. What is important is that sociologists examine the ways that people engage instances of religion and/or secular ideology relative to their broader notions of human knowing and acting in situated, historical, and comparative analytic terms (see Durkheim, 1912).

Moreover, once it is recognized that secular morality is both an extension of, and a functional alternative to, religion as a generalized representation of society (Durkheim, 1912), both religion and secular morality become amenable to study as a humanly engaged process. By approaching people's involvements in religion, secular ideology, or other belief systems as subcultural life-worlds, we can examine the ways that particular versions of reality are developed, promoted, maintained, extended, become fragmented, dissipate, become reconstituted, and so forth within this or that community context. Likewise, we can consider the nature of people's involvements in particular religions or other belief systems as well as the ways that the people involved in these life-worlds deal with outsiders of various sorts.

Attending to reference points of more distinctively religious sorts as well as the other sets of moral frames that people may invoke in defining and judging the acceptability or disrespectability of the viewpoints, activities, appearances, possessions, and associates of others as well as themselves, the concepts of *deviance and regulation* (see Blumer, 1971; Prus and Grills, 2003) also merit extended attention in the viable public sociology.

Thus, while adopting the viewpoint that nothing is inherently deviant in itself, but that all definitions of deviance reflect the perspectives of the audiences involved, it is most important that sociologists attend to the humanly achieved "realism of deviance."

Insofar as people define things as troublesome, immoral, disreputable, evil, and the like, deviance has a reality. Even though people in various communities may differ in their notions of what is and is not deviant and, likewise, may change their views on these matters over time, as well as disagree among themselves about the definitions of deviance and deviants at particular times, this does not eliminate deviance as a consequential social phenomenon. Moreover, as long as people act towards others whom they define as deviant in more particularized manners (as in avoidance, exclusion, or other selective modes of informal and formal interchange) they further affirm the realism of deviance.

As well, although some sociologists may be inclined to be highly critical of those who assume regulatory roles in dealing with deviance, it is most important to consider the ways in which people (as both insiders and outsiders to particular subcultural life-worlds) become involved in attempts to establish and maintain the moral order of the community.

Relatedly, as with people's involvements in other fields of activity, it seems most instructive to examine people's regulatory practices (including the control endeavors of external critics and activists!) within the context of subcultural life-worlds and people's participation therein.[4] Indeed, once regulators as well as those involved in particular deviance-making ventures are approached mindfully of their participation in subcultural life-worlds, the parallels across these two seemingly opposed realms of activity become strikingly evident (Prus and Grills, 2003).

Because the matters of defining, participating in, and regulating deviance are relevant to all known communities (ergo have a transcontextual as well as a transhistorical presence) those who pursue a public sociology have an obligation to examine the various life-worlds and processes associated with deviance and control in careful, sustained, nonpartisan ways.

Like morality and deviance, the matters of education, philosophy, and science also have great importance for comprehending community life. Although sociologists often define *education* in more formal, conceptually restricted terms, it is important to recognize that the teaching, learning, and resistance processes associated with classroom contexts are much more encompassing, generic phenomena than commonly supposed and have great relevance across the broader realms of community life as well as throughout people's entire lifetimes.

Moreover, even classroom contexts denote extended sets of activities and wide ranges of social processes. As well, although attention typically is focused on instructors and students, a broader array of others (student associates, administrators, parents, religious leaders, secular moralists, and politicians) commonly assume significant roles as tacticians and targets with respect to the others in the educational arena.

Further, once one recognizes that all instances of formal education typically represent a series of fields of activity as opposed to settings in which "knowledge is poured into mindless receptacles," the follies of trying to reduce the educational experience to sets of structures, factors, and the like become more apparent. Like the realms of morality and deviance, the field of education offers a great many departure points for more sustained instances of ethnographic and historical inquiry into the ways that consequential aspects of human group life are accomplished (also see Durkheim, 1902-1903, 1904-1905).

Denoting more extended features of the broader educational process (especially religion, Durkheim, 1912), philosophy and science also become demystified when approached as sites of subcultural life-worlds. Here, as in the other areas of community life, it is by examining the historical developmental flows as well as the more immediate emergent, situationally enacted instances of human knowing and acting of those involved in philosophy and science that sociologists may be able to better comprehend and articulate the processes by which instances of knowing are accomplished in these more focused contexts. Moreover, because philosophy and science, as realms of knowing, exploration, discovery, analysis, and conceptual development are so fundamental to community life, more systematic ethnographic and historical examinations of these realms of knowing and acting represent yet other ways that sociologists can contribute substantially to a more consequential public sociology.

In all of these areas, it is important that sociologists examine instances of the emergent, problematic nature of the world that humans experience and attempt to see how people manage ambiguity, exercise intentionality, and make adjustments in all manners of contexts. If sociologists are to generate information of more enduringly valuable sorts, it will not be through advice, admonishments, or activism. It will be by developing concepts, research, and analyses that are thoroughly attentive to the ways that people encounter, enter into, and engage these aspects of community life.

Intersubjectively accomplished

> Every word, every sentence, every gesture or politeness, every work of art, and every historical action are only comprehensible because of a community that binds the expresser with the interpreter; every person lives, thinks, and acts constantly in a sphere of community and only in such a sphere does he understand. (Dilthey, in Ermarth, 1978: 278)

Addressing the matter of meaning in a most comprehensive sense, the preceding quotation from Wilhelm Dilthey focuses attention on the fundamentally enabling features of language for all that is humanly known. Still, more than just sets of sounds or signifiers and their referents, words achieve their relevance, potency, or realism because of their collectively shared, multiplistically experienced, and humanly enacted qualities.

In learning and using words, thus, people not only "become one with the linguistic community of the other," but they also "become one with the community of the other in behavioral, emotional, and contextual terms." Moreover, whereas words and the concepts embedded in words enable people to think, plan, implement, assess, and adjust their activities mindfully of the situations they encounter, the learning of words also requires that people adopt the viewpoints and behavioral inclinations of the community-based other (Mead, 1934).

The words that people use enable them to deal with all sorts of immediately situated circumstances. However, words are not merely situated phenomena. Thus, as Durkheim (1912) emphasizes, when people use words in meaningful ways they not only invoke the intellectual heritage of the past through the collective memories that are embedded in language, but they also access some of the vast array of resources (conceptual, behavioral, emotional, and contextual) that these words have come to imply. Although they typically engage these matters in unwitting or taken for granted fashions, it is in using language that people invoke and employ the greatest of all human technologies.[5]

Further, as Mead (1934) suggests, there is a particularly consequential metamorphosis or transformation in species that occurs with the acquisition of language, wherein people (Shibutani, 1955) become "societies in miniature." Thus, even though these transformations may be notably partial at the outset, as well as highly uneven in their subsequent realizations, it is through this "pragmatizing process"—in acquiring language and actively participating in human group life—that people become "one with the community."

However, it is only in achieving a oneness with the community (by attending to the conceptual, emotional, behavioral, and contextual whatness of the other) that people are able to act in intentioned, meaningful terms. Further, it is this process of achieving intersubjectivity with, and fitting into the life-world activities of, the other (not some abstracted sets of factors or structures) that makes community life possible.

It also is in acquiring intersubjectivity with the community-based other and by participating in the pragmatizing process implied therein that people develop (a) capacities for reflective thought, (b) a sense of purposive, deliberative agency, and (c) an awareness of the prospects, processes, and problematics of coordinated behavior. It is only as people engage in "joint activity" (Blumer, 1969) or knowingly fit their lines of activity together into those of their associates, that they achieve a more complete sense of oneness with the community of the other.

As well, because each of the multiple life-worlds that constitute community life assumes a somewhat particularized version of the broader reality of the community, it also is to be appreciated that the (intersubjectively-enabled) pragmatizing process is a highly pervasive, ongoing phenomenon with which people deal as they move from one community context to another; engage multiple subcultural life-worlds on a more or less simultaneous basis; or even attempt to come to terms with the ongoing, emergent features of a single subcultural setting.

If sociologists are to develop a more genuine public sociology, it will be necessary to embark on closer, highly sustained examinations of the intersubjectively-enabled pragmatizing processes that people experience as they move from one setting to the next and develop their activities in conjunction with others in each theater of operation. Further, whereas it is words that allow species humans to share meanings with one another, to access various stocks of knowledge built up by their predecessors and engage in wide ranges of meaningful instances of coordinated activity, it is also the words shared in common that provide the basis of memory (discussed later)—without which meaningful human behavior would not exist.

Relationally engaged

> Social psychology studies the activity or behavior of the individual as it lies within the social process; the behavior of an individual can be understood only in terms of the behavior of the whole social group of which he is a member, since his individual acts are involved in larger, social acts which go beyond himself and which implicate the other members of that group.
> We are not, in social psychology, building up the behavior of the social group in terms of the behavior of the separate individuals composing it; rather, we are starting out with a given social whole of complex group behavior, into which we analyze (as elements) the behavior of each of the separate individuals composing it. We attempt, that is, to explain the conduct of the individual in terms of the organized conduct of the social group, rather than to account for the organized conduct of the social group in terms of the individuals belonging to it. (Mead, 1934: 6-7)

Whereas the concept of intersubjectivity is of the greatest importance for comprehending the relationship of the individual to the group, it also is essential that a public sociology attend to the interpersonal relations that people develop with one another. Those focusing on structures, variables, factors, and the like may disregard or minimize the importance of people's interpersonal relationships in their analyses, but this most certainly is not the case for members of the community at large. Indeed, people often place great emphasis on kinship, friendship, love, and animosity as well as on the particular activities, commitments, senses of self, and modes of emotionality associated with these realms of interchange.

Further, even though a great many instances of meaning and purpose revolve around the particular objectives, activities, concepts, and roles that people develop in organizational contexts of various sorts, some of the most intense and sustained senses of meaning and purpose emerge within the interpersonal relationships that people develop in more formal as well as more casual settings.

A sociology that disregards people's interpersonal relationships, the processes these signify, and people's fuller senses of participation within will lack potency as well as relevance and authenticity. Consequently, if it is to be even minimally adequate, a public sociology must be directly and openly mindful of the relationships that people develop and the associated identities and senses of self that people experience on an interpersonal level.

Whereas people's relationships with specific others may vary greatly in duration, intensity, and importance, it is within these relational contexts that people experience love and other affection, dedication, intrigue, and loyalty as well as animosity and other disaffection, jealousy, fear, disputation, and the like.

It is here, amidst the interchanges of human group life, that people experience more distinctive and rigid as well as more ambiguous, multiple, and shifting senses of self and the other along with the challenges of acceptably managing a fuller range of emotions within emergent mixes of expectations, proscriptions, purposes, desires, successes and satisfactions, and failures and frustrations. Likewise, even as they develop some senses of self as objects in the world of the other, people are apt to encounter broad arrays of influence work and resistances as they engage the various relationships in which they find themselves.

When viewed thusly, it becomes apparent that all of people's interpersonal relationships may be seen as instances of subcultures within the broader community. As somewhat unique sets of life-worlds unto themselves, people's interpersonal relations also can be examined mindfully of the perspectives, identities, activities, commitments, emotions, linguistic fluencies, collective events, and so forth.

Thus, rather than requiring a special methodology and theory for interpersonal relations, researchers and analysts can study people's relationships ethnographically and build on (as well as assess and extend) the same sets of social processes (i.e., concepts) that they might use in comprehending other realms of community life.

Activity minded

> The essence of society lies in an ongoing process of action – not in the posited structure of relations. Without action, any structure of relations between people is meaningless. To be understood, a society must be seen and grasped in terms of the action that comprises it. (Blumer, 1966: 541)

When I say that the preceding canons not only are of limited consequence for understanding the human community without activity but also
that *the study of activity is the key to comprehending community life*, some
may wonder why I have left a more focused consideration of activity to
this later point in the chapter. Moreover, even though activity has been a
conceptual companion to all of the preceding discussions, my reasoning
is this: It is essential that we envision human activity as something much
more multifaceted, involved, and consequential than mere instances of
motion in process or something that emerges as a behavioral byproduct
of social structure or other "factors."

Ironically, although it is activity (e.g., Durkheim, 1912; Blumer,
1969) that gives life to all matters of social organization, activity has
been almost completely disregarded as a consequential feature of community life in mainstream sociology. As with intersubjectivity and
interpersonal relationships, mainstream sociology (following Marx and
Weber; and the earlier Durkheim, 1893, 1895, 1897) with its emphasis
on structures, factors, and variables also has failed to address activity
as a socially accomplished phenomenon. It is because of this neglect of
activity as well that sociologists generally have done such an inadequate
job of establishing more direct, humanly engaged linkages between the
concepts that they present as structures and outcomes (also independent
and dependent variables).

Indeed, there has been a persistent failure across the social sciences to
recognize that human activity is a social process of the first order. Human
activity is not the mere behavioral manifestation of people's physiological
capacities or their cognitions, tendencies, beliefs, attitudes, perspectives,
or definitions of situation. Nor does human behavior represent the ex-
truded products of the organizational machinery that is often referenced
as "social structure."

Activity, as Blumer (1969) stresses, is a formulative process in its
own right (also see Durkheim, 1912) and needs to be studied as such.
All instances of meaningful human activity are to be understood as
"something in the making," and even simple instances of meaningful
activity are possible only because of people's participation in a pragmatizing process wherein newcomers to the group become one with
the community-based other. Not only is this linguistically-enabled
participatory process pertinent to all overt instances of meaningful
behavior, but it also is basic to all matters of knowing as well as the
capacity for selective, deliberative agency assumed within the context
of meaningful behavior.

Whereas human behavior often seems to defy a sociological base because people do so many things on their own and often in ways that seem comparatively unique, it should be acknowledged that individual behavior only makes sense through the concepts that people acquire from the broader community.

Further, even though a great deal of activity is embedded within and often seems demanded by particular organizational units, these latter instances of activity—as with all instances of meaningful solitary behavior—are to be understood not only relative to people's capacities to assume roles as agents but also in terms of people's reliance on group-based memory.

By agents, I am not simply referring to something that in some way might impact on something else, but to people entering into the causal process as knowing, reflective, purposive, adjustive essences. Indeed, not only can people take other people (both generally and particularly) as well as themselves (as objects unto the themselves) into account when formulating, assessing, and adjusting their activities (Mead, 1934) but, as Mead (1932, "The Physical Thing") further indicates, people also develop abilities to take the role (attend to the potential capacities and resistances) of wide ranges of nonhuman (animate and inanimate) objects that they may act toward in some way.

As well, although people need not be accurate in the attributions or inferences they make about things, they nevertheless can make assessments of and adjustments to their activities even as they are in the process of developing (and entering into) the specific instances of processes that the pursuit of particular purposes or ends might entail.

Still, as noted earlier, meaningful human activity cannot be understood apart from group-based memory. Because all knowing presumes reference points of some sort, there can be no meaningful activity without an accompanying conceptual sense of whatness (also see Durkheim, 1912). Moreover, it is not just the capacity to retain concepts and other information about things through associations of sounds, images, motions, and other sensations that defines human memory. As Aristotle (*On Memory*) observes, human memory also is rather uniquely enabled by the capacity for deliberate recollection—by people's abilities to intentionally recall particular instances of information (as in images, sensations, concepts, objects, events) that they earlier had experienced and to draw inferences (through comparisons of recollected information and the situation at hand) about the ways that they might deal with the particular matters under consideration.

However, rather than denoting the spontaneous ability of the human species, remembering both in general, knowledgeable and specifically focused, recollectable terms is contingent on linguistically-enabled people accessing the concepts and categories of the human group. Indeed, until individual humans acquire intersubjectivity, or become one with the community-based other, there would be nothing of a meaningful sort to be remembered in either general or intentioned ways.

Although it may seem odd to emphasize the sociological rather than the physiological or psychological qualities of human memory, it is to be appreciated that (a) the meaningful contents of specific memories, (b) the ways that memories are meaningfully coded, and (c) the relevance of particular memories all are steeped in community conceptions of whatness. By approaching memory as a social process and by ethnographically studying memory within the context of people's (conceptually informed) lived experiences, sociologists can contribute notably to understanding human memory.

Without delving further into the parameters of human knowing and acting, enough may have been said to make it apparent that a public sociology that respects the nature of human group life should be prepared to focus on activity in highly central and sustained terms. Still, to contribute more viably to a genuine public sociology, it will be necessary to examine instances of activity in the making in highly sustained detail; to take instances of activity apart, piece by piece; and then employ comparative analysis to see more precisely how people, as agents, causally (purposively) enter into the processual flows of human group life.

This means examining matters such as (a) people's definitions of the situation and associated ambiguities and dilemmas; (b) the roles that people's associates assume in focusing, sustaining, coordinating assessing, adjusting particular instances of activity; (c) the ways that people perform instances of activity (and deal with resistances) on a solitary basis as well as engage in all manners of coordinated activity and participate in a wide range of collective events; (d) the ways that people engage (enter into, adjust, sustain, extend, promote, challenge, reject, and resurrect) organizational features of human community life; (e) manage information (concealing and revealing) pertaining to self, others, and the broader organizational units in which they participate (see Goffman, 1959; 1961); and (f) embark on instances of influence and resistance across the full range of humanly engaged theaters (Prus, 1999) as well as attend to (g) memory as a socially engaged process.

Still, as the following discussion of technology indicates, activity as a social process is yet more multifaceted.

Technologically enabled

Now, isn't it of the greatest importance that warfare be practiced well? And is fighting a war so easy that a farmer or a cobbler or any other craftsman can be a soldier at the same time? Though no one can become so much as a good player of checkers or dice if he considers it only as a sideline and doesn't practice it from childhood. Or can someone pick up a shield or any other weapon or tool of war and immediately perform adequately in an infantry battle or any other kind? No other tool makes anyone who picks it up a craftsman or champion unless he has acquired the requisite knowledge and has had sufficient practice.

If tools could make anyone who picked them up an expert, they'd be valuable indeed. (Plato, *Republic*: 374c-e [Reeve translation])

If a public sociology is to be viable, it also must be attentive to the technologically enabled nature of human group life. It is not enough to say that people act mindfully of a socially constructed world of objects or that "people are toolmakers." It will be necessary not only to indicate the ways that people engage objects of all sorts as they go about their activities but also to consider the ways that people develop and utilize enabling devices as a more particular subset of objects (i.e., anything to which people may refer).

This latter emphasis requires an examination of the ways in which people experience, conceptualize, produce, test out, distribute, access, utilize, adjust, reconfigure, extend, and reject instances of technology, rather than restrict images of technology to those material items that seem more complex, ingenious, or scientistic in some way. Once one envisions technology as more fundamentally consisting of enabling devices, it becomes apparent that the humanly known and enacted world is a world of technologically-enabled adjustments.

Furthermore, since instances of technology, no matter how sophisticated or rudimentary these may seem, would have no value except in relation to particular purposes, applications, interconnected objects, procedures, and user competencies, it is most instructive to consider the ways that people both fit technology into aspects of existing situations and how they modify aspects of the existing situations to incorporate instances of technology. Approached thusly, people's experiences with technology provide a highly consequential sociological window for studying aspects of change, continuity, ambiguity, and adjustment as these take place within the developmental flows of community life.

Because all instances of technology also are instances of objects, it is instructive to acknowledge at least briefly some ways that people might deal with objects. Since "objects" signify anything to which people may refer, indicate, designate, or otherwise act toward, a more substantial public sociology would direct extended attention to the matters of people delineating, naming, knowing, developing, using, making, changing, owning, trading, maintaining, retiring, resisting, disposing of, and salvaging objects. This would include animate and inanimate phenomena, concepts and connections, and enabling devices of all sorts. Because people live, act, and think in a world of objects, each of the preceding processes introduces a consequential set of departure points for inquiry into the ways that human group life is accomplished.

Still, it also is useful to distinguish (a) *objects* or the particular things that people might reference, (b) people's *knowledge about* or understandings of particular things, (c) the ways that people deal with other objects from, and (d) the ways that people *develop and use instances of enabling devices* in their concerns with accomplishing things in the world of objects.

It may be tempting to use the term technology to refer to the latest and most sophisticated instances of enabling devices currently available and/or more exclusively to material goods (e.g., physical items, electronic processing) but it also should be appreciated that contemporary instances of particular enabling devices would not exist were it not for both the most rudimentary and subsequent instances of associated technology that people had developed along the way. When viewed thusly, it also becomes evident that rather than a seemingly unlimited set of material items, technology much more fundamentally *is a socially engaged process.*

Moreover, when the "technology-making venture" is viewed as an adjustive, historically enabled social process it becomes apparent that the specific products (and the actual physical materials associated with those instances of technology) are among the least consequential aspects of the process. Despite the apparent marvels of the many unfolding instances of technology throughout recorded history, all "new" instances of technology are dependent on earlier modes of human knowing and acting. Quite directly, as the quotation from Plato suggests, technology is centrally contingent on the applications, contextual frames, and skills with which people engage those particular enabling devices.

Notably too, like other habits, practices, and dependencies that people develop in dealing with the situations in which they find themselves, instances of technology often represent more systematic or patterned ways in which people may engage their environments. For this reason, it is so important that a public sociology be highly mindful of the ways that people develop and use enabling devices, as well as people's tendencies to take wide ranges of earlier technologies for granted (and blend these into broader, background "object" contexts) over time as these particular matters become more thoroughly synthesized into the day to day practices of community life.

Although technology generally is intended to enhance activity, if not also to eliminate certain realms of activity, technology does not in any way diminish the relevance of activity for comprehending human group life. To the contrary, whereas (a) technology cannot be understood apart from activity, human activity is to be understood relative to (b) all of the objects to which people refer when defining, approaching, and adjusting to the situations at hand and (c) the ways that people build on, accommodate, and extend their notions of "whatness" (and the objects referenced within) through the development and use of enabling devices.

Memorably historical

> The younger generation of sociologists and psychologists explicitly claims that nothing important has been discovered in their fields during all the preceding centuries; that there were only some vague "arm-chair philosophies"; and that the real scientific era in these disciplines began only in the last two or three decades with the publication of their own researches and those of members of their clique. Claiming to be particularly objective, precise, and scientific, our sociological and psychological Columbuses tirelessly repeat this delusion as a scientific truth. Accordingly, they rarely make any references to the social and psychological thinkers of the past. When they do, they hardly veil the sense of their own superiority... As a result, the indexes of their books list none, or very few, of the thinkers of preceding centuries... (Sorokin, 1956: 3-4)

Like most other social scientists, sociologists have tended to focus on the present and generally have neglected memory as a consequential feature of community life. However, a public sociology will be most valuable when it is attentive to the contributions of "perspective" and "contextual substance" that earlier accounts of human group life have to offer. These can be invaluable both for better situating and comprehending the immediate present and for developing yet broader conceptual understandings of particular phenomena through comparative analysis.

Indeed, as Durkheim (1904-1905) so cogently stresses in *The Evolution of Educational Thought,* the present cannot be adequately understood as something unto itself but is best comprehended relative to that which preceded it. Moreover, Durkheim insists, it is not enough to develop comparisons with the events of the last few centuries (i.e., following the Renaissance, the Protestant Reformation, and the New World explorations of the sixteenth century and the scientistic emphasis of the seventeenth century). Thus, he observes that it is only by returning to the classical Greek roots of Western social thought that a great many conceptual and procedural aspects of the present can be more thoroughly comprehended.

Without a more complete sense of history, Durkheim emphasizes, people lack more viable understandings of the present, including a base for distinguishing between the superficial novelties and the more substantial changes of the present. Likewise, they are unable to benefit from either the wisdoms or the follies of the past.

Hence, instead of building on the more viable accomplishments of their predecessors, those who do not know much about the past not only may reinvent weaker variants of previous matters rather than benefiting from earlier intellectual achievements, but they also are apt to magnify the importance of their own productions. Unfortunately, as Durkheim observes, those who disregard the past also may unwittingly generate variants of some of the most unproductive failings of the past.

Still, if a public sociology is to be memorably historical, it is not just enough to attend to the scholarship of the past. It also will engage that which is memorable in reflective sociological terms. Thus, a more informed public sociology also would examine memory as a socially accomplished process.

This not only means attending to the social whatness (concepts and other content) of memory, but also to the ways that memories (as instances of humanly engaged phenomena) emerge, take shape, are sustained, embellished, challenged, contested, reformulated, neglected, and resurrected, as well as the ways that people "give memories" to their associates and themselves in the course of everyday life.

Moreover, whereas particular subject matters may become more notably entrenched or objectified in certain communities or sectors within, it is not enough to make vague claims about the structural or institutionalized nature of human memories. Instead, it is essential that those concerned about developing a more viable public sociology attend to the nature of human memory in much more comprehensive enacted terms.

At one level, it is necessary, as Durkheim (1912) stresses, that scholars of the human condition attend to the historically-enabled accumulations of all modes of memory in the broadest cultural sense. Thus, he encourages sociologists to consider the temporal linkages and developmental flows of all manners of practices, language, tradition, organization, policies, technology, objects, and so forth—focusing as much as possible on the ways that people enter into these processes in both more immediate and temporally sustained ways (also see Durkheim, 1904-1905).

Amongst other things, this means attending to the careers or processual flows of particular ways of life, specific events, and people's involvements in particular situations. This also means pursuing pertinent connections or linkages as carefully as possible in historically and ethnographically informed terms. Relatedly, it implies attending to more particular instances of the transformation process, being mindful of the interfusions of change and continuity as people experience, define, and otherwise engage these matters within the context of ongoing community life.

Further, rather than view memory as a function of that which is intrinsically important it is essential, as Durkheim (1912) stresses, to recognize that virtually anything may become a prominent subject matter of memory. Moreover, whereas things achieve an importance because they are remembered, Durkheim also emphasizes the point that many things are remembered more specifically because they are thought to be enabling or desired in some way.

Accordingly, it is most desirable that those contributing to a more genuine public sociology examine the entire set of social processes that develop around instances of "memory in the making." Even though some memories become highly established, clearly assuming a prominent "object" status in the community, it is important to consider the ways that all sorts of things both do *and* do not become memories within the community.

Not only is remembering a collectively achieved realm of activity, but memory also represents an enabling device of paramount importance for comprehending ongoing community life. As a result, it is most instructive to ask when and how people attend to particular matters as well as emphasize or neglect specific things in actual instances. Thus, it is important to know when particular matters of reference are invoked, shared, instructed, learned, utilized, promoted, extended, dramatized, accepted, taken for granted, challenged, compromised, rejected, lost, and possibly resurrected.

Rather than focus on those matters that analysts might personally find more intriguing, morally disturbing, or otherwise emotionally engaging in some way, the goal is that of better comprehending all aspects of the memory-making process in more generic terms.

Enduringly humanist

(T)hey say that if a group of people should collect from all the nations of the world their disgraceful customs and then should call everyone together and tell each man to select what he thinks is seemly, everything would be taken away as belonging to the seemly things. (Dissoi Logi or Dialexeis, circa 400BCE; Sprague, 1972: 284)

If a public sociology is to be enduringly humanist, it will not be selectively inclusive or partially public. It will be pluralist, impersonal, and universal in its emphasis. Further, while attentive to wide ranges of situated instances and generic conceptualizations, it also will be a sociology that is multiplistic; one that is interested in all aspects of human knowing and acting; one that would be applicable to any and all realms of community life. It will be relevant to the entire range of human behavior and interchanges and will not be concerned with the matters of praise or condemnation except as realms of scholarly inquiry.

It is not to be a sociology that favors one morality over another, one sector of the community over another, or one society or era over another. Nor, will it assign equality to all groups, societies, peoples, moralities, and the like. It will not adopt yet another standpoint; suggest that everything is arbitrary; or, relatedly, as is sometimes done, contend that nothing has any truth value and/or that human group life is little more than an elaborate set of linguistic charades. Indeed, if a public sociology is to be more viable, more universal, judgments of all of these sorts are to be avoided. What is required is the more fundamental quest to examine and comprehend the enacted nature of human group life in all of its variants. The emphasis, thus, is on the ways in which people, in whatever settings they may be located, engage the world in knowing and acting terms.

Focusing on "what is," rather than what should be, an enduring humanism will place great stress on authenticity of representation and attend to human lived experience as people do things in instances. It will be openly attentive to the viewpoints of the participants in examining, analyzing, and representing the activities and viewpoints of the other. It will be intended to enable the understanding (and study) of community life, not to sensationalize, arouse, impress, entertain, or please audiences.

Likewise, if it is to have a more enduring value, a public sociology cannot be temporally encapsulated. It is to be fully transsituational (transcontextual and transhistorical). Although attentive to all sorts of human experiences, it is to be an approach that transcends the particular moralities, fads, fashions, temptations, excitements, disappointments, agonies, and losses of the ever-shifting present. As well, even though certain communities and contexts may be given more attention than others as a consequence of the available materials therein, each era and each setting within achieves a potential viability as a realm in which to learn more fully about the nature of human group life.

Still, something more is required. This pertains to the matter of *attending to socially encoded categorical subcultures*. Despite the awkward nature of this term, this topic merits explicit attention because of the notably dehumanizing quality of much structuralist sociological analysis. Thus, whereas sociologists commonly invoke constructs such as class, gender, race and ethnicity, and age as the determining features (also structures, forces, factors, variables) and explanations of various aspects of community life, these categories lack authenticity because they typically are used in ways that fail to acknowledge the fundamental humanly engaged features of community life.

Although (a) statistics using these categories can be of value for describing certain proportionate aspects of community life and (b) the sociological categories most commonly invoked as independent variables (class, gender, ethnicity, and age) point to important aspects of community life, (c) a humanist sociology would need to revise extensively the ways that categories of these sorts are comprehended, conceptualized, discussed, and studied within the sociological venture.

Sociology has tapped into some categories that have a notably pervasive relevance across a fuller range of communities, but the significance of these categories is substantially different than is commonly assumed in the sociological literature. The relevance of categories of these sorts does not reside in the categories as "forces in themselves" but is located much more centrally in the ways that people attend to these categories. It is the more particular qualities of human group life that people in various communities associate with these categories that gives vitality to these terms of reference. The reality of these categories most fundamentally resides in the enacted subcultural life-worlds that these categories (and divisions within) signify (Grills and Prus, 2006).

Even though these categories may have some physiological and/or material correlates (as with gender, age, class) it is the ways that people more selectively engage (envision and act toward) those encompassed by these categories as situated, living, acting, interacting participants of certain subcultural life-worlds that connotes the essential humanist quality of categories of these sorts.

Consequently, instead of dealing with these categories (of people) as factors or variables that somehow account for (also predict, control) particular outcomes, a humanist sociology would examine the ways that (a) people (both insiders and outsiders) delineate and assign qualities to particular sectors of the community and act toward those so designated (as well as those associated in some way with particular categories of people) and (b) the people in the subcultures signified by these categories acquire perspectives on aspects of the world, do activities, develop relationships, experience emotionality, achieve linguistic fluency, deal with outsiders, and so forth as active participants in these categorically delimited life-worlds.

When the categories of class, gender, race, age, and the like are reconceptualized thusly, the sociological venture almost at once becomes less mysterious, more authentic, and more attentive to the human community as a dynamic, multifaceted field of activity.

Relatedly, it becomes possible to examine more directly, comprehend, and articulate the linkages that people develop in both more situationally enacted and longer-term developmental flows of community life. It is humanism in both contextual and transhistorical terms.

Given the prominence of structuralist thought in our discipline and the broad ranges of commitments that sociologists have made to structuralist theories and variable analysis, there is apt to be considerable resistance to a more thorough humanist reconceptualization of these sociological constructs. Indeed, an emphasis of this sort strikes at the heart of some longstanding practices in the discipline. However, if we are to develop a public sociology that has an enduringly humanist quality it will be necessary to embark on an agenda along these lines.

Conclusion

The present statement has been developed around the question of, What might the conceptual parameters of a public sociology, one that focuses centrally *on the public* in broadly comprehensive and enduring terms, look like? And, relatedly, How might this sociological enterprise be pursued?

Reiterating the canons addressed herein, it was said that a public sociology not only is one in which (1) authenticity is emphasized, but also one that is (2) empirically grounded, and (3) conceptually articulated. Moreover, a scholarly public sociology must be (4) community-based and (thereby centrally) attentive to the (5) intersubjectively accomplished, (6) relationally engaged, (7) activity minded, and (8) technologically enabled nature of human group life. As well, a public sociology is to be (9) memorably historical and (10) enduringly humanist in its emphasis.

وِثّرِ كَى هاى كه اين از عُموِم انْظار دارِه

Interestingly, even though an early concern in developing this statement was to protect the integrity of the discipline from those who seemed
intent on using sociology as a mechanism for promoting moral agendas,
a set of other no less consequential emphases emerged as I grappled with
the canons of a public sociology. Thus, although insisting on the importance of maintaining the sociological mission as a scholarly endeavor
in its own right, this statement also has identified a number of ways in
which mainstream sociology is disconnected from the world of human
lived experience.

Mindful of these matters, one may ask, "What are the implications
of the canons introduced here for revitalizing the broader discipline of
sociology? How can sociology be made more relevant to the public and
become more authentic as a realm of scholarly endeavor?"

One major implication is that sociologists need to venture into the
humanly engaged world, not as activists, but as scholars who want to
learn more about the nature of community life by achieving intimate
familiarity with the things that people actually do. Sociologists need to
engage people in much more direct and concerted terms. They need to
spend time relating to people in all manners of contexts, watching how
they do things, and especially listening to them describe their viewpoints,
practices, and other experiences in extended detail. They also need to
keep records of these matters and subject these to sustained levels of
comparative analysis so that they can begin to take instances of the
activities that people do apart in process-related terms and, thus, follow
the connections that people (as minded agents and interactors) make as
they enter into the ongoing flows of human group life. It is on this basis
that sociologists may better understand the great many subcultural life-
worlds that constitute community life.

However, more is involved than accumulating hundreds of ethnographic accounts of people's life-worlds. These materials need to be
examined in conceptual terms. This will require comparing specific
studies of this and that aspect of community life with other ethnographic
inquiries mindfully of any associated process-related concepts that may
been developed to that point. It is here, through comparisons of instances
and the associated development, assessment, and refinement of concepts,
that we may learn more about the nature of human group and develop
more precise, informative materials that can be shared with others both
inside and outside the academic world.

Still, despite the essential base provided by ethnographic inquiry and
comparative analysis, something else is required for a more adequate

sociological enterprise. Whereas the existing stocks of ethnographic work can be highly instructive for acquiring a more general awareness of the nature of community life, developing analytic comparisons, and achieving conceptual refinements, Durkheim (1904-1905, 1912) is correct in emphasizing the importance of history (attending to both the broader historical flows and the materials developed by earlier scholars). This is essential for gaining a more comprehensive scholarly sense of perspective, a more general wisdom about human affairs, and a greater awareness of both the accomplishments and the follies of earlier scholarly ventures as well as learning about the appeals and vulnerabilities of intellectual endeavors in the shifting contexts of community life.

In addition to these historical advantages, a public sociology will be even more viable when scholars extend their analyses to include more sustained descriptive and analytic accounts of human group life from the past. Because of the exceptional value that numerous texts, from the classical Greek era (circa 700-300BCE) to the more recent past, offer for comparative analysis, a more viable public sociology is one that would have an explicit transhistorical quality.

Relatedly, if mainstream sociology is to become more relevant, more meaningful, more viable or, conversely, less nebulous, less speculative, and less pretentious, it will be necessary to replace an emphasis on structuralist analysis with an emphasis on human activity and interchange. It will be necessary to replace the reductionistic methodological emphasis on quantification, factors, and end products with the humanly engaged methodologies of ethnography, history, and process-related comparative analysis.

Although we may recognize the scientific attitude and associated concerns with rigor, impartial inquiry, assessment, and conceptual analysis that characterizes much mainstream (positivist) sociology, along with the general sociological insistence that people's circumstances cannot be understood except in reference to the broader communities in which they are located, the key will be whether mainstream sociology can connect empirically and conceptually with people as living, breathing, acting, and interacting beings who constitute and generate community life. If mainstream sociology cannot do that; if sociologists generally treat people as marginal to the discipline and continue to stress factors, variables, structures, and other impersonal forces as the central features of human group life; mainstream sociology may remain "scientistic" but it also will remain inauthentic and disconnected with the human subject matter of community life.

However, the challenges facing the discipline are not purely intellectual matters. A public sociology of the sort addressed here will encounter substantial realms of resistance of both more situated and developmental sorts. That is, despite a general recognition of the importance of more directly attending to our human subject matter on the part of a great many scholars in the field, intellectual wisdom often gives way to other concerns and resistances.

To put some of these matters briefly in perspective, it might be first observed that most sociologists have not been trained in pragmatist social thought, ethnographic methods, historical research, or analytic induction (as situated, concept-oriented comparative analysis). Like people more generally, sociologists also tend to do things in more familiar ways. Some also will look at the commitments they have made to earlier programs of study and feel that these investments owe them something.

Still others, who think of the human sciences only in ways that parallel the more overt practices of the physical sciences, will not acknowledge limitations of the sort referenced herein and are apt to define the canons outlined here as threats to their current states of scholarship, prestige, and persona. Further, in examining the literature and observing their more immediate associates at work, these people and others will see that many sociologists are deeply entrenched in structuralist/positivist productions and may take solace in these reference points.

As well, there are others who will more privately acknowledge the canons addressed in this paper but fear that, if they fail to stay close to prevailing practices, they may lose opportunities to graduate, publish in the major journals, secure desired academic positions, obtain research grants, achieve scholarly prestige, and such.

Another set of resistances to a public sociology of the sort outlined here comes from administrators in government, public agencies, business arenas, and other sectors of the community. Attending to organizational demands for immediate information, (superficial) program assessments, and other modes of accountability as well as longstanding promises made by those promoting positivist sociology that they can predict and control aspects of community life, these bureaucrats may seek "quick fixes" to their organizational challenges by investing in positivist research. When money is on the table, there appears to be no shortage of sociologists who are willing to help them perpetuate these hopes and images.

Somewhat parallel emphases may be seen in community colleges, as well as in some university programs, wherein an emphasis on "social engineering" and associated "practical applications" far outstrips concerns with theory and research, especially of more sustained, comprehensive, comparative, patient, and demanding types.

Although universities may be seen as havens for the pursuit of intellectual emphases of the sort addressed in this paper, it may be observed that a great many universities also contribute to the positivist emphasis (and *mythos*) in the social sciences. In their quests to have their institutions grow and become more important features of community life under their leadership, as well as support various educational programs, administrators often place considerable value on the grants that academics bring into the university. Because universities typically assume percentages of research funds, "big grant" researchers may be seen as particularly valuable commodities.

Policies vary across universities, but the emphasis on large grants frequently assumes more localized (departmental) dimensions and may directly affect hiring decisions as well as impact on people's subsequent careers in the university setting. Whereas those involved in ethnography, historical research, and theoretical analysis seldom require substantial outside funding for their work, the pressures to pursue larger research grants (and associated positivist research) can be considerable even when scholars know that the projects being developed are likely to be of marginal value at best. As well, insofar as departments become more extensively populated with people assuming positivist mentalities on the one hand, and/or moralist and activist standpoints on the other, there may be very little localized tolerance for a sociology that attends to the study of human knowing and acting on a more sustained basis.[6]

One more consequential source of resistance to a viable public sociology pertains to the prevailing practices in the social sciences more generally. Thus, although I may seem severe in assessing the limitations of mainstream sociology, there is no justification for smugness on the part of the other disciplines in the social sciences or those adjunct departments and programs that build so centrally on sociology and psychology (also see Sorokin, 1956). Indeed, although some other disciplines and programs may be less distracted by moralist issues than is sociology, most also are much more exclusively mired in positivist methodologies than is sociology. With its heavy emphases on reductionism and individualism, psychology may be particularly culpable in that regard, but, clearly, the problem of disregarding the study of human knowing and acting is much more extensive than implied in sociology alone. Indeed, despite the centrality of activity for all realms of community life, activity as a mindfully engaged social process has been given very little direct attention in the social sciences.

With these emphases and resistances in mind, one might ask, "What is the future of a public sociology of the sort proposed here? Can it be accomplished in the situated instances in which research and analysis takes place? Can it survive and become more consequential within the developmental flows of contemporary scholarship?"

Although dependent on the general sincerity and courage of social scientists and their more explicit dedication to "the public," along with the receptivity of the general public to longer term scholarship, one of the most important elements fostering continuity revolves around the opportunities that like-minded scholars have to pursue these ventures in more sustained, interactive contexts—within departments and universities more broadly, through conferences and professional associations, through journals and other publications, and through more sustained scholarly contact with the public. Still, if history is an indication (Durkheim, 1904-1905), the optimism that one might associate with the future of any specific scholarly venture, including a broad, enduring public sociology of the type outlined here, is best viewed as tentative. It is for this reason that we need to develop as many conceptual life-lines as possible so that we might better enable scholars who are pursuing the study of human lived experience to reach across the boundaries of place and context as well as the corridors of time. Because the study of knowing and acting is so consequential for comprehending all matters human, we need to preserve a stronger pluralist, encompassing, and enduring vision of the public and the things that people actually do—not just for ourselves or present day scholarship more generally but for those who follow.

Notes

1.   I would like to thank Michael Burawoy, Ines Fritz, Lorraine Prus, Tony Puddephatt, and Silvia Stekar along with Larry Nichols (editor of *TAS*) for their thoughtful commentaries on earlier drafts of this paper.

2.   Although it is not possible to address the central features of symbolic interactionism (especially the much overlooked ethnographic research tradition and subsequent conceptual developments) in fuller terms at this time, readers may find the following list of premises useful in developing a more holistic image of the emphasis of this approach to the study of community life: Human group life is (1) *intersubjective* (human knowing is fundamentally conceptual in essence and is contingent on community-based linguistic interchange); (2) *knowingly problematic* (with respect to "the known" and "the unknown;" as in distinguishing between things that are humanly delineated, named, defined, tested, and objectified versus matters considered ambiguous, unexperienced, hidden, and inaccessible); (3) *object-oriented* (wherein humanly referenced things constitute the contextual

and operational essence of community life); (4) multiperspectival (as in variable viewpoints, conceptual frameworks, or notions of reality); (5) *reflective* (minded, interpretive, purposive, deliberative); (6) *sensory-embodied* (acknowledging human capacities for stimulation and motion, as well as the practical enacted, material capacities, limitations, and fragilities of human essences); (7) *activity-based* (as implied in people meaningfully doing things, assuming agency, engaging objects of their awareness); (8) *negotiable* (whereby people may anticipate, influence, cooperate with, resist, and adjust to others); (9) *relational* (denoting particular associations, affiliations, identities, commitments, expectations, and affinities); and (10) *processual* (signifying emergent, ongoing, or temporally developed) flows. For more extended considerations of these premises and their relevance for the study of human group life, see Blumer (1969), Strauss (1993), Prus (1996, 1997, 1999), and Prus and Grills (2003). Still, as indicated elsewhere (Prus, 2003, 2004) somewhat parallel pragmatist notions can be located in the classical Greek tradition (especially Aristotle's consideration of the human condition in *Nicomachean Ethics*, *Politics*, *Rhetoric*, and *Poetics*). Likewise, those who know Durkheim's *The Elementary Forms of the Religious Life* will find much in Durkheim's "sociological pragmatism" that resonates with the premises addressed here. Those working in the phenomenological tradition of Alfred Schutz (1962, 1964) and its constructionist (Berger and Luckmann, 1966) and ethnomethodological (Garfinkel, 1967) offshoots also will find much in the premises listed here that corresponds with their approaches to the study of human group life.

3. Grills and Prus (2006) provide a fuller statement on the problematic/mythical status of the independent variable.

4. If we may judge from Plato's *Laws*, the concern about "regulating the regulators" clearly is not a novel emphasis in Western social thought.

5. This point is expressed particularly cogently by Thomas Hobbes, chapter IV:

> The invention of printing, though ingenious, compared with the invention of letters is no great matter . . . A profitable invention for the continuing the memory of time past . . . But the most noble and profitable invention of all other was that of SPEECH, consisting of names or appellations, and their connexion, whereby men register their thoughts, recall them when they are past, and also declare them one to another for mutual utility and conversation, without which there had been amongst men, neither commonwealth, nor society, nor contract, nor peace, no more than amongst lions, bears and wolves. (Hobbes, 1668; in *Leviathan*, Curley, 1994: 15-16)

6. Although written with other objectives in mind, readers also may appreciate discussions of the cross-pressures (notably including positivist emphases and moralist/reform agendas) characterizing the discipline in the works of Sorokin (1956) and Horowitz (1993).

References

Aristotle (384-322 B.C.E.). *The Complete Works of Aristotle*. Jonathan Barnes (ed.). Princeton, NJ: Princeton University Press (1995).

Berger, Peter and Thomas Luckmann. 1966. *The Social Construction of Reality*. New York: Doubleday-Anchor.

Blumer, Herbert. 1928. "Method in Social Psychology." Doctoral Dissertation. University of Chicago.

_____. 1969. *Symbolic Interaction*. Englewood Cliffs, NJ: Prentice-Hall.

_____. 1971. "Social Problems as Collective Behavior." *Social Problems* 18: 298-306.

Boyns, David and Jesse Fletcher. 2005. "Reflections on Public Sociology: Public Relations, Disciplinary Identity, and the Strong Program in Professional Sociology." *The American Sociologist* 36 (3-4): 5-26.

Burawoy, Michael. 2005a. "2004 Presidential Address: For Public Sociology." *American Sociological Review* 70 (1): 4-28.

_____. 2005b. "Third Wave Sociology and the End of Pure Science." *The American Sociologist* 36 (3-4): 152-165.

Cicero, Marcus Tullius. (106-43 B.C.E.). *De Natura Deorum* [On the Nature of the Gods]. Trans by H. Rackham. Cambridge, MA: Harvard University Press (1951).

Durkheim, Emile. 1893. *The Division of Labor in Society.* Trans. by George Simpson. New York: Free Press (1947).

_____. 1895. *The Rules of the Sociological Method.* Trans. S.A. Solvay and E.G. Catlin. New York: Free Press (1958).

_____. 1897. *Suicide.* Trans. by J.A. Spaulding and G. Simpson. New York: Free Press (1951).

_____. 1902-1903. *Moral Education.* Trans. by Everett K Wilson and Herman Schnurer. New York: Free Press (1961).

_____. 1904-1905. *The Evolution of Educational Thought in France.* Trans. by Peter Collins. London: Routledge & Kegan Paul (1977).

_____. 1912. *The Elementary Forms of the Religious Life.* Trans. by Joseph Ward Swain. London: Allen and Unwin (1915).

_____. 1913-1914. *Pragmatism and Sociology.* Trans. by J. C. Whitehouse. New York: Cambridge University Press (1983).

Garfinkel, Harold. 1967. *Studies in Ethnomethodology.* Englewood Cliffs, NJ: Prentice-Hall.

Goffman, Erving. 1959. *The Presentation of Self in Everyday Life.* New York: Anchor.

_____. 1961. *Asylums.* New York: Anchor.

Grills, Scott and Robert Prus. 2006. "The Myth of the Independent Variable: Reconceptualizing Class, Gender, Race, and Age as Subcultural Processes." Paper presented at Symbolic Interaction and Ethnographic Research Conference. Niagara Falls, Ontario, May 16-18.

Horowitz, Irving Louis. 1993. *The Decomposition of Sociology.* New York: Oxford University Press.

McLaughlin, Neil, Lisa Kowalchuk, and Kerry Turcotte. 2005. "Why Sociology Does Not Need to be Saved." *The American Sociologist* 36 (3-4): 133-151.

Mead, George H. 1932. *The Philosophy of the Present.* Arthur E. Murphy (ed). Amherst, NY: Prometheus (2002).

_____. 1934. *Mind, Self and Society.* Charles W. Morris (ed.). Chicago: University of Chicago Press.

Plato (427-347 B.C.E.). *Plato: The Collected Works.* John M. Cooper (ed.). Indianapolis: Hackett (1997).

Prus, Robert. 1996. *Symbolic Interaction and Ethnographic Research.* Albany: State University of New York Press.

_____. 1997. *Subcultural Mosaics and Intersubjective Realities.* Albany: State University of New York Press.

_____. 1999. *Beyond the Power Mystique.* Albany: State University of New York Press.

_____. 2003. "Ancient Precursors." Pp. 19-38 in Larry T. Reynolds and Nancy J. Herman-Kinney (eds.), *Handbook of Symbolic Interactionism.* Walnut Creek, CA: Altamira.

_____. 2004. "Symbolic Interaction and Classical Greek Scholarship: Conceptual Foundations, Historical Continuities, and Transcontextual Relevancies." *The American Sociologist* 35 (1): 5-33.

Prus, Robert and Scott Grills. 2003. *The Deviant Mystique: Involvements, Realities, and Regulation*. Westport, CN: Praeger.

Schutz, Alfred. 1962. *Collected Papers I: The Problem of Social Reality*. Hague: Martinus Nijhoff.

_____. 1964. *Collected Papers II: Studies in Social Theory*. The Hague: Martinus Nijhoff.

Shibutani, Tamotsu.

_____. 1955. "Reference groups as Perspectives." *American Journal of Sociology* 60: 562-569.

Sorokin, Pitirim. 1956. *Fads and Foibles in Modern Sociology and Related Sciences*. Chicago: Henry Regnery.

Sprague, Rosamond Kent. 1972. *The Older Sophists*. Columbia, SC: University of South Carolina Press.

Strauss, Anselm. 1993. *Continual Permutations of Action*. Hawthorne, NY: Aldine de Gruyter.

Waller, Willard Walter. 1932. *The Sociology of Teaching*. New York: Russell (1961).

Weber, Max. 1958. "Science as a Vocation." (1918) in *Max Weber: Essays in Sociology*. Trans. by H. H. Gerth and C. Wright Mills. New York: Oxford University Press.

10

Guide for the Perplexed:
On Michael Burawoy's "Public Sociology"[1]

Steven Brint

If you scratch the surface of a sociologist, you are likely to find a person who was initially attracted to the field either by its unconventional way of looking at the social world, or by the criticisms it offered of existing social relations. Most of us had (and many still have) a strong desire to "change the world"—to help it become more just, more equal, more accepting, more aware.

Add to this another factor. Much of our work as sociologists is directly relevant to public issues. We study race and immigration, religion and politics, environmental changes due to urban growth, educational success and failure, global inequalities. We know things that decision-makers should know: that bilingual students often do better in school than monolingual students, because they have wider networks (Rumberger and Larson, 1998); that religious politics is a form of status group assertion more common among uprooted peoples (Evans, 1996); that secrets in organizations can be corrosive and lead to disaster (Vaughan, 1996); that the interests of corporations lie behind the crisis in personal finances (Sullivan, Warren, and Westbrook, 2000). Our research touches directly on public issues—if only decision-makers would listen!

Add to this a third factor. Many people of progressive convictions understandably feel the need to fight back on behalf of the poor and dispossessed at a time when the rightward drift of the country has been apparent for a quarter century—and the right seems to be ever-better organized. The situation of the poor is often desperate and has not been improving, either globally or nationally. If we needed any additional proof, the suffering following the recent devastation of New Orleans and other Gulf Coast cities shows us clearly how many people have been left behind in our own prosperous country, and how little the government seems to care about these people. If we do not respond now, when will we?

In view of all this, it is not surprising that Michael Burawoy's call for "public sociology" has found a receptive audience in the discipline. Since his electrifying presidential address at the 2004 annual meeting of the American Sociological Association, the pages of *Footnotes* have been filled with encouragement for "public sociologists," and the ASA has set up a committee to institutionalize "public sociology." Burawoy has discussed his ideas at dozens of campuses. This symposium is additional testimony to the powerful stimulus of his ideas.

I will focus on the best known of Burawoy's works on "public sociology," the version of his presidential address published in the *American Sociological Review* under the title "For Public Sociology" (Burawoy, 2005). This is Burawoy's most influential statement. I regard it as a learned analysis of the current condition of the discipline. It is thoughtful, subtle, and it strives to be balanced. It presents an attractive proposal for resolving the conflicts that have arisen among sociologists of different orientations. Where others have seen only continuing discord, he sees possibilities for "reciprocal interdependence" among four sociologies, which he calls "professional sociology," "policy sociology," "public sociology," and "critical sociology." Although I disagree with Burawoy's assessment of the relations between these sociologies and his proposed resolution to the conflicts that divide us, I respect his efforts to create compatibility out of discord and to inspire future achievements in the discipline.

Here are the key passages in the article describing the four sociologies and the relations Burawoy sees among them:

> There can be neither policy sociology nor public sociology without a *professional sociology* that supplies true and tested methods, accumulated bodies of knowledge, orienting questions, and conceptual frameworks. (2005: 10)

> Policy sociology is sociology in the service of a goal defined by a client. Policy sociology's *raison d'etre* is to provide solutions to problems that are presented to us.... (2005: 9)

> Public sociology ... strikes up a dialogical relation between sociologist and public in which the agenda of each is brought to the table, in which each adjusts to the other.... In the ... genre of what I call *traditional public sociology* ... are (books and articles) read beyond the academy and (which) become the vehicle of public discussion about the nature of U.S. society.... (A)nother type of public sociology (is) *organic public*

sociology in which the sociologist works in close connection with a visible, thick, active, local, and often counter-public. (2005: 9, 7—passages reorganized for clarity)

It is the role of *critical sociology* ... to examine the foundations—both the explicit and the implicit, both normative and descriptive—of the research programs of professional sociology. (2005: 10)

Unfortunately, the program Burawoy offers is likely to prove a mischievous diversion, because it follows from a basic misperception of the strengths of the discipline. To the extent that it succeeds in shifting attention away from "professional sociology," it will reduce the achievements and legitimacy of the field rather than increase its influence. To Burawoy's 11 theses, I will therefore offer 11 of my own. For the most part, they address problems in the logic and rhetoric of Burawoy's argument. They also address weaknesses in Burawoy's conception of the environments the "four sociologies" face and in his conception of the relation of the four to one another. Finally, they address problems with the treaty he has designed to resolve the conflicts among us, and they propose a different direction, which I believe will lead to a much more productive peace. These themes are interconnected: flaws in the logic of Burawoy's argument help to explain flaws in the program he proposes.

Thesis I: The Ph.D. Is a Research Degree

Burawoy hopes to turn the focus of more sociology in the direction of disciplinary self-criticism ("critical sociology") and concrete contributions to society ("public" and "policy" sociologies). Because I think his program could undermine the development of our disciplinary core, let me start with a basic point. The doctoral degree is, at bottom, a research degree. The reason why students are admitted into a doctoral program is to learn theory and methods in sociology, to learn the literature of their fields of specialization, and to learn how to conduct research. Following completion of their dissertations, it is true many new Ph.D.s prefer to concentrate on teaching, and there is obviously nothing wrong with that. But, alone among all the courses of study in universities, the Ph.D. provides a qualification to conduct research for those who wish to do so. The culminating requirement of the degree is the production of a research report. The master's degree provides much less advanced training in research, and professional degrees like the M.D. and J.D. are qualifications for clinicians and practitioners, not researchers.

Similarly, professors in doctoral-granting institutions have no other central purposes than to conduct research, to develop the theories and methods that underlie research, and to teach students the best current thinking in their fields of study. They have no warrant as politicians, although the findings of their research may lead them at times to become involved in public affairs. The only reasonable basis that any public has for listening to sociologists is that their research or their discipline's insights bear on issues of public moment. Everyone has passions and values; but only professors and doctorate-level researchers have the accumulated knowledge and research of an academic discipline to offer. They alone have the rigorous methods to prove or disprove ideas that have gained currency.

Thesis II: Discomfiting Truths are Marks of a Mature Discipline; Some of these Discomfiting Truths Challenge our Moral Passions and "Good Values"

In the humanities and social sciences, one of the hallmarks of mature and fruitful disciplines is that they can tell us discomfiting truths. The foundation of classical microeconomics, after all, is that "greed is good"—an appalling but intellectually productive observation about markets. I remember the singe of disappointment I felt when I first encountered, what were to me, equally disturbing propositions in classic works of political sociology. Yet, this sense of disappointment was simultaneously the first stirring of a maturing consciousness. From Robert Michels (1911 [1962]), I learned that even the most democratic organizations give rise to self-perpetuating oligarchies. My faith at the time was in participatory democracy, as captured in the stirring words of the Port Huron Statement. Imagine the bucket of cold water that Michels' work represented for me! From Max Weber (1919 [1946]), I learned that the "ethic of responsibility" required understanding the strength of contending powers and, very often, compromising for the good of one's cause. I was certain at the time that the "ethic of absolute ends" I shared with so many in Berkeley would triumph, even in the face of misguided opponents. Another bucket of cold water! But how true. My fellow protestors and I may have hastened the end of the war in Vietnam, but in our arrogance we also hastened the rise of Reaganism, which began as the visceral reaction of conservative America to rowdy protestors in the streets.

The value of sociology has something to do with social justice, but it is far from co-extensive with it. Its value comes primarily from telling us things we would never have known without it. Moreover, some of the things it tells us directly challenge our moral passions and "good values." We learn that communities often endure, not so much out of the spirit of comradeship, as from mutual dependence in the face of external discrimination (Hechter, 1987). We find that divisions among elites and resource mobilization through threats and incentives may be more important to the success of social movements than the justice of their cause (Gamson, 1990). We find that the strong forms of social reproduction theory are wrong: academic ability may be more important in status attainment than family background and that only about 40 percent born into the top income quintile end up in the top quintile as adults (Bowles and Gintis, 2002). We find that "oppressed" kids may be more interested in using sports and gangs as mechanisms for gaining a reputation in the community than in fighting the source of their oppression (Anderson et al., 2004). We find that two adults in a household might actually be better for kids than one adult (Entwisle, Alexander, and Olson, 1997: Chapter 5). If we are honest sociologists, we take in all well-validated findings, both those that confirm our expectations and those that do not, and we adjust our theories accordingly. If we are political actors instead, we may look for ways to hold on to our worldviews, tied as they are to our deepest beliefs, even in the face of apparent disconfirmation.

Thesis III: The Heart of Sociology Should Not Be Faint

Burawoy places "professional sociology" squarely at the center of his scheme of "four sociologies." He defines "professional sociology" as supplying "true and tested methods, accumulated bodies of knowledge, orienting questions, and conceptual frameworks." Further, "(p)rofessional sociology is not the enemy of policy and public sociology but the *sine qua non* of their existence—providing both legitimacy and expertise..." (p. 10). Professional sociology is, he writes, the "heart" of the other sociologies (p. 15).

Yet, in Burawoy's treatment professional sociology supplies only a very faint heartbeat. We might expect at least *some* discussion of the theories, methods, and findings that have "supplied" public sociology with the "legitimacy and expertise" that allow it to be strong and effective. But there is nothing of the sort. We have no sense at all of the nutrients this heart pumps into the other sociologies. Professional sociology emerges instead as a vaguely perceived, distantly nurturing parent—necessary somehow, but not very interesting.

Instead, moral passion is the real pump. This is evident from the very beginning of the article, in the epigraph from Walter Benjamin. This epigraph associates with the "angel of history" and the moral sentiments of humanity, which are turned backward to grieve over the wreckage of the past. But the "angel of history" is caught in the "storm" of progress which "irresistibly propels him into the future…." The "angel" cannot help but be propelled forward by the storm. Later, on page 5, we find echoes of C. Wright Mills' (1959) contention that the postwar profession-als—from Talcott Parsons and Robert Merton to Neil Smelser and S.M. Lipset— buried the moral concerns that motivated the founders of the discipline.[2]

This condemnation of mid-century professionals is followed by more criticism of the "heart" of the discipline: "The original passion for so-cial justice, economic equality, human rights, sustainable environment, political freedom or simply a better world … is channeled into the pursuit of academic credentials" (p. 5). He does not say "unsatisfying" or "unrewarding" credentials, but the implication is clear: "a battery of disciplinary techniques—standardized courses, validated reading lists, bureaucratic rankings, intensive examinations, literature reviews, tailored dissertations, refereed publications, the all-mighty CV, the job search, tenure file, and then policing one's colleagues to make sure we all march in step" (ibid.). Burawoy appeals as directly as possible in this passage to people whose *values* and *advocacy* of social change underlie their feelings of having more to offer society than professional life can sup-ply. If "professional sociology" is the core, the core appears to be quite rotten with useless requirements and disillusionment. But, fortunately, he writes, the originating "moral impetus" cannot be "extinguished so easily" (ibid.).

Instead of dwelling lovingly (as others might) on the scholarly ap-paratus that turns some talented, hard-working, dedicated raw recruits into competent professionals, Burawoy offers a swift tour of political and social issues of our age—the war in Vietnam (including attacks on the complicity of "fat-cat" sociology), "the corruption of academe by money and power," racism, gay rights, the War in Iraq— and a conviction about the importance of taking a stand on these issues. Indeed, heart and limb seem to be reversed by the end of the article, where "public sociology" emerges as the higher calling—or, to use Burawoy's terms, "the best possible terrain for the defense of humanity" (p. 25).

One wonders what is behind this conflicted attitude toward "profes-sional sociology." Is this an Oedipal conflict writ large? Is it an effort to supply academic legitimacy for the ideological passions of the left? Is it a peace treaty constructed by a diplomat representing one party to the argument? Perhaps all of the above are true. But one conclusion that seems doubtful is that Burawoy truly finds "professional sociology" central to the content and mission of "public" and "critical" sociology. I doubt that more than a handful of articles published in the pages of the *American Sociological Review* have been as severe in their criticism of the "heart" of the discipline.

Thesis IV: Public Sociology Is a Political Orientation in Non-Partisan Clothing

Burawoy's conception of "public sociology" has a distinct political orientation. As he presents it, it would be more accurately described as "left-liberal public sociology." Burawoy uses the term "public sociology" in much the same manner as Russell Jacoby (1987) used the term "public intellectual"—to criticize the narrowness of academics and to re-align the adjective "public" with a left-liberal agenda among writers interested in broad issues of political and social import.

Burawoy's own preferences regarding the orientation of public sociology are evident in the passages quoted above, and in others such as the following: "(During the Vietnam Era) campuses—especially those where sociology was strong— were ignited by political protest for free speech, civil rights, and peace, indicting consensus sociology and its uncritical embrace of science…" (p. 5). By my count, he mentions ten examples of "public sociology." Nine involve advocacy of left or liberal positions. He fails to mention "public sociologists" who do not easily or consistently fit on the contemporary liberal left, such as Daniel Bell, Amitai Etzioni, James Davison Hunter, Rosabeth Moss Kanter, Orlando Patterson, Pepper Schwartz, or Paul Starr, and he remembers only the more "critical" or dissenting efforts of earlier "public sociologists" whose entire body of work is not easily categorized by political orientation. David Riesman, for example, is remembered for his critique of the "other-directed" personality (1950), but not for his opposition later in life to "sunshine laws"[3] and affirmative action.

Burawoy is understandably concerned about the relationship between the term "public," which still carries non-partisan connotations for many, and his advocacy of a political agenda in the name of "public sociology." In response to this concern, he offers a number of improvements on Russell Jacoby. First, he distinguishes between two kinds of "public sociology": "traditional public sociology" (writing popular books and magazine articles) and "organic public sociology" (working with community organizations of various types). Second, he asserts that no one "public" exists, but a multiplicity of "publics"—and public sociologists are free to address any of these "publics." Third, public sociologists are expected

to address these publics through Habermasian (1984) methods—"open
dialogue ... free and equal participation of (the) membership ... (and)
deepening ... internal democracy" (p. 8). Fourth, public sociology has
"no intrinsic normative valence" other than "the commitment to dialogue
around issues raised in and by sociology." He writes that public sociology can "as well support Christian Fundamentalism as it can Liberation
Sociology or Communitarianism" (pp. 8-9).

This last point would seem crucial in that it retains the formally
non-partisan expectations we have of the word "public." But, fatefully,
he veers: "If sociology actually supports more liberal or critical public
sociology that is a consequence of the evolving ethos of the sociological
community." Instead of throwing his weight on the side of pluralism—or,
better, the well-investigated insights and findings of the discipline—he
aligns with the party politics of the sociological community's "evolving
ethos." The use of sociological knowledge in public life is turned into a
matter of majority opinion. Public sociology is formally plural and non-
partisan, but it can become singular and partisan, if those who identify
as "public sociologists" want it to be.

Thesis V: The Public Recedes;
Political Coalitions and Market Segments Persist

Burawoy draws on a Habermasian image of "the public"—or "publics," as he prefers. The realm of the public is the realm of discussion
and deliberation. Burawoy acknowledges the warnings of Habermas
(1973 [1989]), Skocpol (2003), and others "that publics are disappear-
ing—destroyed by the market, colonized by the media, or stymied by
bureaucracy" (p. 8). But he dismisses these doubts: "The existence of
a vast swath of public sociology ... does suggest there is no shortage
of publics if we but care to seek them out" (ibid.) Let me suggest that
the concerns of Habermas, Skocpol, and others merit further investigation. Money, technology, and power—and the networks that connect
them—are strong forces shaping public discourse in the United States
(see e.g., Ganz, 1994).

Who are the publics? It seems unlikely to me that Burawoy is interested
in the entire range of voluntary associations—from church ritual committees, to book clubs, to gardening clubs, and youth sports clubs. These are
not the kinds of associations that sociologists have traditionally engaged.
And, if sociologists did begin to engage them, what would they have to
offer that participants themselves cannot supply? Problem-solving does
not always require professional expertise (Lindblom and Cohen, 1979).

Instead, by "publics" I think Burawoy has in mind mainly community groups that are challenging the power structure in some way (the domain of his "organic public sociologists"). He implies as much when he writes: "The bulk of public sociology is indeed of an organic kind—sociologists working with a labor movement, neighborhood associations, communities of faith, immigrant rights groups, human rights organizations" (p. 8).

Do discussion and deliberation prevail in these arenas? Many groups struggle to work out issues collectively. At the same time, deliberation frequently takes place in the context of an active, well-organized leadership and a more passive, less well-organized membership. Indeed, I would add another (albeit minor) reason for the disappearance of "publics": the tendency for members of voluntary associations to "free ride" on the efforts of a minority can create conditions unfavorable to broad participation in collective decision-making (Olson, 1971; Swidler, 1979). As in the military, challenging groups are often most effective when a small circle around the leader makes most of the tactical decisions (Gamson, 1990; Michels, 1911 [1962]; Jankowski, 1991). In many challenging groups, the leadership consults when it knows it has the votes to prevail or for purposes of consensus-building. When the leadership is ineffective, it is opposed by an alternative faction, usually running under the banner of "greater democracy." Sociologists can try to bring reflexivity into community groups struggling against a power structure, but it will not be easy (see e.g., Polletta, 2002).

Burawoy is also interested in the readership of the more intellectually oriented periodicals and books (the domain of his "traditional public sociologists"). Something short of deliberation also characterizes the book and magazine trade. In the early 1990s, a graduate research team and I coded the content of some 300 articles in periodicals aimed at "educated general readers." These periodicals included *The New Republic, Dissent, The New York Review of Books,* and *The New York Times Magazine.* I concluded that the dominant cognitive frame of the majority of articles had nothing to do with taking stances on public issues, but rather could be characterized as "particularistic refinement." This frame required close observation and analysis of particulars on a subject, event, or person—without appeal to values, theories, or ideologies. Indeed, explicitly political comments were rare. Even authors in periodicals of the left rarely mentioned labor, the poor, or provisions for basic social welfare. Not surprisingly, professors from particularizing disciplines, such as history and literature, were far more common among authors than social scientists (Brint, 1994: Chapter 7).

The orientation of public taste is a constraining factor. We are a long way here from the idealized coffee house discussion of the eighteenth century. Editors ask themselves: "What will be interesting to the people our work reaches?" Most of the few sociological pieces that make their way into the marketplace fit a mood of the time (concerns about conformism for Riesman; worries about the individualism of the "me generation" for Bellah and his co-authors). They appeal to the preoccupations of Americans with effective interaction styles (as in Goffman's dramaturgy of everyday life), or with the application of utilitarian ideas to new fields (as in Putnam's social capital). They offer a strongly defined conceptual grid (as in Erik Erikson's seven stages of identity). Sometimes they attempt to forecast the future (as in Bell's post-industrial society). They are often written in a journalistic style—with characters and identifiable narrative structures—as well as quantitative patterns.

Is Burawoy's treatment of the contexts of "professional" as opposed to "public" sociology sufficient? One institution, the university, is described as drowning in red tape and irrelevance, while two others, community organizations and the book and magazine trade, are described as invitingly open vistas for collective reflection. It is clear to me that these images are developed more for rhetorical effect than analytical purposes.

Thesis VI: Civil Society is Not the Only Arena and Social Justice is Not the Only Tool for the "Defense of Humanity"

Burawoy identifies sociology with civil society (as opposed to markets and states), and he associates civil society with the "interests of humanity" (p. 24). Because public sociology addresses the various publics that constitute civil society, it too is associated with the "interests of humanity." The argument goes as follows: "(W)e can define (civil society) as a product of late-nineteenth-century Western capitalism that produced associations, movements and publics that were outside both state and economy—political parties, trade unions, schooling, communities of faith, print media, and a variety of voluntary organizations.... For the last 30 years ... (the) three-way separation (between market, state, and civil society) has been undergoing renaissance, spear-headed by state unilateralism on the one side and market fundamentalism on the other.... (S)ociology's affiliation with civil society, that is public sociology, represents the interests of humanity—interests in keeping at bay both state despotism and market tyranny" (p. 24).

But sociology is not the study of civil society. It is the study of all forms of social structure, cultural structure, and social relations. Social control is as much a part of it as voluntary interaction. Sociology looks at markets as a form of developing social organization, and it looks at states as a developing form of social organization. Of the institutions mentioned by Burawoy in the passage quoted above, none are completely separate from state or economy. Indeed, most schooling comes under state control during the course of the nineteenth century, while print media is clearly, among other things, a product of commerce by the eighteenth century.

Civil society, as Burawoy recognizes, is as much an arena of power and inequality as state and economy: "Civil society, after all, is not some harmonious communalism, but it is riven by segregations, dominations, and exploitations. Historically, civil society has been male and white...." (pp. 24-25). Still, he argues, "in the present conjuncture (it) is the best possible terrain for the defense of humanity—a defense that would be aided by the cultivation of a critically disposed public sociology" (p. 25).

Is civil society truly the best possible terrain for the "defense of humanity"? As currently constituted, civil society is an arena of material and ideal interests voluntarily pursued in a relatively autonomous way outside market or state institutions. As nearly anyone who has spent time in labor unions, neighborhood associations, religious organizations, youth sports clubs, or other community organizations can attest, these arenas can be at least as rife with prejudice, indifference to the lot of distant others, self-interest, inequality, and power-factions as any other realms of humanity. They are often arenas of discussion and human community, too, I agree, but they can lack the formal equity of access of market structures, and they sometimes lack the self-correcting mechanisms of democratic governance, because they rely so much on the activation of personal bonds and obligations. It is a bit distressing to see civil society treated with such gauzy romanticism, while the state is described as "despotic" and the market as simply a "tyranny." Here again, rhetoric is stronger than analysis.

If we think more about the issues, we can see the arbitrariness in the connection Burawoy draws between civil society and "the defense of humanity." A number of answers are plausible to the question of how to build a "defense for humanity," but few philosophers would limit themselves to civil society as the singular ground for improving human social relations, or social justice, even if defined well (not an easy task), as the primary discourse.

What institutions and discourses might figure in the "best possible" defense of humanity? Here is a one (highly conventional) answer that I will offer only to suggest how much is left out by Burawoy's focus on civil society: First, start with a good constitution, with checks and balances between and within the major branches; and protection for the people's rights and liberties, with special attention to the rights of minorities. Second, provide an acceptable level of social provision for all in the absence of available work, living wages, and economic opportunities for all to the extent possible. Third, as a source of judgment and productive skill, provide a high quality education to all. (As John Adams wrote: "I must judge for myself, but how can I judge, how can any man judge, unless his mind has been opened and enlarged by reading...." See McCullough, 2003: 223.) Fourth, design social institutions—from family and religion to the democratic state—to support discourses that are conducive both to the continuity of society and the autonomy of individuals. Finally, encourage a vital civil society, with high levels of participation and strong Habermasian norms of discussion and deliberation. Markets and states can work well within the framework of such a design, though of course they will not work well in every instance.[4]

At the ideological level, Burawoy's conception of the best possible defense of humanity can be criticized on similar grounds; he focuses too narrowly on the pursuit of social justice (and a few other values connected to the contemporary left). In addition to social justice, we might wish to maintain discourses about compassion, open-mindedness, rationality, persistence, honesty, independent thinking, and courage, among other desirable qualities.[5]

Thesis VII: "Critical Sociology" is Essential, but Ardent Passions Will Not Necessarily Stay Put in Their Assigned Boxes

Burawoy writes of a circumscribed "role" for "critical sociology." The "role" of "critical sociology" is to "examine foundations" and to provide a "conscience" for the discipline. This phrasing suggests that "critical sociology" is meant to be an inquiring and correcting superego, more polite and reserved than some superegos. But the role of "critical sociology" in Burawoy's scheme is not quite as clear as it seems at first. He also enthusiastically recounts Martin Nicolaus's "fearless attack" on "'fat-cat' sociology" during the "turbulent" annual meeting of 1968 and the "forthright demands" of radical sociologists of the time (p. 6). And he expresses elsewhere his emotional allegiance to the insurrectionary spirit of "critical sociology." For example: "Feminism, queer theory, and critical race theory have hauled professional sociology over the coals for overlooking the ubiquity and profundity of gender, sexual, and racial oppressions" (p. 10).

Perhaps Burawoy can cheer on "critical sociology" because he assumes the unchallenged structural centrality of "professional sociology." Professional sociology is, he writes, "larger and better differentiated" than the other sociologies; and they are "less internally developed" (p. 12). Elsewhere, he writes, professional sociology constitutes, with policy sociology, "the ruling coalition," while critical and public sociology form a "subaltern mutuality" (ibid). The superego may be as unruly as the id at times, but the ego nevertheless remains firmly in charge.

Like Burawoy, I see an important role for "critical sociology." Sociology has undoubtedly gained valuable new perspectives and new research programs from the insistence of "critical sociologists" on the importance of gender and racial inequalities, sexual orientation, and the global division of labor. We have learned a tremendous amount about how subordinate identities are simultaneously enacted and challenged, and the complex ways they are related to social control and economic experiences (see, e.g., Fenstermaker and West, 2002; Scott, 1990; Thorne, 1993).

"Critical sociology" often supports an activist orientation in the name of greater social justice. American society is heavily skewed toward the wealthy. It can use more activism on behalf of the poor and the marginalized—and, more generally, it can use organizations designed to provide alternatives to conformity and passivity. But here we also run into a serious problem. The drive for social justice and the drive for social explanation are far from the same in principle. By encouraging a larger role for "critical sociology," Burawoy's program will amplify the role of activism within the discipline. In my view, this is unlikely to prove a positive development.

I doubt that anyone will deny that the activist spirit of "critical sociology" is already an important presence in many departments. We now often hear testimonials from colleagues about the close connection between the "new," the "innovative," the "fundamental," the "critical," and the "first-rate." Burawoy might also agree in the end that the passion for social justice among "critical sociologists" will not necessarily stay put within the neat box he assigns to it. It is an ardent passion; and it is, as he indicates, morally righteous. If it finds sufficient support among elites, the chances that "critical sociology" will be content with polite inquiry and examination are slim.

More broadly, we should consider the extent to which the outlook of science and scholarship is being challenged on many fronts by the resurgence of faith-based activism, which demands far-reaching change and has little interest in judiciously weighing evidence. Even in the natural sciences, a critical school, intelligent design, which is closely linked to the Christian conservative movement, has challenged evolutionary theory. The advocates of intelligent design have published nothing in the leading peer-reviewed scientific journals, and, yet, the President of the United States has gone on record as suggesting that schools "teach the controversy." If evolutionary theory now totters in the face of a political-intellectual mobilization of the faithful, why should we imagine that professional sociology is less susceptible? Instead, we should realize that the centrality of the scholarly and scientific mentality is an achievement, not a given, and one that requires constant, deliberate reproduction based on excellent standards, outstanding appointments, and careful buffering of the intellectual core.

Thesis VIII: Burawoy's Peace May Encourage Conflict, Rather than Prevent It

"For Public Sociology" is, among other things, a proposal for peace. Burawoy writes: "As a community, we have too easily gone to war with each 'other,' blind to the necessary interdependence of our divergent knowledges. We need to bind ourselves to the mast, making our … sociologies mutually accountable" (p. 17). Relations between the four sociologies are spelled out in four-fold boxes, which, as Burawoy notes, bear "an uncanny resemblance" to the work of Talcott Parsons (1951).

To review, neither "policy" nor "public sociology" can exist without "professional sociology" to supply knowledge, methods, orienting questions, and conceptual frameworks. "Professional sociology" addresses an academic audience. Both "policy" and "public" sociologies use "professional sociology" to address extra-academic audiences, but "policy sociology" is based on "instrumental" knowledge, while "public sociology" is based on "reflexive" knowledge. Finally, "critical sociology … examine(s) the foundations … of the research programs of professional sociology." It addresses an academic audience, and is "reflexive" rather than "instrumental." The level of complexity in Burawoy's system is actually higher than this, with each one of the four sociologies having "moments" involving the other three types and each sharing a tendency to stereotype the others. Each of the four also has its own distinctive forms of knowledge, truth, legitimacy, accountability, politics, and (in good functionalist style) also its own pathology. Mutual critique, he argues, can trim the worst excesses of each of the sociologies.

Burawoy is exceptionally talented as a systems theorist. The layering of boxes within boxes is original in content and ingeniously executed.

The theorist in me appreciated this part of the paper, and particularly his comments on the "pathologies" of the "professional" and "critical" sociologies: "In the pursuit of puzzle-solving, defined by our research programs, professional sociology can easily become focused on the seemingly irrelevant.... (C)ritical sociology has its own pathological tendencies toward ingrown sectarianism—communities of dogma that no longer offer any serious engagement with professional sociology...." (p. 17). (The characteristic pathology of policy sociology is "servility" and that of (traditional) public sociology "faddishness"—also fair enough.)

But how does this section accord with what we know about the world? To Burawoy's systems approach, we might juxtapose the different illumination provided by a conflict theory approach. For a conflict theorist, the real world is ordered by dominant groups and organizations, backed up by supporting rules and resources (and, not infrequently, by the coercive powers of the state) (see e.g., Collins, 1975). Social movement organizations mobilize to challenge these dominant groups, and are not very much interested in respecting their "centrality." Indeed, their centrality is precisely the problem.

"Critical sociologists" and "organic public sociologists" are very nearly one and the same in membership and goals. They could be considered to constitute the challenging group in our arena. For a Robert Park-influenced conflict theorist, the original source of change is competition. Where a stable and reproducing structure of domination exists, no real competition occurs. However, at some point, the system breaks down sufficiently to allow people from rising groups to begin competing for some scarce rewards. Inter-group competition leads over time to the formation of conflict groups and, after a period of increased tension and (sometimes) an overt conflict, either the re-establishment of the dominant structure, or the creation of a new accommodation. The latter frequently includes the succession of the new group into some positions of the old (Park and Burgess, 1921: 505-510). Burawoy's article can be interpreted, again in the Park framework, as an attempt to bring about a new accommodation. "Professional sociology" is acclaimed as the heart of the discipline, while "critical" and "public" sociology are encouraged to take a larger role. Professional sociologists have the satisfaction of *structural centrality*, and the others are granted a more widely appreciated legitimacy—and, more important, *moral centrality*.

Burawoy's peace is intended to reduce conflict, but it may have the opposite effect. Burawoy's emotional identification with "critical sociology" and his emotional distance from "professional sociology" tell us at least as much as the formal architecture of his system. Formally, "professional sociology" has the dominant role in the system, but, reading between the lines, we can readily see that its true value is in doubt. "Public" and "critical" sociologies have subordinate roles in the system, but their moral value is higher.

The tensions in Burawoy's article reflect, in my view, important tensions in the discipline itself, with both "professional sociology" and "critical sociology" claiming moral centrality. For all his efforts as a peacemaker, Burawoy does not resolve the issue. In fact, he creates a symbolic universe in which moral centrality is divided from structural centrality. As any reader of genre fiction knows, this is a recipe for an unstable literary order. Although it may not be his intention, Burawoy contributes in other ways to an uneasy peace: through his derisive comments about professional sociology, through his enthusiasm for moral passion as a singularly important source of intellectual energy, and by providing reasonable-sounding, but emotionally uncommitted formulations about the roles of "professional" and "critical" sociologies.

Thesis IX: New Lines of Division Develop in Universities; and University Administrators Are Not in a Position to Resolve Disputes

Why do new schools of thought come into being? I accept it as axiomatic that for schools to grow, they must illuminate parts of the world that were previously obscured from view. Once they are institutionalized, of course, they will attempt to reproduce themselves. Moreover, new schools are not required to subscribe to "traditional" norms. Indeed, part of their appeal may come from their rejection of traditional norms. If the work of "traditional" professionals has been found to leave important features of social reality out of the picture, it is reasonable to conclude that this may be because professionals are biased (and would not admit to it). If so, the field definitions, academic purposes, epistemologies and methods of "traditional" professionals will be of little interest to new schools.

The question is how different are "professional" sociologists and "critical" sociologists? Scholars have complex views, and few fall neatly along a set of distinguishing dimensions. Yet our experience suggests that some colleagues identify more closely with the "professional" and others with the "critical" ideal of scholarship. In ideal-type contrast, how would we describe the distinguishing characteristics of these two types of scholars?

"Professional sociologists" subscribe to the ideal of theory-guided empirical research in which any conclusions related to social change require quite a bit of data analysis first. They pursue their work in a scientific or scholarly spirit; but far from being naïve positivists, most acknowledge that concepts and ideas play an important role in social life. Their major goal is to understand social phenomena. They try to keep their political views out of their research procedures and interpretations. And, while they might be active in community social action outside of work, their interest in activism on campus is likely to be limited.

By contrast, "critical sociologists" work from a self-consciously critical perspective on human social organization, in which empirically existing social life is seen as highly problematic, because it reflects the oppressions and inequalities of the world. They are distrustful of established research methodologies, because these methodologies tend to accept as given the oppressions and inequalities of the world. "Critical" scholars look at social relations as culturally constructed within a framework of power. They are less interested in explaining patterns of variation in the empirically existing world than in exposing the injustices created by inequalities of wealth, status, and power. A major goal is to help bring about social change in the direction of greater social justice. "Critical" scholars are less likely to accept a strict separation of political commitments and scholarly engagements. Their support for activism on campus is likely to be high.

When people differ from many of their colleagues along such important lines as underlying field definition, the purposes of academic inquiry, and in their epistemological assumptions and methodological preferences, they naturally look for support from others whose views resemble their own. In the contemporary university, both "professional" and "critical" scholars find allies across departmental lines. The structure of university advancement—with its continuous counting of publications, awards, lecture invitations, and all the rest—ensures that "professional" sociologists will be well supported within the university community. But the university's interest in "creating the future" (Brint, 2005) and its increasing emphasis on "social embeddedness" (Ramirez, 2005) ensures that "critical" scholars will be well supported, too.

Often, "professional" and "critical" scholars can get along, dividing hiring and specialization fields in ways that avoid controversy. Academic politics, like all politics, searches for a middle ground. But tensions can also crystallize—often over new appointments and promotions. In these instances, we do not find the "roles" and "reciprocal interdependencies" of Burawoy's system, but rather the mobilization of network ties and the formation of what Max Weber (1921 [1946]) would call "parties"—vertically organized groups pursuing power. We should therefore supplement Burawoy's systems theory, with an analysis of the potential for conflict and party politics in academe.

We should also consider the capacity of university administrators to resolve disputes between parties. Indeed, university administrators are placed in a difficult position. Most administrators will not take sides in conflicts between "traditional" professionals and "critical" scholars. Instead, they will try to manage the conflicts— leading to a "split the difference" outlook, or, even, to an assessment of which side can do the most damage to the university's reputation. No administrator will want an incident to occur on his or her watch. University administrations are not capable of solving disputes over field definition, the purposes of inquiry, and the other matters that divide "professional" and "critical" scholars. The most they can do is to try to ensure that ethical norms are respected and that scholarly contributions, rigorously examined, continue to be decisive considerations in personnel cases. They can also try to ensure that decisions are made within the context of an abiding and serious concern for diversity. These are tough, case-by-case assessments that no peace treaty can resolve.

It is difficult to imagine that, as a sociological community, we will easily escape the many possible conflicts in the future between "elitism" and "new approaches," or between empirical science and the activist spirit. We can hope to make these oppositions into our strength as a discipline, but we must recognize that they are not mutually reinforcing in principle. In the natural sciences, the leadership of elites and skeptical empiricism go essentially unchallenged. Progress has depended on them, and no one doubts that progress will depend on them in the future. The case is different for sociology. We are now well beyond the time when the discourse of scientifically oriented elites held an unrivalled position. But relatively few dispute the pre-eminence of theory-driven empirically grounded social science as the foundation for disciplinary strength. This is a position with which Burawoy, in fact, agrees in principle. More important, I think a strong case can be made that "professional" sociology is both the *structural* and the *moral* center of the discipline.

Thesis X: The Core Departments in Sociology Are Strong, but the Periphery and Semi-Periphery May Be in Danger

Like Burawoy, I believe sociology has rarely been stronger. The discipline has benefited from a number of intellectual breakthroughs in recent years, ranging from the elaboration of world-systems theory (Hall and Chase-Dunn, forthcoming) to the maturation of neo-institutionalism in organizational studies (DiMaggio and Powell, 1991) to the continued development of network analysis (Watts, 1999). We have had methodological breakthroughs as well, from hierarchical linear modeling (Bryk and Raudenbush, 1990) to sequence analysis (Abbott, 1995). NSF has recognized sociology in a unique way, by bestowing the Alan T. Waterman award for the first time on a sociologist, Dalton Conley, who has already told us several things we did not know before—for example, that many families pick winners among their children for unequal investment, and that middle children have a particularly difficult time gaining parental attention due to their structural position (Conley, 2003). Sociologists are appearing more frequently in the press, and efforts to solve social problems, which have accumulated over a quarter century, may at long last be coming back onto the public agenda. Intellectually, sociology's successes have been built on the critical mass of high quality graduate programs, creative research programs, and the growth and integration of specialized knowledge.

To continue to succeed intellectually, sociology must take the whole social world as its object: men as well as women; whites as well as people of color; heterosexuals as well as homosexuals; religious identities as well as gender and racial identities; rich and middle-class as well as poor; suburbs and exurbs as well as inner cities; markets, corporations and states, as well as civil society. It must continue to look at the relationships among people and the structure of social and cultural organization, writ both large and small. It must continue to look at social structures in comparative and historical perspective, rather than concentrating solely on the problems of our own time. Above all, it must continue to tell us surprising things; things that we would not have known without it. If it becomes a mere partisan tool, it will no longer attract talented thinkers or train its new recruits competently. In some universities the discipline will die intellectually, even if it continues to find a home due to institutional inertia, or for other reasons.

One hundred research universities conduct more than 85 percent of sponsored research; the next 100 conduct nearly all of the rest (National Science Board, 2004: Chapter 4). Every institution teaches sociology to potential new recruits to the discipline—and to thousands of others who can use it to illuminate their lives and the lives of those around them. Professional sociology will be strong at the top graduate departments, but its continued strength in institutions below the top 25 to 30 must be considered uncertain. Those committed to the centrality of "professional sociology" should realistically gauge the nature and extent of the challenge presented by "critical sociology," and they should make their judgments about the desirability of Burawoy's program for peace accordingly. Burawoy's peace will be empty if it cannot truly renew the discipline where it is most in need of renewal.[6]

We must ask ourselves, what benefits can the sociological community derive by agreeing to Burawoy's half-open, half-hidden attack on "professional sociology," or his half-open, half-hidden encouragement for "critical sociology" and (organic) "public sociology" to assume larger roles than they have? As more "critical sociologists" enter the discipline, I suspect that others who could contribute may be deciding that sociology is not for them. Certainly some important research areas are not as visible as we might expect them to be, at this point more than 150 years into our collective project of understanding. Do we have sufficient breadth and depth in our studies of the social changes wrought by new technologies, of the middle and upper classes, of exurban communities and cultures, of religious believers, of organizational successes, of societies other than the United States, of the growth and development of human societies from the beginning to our own time?

Thesis XI: Toward a More Productive Peace: Building a Curriculum for the Future and Emphasizing the Moral Centrality of "Professional" Sociology

As we look for solutions to our problems, we can begin by embracing Burawoy's four sociologies as legitimate expressions of the discipline. We can appreciate the important work Burawoy has accomplished in defining and showing the ideal relations among these four sociologies. We can try to use our insights and research for the public good. Sociologists address vital issues of social concern, such as crime, family problems, substance abuse, unjust authority, war and destructive conflict, and many others. Neither "public" nor "policy" sociology represents any threat to the discipline, if they are based on strong research and the legitimate insights of the discipline. Therefore, let us have more organizations—foundations, think tanks, and policy institutes—that use sociological work, and let us have more sociologists who are comfortable working in the public arena. In all of this, I stand at Burawoy's side.

Critical sociology is essential, too. A passion for social justice can inspire good research. I do not deny this for a second. Moreover, the university is a place for questioning "all aspects and all values of society." A leading statement on the role of criticism and dissent in the university is the University of Chicago's Kalven Committee's "Report on the University's Role in Political and Social Action": "A university faithful to its mission will provide enduring challenges to social values, policies, practices, and institutions. By design and by effect, it is the institution that creates discontent with the existing social arrangements and proposes new ones. In brief, a good university, like Socrates, will be upsetting" (Kalven Committee Report, 1967: 1).

Nevertheless, to preserve what is *much more* essential in the discipline, we will have to find ways to direct some of the activist energies of "critical sociologists" outward into the institutions of society, while focusing the largest part of the energies of all professors and graduate students on the teaching and further development of the discipline in a scholarly and scientific spirit. Again, the Kalven Committee Report makes this case eloquently: "The mission of the university is the discovery, improvement, and dissemination of knowledge.... The university is the home and sponsor of critics; it is not itself the critic. It is, to go back once again to the classic phrase, a community of scholars. To perform its mission in the society, a university must sustain an extraordinary environment of freedom of inquiry and maintain an independence from political fashions, passions, and pressures. A university, if it is to be true to its faith in intellectual inquiry, must embrace, be hospitable to, and encourage the widest diversity of views within its own community. It is a community, but only for the limited, albeit great, purposes of teaching and research. It is not a club, it is not a trade association, it is not a lobby" (ibid.).

An activist faith can be important in social change, but it can be harmful to the definition and methodology of social science. The characteristics weaknesses of "critical sociology"—dogmatism, tendentiousness, overheated rhetoric substituting for evidence—can threaten essential tenets of scholarship. To the extent that Burawoy's program encourages a new definition of the discipline—"Sociology equals social justice," in the words of a young colleague—I predict it will have a pernicious effect. It could open sociology to external attacks, and it will bore away at sociology's "heart," even as it declares its fealty to that weakened muscle. This waste of culture is not the outcome Burawoy intends, but it is the outcome his peace would likely render.

To strengthen the heart of the discipline, sociologists may need to rethink undergraduate and graduate education. Sociology must continue to be an inclusive discipline that welcomes everyone, but we must then transform people so that they can become, in their role as sociologists, agents and creators of the discipline's knowledge base. The electrical charge of knowing new things and the thrill of conducting research should be at least as much a part of the student experience as the passion for social change. To encourage a passion for learning and for conducting research, we might try to focus, first, on fruitful ideas and intellectually inspiring texts, rather than on drier fare, and we might try to get students started right away on research. We can expose them from the beginning to competing explanations for outcomes that are of interest to them. Formal courses in theory and methods might come later in the process, and be supplemented by their integration into research projects.

Equally important will be the restoration of professional sociology to a position of centrality in the moral sphere. I say this a bit reluctantly, because I am no fan of moral righteousness, and I believe the whole issue of morality has been badly corrupted in the United States by the efforts of some conservative religious groups to claim status and power on the basis of their "moral values." Nevertheless, the issue must be addressed in some way. Burawoy has created a system in which structural centrality and moral centrality are set at odds to one another. I see no reason for "professional" sociologists to accept this separation, and I see many reasons to question it. Professional sociologists should appreciate that their work has deep moral roots.

In the first place, work that meets craft ideals is a form of moral life. If a sociologist likes her work to be done precisely and well, does not cut corners, and puts her full concentration into her work, she is acting morally in the profession. Teaching is a moral activity. For "professional" sociologists in their capacity as teachers, moral passion is directed primarily toward teaching the leading ideas of sociology's sub-fields and doing so with the conviction that comes from knowing that reaching receptive students really matters for how they see and live in the world. Research is a moral activity. For "professional" sociologists in their work as researchers, moral passion is directed primarily toward discovering truth; and it is based on methods that allow the truth to be known; and for the fair assessment of competing explanations. If a sociologist searches for the truth, even in places he might prefer not to go, he is embodying the very expression of morality in research.

What is "moral passion"? I would define it as the energy that drives us toward the accumulation of symbolic credit for pursuing a higher social "good" through devoted (often misrecognized as "selfless") activity. Some say the morality of the teacher-scholar is an abdication of a larger responsibility to society. I disagree. As students and professors, we have a responsibility to the vigor and autonomy of reason. Our legitimacy and our strength flow ultimately from the hard work of generations of sociologists who have created the conditions for intellectual freedom and progress. From the shielded, competitive places they have created—places in which ideas can be nurtured, and can encounter and clash with one another and grow stronger—we have built the social structure and the tools we need to bring the benefits of sociological ideas and social research into the larger world.

From this, the last follows: our learning communities and their interests in understanding are the angels of our history.

Notes

1. I would like to thank Andrew Abbott, Michael Edward Brint, Vincent Jeffries, John Christian Laursen, Neil McLaughlin, Raymond Russell, Michele Renee Salzman, and Jonathan H. Turner for comments that helped to improve the quality of this essay.

2. Some founders of sociology—Comte, Spencer, Simmel, and Mead, for example—disappear in Burawoy's foundation story. Others—such as Marx and Durkheim—are presented as moralists, when in fact they mixed moral concerns with purely descriptive and explanatory interests. Weber's efforts to "extract the meaning from disenchantment" are commended, but Burawoy ignores the remaining 1,400 pages or so of *Economy and Society* (Weber 1921 [1987]), and much else in Weber.

3. "Sunshine laws" guarantee public access to previously confidential meetings of administrative or selection committees. See McLaughlin and Riesman (1990).

4. Many of the outcomes of modernity that sociologists (and other people) like—from personal liberties, to popular culture, to new technologies, to the expansion of economic resources—are connected to markets. Market productivity and market freedoms are as important to sociological analysis as market "tyrannies." This was once widely appreciated. At the time of the revolutions of 1848, two early "critical sociologists" wrote: "The bourgeoisie, during its rule of scarce one hundred years, has created more massive and more colossal productive forces than have all preceding generations together. Subjection of nature's forces to man, machinery, application of chemistry to industry and agriculture, steam navigation, railways, electric telegraphs, clearing of whole continents for cultivation, canalization or rivers, whole populations conjured out of the ground—what earlier century had even a presentiment that such productive forces slumbered in the lap of social labor?" I wonder how many "critical sociologists" today would agree.

5. One philosopher, Michael Oakeshott (1991), has written: "Too often the excessive pursuit of one ideal leads to the exclusion of others, perhaps all others; in our eagerness to realize justice we come to forget charity, and a passion for righteousness has made many a man hard and merciless" (p. 476). Indeed, a passion for social justice has sometimes devolved into populist authoritarianism, as in the cases of Jacobinism, Bolshevism, Maoism, and Peronism.

6. The engagement of the teaching staff in *any* of Burawoy's "four sociologies" is an important issue at some institutions. Some professors (and many part-time instructors) teach and do committee work, but do not give issues in the discipline or ASA a second thought. Can these professors and instructors be drawn into a deeper

engagement with issues in the discipline, or will they become "de-professionalized" workers? The ASA and the regional associations might consider appointing task forces to discuss ways to increase the involvement of these disengaged instructors in the life of the discipline.

References

Abbott, A. 1995. "Sequence Analysis: New Methods for Old Ideas." *Annual Review of Sociology* 21: 93-113.

Anderson, E. et al (Eds.) *Being Here and Being There: Fieldwork Encounters and Ethnographic Discoveries.* Thousand Oaks, CA: Sage Publications.

Bell, D. 1973. *The Coming of Post-Industrial Society: An Essay in Social Forecasting.* New York: Basic Books.

Bellah, R., Madsen, R., Sullivan, W.M., Swidler, A., and Tipton, S. 1985. *Habits of the Heart: Individualism and Commitment in American Life.* Berkeley, CA: University of California Press.

Bowles, S. and Gintis, H. 2002. "Schooling in Capitalist America Revisited." *Sociology of Education* 75: 1-18.

Brint, S. 1994. *In an Age of Experts: The Changing Role of Professionals in Politics and Public Life.* Princeton, NJ: Princeton University Press.

_____. 2005. "Creating the Future: 'New Directions' in American Research Universities." *Minerva* 43: 23-50.

Bryk, A.S. and Raudenbush, S.M. 1988. "Toward a More Appropriate Conceptualization of Research on School Effects: A Three-Level Hierarchical Model." *American Journal of Education* 97: 65-108.

Burawoy, M. 2005. "For Public Sociology." *American Sociological Review* 70: 4-28.

Collins, R. 1975. *Conflict Sociology.* New York: Academic Press.

Conley, D. 2003. *The Pecking Order: Which Siblings Succeed and Why.* New York: Pantheon.

Entwistle, D., Alexander, K.L. and Olson, L.S. 1997. *Children, Schools and Inequality.* Boulder, CO: Westview Press.

Erikson, E.H. 1968. *Identity, Youth and Crisis.* New York: W.W. Norton.

Evans, J.H. 1996. "'Culture War' or Status Group Ideology as the Basis of U.S. Moral Politics." *International Journal of Sociology and Social Policy* 16: 15-34.

Fenstermaker, S. and West, C. (Eds.). 2002. *Doing Gender, Doing Difference: Inequality, Power and Institutional Change.* New York: Routledge.

Gamson, W. 1990. *The Strategy of Social Protest, 2nd edition.* Belmont, CA: Wadsworth Publishers.

Ganz, M. 1994. "Voters in the Crosshairs: How Technology and the Market Are Destroying Politics." *Current* (Washington D.C.) 362 (May): 4-10.

Goffman, E. 1959. *The Presentation of Self in Everyday Life.* Garden City, NY: Doubleday.

Habermas, J. 1973 [1989]. "The Public Sphere." Pp. 231-236 in Steven Seidman (Ed.) *Jurgen Habermas on Society and Politics.* Boston, MA: Beacon Press.

_____. 1984. *The Theory of Communicative Action.* (Two volumes). Boston, MA: Beacon Press.

Hall, T.D. and Chase-Dunn, C. Forthcoming. "Global Social Change in the Long Run." In Christopher Chase-Dunn and Salvatore Babones (Eds.) *Global Social Change: Comparative and Historical Approaches.* Baltimore, MD: John Hopkins University Press.

Hechter, M. 1987. *Principles of Group Solidarity.* Berkeley, CA: University of California Press.

Jacoby, R. 1987. *The Last Intellectuals: American Culture in the Age of Academe.* New York: Noonday Press.

Jankowski, M.S. 1991. *Islands in the Street: Gangs and American Urban Society.* Berkeley, CA: University of California Press.

Kalven Committee. 1967. *Report on the University's Role in Political and Social Action.* Chicago, IL: University of Chicago.

Lindblom, Charles E. and Cohen, D.K. 1979. *Usable Knowledge: Social Science and Problem-Solving.* New Haven, CT: Yale University Press.

Marx, K. and Engels, F. 1848 [1998]. *The Communist Manifesto: A Modern Edition.* London: Verso.

McCullough, D. 2001. *John Adams.* New York: Simon and Schuster.

McLaughlin, J.B. and Riesman, D. 1990. *Choosing a College President: Opportunities and Constraints.* Princeton, NJ: Carnegie Foundation for the Advancement of Teaching.

Michels, R. 1911 [1962]. *Political Parties.* New York: Free Press.

Mills, C.W. 1959. *The Sociological Imagination.* New York: Oxford University Press.

National Science Board. 2004. *Science and Engineering Indicators 2004.* Arlington, VA: National Science Foundation.

Oakeshott, M. 1991. *Rationalism in Politics and Other Essays.* Indianapolis, IN: Liberty Press.

Olson, M. 1971. *The Logic of Collective Action: Public Goods and the Theory of Groups.* New York: Schoeken.

Park, R.E. and Burgess, E.W. 1921. *An Introduction to the Science of Sociology.* Chicago, IL: University of Chicago Press.

Parsons, T. 1951. *The Social System.* Glencoe, IL: The Free Press.

Polletta, F. 2002. *Freedom Is an Endless Meeting: Democracy in American Social Movements.* Chicago, IL: University of Chicago Press.

Powell, W.W. and DiMaggio, P.J. (Eds.) 1991. *The New Institutionalism in Organizational Studies.* Chicago, IL: University of Chicago Press.

Putnam, R. 2001. *Bowling Alone: The Collapse and Revival of American Community.* New York: Simon and Schuster.

Ramirez, F.O. 2005. "The Rationalization of Universities." In M.-L. Djelic and K. Shalin-Andersson (Eds.) *Transnational Governance: Institutional Dynamics of Regulation.* Cambridge, England: Cambridge University Press.

Riesman, D., Glazer, N., and R. Denney 1950. *The Lonely Crowd: A Study of the Changing American Character.* New Haven, CT: Yale University Press.

Rumberger, R.W. and Larson, K.A. 1998. "Toward Explaining Differences in Educational Achievement among Mexican American Language Minority Students." *Sociology of Education* 71: 69-93.

Scott, J.C. 1990. *Domination and the Arts of Resistance: Hidden Transcripts.* New Haven, CT: Yale University Press.

Skocpol, T. 2003. *Diminished Democracy: From Membership to Management in American Civic Life.* Norman, OK: University of Oklahoma Press.

Sullivan, T., Warren, E., and Westbrook, J.L. 2000. *The Fragile Middle Class: Americans in Debt.* New Haven, CT: Yale University Press.

Swidler, A. 1979. *Organization without Authority: Dilemmas of Social Control in Free Schools.* Cambridge, MA: Harvard University Press.

Thorne, B. 1993. *Gender Play: Girls and Boys in School.* New Brunswick, NJ: Rutgers University Press.

Vaughan, D. 1996. *The Challenger Launch Decision: Risky Technology, Culture, and Deviance at NASA.* Chicago, IL: University of Chicago Press.

Watts, D.J. 1999. *Small Worlds: The Dynamics between Order and Randomness in Social Networks*. Princeton: Princeton University Press.

Weber, M. 1919 [1946]. "Politics as a Vocation." Pp. 77-128 in H.H. Gerth ad C.W. Mills (Eds.) *From Max Weber: Essays in Sociology*. New York: Oxford University Press.

_____. 1921 [1946]. "Class, Status, Party." Pp. 180-195 in Hans H. Gerth and C. Wright Mills (Eds.) *From Max Weber: Essays in Sociology*. New York: Oxford University Press.

_____. 1921 [1978]. *Economy and Society*. Berkeley, CA: University of California Press. Edited by Guenther Roth and Claus Wittich.

11

"Is Public Sociology Such a Good Idea?"

Jonathan H. Turner

Michael Burawoy's call for a public sociology disciplined by professional and policy sociology, on the one side, and driven by critical sociology, on the other, exposes the ideological biases of sociology to publics. In so doing, public sociology will thwart non-ideological efforts for sociology to exert influence on broader publics and on political decision-makers. In order for sociology to be able to influence public opinion and the decisions of key players in the political and economic arenas, it will need to earn respect through a long evolutionary process of careful research and explanation without ideological fervor. To expose the ideological biases of sociology will thwart this evolutionary process. In contrast, sociology would be much better to develop an engineering mentality in addressing issues, problems, and concerns of publics in present-day societies.

It is striking that a discipline devoted to the study of human organization is, at best, a marginal player in public debates and important policy decisions. Since most public debates and policy decisions deal with problems of social organization and with proposals to reorganize some aspect of society, it would seem natural that sociology, as a discipline, should be a major player in the "public sphere," in the halls of political and economic decision-making, and in most social arenas. Sadly, such is not the case; we are left standing on the sidelines, while presidential historians, economists, political scientists, lawyers, and even psychologists engage the public and whisper in the ears of those who have the power to make decisions that affect the organization of society and, hence, people's lives.

American sociology appears to be embarrassed by the fact that it has very little impact on the public and on policy decisions by both governmental and economic actors. The listing of sociologists who are "In The News" with each issue of *Footnotes* is, I think, confirmation of

sociology's small impact on public and political issues. If we were secure in our position, we would not need to trumpet those relatively few
occasions when sociologists are asked by the press to say something.
It is almost as if we needed to say to ourselves: "See, we influence the
public, really we do." It is this sense of being marginal, if not impotent,
that provides the context for Michael Burawoy's (2004a, 2004b, 2004c,
2005) call for "public sociology." Sociologists rightly perceive that as the
field of inquiry that studies virtually all dimensions of human societies,
we should be players when issues, debates, and decisions affecting the
organization of society are being made. The call for a public sociology,
alongside other types of sociology, might signal a new strategy for getting our foot in the door that has been closed to most sociologists but
open for many other kinds of social scientists and even scholars in the
humanities. Burawoy is to be commended for offering a strategy and
forcing American sociology as a discipline to think about why we are
left out, and what can be done about our marginality.

Yet, for all its elegant symmetry, Burawoy's proposal is not likely to
open many doors; and in fact, I think that the approach advocated will
cause even more doors to be slammed in our faces. Moreover, the approach will further erode the only type of sociology that has any hope of
being influential—professional sociology committed to the epistemology
of science. I have reached this conclusion as a former activist, and as
one who has written normative works that are explicitly ideological (e.g.,
Turner, 1972, 1976, 1977, and 1985), but I am now convinced that, as
frustrating and unfair as it might seem, sociology and sociologists need
to "go slowly" when entering the public sphere and when trying to knock
down the doors behind which the powerful make important decisions.

Burawoy's Proposal for Public Sociology

The essence of Burawoy's argument is that there are four basic types
(and various subtypes) of sociology: (1) professional sociology, (2)
policy sociology, (3) public sociology, and (4) critical sociology. These
four types of sociology are seen by Burawoy to "complement" each
other. Professional sociology is committed to science, emphasizes peer
review of work, and seeks to accumulate knowledge about the empirical
world; policy sociology uses sociological knowledge to meet the needs
of clients and patrons, suggesting strategies for interventions based
upon sociological knowledge; public sociology engages publics (both
the general public and various local publics) over present-day problems,
questions and issues;[1] and critical sociology questions the moral vision

and foundational assumptions of all other sociologies, but particularly professional sociology. Each type of sociology reveals its own potential pathology: For professional sociology, it is self-referentiality; for policy sociology, it is servility to the demands of clients; for public sociology, it is faddishness; and for critical sociology, it is dogmatism. For each of these pathologies, the other three sociologies provide the remedy. I think that Burawoy has correctly identified the potential problems with each sociology, but I do not think his therapy for each pathology will cure the disease of any one sociology, let alone the problems that sociologists have in getting a public hearing, in securing clients who seek our knowledge, in convincing both general and local publics of the relevance of our perspective, or in providing a moral vision that anyone will accept. Burawoy admits that the pluralism in sociology may work against success in the policy world, as clients shy away from a discipline that speaks with so many tongues, but this pluralism should, he argues, allow us to hold sway with publics.

I think that this is a wrong diagnosis for the simple reason that, as Burawoy has emphasized, the morality of sociologists is several standard deviations from that of the publics we might influence. They are not likely to listen to left-wing ideology of sociologists; and indeed, if the public finds out that the discipline is so left and so mired in political correctness, we could permanently hurt our chances of influencing anyone–client, public, or fellow social scientists. Let me say at this point that I share the left-wing or at least left-leaning ideological commitments of most sociologists (although I am just an old-fashioned liberal, and certainly not a Marxist), and I firmly believe that, on net balance, affirmative action and other policies designed to redress past patterns of discrimination have been effective and, no doubt, must continue well into the future. So, it is not my politics that leads me to my critical remarks on Burawoy's proposals, but my sociology. What Burawoy proposes looks good on paper, but if analyzed sociologically, I do not think that it will help the discipline. In fact, I think just the opposite: it will hurt the discipline.

As I will argue, sociology needs to re-commit itself to the epistemology of science; it needs to seek out clients for sociological knowledge; and it needs to demonstrate that our knowledge is useful. Only then will we begin to make inroads on broader publics; and rather than preaching to these publics, as Burawoy's proposal would surely promote, we need to tone the moral debate down and offer sociological analyses of the outcomes of various lines of argumentation in the public sphere. Jumping into public debate waving our moral flag might get some attention, for a short moment, but it will erode our long-term credibility. I am committed to a sociology that becomes influential because the problems of the world are far too serious to leave to economists, political scientists, psychologists, and presidential historians, to say nothing of all the "talking heads" in the media. Sociology does not need to become a discipline of "talking heads" but a respected corpus of knowledge that all sectors of society find useful. Burawoy's strategy will inevitably expose our ideological leanings to the public, an outcome that would be a disaster for the discipline in the long run. We need to downplay our moral commitments and subordinate them to scientific inquiry. This kind of advocacy may sound "old school," but it is nonetheless sound advice. We will become even more marginal players when critical sociology and public sociology drive the public's perception of who and what we are. Now, let me backtrack and develop this line of argument in more detail.

The Public and Sociologists

For Burawoy (2004c: 5), "public sociology engages publics beyond the academy in dialogue about matters of political and moral concern," although he also offers broader definitions like (Burawoy and Van Antwerpen, 2001):

> Public sociology is less a vision of than it is an orientation toward the practice of sociology. It is a sociology that is oriented toward major problems of the day, one that attempts to address them with the tools of social science, and in a manner often informed by historical and comparative perspectives. It is a sociology that seeks as its audience not just other sociologists, but wider communities of discourse, from policy makers to subaltern counter-publics.

This broader definition seems harmless enough, but in so many other places, Burawoy reveals his hand: public sociology is to be moral; it is to involve bringing sociology's critical approach to the issues of the day. True, Burawoy almost always qualifies such statements by arguing that professional and policy sociology curb excesses and the pathologies inherent in critical and public sociology, but I remain unconvinced that such would be the case. Critical sociology will be the rocket fuel of public sociology; and as it does today, public sociology will target both professional and policy sociology.

Burawoy's real program becomes more evident when distinguishing between traditional and organic public sociologies. There is a "traditional" public that sociology addresses at "arms length" when, for example, sociologists become talking heads, op ed writers, or commentators; and then there is an "organic" grassroots public sociology that engages more delimited publics—specific organizations, neighborhoods, and communities. Engagement is to be moral; it is to propose and challenge ethical foundations of issues, debates, and decisions. Burawoy recognizes that there is a fine or fuzzy line between policy sociology—where sociological data and analysis are prepared for a client with a specific need—and public sociology—where the moral implications of situations are debated. Indeed, the examples he cites of the Moynihan Report, Diane Vaughan's book on the Challenger accident, or of James Coleman's report on school facilities and segregation were all policy reports that entered the public sphere and became the basis for moral and political discourse. Thus, almost anytime that social science knowledge enters the public sphere, it is used to buttress moral and ethical arguments, regardless of whether or not the scientists intended the work to have such an impact. This kind of infiltration of sociological knowledge into the public area is typically backed up by high professional standards of data collection and analysis. More recently, Douglas Massey and various coauthors (Massey and Denton, 1993; Massey, Durand, and Malone, 2002) have written works on ethnic segregation in America and immigration from Mexico that employ careful collection of data and reasoned analysis of the data; and these works have influenced public and political policy in ways that, potentially, can make a difference in political decisions. The data themselves make the critical case, without undue moral preaching. And while the findings can arouse political resistance, the data cannot be faulted. In contrast, if sociologists simply throw their ideological hats into the ring, spouting off their own moral judgments, their credibility will be lost; and political counterattack will be easy. We become just another set of talking heads engaged in a moral crusade.

If sociologists vent their morality, we will expose to the public our left-of-center political commitments; and we will immediately lose credibility with a public that is far more conservative. We will preach to our own choir of fellow sociologists, or seek self-satisfaction from reflexive gazes into our "looking-glass self." The one thing that we will not accomplish is to shift the debate or to influence the public in a significant way. What we will do is erode our credibility as scholars who have useful and important knowledge that can inform public issues. Let me offer an example. I have a colleague who is a self-proclaimed Marxist and who has done interesting research on the sweatshops and outsourcing in clothing manufacturing/ distributing and on Wal-mart's buying and distributing practices. The data are very convincing that there is something "wrong" in these practices, and they are given a Marxist twist about the evils of capitalism. This colleague received a certain amount of public attention for this work, but I think that if the underlying Marxism is vented in the public sphere, the credibility of the data will be lost. The data, in essence, speak for themselves; there is no need to moralize about what the data show; it is far better to let publics or policymakers draw their own conclusions. Once we start up the slippery slope of moralizing, we soon lose our credibility as social scientists; and while it may make us feel better about ourselves to engage the morality of certain industries, it is not likely to increase our credibility with most of the public—save for a more delimited public like labor unions. Recently, Massey (2005) called for a "weak politics" in which the researcher's politics are recessive and subordinated to the collection and analysis of data; there is, as he notes, "a strength in weak politics" because it is the data and its careful analysis that is front stage, not political ideology. We do not need to poke people in the eye with ideological pronouncements; instead, we need to demonstrate the power of sociological analysis to say important and relevant things.

My view is that the public's trust in our diagnoses of issues must be earned in a slow process of demonstrating to academics, non-academic clients, patrons, and eventually publics that the kind of knowledge generated by sociologists is relevant and useful. Burawoy implicitly agrees with this argument in his view that public and policy sociology depend upon the integrity of professional sociology, but if we start out trying to influence publics and to address moral issues with our own ethical standards, we short-circuit what needs to be *a long evolutionary process*. American sociology has had opportunities in the past to demonstrate its value, but in most cases it has fumbled the ball by either sloppy research or moralizing for its own sake (see Turner and Turner, 1990, for a history of sociology's failed efforts at public sociology). Respectability and credibility must evolve over a long time as a wide range of publics and clients recognize that our knowledge is useful.

With this line of argument in mind, let me comment on another example that Burawoy uses—ASA's stand against the war in Iraq. The vast majority of sociologists were, as Burawoy (2005) illustrates with opinion data, against the war, while the public was just the opposite and overwhelmingly supported the war, at least until recently. A proclamation from ASA was, first of all, hardly a very significant statement; no one is really listening to us anyway. But, it reflects a moral vision— unprovoked invasion of another nation is bad (a view I share, let me emphasize)— and let us assume the improbable event that sociologists were asked to go on the media and let fly their moral outrage. What would this accomplish, aside from allowing us to collectively vent our morality? We would have turned off the very public whom we want to influence; and we might have done further harm to the profession because the public and potential clients may come to believe that we do not produce useful knowledge. Instead, what the association should have done is have sociologists who study war, geopolitics, empires, collective behavior, and other relevant topics become resources to various publics, and especially the media. These "experts" would remain neutral in their public presentations, providing sociological insights that would allow the public to make their own decisions. Indeed, if we had been effectively doing this for the last 50 years, we might well have had insiders (in the Pentagon, Congress, and even the Executive Branch) who would have provided sociological analyses of what it means to invade and control a large territory, or at the very least, the sociological insiders could have steered decision-makers to relevant experts. As long as we keep our own politics and moral opinions in the background, while presenting data and theory that are relevant to big public and policy issues, people will be willing to listen to us; and over time, after years of successful consultation across a wide array of private clients and public debates, the credibility of sociology will rise, allowing us to have an influence on policy decisions that affect people's lives. If, on the other hand, we impatiently leap into the public sphere, sign petitions, and shout our morality, we will turn off the public and alienate potential clients. Sociology will not be better off for such zeal. It will be defined as yet another left-wing academic discipline whose knowledge is so corrupted by political ideology that it is not worth listening to.

This potential is aggravated by changes in the nature of publics. Small local publics may still exist, but the general public has been transformed by the media. The literate lay public that scholars like David Riesman, Robert Bellah, Daniel Bell, and my former colleague, Robert Nisbet, addressed has receded, although there is still a large reading public (with whom surprisingly few sociologists make contact). But, the public is now mediated through cable television and the Internet; and these forms of media want instant analysis in a few sound bites. There is little opportunity for a more nuanced analysis; and even if it is given, editing soon finds the best sound bites and ignores the more general and nuanced argument in which these bites were uttered. I have been amazed at the outcomes of my own interviews with the media; what may have been a one-half to full-hour interview becomes a few sentences in a newspaper. I am very careful in such interviews to avoid moral preaching; instead,

I try to demonstrate the extra degrees of insight and understanding sociology can contribute to an issue. As a result, the few sentences where I am quoted are not inflammatory; rather, they are simply filler words for a point the reporter wants to validate. Imagine what a more inflamed public sociologist will say; and since controversial sound bites are more entertaining to publics, they would get reported. But extreme statements can be credibility killers when they go against the biases of the public whom we seek to influence. Sociology does not need to become like *Fox News* on the left.

As long as the public's opinions on most issues are so divergent from those of sociologists, we need to tread lightly. We need to practice a "weak politics" (Massey, 2005)—indeed, in my view, a virtually invisible politics. And such should be the case even if the general public's views or those of a specific public coincide with those of sociologists; we still need to be very cautious. It is far wiser to offer our knowledge in as an objective manner as possible; and if we do so, we will gain credibility and be invited back by the public and key decision-makers.

The Dangers of Critical Theory

My sense is that Burawoy has a not-so-hidden agenda—the further institutionalization of the critical wing of the discipline. True, he emphasizes that critical sociology can be dogmatic and needs the corrective provided by professional sociology, but in looking at his exemplars of critical sociology, he clearly sees its influence on the discipline in positive terms. He constantly cites some of the common bromides: Sociology for What? Sociology for Whom? Whose Side Are We On? And, he is sympathetic to the argument that policy research and consulting "put values up for sale" and "cede the discursive terrain" to clients. And he is critical of those of us—Jonathan H. Turner (1998, 2001), Irving Louis Horowitz (1993), and/or Stephen Cole (2001), to name a few—who see the infiltration of political social movements as having pernicious effects on the discipline. Indeed, he sees us as lamenting the "fall from grace" of the "putative consensus around structural functionalism" or as seeking to create a discipline around a single paradigm. He approvingly cites Alvin Gouldner, C. Wright Mills, Alfred McClung Lee, and even the late Pitirim Sorokin (see Vincent Jeffrey's article in this symposium); and he commends the early founders—certainly Marx, but also Durkheim and Weber—for their more moralistic assessments of modern societies.

But let me ask a simple question: Has sociological inquiry been advanced and enhanced by critical sociologists and by the more critical pronouncements from theorists of the early canon? My answer is that the pronouncements of critical theorists have not tended to have "legs," even when the figure who made these pronouncements is still revered by contemporary sociologists. In other words, these pronouncements have not significantly increased the knowledge base of the discipline in the long run. True, we still use the term "power elite," but has this assertion significantly increased our understanding of power or has it simply biased inquiry? Or, to take ideas from the early canon, I would make what probably seems like an outrageous statement: most of the moral preaching of the early theorists was probably wrong, even if sociologists still cling to the concepts inhering in these moralistic statements. For example, Marx was clearly wrong about alienation; he had it conceptualized wrong, and his predictions about its effects were wrong. Durkheim's analysis of anomie is very flawed, whether as a cause of suicide or as a potential condition of differentiated societies. Max Weber's concerns about the "steel enclosure" (granted "iron cage" sounds better, even though it is not a correct translation) are obviously overdrawn. My point here is that when concepts reflect moral biases, if not outrage, they almost always miss the point. They fail to denote key processes accurately; they lose precision and nuance; and if theories and analyses are built around such concepts, they will inevitably be highly flawed. And, should it transpire that policy decisions were based upon these flawed concepts, more people might be hurt than helped by policies based upon moral ranting.

Less harmful are ideas that were once a part of at least some public's discourse. For example, have concepts like "inner directed" or "outer directed" from *The Lonely Crowd* (Riesman et al., 1950) endured?; and would we even consider these characterizations of people as accurate? I doubt it. Is Robert Nisbet's analysis of a "quest for community" any more accurate than rather romantic portrayals of preindustrial communities by many early founders of sociology? I doubt it. Or, closer to the present, are the pronouncements of cultural postmodernists about the dominance of culture, the overly reflexive self, the commodificaiton of symbols, and other ills of the postmodern condition accurate? I doubt it. Is the portrayal by Jurgen Habermas—also approvingly cited by Burawoy—of the "ideal speech act," "the public sphere," or "colonization of the life world" accurate? I doubt it. My point here is obvious, but nonetheless fundamental: When analyses becomes interwoven with critique—and even more so when critique is packaged in attention grabbing terms—the analysis becomes not only biased but also distorted; and in most cases, it is empirically wrong at crucial junctures.

Some might argue that these concepts grab the public's attention and encourage discourse and debate—which, after all, cannot be so bad. True enough, but what do they do to sociology? At best, we become public philosophers. At worst, we become talking heads who have only flash fame and little long-term credibility. It may be less appealing to present reasoned analysis in neutral terms, using theory and data carefully, but such an approach to public and policy issues is far more likely to have long-term payoffs for the credibility and power of the discipline to make a difference in policy, in public discourse, and, most importantly, in people's lives.

Burawoy (2004c) argues that a public sociology, fueled by ethical critique, naturally addresses "civil society" and the "autonomy of the social" in much the same way that the object of inquiry for political science is the state, and, for economics, the market. This conception of what public sociology should be is far too narrow, and far too embedded in old philosophical arguments about the public sphere. The state and market are topics of equal or even greater importance to sociology than the public sphere or civil society. It is the state and economy that exert the greatest influence on people's lives; and I, for one, am not ready to cede this topic over to either economics or political science. We can study the dynamics of these institutional systems as well as any other social science; and we can use the knowledge gained in these and other arenas to influence the policy decisions made by those in power. But, first we have to get their attention; and we will not do so by moral preaching or philosophical discourse. They will listen when we have something useful to say.

Part of the agenda for critical sociology is to help the oppressed, downtrodden, disenfranchised, poor, powerless, and other publics not able to enjoy the fruits of a wealthy society. Juxtaposed to this advocacy is the view that powerful decision-makers are evil oppressors; they are the enemy of a sociology that must be committed to helping the downtrodden. This kind of polarization is counterproductive. It is laudable that sociologists might be willing to give their knowledge to the poor and others who could not afford to pay for this knowledge (after all, even greedy lawyers and doctors give their expertise away at times to those in need). But this is not what being a critical sociologist means. Rather, we are to become involved as actors in the social movement that will lead the needy to the promised land. We are to be their ideological spokespersons and advocates. There is, of course, nothing wrong in sociologists as concerned citizens doing such things (as I have done numerous times in my life), but there is a line here that has been crossed: Sociologists who are advocates soon lose their professional detachment to analyze conditions accurately; they are pulled by emotion and ideology into the cause, and almost always, they lose their sociological imagination in the process. We become foot soldiers in a war against evil oppressors.

My view is that if we want to help people, we need to get the ear of those who have political and economic power to change people's lives. Becoming a foot soldier will not allow us to march into the halls of power; indeed, it will be a sure-fire way to remain outside these halls. The notion that sociologists who provide knowledge to those in powers are "sell outs" is absurd and counterproductive. This knowledge can be given away to other publics and groups, but if our knowledge is found useful by those with political and economic power in one context, they are likely to draw upon our knowledge on the dynamics of societies in other arenas where their decisions affect public policy. Questions like "whose side are we on?" simply miss the point. No matter what we may advocate as citizens and as moral actors, we have an interest as a profession and as people who think sociology can inform policy and public opinion in cultivating all kinds of diverse clients and in proving to them that we have important things to say. Sociologists do not have to choose; their obligation as sociologist is to legitimate our discipline in the eyes of all actors in society. Only in this way can we have the power to affect important decisions that influence people's well-being. To man the barricades in a cause simply barricades us from the halls of power. Indeed, the highly critical story in the *New York Times* after the year 2000 annual meeting is a likely result: ridicule for a discipline that still wants to "man the barricades."

As long as I am on the topic of critical sociologies, let me question some of the discipline's sacred cows. From the 1960s to the present day, broader social movements revolving around civil rights, ethnic and gender equity, and concerns for other segments of society that have been subject to discrimination have moved into sociology and politicized the discipline. Burawoy makes the reasonable point that these movements have broadened sociological inquiry and added to both the diversity and vitality of the discipline. But they have also politicized and fragmented sociological inquiry. Since W.E.B. DuBois, sociologists had studied ethnic stratification, and so, it was not essential to have a social movement to alert us to this sociological question. A stronger case can be made for feminism because it is very clear that women had historically been kept out of the academy, even sociology, and that sex and gender as key forces in human relations had not been adequately studied. The same could be said for sexual orientation, since these topics had been confined to the study of "deviance" well through the 1960s and 1970s. Other, less personal topics like ecological disruption similarly came into the discipline on the crest of the environmental movement. The problem with incorporating the ideas of a social movement into the corpus of a discipline is that the justified moral zeal and outrage of those in the movement become a part of how sociological inquiry is conducted. The moral agenda increasingly dictates what can be studied and, more dangerously, what can be discovered.

From its inception, of course, American sociology was populated by those who had an activist agenda, and while many gave lip service to the importance of objective scientific inquiry, their understanding of science was limited and, more fundamentally, they did not practice what they preached (Turner and Turner, 1990). Among most sociologists, the moral agendas of social movements have been a "good thing" for sociology, but I am not so sure. There is, I feel, a tyranny of political correctness from the left which will stone anyone who dares to present findings that contradict ideologically based conclusions about what is and what is real (or what is right). Moreover, certain topics become taboo because they offend moral sensibilities. For example, I am frequently asked why I study the biological basis of human thought and action. Numerous times I have been asked: Am I not resurrecting old and discredited racist evolutionary doctrines? I can only stare at the ignorance and anger contained in such questions. When legitimate modes of inquiry are questioned because they violate someone's (ignorant) perceptions of what such inquiry involves, diversity at the expense of tolerance for the full range of sociological inquiry is not diversity; it is a tyranny by ideologues.

Moreover, I seriously question if critical theory and research have expanded our knowledge of society. Let me take Jurgen Habermas as my poster boy. In my view, Habermas is more of a philosopher than sociologists; and I do find his works interesting—and indeed fascinating, once I get past the prose—*as philosophy*. As sociology, his works (e.g., Habermas, 1981, 1984) about the colonization of the life world and the ideal speech act strike me as naïve and empirically suspect; and as noted above, I do not think that they have greatly expanded sociological knowledge about the dynamics of society. True, this is just one person's opinion but it is based upon a complete and careful reading. The ideas are interesting for public sphere debate, but they do not advance our knowledge; and it is knowledge about *how the social world really operates* that is to be critical in sociology's slow climb to prominence and political influence. Let me take, while I am at it, the case of postmodernism's critique of advanced capitalism, especially the cultural school (the more Marxist-inspired analyses strike me as much more empirically plausible). All kinds of assertions are made about culture and self, and none of them are empirically verified. Indeed, to even pose the question: Is this statement empirically true often invites the retort that I am imposing the standards of a "failed epistemology" (i.e., science) which is so preposterous that it is hard to know what to say to those who make this claim. If we cannot mobilize data to check assertions because we are being "naïve" and invoking the standards of a "failed epistemology," there is not much difference between this tyranny of relativism and solipsism, on the one side, of critical sociology to become "dogmatic," on the other side. But more than dogmatism is involved. There is a commitment to remove scientific sociology from the discipline. Fortunately, these dogmatists are not likely to be successful, but they hardly inspire creative synergy that is supposedly to come from Burawoy's call for intellectual and professional "diversity."

Indeed, Burawoy portrays the typical sociology career as often moving through the four sociologies, or at least several sociologies. Our undergraduates are drawn to sociology because they want to change the world; as graduate students, they are forced to repress or forget such altruistic motives as they learn standard theory, methodology, and statistics. Then, there is the rush to tenure where young professionals must tread lightly. And only later after tenure is granted does the critical impulse re-emerge, when it is safe. This is not an inaccurate portrayal in many cases, but it communicates the agenda contained in Burawoy's advocacy. Activism is to be beaten out of students by a repressive tyranny of scientism. What Burawoy implicitly argues, I believe, is that science—if it is to be a useful science—must nourish students' critical impulses and serve as part of the arsenal of a public sociology fueled by moral outrage at unjust conditions. This is not the constructive interplay in his typology of the four sociologies; it is something much different, and it is a subtle message that the perceived tyranny of science must end.

My experience is that the tyranny of science, if it ever existed, certainly does not exist any more. Political correctness, demographic shifts in the composition of graduate student populations, diffuse anger at unjust conditions, and heavy doses of various ideologies have all made the scientists in most graduate departments run for cover. Attack dogmatism is on the loose, and not likely to be leashed in any time soon; and dogmatism is certainly not considered a pathology by at least one-half of the students that I see in graduate school. Perhaps there are differences between elite and less elite departments, as Burawoy suggests, but I am not even sure that this generalization is true; it is certainly worthy of empirical inquiry. I would suspect that it is science that is being beaten out of students by their fellow students and by activist faculty members. The dwindling number of hard scientists in the discipline has hardly been very success-ful, assuming they tried, in repressing graduate student activism.

Thus, Burawoy need not worry that the critical impulses of sociologists have been unduly repressed; on the contrary, cohorts of storm troopers are being trained for moralizing in the public sphere. If there is a trend in sociology, it is for increased moralizing—mostly to our students and occasionally to the public. The only bright spot in these trends, at least from my view, is that most decision makers and most in the public do not know about us, and hence, do not listen to what is being said in our classrooms. And, this is a good thing because unrestrained moral zeal will hurt the discipline's credibility and turn over even more influence to disciplines like economics that are singularly ill-equipped conceptually and empirically to provide useful advice on most social issues.

The Tower of Babble

Burawoy chides economics for its narrow adherence to the classical paradigm, pushing Marxist economists to the sidelines. He does note that many prominent economists, including several Nobel Prize winners, have begun to incorporate sociological variables into economic analy-sis. I am in general sympathy with the critique of economics which, in my view, enjoys far too much power in decision making at all levels in American society. But, although Burawoy concedes that economics is powerful because of its unity, he does not recognize an essential truth: intellectually coherent disciplines can speak with a unity and power not possible in fragmented ones like sociology. Even as economics expands its horizons— granted in a most limited way—the basic classical model remains intact. Here we have a discipline with an incorrect view of hu-man behavioral propensities, with an isolated view of the dynamics of production and distribution (Pareto would turn over in his grave), with what seem to me to be problematic uses of mathematics, and so it goes. Their reward for this narrow-mindedness and focus: enormous politi-cal and public power. I have sat in meetings with economists at venues like the World Bank, including Nobel Prize winners, and I am typically stunned by how such brilliant scholars (and they are this, even if somewhat narrow) can be so ignorant of the broader social forces surrounding market dynamics. Yet, they dominate the discussion because they have a coherent view—also a view that conveniently reinforces cultural values in America. And, it helps to win Nobel Prizes, although it has always galled me that the Nobel Prize in economics was created so that the Swedish academy could give it to one of their own, Gunnar Myrdal who was certainly more a sociologist than an economist. The only consolation is that his wife, Eva, a true sociologist, received the Nobel Peace Prize as did the American Jane Addams whom we can claim as one of our own. None of this, however, has helped the prestige of the discipline; and I have seen, again and again, the consequences of our low prestige in the academic hierarchy, especially when sociologists and economists are at the same table. This constant reminder of the relatively low prestige of sociology compared to economics underscores my point that sociology must gain credibility and, thereby, slowly raise its standing so that we can sit as equals to economists at the tables of power.

Let me get back to what is my main point: sociology is seriously impaired by the lack of consensus over espistemology and subject matter. There appears to be a congratulatory tone in most commentaries on sociology about the merits and vitality of intellectual diversity, but in fact, this diversity is what keeps sociology from being very influential in the world. In essence, anything goes in sociology—no matter how outrageous. Burawoy's critique of economics and his inclusive fourfold scheme of the "sociologies" attest to his belief that such diversity is a good thing. Perhaps it is a good thing for people who have academic jobs because they can teach anything, find some journal to publish just about anything, and feel that they are true professional sociologists—even if they simply emote their own identity problems onto the students and fellow intellectual travelers in narrow specialties. Burawoy paints those committed to science with a mud-laden brush by arguing that they become self-referential and anal retentive over narrow methodological techniques; and while he is not completely wrong on this point (this is a tendency among *some*, but hardly all), his implication is nonetheless clear: if sociology had only one epistemology, it would become obsessive-compulsive and impose a narrow range of theories and methodological techniques on the rest of the discipline.

When I was in graduate school, it seemed that sociology was ready to take its place at the table of science, but this was clearly an illusion. It was not just that the 1960s burst this bubble and began to politicize the discipline; it was also the case, as it had been for the founding generation of American sociologists, that there was a profound misunderstanding about how science works (Turner and Turner, 1990). Perhaps the spate of theory construction textbooks, to say nothing of methodological and statistical books (and, later, statistical "packages" for computers) attest to a sense that sociologists needed to "bone up" on how to do science. Sociology was, as Burawoy correctly points out, somewhat obsessed with "quantification," much like Franklin Giddings' advocacy at the beginning of the twentieth century. The advent of the computer and the ability to do multiple regressions without a room full of clerks only contributed to what I have sometimes called "quantamania." Coupled with the fact that the dominant theoretical approach was Parsonsian action theory, which in reality was a rather large category system, it is not surprising that there was a reaction against this vision of science. Robert Merton did not help matters by arguing for "theories of the middle range" which, to my mind, simply justified what C. Wright Mills (1959) had termed "abstracted empiricism." In Merton's advocacy, empirical generalizations from studies at particular times and places were considered "theoretical" when, in fact, they were *explicandum* in search of a theoretical *explanans*. Symbolic interactionism, for all its merits, was too limiting; and Parsonsian action theory provided a giant category system which, to say the least, had a lot of unneeded conceptual baggage. There were no elegant theories, save for a few in social psychology (narrow but elegant), which could explain the pro-liferation of empirical generalizations in an ever-increasing number of specialized journals. Thus, there never has been real consensus over the nature of science in sociology; and with the explosion of identity politics and various social movements, it is not surprising that the rather fragile Humpty Dumpty fell off the wall, fracturing the discipline into so many pieces (Abbot, 2001).

We live with the result of this fall. A discipline that speaks with so many tongues is not vibrant; rather, it is in chaos. It sounds good, in the abstract, to say that we can offer a variety of perspectives on our subject matter, but when the variety is so great, we end up saying nothing that people want to hear. There must be a set of common standards by which we judge competent work, and the only viable standards are those of science. If sociology wants to be a humanistic discipline, then other standards can apply—verbosity, for example—but there is no reason to think that the public and certainly those with the power to change things would ever be interested in knowledge produced in accordance with such standards.

We simply cannot have our cake and eat it, too; we cannot be ideological and intellectually chaotic, and still be influential. To be a player in the public forum, it is essential to have a common set of standards as to what constitutes good sociology. Without such standards, we are the ivory tower of "babble." We talk, shout, pout, criticize, emote, and do all manner of things without explaining very much; and if we cannot explain how the social world operates, few people outside the discipline are going to listen to us. We will continue to be irrelevant to the big issues and big concerns of the modern world. What strikes me, and at the same time causes me great dismay, is the impotence of sociology—the very discipline that studies the phenomena at the center of public and private debate. How can we be so irrelevant? The answer is that we are too diverse, too tolerant of any idea, too inclusive, too consumed with political correctness and identity politics, too abusive of the one approach that can save us (science), and too smug in our view that all this diversity is somehow good for the discipline.

Science does not need to be obsessive compulsive; it does not have be to only quantitative (indeed, in my mind, most of the really good empirical studies in the history of sociology have been historical and/or qualitative); it does not have to elevate empirical generalizations to the status of theory; it does not have to have grand theories that only categorize; and it does not have to become overly specialized and narrow. Indeed, the goal of science is to try to explain as much of social reality as is possible with as few principles and models as possible. When we have consensus over some basic principles or laws that have been confirmed with a wide variety of empirical tests employing diverse methodologies, we will have something to bring to the table of policy makers and to the public. If all we have to bring is ideology, few will listen to our message.

Burawoy may chide economics for being so narrow (and I agree with his critique), but look what can be done when there is some consensus over what constitutes good theory and research. Even when a discipline is this narrow, and in many cases wrong or incomplete, it can exert a level of influence that sociologists can only dream of. We need to stop celebrating our intellectual diversity, and find ways to develop common scientific standards for good sociology. My own feeling is that the discipline is now hopelessly diverse; and as a consequence, it needs to be broken into two parts—humanistic sociology, which can go over to the humanities, and scientific sociology, which can stay in the social sciences.

If this differentiation occurred, let us see which branch will exert the most influence on those who make the critical decisions affecting people's lives and on the public debates on critical issues. I think it will be the scientific wing, but not the science of Merton and Parsons. All of the problems addressed by critical theory and identity politics can (and should) be studied scientifically; and the outcomes of such studies and deductions from more general theories to explain generalizations from these empirical studies will contribute far more to public debates than moralizing and preaching by sociologists with their own ideological agenda.

In Defense of Sociological Practice, with a New and Perhaps Outrageous Twist

Recently, I have argued for an engineering wing of scientific sociology (Turner, 1998, 2001). The notion of "social engineering" has unsavory connotations, but all mature sciences have engineering applications of their knowledge. There is no reason that this cannot be true of sociology. Perhaps the idea of social engineering will offend many or most sociologists, but quite frankly, most ideologues in the discipline do not shrink from asserting how the world should be structured. Such assertions are clearly efforts at engineering, albeit in different clothing. What I propose is far less scary than what the critical ideologues in our discipline advocate. I would not be so arrogant as to tell a client or the public about what *they should do* to be morally and ethically pure (I certainly have opinions but this is different than giving advice or demanding that my opinions be the center of public debate). My proposal is much more modest: use sociological knowledge to solve problems that clients bring to us. Most problems in the social world concern how activities are organized; and as the science of social organization, sociologists can provide informative advice that a client is free to use or discard.

Now immediately there will a chorus, which Burawoy appears eager to join, that we are "selling out." Indeed, in his typology, he sees the pathology of policy sociology as its "servility." This is not a wholly wrong-headed diagnosis because a sociology that is oriented to seeking clients runs the danger of pandering and subordinating analysis to the perceived desires of a client. We become a new breed of ambulance chasers. But serious engineers—at least, most of the time—are not servile because they have codes and standards of conduct and because, if they cut corners, things fall apart and lead to lawsuits. There is no reason that an engineering wing of sociology cannot have the same kinds of professional standards; and moreover, social engineers can turn down work that, for whatever reason, is unappealing.

There is also a critique of social engineering that borders on hysteria, arguing that if sociologists are engineers we will somehow be parties to state oppression—a view of Big Brother in an Orwellian world. I have had people tell me that Nazi doctors experimentation on Jews is an example of social engineering and that engineering of the social is inherently evil. Such experiments were not the result of engineering but of ideological mobilization and political abuses justified by this ideology. I suspect that most sociologists would feel quite comfortable in imposing their ideological diagnosis of society's ills, if they had the power to do so, imposing this diagnosis on members of society. The danger is not engineering, *per se*, but abusing power legitimated by extreme ideologies. Public sociology is by its nature ideological because, in the end, it inserts morality (of the sociologist) into public discourse; and, in my view, extremist ideologues are far more dangerous to society than sociological engineers.

Let us now turn to some details of what I have in mind for an engineering wing of sociology. First, we should ask what engineers do. For the most part they provide knowledge that allows for the building of things—from computers and highways to bridges and airplanes. Engineers have a bad reputation as insensitive nerds with pocket liners, but in fact, they do creative things: they make it possible to build new things that, for the most part, make life better. True, engineers often build bombs and weapons as well as structures like intrusive freeways that can tear people's lives apart, but on net balance, we are better off for having engineers. They should, therefore, deserve more respect. Social engineers should similarly have respect. The reason that sociologists fear them is, perhaps, a classic case of projection: assuming that engineers would be like radical sociologies and impose their beliefs on the world, except in this case there is often the presumption that engineers would be political conservatives (as opposed to being the liberator of the oppressed). Why, I ask, would engineers be this way? Indeed, if they are good engineers, their politics and ideology are irrelevant; there is a problem of organization faced by a client, and it is the sociological engineer's job to analyze the problem and then suggest to the client the way to build a structure that solves the problem. We have a considerable body of knowledge that is relevant, but we do not make it available to people who could use it. For example, we as a discipline know the conditions that generate solidarity and commitment. A client comes in with a problem of worker turnover because workers do not seem committed to their jobs. We could be ideologues and say that such is the case because the client is a "capitalist pig" who refuses to pay workers enough or provide benefits. Or, we could review the structure and culture of the workplace and suggest a series of options that, to varying degrees, would increase commitment and solidarity (perhaps including the points made by the ideologue). But there is more to solidarity than just pay and benefits, and we can impart this knowledge to our client. Now, the ideologue will say that we are contributing to the workers' oppression which, to my mind, is the height of arrogance because if workers are happier and more satisfied in their jobs, who has the right to tell them that they should be unhappy because they are, in the eyes of the sociologist, "oppressed." But, the ideologue might say: What if Wal-mart comes to you and asks how to get workers to take less pay and benefits? I would not take work from this client (for ideological reasons; I do not like what Wal-mart is doing to American society and, indeed, the world). But note, the ideology affects my choices of clients, not my actual engineering of social structure and culture. Others might take on Wal-mart as a client and that is their privilege

It is through engineering applications that abstract knowledge is made concrete and relevant to specific situations or problems. To have an engineering wing of the disciplines assures, if we can find clients, that there would be a constant flow of theoretical knowledge to the real world; and conversely, when theoretical knowledge is put into practice, such practice offers one more empirical test of its plausibility and utility (Turner, 2001). The critic might argue that applied sociology, clinical sociology, and sociological practice already do this, and so, my talk of engineering is simply inflammatory. But, in fact, if you look at much of sociological practice, it is a mixture of advocacy (for a local public), descriptive analysis of some situation, and only rarely, the application of theoretical ideas to a concrete problem of a client. Moreover, much sociological practice is another name for what Burawoy advocates: organic, grassroots public sociology, or moral advocacy for a local public. This is not engineering, and it is not good sociological practice. It may be a worthy task as part of our role as morally engaged citizens, but it is not a particularly good sociology. Another part of applied sociology revolves around intuition or seat of the pants experience, thus making sociological practice more clinical than scientific. Still another part of sociological practice involves extrapolation from current trends or from other cases, and here again, there is a considerable amount of guesswork involved.

In contrast, what I have in mind is an engineering that is more rigorous than most applied sociology; moreover, it involves a systematic effort to use theoretical principles and models of social processes to intervene in a problematic situation, to tear down a dysfunctional social structure, or to build a new kind of social structure. Engineering is not description, or census taking; it is not ideological advocacy; it is about building something useful or tearing down something that is not useful.

If you look at the curriculum of an engineering school, students are taught a mixture of theoretical basics and applications of abstract ideas to concrete situations. Often, engineers are given "work formulas" derived from more theoretical knowledge; and the engineering consists of applying these formulas to specific problems. The theories from which these formulas are derived may be unknown or pushed to the background, but the point is that, ultimately, engineering is based upon theories that explain the properties and dynamics of various domains of the universe. Since human behavior, interaction, and organization are part of the universe, they should be understandable by theories that have been tested. In turn, these theories can suggest basic "rules of thumb" that can serve sociological engineers. For example, we could rather easily list the basic conditions that make people feel a sense of injustice (there are clear theories and lots of empirical verifications); the same would be true for various kinds of emotional arousal, alienation, commitment, trust, solidarity, and many other conditions which are often problematic and which require engineering (not ideological/political) solutions.

Despite all the carping by critical sociologists about the lack of verified knowledge (and indeed the very prospects for such knowledge), sociology has made enormous progress over the last forty years. If we compare present-day sociology to the supposed hegemony of functionalism, it is clear that we know so much more, by a larger factor. There has been a steady accumulation of knowledge that can be used to address real-life problems faced by people. To use this knowledge, it needs to be better consolidated and boiled down to basic engineering rules of thumb, but this is relatively easy once one is committed to the task. Sociology knows a great deal, even if many of its practitioners do not because it falls outside their critical worldview. These critics simply refuse to believe that we have knowledge that can be used to make people's lives better in engineering applications; instead, they wish to castigate the current capitalist system, bemoan the fate of some subpopulation, fire up students over real and, in some cases, imagined injustices, and in general light the ideological fires. To the extremists, everything is politics, and scientific sociological knowledge is irrelevant to their cause. If there is a public sociology, which will inevitably be fueled more by critical sociology than professional or scientific sociology, any effort to be a sociological engineer will be considered illegitimate.

My alternative to this polemical world is to re-establish science as the core of the discipline and to work toward an engineering subdiscipline that can use theoretical knowledge that explains social processes to solve real problems brought to us by clients and the public. If we become social engineers, we can choose our clients in terms of many criteria—money or ideology, for example—but we need to remain engineers, pushing our personal ideology and politics out of analysis as much as is possible. We have to be committed to using what we know, not what we feel and believe in our ideological incarnations, to advise clients. If we do not like the morality of a potential client we can "suck it up," "hold our nose," or quit, but we should not become moral preachers and ideologues.

If sociology could serve clients over many years in this manner, we would demonstrate to virtually all sectors of society that we have useful knowledge. And we would increasingly be called upon to comment on public issues. By examining issues from a sociological perspective—bringing theory and data to bear—we can challenge the simplistic analyses inevitably offered by economists and even political scientists on complex, dynamic issues. And we can counter the even more simplistic analysis of talking heads in the media.

We can become public sociologists of another kind: experts who can provide knowledge that can lead the public and the powerful to look at important issues in a different light and to make decisions that can benefit more people. If we enter the public arena as self-conscious ideologues, we will not "energize" public debate; we will turn off those we hope to influence, especially given the disparity in political leanings of most sociologists (including me) and the public. We may pat ourselves on the back for our political correctness, but we will have done little to turn the terms of public debate. We will be just as impotent as we are now, at least in most cases.

I recognize that what I propose is not likely to transpire, at least across the whole of the discipline. It occurs today among relatively small numbers of sociologists who are considered to have expertise that clients seek. My goal is to get more sociologists engaged in social engineering, albeit labeled by another name. At present, we cede too much of this work over to other disciplines that are not as knowledgeable as we are about the dynamics of the social world. But, I am a realist; this will not happen in my lifetime, except on a person-by-person basis; and hence, sociology will not have the impact that it should on public affairs.

As noted earlier, I increasingly believe that sociology should be split apart into a humanistic/activist discipline and a scientific discipline. There is no easy reconciliation between these two sociologies, although many such as I are both scientists and, I trust, humanists in that they want to make people's lives better and to construct a more just society. But, unlike Burawoy's neat four-fold table, we cannot live in peace. We get in each other's way; and rather than serve as a source of synergy, we drain our respective energies. The interdependence implied by the four-fold table on the four sociologies is reification or, worse, utopian; it cannot occur. It has never occurred in the history of the discipline, and it is not going to occur with the advent of a new public sociology.

A much better template for sociological engagement in public debates is the model provided by the Union for Concerned Scientists who often comment on public, political, and moral issues. As social scientists, we could join such a group and enjoy its protective shield. Or, we could create a Union of Concerned Social Scientists to enter the public debate as a coalition of scholars who are morally concerned and who, based upon their *demonstrated expertise* in theoretical, empirical, and engineering science, are likely to have credibility with the public. If sociologists go it alone, they will confirm the public's rather suspicious views of who and what we are. An umbrella group gives us "cover," but more importantly, such groups are given credence because their members are scientists, and science carries a credibility that gets a foot in the door with the public. A screaming sociological ideologue will get the door slammed in his or her face.

Conclusion

It is clear that I do not think that Burawoy's proposal is viable. I do appreciate the effort because it addresses one of the central issues that has confronted the discipline since its founding—the connection between science and advocacy. No matter how hard we try, we can never make this two-headed monster work. To be a scientist, it is necessary to suspend biases and beliefs in order to understand how the *world actually works*, whereas to be an advocate is not to let science get in the way of biases and beliefs about how the *world should work*. These two incompatible goals cannot be reconciled by an armistice, or by a four-fold table. We simply must accept the fact that we must choose one path between the two options, not to the total exclusion of the other but to its subordination. I have chosen the path of science, even given my activist background (that probably exceeds that of most sociologists) and despite having written sociological works that mix science and ideology. But, I do not think that open activism or a mix between science and activism is the way to go. In my 40 years as a sociologist, we have not made great headway in penetrating the public or the halls of decision-making. We have dramatically increased what we know about the operation of the social universe, but we have not made significant inroads in those areas where Burawoy sees public sociology as taking us. I think that his proposal would have the exact opposite effect on sociology; it would isolate us more from those areas where we should have more influence.

We will penetrate the public's consciousness and places where important decisions are made when we demonstrate again and again over a period of some decades that we possess an important body of knowledge. The only way for sociology to become more influential is to be a discipline committed to science and engineering, however you want to re-label the latter. Sadly, the years since I received my Ph.D. have seen just the opposite trend: inclusion of politicized social movements and their attendant ideology as not only subject matter (a quite legitimate activity for a scientist) but also as epistemology and as a world view. We have critical this and critical that; many sociologists do not educate students as much as they seek to indoctrinate them into their identity politics or their moral vision of how the world should be. Of course, not all sociologists do this. I would guess that the discipline is split right down the middle between those who use the lectern as a pulpit and those who teach knowledge in an objective manner and let students decide for themselves how they will use this knowledge to frame their own beliefs.

Given this even split, the best solution is to institutionalize this split into two sociologies—humanistic/activistic sociology (or some such label) and scientific sociology (or some alternative label, with my preference being "social physics"). Burawoy's solution is inclusive, and on first glance it really does seem reasonable and reasoned, offering a strategy where we don't have to echo Rodney King and wonder, "can't we all get along?" We can perhaps get along in a personal sense, although surface politeness and, in a few cases, genuine friendships, represent an uneasy armistice. But, my experience is that the tension is always there between the scientists and activists; we really do have different worldviews and priorities about how sociology can inform the outside world. Drawing a four-fold table, and extolling the virtues of interdependence and synergy sounds good (I only wish it were so), but it is not a viable roadmap to our future.

Our future would be better served by separating the discipline; I am even willing to give up the name sociology to critical and activist sociologists, if this will facilitate the separation. We spend far too much time in faculty meetings, in professional debates, in competing for students' minds, and in so many activities revolving around a battle that will never end. We have our own version of Dante's *Inferno*, but we have a way out. Many sociology departments are in this inferno; true, they may have peace for a while, but the conflict will erupt again and demonstrate to all that they have not escaped the hell in which they find themselves. We would be much better off to spend less energy in fighting rear guard battles with those who do not accept our epistemology; instead, let us spend our energies collaborating with those who do share our views on what sociology should and can be. Both sides of this conflict will be happier.

Seeing public sociology as one mechanism for integrating the two sides of the conflict—ultimately critical sociology vs. scientific sociology (I won't say "professional sociology" because critical sociology can be professional)—will not work. It did not work at the beginnings of American sociology in the first decades of the twentieth century, and it will not work at the beginning of twenty-first century. Let us simply part ways with a certain amount of mutual respect and move forward with less rancor and acrimony.

Note

1.   Burawoy presents several definitions of public sociology. At times, he makes clear that public sociology is about moral issues; at other times, he argues for public sociology to be civic engagement in the "public sphere"; and at other places, he sees public sociology as assessing the values of society and of sociologists. No matter the definition, public sociology becomes a version of critical sociology, and this outcome will be harmful to sociology.

References

Abbott, A. 2001. *Chaos of Disciplines*. Chicago, IL: University of Chicago Press.

Burawoy, M. 2004a. "Manifesto for Public Sociologies." *Social Problems* 51: 124-130.

_____. 2004b. "Introduction." *Social Problems* 51: 103-106.

_____. 2004c. "Public Sociologies: Contradictions, Dilemmas, and Possibilities." *Social Forces* 82: 1613-1626.

_____. 2005. "For Public Sociology." *American Sociological Review* 70: 4-28.

_____, and Van Antwerpen, J. 2001. "Public Sociology at Berkeley: Past, Present and Future." *Unpublished paper*.

Cole, S. 2001. *What's Wrong with Sociology?* New Brunswick, NJ: Transaction.

Habermas, J. 1981/1984. *The Theory of Communicative Action*. Two volumes. Boston: Beacon.

Horowitz, I.L. 1993. *The Decomposition of Sociology*. New York: Oxford University Press.

Massey, D. 2005. Presentation in Centennial Session: "Assessing Scientific Basis of American Sociology," American Sociological Association meetings, August, Philadelphia, PA.

_____, and Denton, N.A. 1993. *American Apartheid: Segregation and the Making of the Underclass*. Cambridge, MA: Harvard University Press.

_____, Durand, J., and Malone, N.J. 2002. *Beyond Smoke and Mirrors: Mexican Immigration in an Era of Economic Integration*. New York: Russell Sage.

Mills, C.W. 1959. *The Sociological Imagination*. New York: Oxford University Press.

Riesman, D., et al. 1950. *The Lonely Crowd*. New Haven, CT: Yale University Press.

Turner, J.H. 1972. *American Society: Problems of Structure*. New York: Harper and Row.

_____. 1977. *Social Problems in America*. New York: Harper and Row.

_____. 1985. *American Dilemmas*. New York: Columbia University Press.

_____. 1989. "The Disintegration of American Sociology." *Sociological Perspectives* 32: 419-433.

_____. 1998. "Must Sociological Theory and Practice Be So Far Apart?" *Sociological Perspectives* 41: 133-162.

_____. 2001. "Social Engineering: Is This Really as Bad as It Sounds? *Sociological Practice*.

_____, and Starnes, C. 1976. *Inequality: Privilege and Poverty in America*. Santa Monica, CA: Goodyear Publishing.

Turner, S., and Turner, J.H. 1990. *The Impossible Science*. Newbury Park: Sage.

12

Why Sociology Does Not Need to Be Saved: Analytic Reflections on Public Sociologies*

Neil McLaughlin, Lisa Kowalchuk, and Kerry Turcotte

After reviewing the debate about public sociologies in the American Sociological Association over the past few years, we offer a response to calls for "saving sociology" from the Burawoy approach as well as an analytic critique of the former ASA president's "For Public Sociology" address. While being sympathetic to the basic idea of public sociologies, we argue that the "reflexive" and "critical" categories of sociology, as Burawoy has conceptualized them, are too ambiguous and value-laden to allow for empirical investigation of the different major orientations of sociological research and the ways the discipline can address non-academic audiences. Debates about the future of sociology should be undertaken with empirical evidence, and we need a theoretical approach that can allow us to compare both disciplines and nations as well as taking into account the institutional context of the universities in which we operate. Research into the conditions under which professional, critical, policy, and public sociologies could work together for the larger disciplinary and societal good is called for instead of overheated rhetoric both for and against public sociologies.

The emergence of "public sociologies" as a conference theme, an intellectual movement and vision for the discipline is one of the most exciting, productive, and important events in the recent history of sociology. The American Sociological Association conference "Public Sociologies" in 2004 organized in San Francisco was interesting, extremely well attended, and has injected renewed energy into the discipline. We have been discussing the issue in Canada as well,[1] appropriately so, since Burawoy's (2005b) original notion of "provincializing American sociology" suggests a truly global vision for sociology. Certainly the exciting international presence at the annual meetings in San Francisco bodes well for the future.

289

This movement towards public sociologies, however, is not controversial. In addition to numerous dialogues and debates about the trend, there has also emerged a countermovement to "save" sociology as a science from public sociology. After outlining the contours of the debate so far among both mainstream and radical sociologists, this essay will argue that sociology most certainly does not need to be "saved" from public sociologies. We will pay particular attention to the perspective of Mathieu Deflem, probably the most vocal critic of public sociologies with his web site "Save Sociology" (Deflem, 2004a). There is a danger, we will argue, that Deflem's perspective could help to destroy sociology in order to "save it," if we can be excused for using this Vietnam era metaphor. While he makes some important points, the tone of the "save sociology" perspective is problematic and divisive. Moreover, his vision of a purely "scientific sociology" undermines the intellectual and moral energy of the discipline in a time of complex institutional transformations within modern universities.

There is something, however, to be discussed in the issues Deflem raises. The argument outlined in Michael Burawoy's (2005a) "For Public Sociology" requires analytic unpacking. Burawoy's public sociology argument in his 2004 Presidential address to the ASA made for a terrific speech, and has helped lay the foundation for a revitalized sociology for the twenty-first century. But his model of the different forms of practicing sociology works better as a political program and diplomatic compromise within the profession than as an outline for an empirically grounded understanding of sociology and other organized forms of knowledge production today. The contradiction between public sociologies as an inspiring agenda for action on the one hand; and an analysis of the trade-offs, institutional dynamics, and comparative dimensions of public intellectuals, popular intellectuals, and academic professions on the other, leaves the space for an ultimately counterproductive movement to "save" sociology. Debates about the future of the discipline can be undertaken in a more productive way if the issues raised by public sociologies are translated into researchable questions. This argument will be laid out as we proceed towards offering an alternative way of thinking about the issues.

This essay is organized in three sections. First, we will outline the basic critique of public sociologies developed by mainstream and radical sociologists, with a particular focus on the perspective developed in the "save sociology" website. What is the basic case against public sociologies, and does it hold up to scrutiny? Our view, as we have suggested above, is that this "save sociology" perspective is misleading. Nonetheless there are, in fact, contradictions with the model Burawoy has developed. We will discuss the problem with the use of the notion of reflexivity in Burawoy's model, the ambiguities of what he means by "critical sociology," and the need to develop a model that will work for both comparative research on various national sociologies, as well as for thinking about different disciplines. Finally, we will present some tentative ideas about how to move forward towards an alternative perspective for studying public sociologies, something we will present in more developed form elsewhere. This analytic perspective, we believe, can help us talk about the future of our discipline in comparative context beyond the case of the United States and the blinders of our own disciplinary perspective.

Does Sociology Need to Be Saved?

Academic respectability in the modern research university, we know, comes from reputational autonomy that flows from technical language, clear boundaries between science and non-science and the restriction of audience to academic peers not the general lay public (Whitely, 1984; Fuchs, 2000). At least that is the conventional wisdom. Sociology as an academic discipline is a relative newcomer to the research university, and has fought a long battle distinguishing itself from the academically low status social work, social reform, religious advocacy, and socialist movements it emerged from, on the one hand, and the more established natural sciences, humanities, and social sciences on the other (Turner and Turner, 1990; Halliday, 1992). As a result, the discipline's history could be read as a debate between the reformers, activists, and utopian visionaries (of both the left and the right) on the one hand, and the professionalizing proponents of a scientific sociology and an autonomous academic discourse on the other.

Michael Burawoy's (2005a) presidential address "For Public Sociology" is such an important and inspiring break from the past, *precisely* because he attempted to break out of these old debates. He offered us not the same old internal battle between radical and mainstream sociology, but a new framework that sees professional sociology and policy sociology in a complementary, not antagonistic, dialogue with the critical sociology promoted by the likes of C. Wright Mills (1959), Alvin Gouldner (1970) and Dorothy Smith (1991; 1995). In Burawoy's vision, critical sociologists and the professional establishment can come together in this period of sociology's history, in order to move forward as a discipline and prosper with a workable division of labour. Moreover, we have now, entered a new era of public sociologies, at least in the United States, as Burawoy tells the story (Burawoy, 2004a; 2004b; 2004c; 2004d; 2005a; 2005c).

The basic vision is compelling. First-rate academic knowledge about society can be produced by professional sociologists armed with our best theories and methods in the context of well-developed and competing research traditions. Policy sociologists can take this knowledge and sell it to clients in governments, non-profits and the corporate sector thus legitimating our disciplinary project to powerful and resource rich sponsors by helping solve specific social problems with reliable quality research. Critical sociologists can argue about the ethical foundations of our practice, raising the big questions regarding "knowledge for what," "knowledge for whom," and issues around the normative relationships between sociology, the university, and civil society. This critical debate can help us find the right balance between various competing methods, theories, and research traditions with a reflexive eye towards substance. The moral energy that critical sociology mobilizes helps recruit talented and energetic young people to our craft inspired by the moral and intellectual possibilities of the sociological imagination. At this stage of our professional development, Burawoy persuasively argues, we are ready to build a productive and peaceful compromise between these various elements of our discipline, putting aside old debates between professional, policy, and critical perspectives. We then can bring sociology's unique defense of "civil society" to political and public debate outside of purely professional and policy circles, in a new era of public sociologies.

Figure 1
The Division of Sociological Labor (adapted from Burawoy 2005a)

	Academic Audience	Extra-Academic Audience
Instrumental Knowledge	PROFESSIONAL	POLICY
Reflexive Knowledge	CRITICAL	PUBLIC

Sociology has a unique historical role to play in the contemporary political and intellectual climate, according to Burawoy. The natural sciences are too purely instrumental to help us address important social issues, beholden as they are to powerful institutional forces and interests. Of our major competition in the social sciences, political science is too wedded to the state, and modern economics all too often serves as an apologist for the market.[2] Only sociology, among the human sciences, can combine theoretical and empirical research with a commitment to the human dimensions of modern society, as they play out in communities, social movements, families, voluntary organizations and face-to-face interaction. Heady and inspiring stuff as anyone who witnessed Burawoy's ASA presidential speech can attest. What is the catch?

Responses to Burawoy's Vision for the Discipline

Mainstream Critique: Keeping It Professional

Not everyone who has heard Burawoy's call for a greater legitimation of public sociology is fully persuaded by it. One stream of critical response to his vision concerns the trade-offs between academic scholarship and public activism. In this perspective, sociology's precarious place in the research university could suffer from too close an association with left activism. We have struggled long and hard to be considered social science, not socialism or social work, and many sociologists worry about losing professional legitimacy, resources and public support. An additional concern is that the reformist zeal of our activism could hide arrogance in public sociology, if it assumes that the left-liberal values that most sociologists hold are superior to the views of others (Tittle, 2004). Attempts to make sociology matter assumes, it can be argued, that sociologists get to decide the moral vantage point too quickly on our own without the need for dialogue with those with different viewpoints (Fuchs, 2002). Others simply want to stress the importance of disinterested scholarly inquiry and education against the applied and activist directions in which public sociologies would take us (Wolfe, 1989; 1998; 2003; Brady, 2004; Burawoy 2004a; Neilsen, 2004; Tittle, 2004).

To some extent, Burawoy's writings and speeches already answer these concerns. Both professional *and* policy sociology, in his view, must be strong and supported in the profession, even as we develop a new focus on public sociologies alongside critical sociology. This compromise allows us to maintain our scholarly integrity by isolating our profession somewhat from the non-academic values of powerful supporters of policy research and passionate social movement activists alike, while preventing the insularity that is the pathology of professional social science. Nonetheless, Burawoy's mainstream critics remain leery of efforts to cultivate further and promote society's public side, evidently skeptical that this balance would be easily achieved.

An additional criticism of Burawoy's typology concerns the dichotomy he draws between the policy and public branches of the discipline (Brady, 2004; Tittle, 2004). This pertains more to empirical sociology that, to use Burawoy's terminology, is geared to "thick" publics (such as community groups), rather than to other ways sociologists may address non-academic publics (for example by addressing "thin" publics on some issue through the mass media). The policy-public distinction is problematic in maintaining that as researchers, only public sociologists have intellectual autonomy from particularistic interests, whereas the policy-oriented sociologist contracted by the state or some other client is "a servant of power" and is constrained by their "limited concerns." Just because a public sociologist doing research to help a community group does so voluntarily rather than for pay does not mean she faces less pressure than policy sociologists to ignore or suppress findings that do not advance certain goals. The less friendly of Burawoy's critics even argue that this kind of interference with scientific rigor is inevitable with public sociology and is one of its gravest defects (Tittle, 2004).

Radical Critique: Fine-Tuning and Globalizing Public Sociologies

A different set of concerns arises from left-leaning scholars who fully share Burawoy's passion for public sociology, yet criticize his sketch of how it complements and integrates with the other major types of disciplinary practice. Less concerned than mainstream critics with addressing questions of the institutional health of the discipline as a whole, these sympathetic recipients of Burawoy's ideas nonetheless raise important points. For example, Burawoy sees professional and public sociologies as making markedly different contributions to the discipline. At the same time, he regards the former is the *sine qua non* of all other types of sociology for its provision of "legitimacy and expertise" (Burawoy, 2005a: 10). The implication of this is that publicly engaged sociology does not build theory or generate questions that can be taken on by professional sociologists. The flaw in this division of labour, critics from the left point out (Acker, 2005; Ghamari-Tabrizi, 2005), is the notion that only professionally oriented, disengaged research is conducted with rigor and is capable of yielding methodological and theoretical innovation, while publicly oriented sociologists merely apply this knowledge to the questions and problems of movement activists and other lay communities. To put it another way, the objection here is to Burawoy's notion that a purely professional sociology should lead the other branches. The problem with the "professional leads the way" approach is that it can miss opportunities where public sociological work can lead to first rate scholarly work as well as political interventions (Light, 2005; Gamson, 2004; Burawoy et al., 2004). Few better examples of this can be found than the decades of politically inspired *and* scholarly influential contributions of Frances Fox Piven, the president-elect of the ASA.

Supporters of Burawoy's overall project also criticize specific aspects of the role he envisions for public sociology. Burawoy's advocacy of support for civil society as the raison d'etre of public sociology needs a heavy dose of caution; in the U.S. case in particular, it is dangerous to romanticize civil society that is plagued by patriarchy, xenophobia, and numerous entrenched inequalities (Brady, 2004; Acker, 2005). Furthermore, in light of the intolerance and political apathy in the United States, some feel that Burawoy is overly optimistic regarding public receptiveness to the work of progressive minded sociologists (Brady, 2004). Acker (2005) also suggests the danger of condescension in Burawoy's view of public sociology's mandate, which could be (mis)understood as trying to solve problems for oppressed or aggrieved groups instead of accompanying them in their own efforts to understand and change their situations. This point is sure to resonate with feminist and other practitioners of participatory action research. Burawoy also needs to pay more attention to civil society's transnationalizing tendencies in recent years, as illustrated by the anti-globalization movement (Urry, 2005). For public sociology, particularly in the United States, presumably this would entail overcoming the tendency to rely on theoretical perspectives derived largely or solely from the national setting.

Burawoy's friendly left critics also argue that his defense of a disciplinary consolidation for sociology misses the radical implications of interdisciplinary perspectives and visions (Acker, 2005; Aronowitz, 2005; Baiocchi, 2005; Braithwaite 2005; Brewer, 2005; Calhoun, 2005; Ghamari-Tabrizi, 2005; Katz-Fishman and Scott, 2005; Urry, 2005). For example, to insist that sociology's focus is civil society, whereas the market is strictly the purview of economics, may reinforce the erroneous patriarchal idea of separate public and private spheres, perpetuating the invisibility of women's contribution to the economy through their reproductive labour (Acker, 2005). Others worry about elitism in public sociology, and in the discipline more generally (Bute, 2005). Still others are concerned about possible unintended conservative consequences of public intervention (Stacey, 2004).

Professional Backlash: Saving Sociology from a Marxist Conspiracy

For the most part, the dialogue between proponents and skeptics of public sociology has been productive. The intellectual tone of the debate is disrupted, however, by the emerging "save sociology" critique. This sharper, more rancorous response to Burawoy's entreaty to legitimize further and institutionalize public sociology is led, it seems, by Mathieu Deflem, and seeks to expose public sociology as purely politically motivated and as a threat to the essence of our discipline.

Though Deflem's thoughts on public sociology, as presented in the "save sociology" website, are fragmented and brief, several basic objections to its place in the discipline can be discerned. Deflem's concerns overlap to some extent with those of the mainstream critics of Burawoy's project. Like Tittle (2004), for example, he would restrict the role of the discipline to generating accurate knowledge about the social world. Sociologists should not "set the agenda for their work" out of the issues important to counter-hegemonic audiences (Deflem, 2004b: par. 6). In aiming to change and challenge society, public sociology abandons the value neutrality that is the hallmark of science. Its moral stance also trespasses on the domain of other disciplines like philosophy, Deflem argues. But he goes further than the mainstream critics by alleging that the term public sociology is merely a ruse for bringing leftist activism into the university and giving it institutional legitimacy. "The true face of public sociology is Marx," he asserts (Deflem, 2004c: par. 7).

Deflem believes that public sociology has already done serious damage to the discipline. One of its effects, he argues, has been to squelch debate and erode plurality of viewpoints among sociologists, particularly within the ASA. To illustrate this he refers to the process by which the ASA under Burawoy's presidency passed a resolution condemning the U.S. occupation of Iraq in 2004, a topic on which sociological knowledge, he argues, offers no relevant insight. So tyrannical was the force of public sociology within this process, according to Deflem, that it intimidated many of the more vulnerable members of the Association, particularly graduate students, from expressing disagreement (Deflem, 2004d). Deflem concurs with other critics of Burawoy (for example Tittle, 2004) in arguing that public sociology undermines the credibility of the discipline in the broader society. He sees this as the outcome of overt political stance-taking by sociologists on issues on which they have no special expertise *qua* sociologists.

Deflem, to be sure, has raised some important issues. There are legitimate questions to be asked about the appropriate boundaries between scholarship and advocacy, and Deflem is in the company of many thoughtful scholars in arguing that we should limit the resolutions we pass at the American Sociological Association to questions within our professional competence. There *is* a danger of public sociologies being framed as purely radical sociology, inappropriately marginalizing liberal and conservative examples of our discipline's engagement in the public sphere. It is not appropriate, it should be said, for the leaders of our discipline to assume that everyone within it places themselves on the left of the mainstream political spectrum.

At the same time, Deflem has crossed over the line of legitimate debate into personalized attack in this crusade. Deflem's attack on the ASA staff for contaminating sociology's allegedly purely scientific essence with commercialization by selling merchandise with the ASA logo verges on the absurd, sounding more like a Herbert Marcuse rant than a serious political or intellectual analysis. More important, trying to discredit "public sociologies" as a Marxist conspiracy led by Burawoy verges on red-baiting. This is especially irresponsible at a time when the organized right-wing in the United States is undertaking an energetic and hate filled campaign to "expose" left-wing professors throughout the United States. Given Deflem's complaint that public sociology "narrows the debate," his annoyance with Burawoy's "inviting activists to the ASA meeting" (Deflem, 2004d) is ironic indeed.

To summarize, Burawoy's call for a renewed appreciation and cultivation of public sociology, facilitated by a new understanding of its complimentarity with the other major orientations within the discipline, has met with a range of critical responses. Those who embrace his project, nonetheless, question the basis for regarding professional sociology as leading the other orientations. They also question some of the distinctive traits, contributions, and focus that Burawoy has ascribed to public sociology relative to the other types of sociology. Those who are less accepting of public sociology—both from a mainstream academic and a more politically conservative or centrist perspective—share a common concern for preserving the rigor and value-neutrality that has helped earn the discipline respect and influence within the academy. Where Deflem parts company with the mainstream critics is his claim that public sociology represents the left's attempt to hijack the whole discipline.

The Case for Burawoy's Public Sociologies

Burawoy has managed to place himself carefully and creatively between the defenders of sociology's mainstream orthodoxy, on the one hand, and the discipline's radical internal critics. His intervention in the debate could be read as part of the long history of competition between the American Sociological Association's mainstream ASR/AJS elite research oriented establishment and the teaching- and activist-oriented element of the discipline spread throughout sociology departments and other institutional environments outside the most elite universities in the United States. Every few years, it seems, a famous radical sociologist with a base among the more activist and teaching oriented wings of the discipline will win the presidential position in the American Sociological Association, to be followed after that by a more mainstream oriented but equally famous and accomplished scholar. Moreover, there are many followers of the mainstream professional/policy approach teaching at the hundreds of less prestigious colleges throughout the United States. The coalitions that emerge in all this are clearly complicated. Be that as it may, the pendulum tends to swing back and forth, and in the larger picture, everyone in sociology seems relatively happy with the compromises struck between the competing elites in the discipline who are able to mobilize different professional and political bases of support. Burawoy's great accomplishment, in his presidential address at least, was to make the case for a new vision for the discipline without self-righteousness that can flow from the radical reformers who do not recognize the extent to which their own academic fame or elite position shapes the debate.

To his credit, Burawoy has emphasized the importance of looking at the role hierarchy plays in the very particular system of higher education in the United States, as we think about the social origins of radical and public sociologies. As a Berkeley sociologist, Burawoy has access to cultural capital, powerful networks, resources and highly motivated and well-trained graduate students that help his efforts in promoting a vision for public sociologies. Instead of ignoring or obscuring this dynamic, Burawoy develops the point in his thesis VIII, "History and Hierarchy," from his ASA presidential address (Burawoy, 2005a: 19). This helps us understand that the maturity of professional sociology that we see today in the United States is the end result of a long historical process and the steeply hierarchical division of labor within the discipline that has centralized enormous cultural capital and resources in the elite private and public research universities in the country. These institutions stand at the top of a system that includes hundreds of lesser status sociology departments engaged primarily in teaching. It is impossible to understand conflict within the American Sociological Association, or the wider debate about "public sociologies" without attention to this institutional context.

The "save sociology" perspective is such a counterproductive force in the discipline because it has taken these spirited and even conflictual debates between competing visions and material bases for the discipline and turned towards a militant attack on public sociology and its advocates. This is happening, ironically, just when there is a possibility that the vocal critical sociologists and militant mainstream sociologists among us are ready to put aside the grudges and counterproductive debates from the past. At the same time, it must be said that part of the reason for polarized debate flows from some intellectual contradictions and problems in Burawoy's intellectual framework for public sociologies. Contrary to Deflem's approach, we need to address Burawoy's ideas on their own terms—we cannot engage in personal attacks or the dredging up of old stale battles within this or that ASA committee meeting or e-mail list. Burawoy's own radical politics as well as his scholarly credentials are quite clear and out on the table, so the next step must be to evaluate critically his analytic model for thinking about public sociologies in a scholarly way.

Relying on an old fashioned two by two table (paradoxically for someone associated with critical sociology, something Burawoy himself acknowledges with good humor!) has left the door open for Deflem's polemics by giving us a model that does not address some of the intellectual and political contradictions within what he outlines as "critical" and "public sociologies." In addition to the normative and practical questions raised by various critics, more theoretical and conceptual work must be done before Burawoy's approach can serve as a framework for a research agenda on public sociologies. A research agenda will allow us to move the debate beyond political differences, personal self-interest and professional grudges, bringing us together and taking the polemics down a volume notch—we should debate the future of the discipline with analysis and evidence. With this agenda in mind, there are four major problems with Burawoy's analytic model.

Is Public Sociology Inherently Reflexive?

First, the notion that the instrumental axis represented by professional and policy sociology can be contrasted with the reflexive approach of critical and public sociology is problematic. Reflexivity is a complex notion that Burawoy could spend more time explicating. As we understand his thinking on this, reflexive sociology involves some kind of dialogic communication between the researcher-scholar who is practicing it, and those who comprise the audience for her work. In the case of public sociology, this is a dialogue with groups outside of academe regarding "matters of political and moral concern" (Burawoy, 2004a: 5), while for critical sociologists the dialogue is with one's peers in the discipline and focuses on ethical or questions about the discipline itself (Burawoy, 2004a). This stands in contrast to the instrumental orientation of policy and professional sociology, the practice of which is geared to "pre-determined ends" as defined by a client or by the norms and/or puzzle solving projects of scientific research (Burawoy, 2004: 4).

The idea, however, the public sociology is necessarily more reflexive in either intent or consequence than other forms of our disciplinary practice simply does not hold up to scrutiny. An examination of public sociologies in practice from a sociological perspective is illuminating. Public sociology is often written for a book or magazine audience or spoken on radio or television, where market niches, the need for interesting, sometimes sensationalized, writing and the often polarizing consequence of political polemics make it arguably harder, not easier, to be reflexive than in purely academic publication forums. Whatever one thinks of the specifics of the contentious debate between Loïc Wacquant and various sociological ethnographers in the *American Journal of Sociology* a number of years ago (Anderson, 2002; Duneier, 2002; Newman, 2002; Wacquant, 2002), the level of reflexivity of public ethnographies was at the centre of the disagreement. Similar dynamics may be operating in the new blog environment.

Writing for, and engaging, the public with our scholarship can certainly be reflexive and give rise to dialogue and debate. It can also, however, feed into the celebrity dynamics of the modern "fame game" in academics. It creates reputations for influential scholars based on polarizing arguments. It can reinforce the worst of public perceptions of the poor and oppressed or provide evidence that is used by powerful political forces for their own purposes. Was William Julius Wilson being "reflexive' when he allowed his excellent piece of historical sociology to be titled "the declining significance of race" by a sale conscious editor, creating a media storm, a heated political debate within our profession, and a major reputational boost to his career (Steinberg, 1995)? Was C. Wright Mills being "reflexive" when he penned *Listen Yankee*, an anti-imperialist polemic that seems, in retrospect, to be less critical of Castro's version of communism than might be called for, at least from the perspective of many thoughtful scholars and intellectuals? Was the great American public sociologist David Riesman particularly reflexive when he publicly critiqued the Equal Rights Amendment (ERA) campaign based on his own particular version of old fashioned elite liberalism (Riesman, [1954] 1993)? Personally, we are sympathetic to all these three examples of public sociologists, despite this or that political or intellectual disagreement. Our sense is that the question of whether these particular thinkers are being reflexive, however, is often a proxy for the question of whether one agrees with their particular politics.

There is nothing in public sociology that is, *by definition,* reflexive. Michael Lynch (2000) provides an extensive overview of the various meanings of reflexivity in sociological thought. He identifies six main categories of reflexivity, and a variety of subcategories, sharing a process of "recursive turning back, but what does the turning, how it turns, and with what implications differs from category to category and even from one case to another within a given category" (34).[3] For him, reflexivity is not necessarily radical or critical, although many proponents of reflexivity characterize it in just this way.

Burawoy (2005a) uses reflexivity quite broadly, saying that "[r]eflexive knowledge interrogates the value premises of society as well as our profession" (11). His purpose is simply to define reflexive sociological practice in opposition to what he calls "instrumental" sociology, or sociology for the purposes of "solving" (11) a puzzle or problem of the social world. For Burawoy, then, reflexivity—with its focus on the ends, rather than the means of sociological practice—is not what Lynch (2000) would call methodological, but perhaps closer to a substantive, modernist conception. Reflexivity is not the exclusive domain of sociologists who consider themselves "public" or "policy" sociologists, but is integral to the practice of sociology, regardless of audience. Burawoy's reliance on a substantive, critical sense of reflexivity allows him to make this distinction, which is (as Lynch (2000) demonstrates so effectively), quite an oversimplification. The only way in which public and critical sociologies can be considered less instrumental is to ignore the fundamental fact of the market/audience forces at work in those pursuits. They are different, to be sure, than those which drive Burawoy's "instrumental" knowledge production, but they cannot be distinguished on the basis of an overly-broad conception of reflexivity.

Professional, policy, and public sociologies, however, can all be defined clearly and unambiguously by the nature of the audience for the work.

Professional sociologists write for their peers, policy sociologists have a client audience among policy makers in mind when they write, and public sociologies engage the public outside their professional mandate as teachers and textbook writers.[4] Critical sociology, in contrast, is defined by a combination of the audience (work written to an audience of professional scholars, as well as possibly students) and the nature of the ideas (it must deal with foundational ethical concerns). Public sociology's place in the two by two table simply does not capture these complexities, and creates a not totally unreasonable suspicion that Burawoy is trying to sneak his politics into the analysis by stealth.

Burawoy's analysis offered in "For Public Sociology" seemed to open up the possibility that he would accept the liberal Riesman, the neo-conservative Daniel Bell, Philip Reiff, or even Herbert Spencer as legitimate parts of the history of public sociologies. But would he? One suspects that the type of public sociology Burawoy supports will be defined in good Gramscian terms as "organic" versus "traditional" forms of public sociologies, the organic version of the social type being heralded as the truly reflexive ideal. But are "organic intellectuals" necessarily more reflexive than professional sociologists? Gramsci certainly was an important contributor to radical political thought and the sociology of intellectuals, but was his relationship to Italian peasants and the Communist Party fully reflexive, or were there not serious problems of representation and elitism embedded in his analysis alongside his undoubted insights (Gramsci, 1971; Walzer, 1988)?

The same question can be asked of DuBois, a sociologist one can admire, while disagreeing with his relationship to the Communist Movement. While critical sociologists such as Gouldner are highly reflexive in some of their writings, however, one cannot argue that all of Gouldner's theoretical arguments, political interventions and professional activities can be defined by their reflexivity (Chriss, 1999). The same is certainly true with Bourdieu, another great representative of reflexivity and someone certainly capable of dogmatism (Bourdieu, 1984; Bourdieu and Wacquant, 1992; Swartz, 2003).[5] And then there is Anthony Giddens, a thinker who writes extensively about reflexivity but is engaged in marketing his textbooks as much as anything else, while being a very instrumental "public intellectual" for the New Labour (Fuller, 2000)![6] Reflexivity is possible, we think, and should be a goal to aim for, but it cannot serve as a major criterion for a researchable model for understanding the sociology of academic knowledge. Reflexivity, all too often, is a term used in legitimizing rhetoric not analytic inquiry. Our preference would be to drop the reflexive versus instrumental axis of the Burawoy model, define the question to be discussed based on audience (professional, policy and public sociologies, for example), allow for political diversity among public sociologies and then unpack further the notion of critical sociology.

What Is Critical Sociology?

This unpacking of "critical sociology" is our second major critique of the Burawoy model. There are, unfortunately, real ambiguities in his implicit definition of this type of sociology. We know that C. Wright Mills' critique of mainstream sociology in *The Sociological Imagination* (1959) was, at least to some extent, motivated by his professional ambitions and desire for intellectual attention (Oakes and Vidich, 1999). One can identify with Mills' vision for sociology, as we do, without ignoring the complexities of this notion of "critical sociology." Is it unreasonable to suggest that much of the "critical theory" we see in contemporary academic work is, for example, an element of the professional academic competition we see all around us? Are the mountains of academic "critical theory" in our libraries today a pure critical attempt to develop a consensus on "knowledge for what" or is much of this work part of professional academic competition itself, undertaken by other means?

A closer look at the example of the original critical theory represented by the Frankfurt School suggests the latter is often the case. There is no question that the Frankfurt School critique of instrumental rationality has had enormous influence in social science, and has been integrated into Burawoy's own typology. But is his account of the critical theorists really accurate and illuminating for us today, or does it contribute to various "origin myths" about the purity of "critical theory"? A closer look at the actual history of the Frankfurt School and its reception shows an enormous amount of professional manoeuvring and instrumental academic politics undertaken behind the scenes (McLaughlin, 1999). Adorno, in particular, played a central role in making sure that the authors for *The Authoritarian Personality* (1950) volume were listed in alphabetical order, resulting in hundreds of citations to Adorno et al. (Wiggerhaus, 1994). Moreover, it should be said, the critical theorists exhibited an enormous lack of reflexivity as to how the values, class, gender and national positions of the critical theorists themselves shaped their own intellectual and political views. The great unwritten story of the Frankfurt School is how they used the effective grant writing skill of their former collaborator Paul Lazarsfeld during the 1930s and 1940s to replenish the depleted funds they were bestowed with in the 1920s from a wealthy German grain merchant, later repaying Lazarsfeld's help with the infamous and polarized attacks on 'positivism" when they returned to Germany (Wiggerhaus, 1994; Fuller, 2004). After following this history, when someone claims the mantle of a critical sociologist today, one is justified in wondering whether there are professional or political goals being covered up (McLaughlin, 1999). Being critical is a normative goal (Hammersley, 2005), and like reflexivity it is not a researchable analytic category for sociological analysis.

Part of the problem here is that Burawoy (2005a) uses critical to mean two different things. In "For Public Sociology" critical means a reflexive and critical engagement with the core moral priorities of social science research. But in other writings, particularly in Burawoy's contribution to the *Critical Sociology* exchange, he clearly means political radical and left wing, a subset, it seems to us, of the critical sociologies that surely would include liberals and even conservatives. The issues get interesting when one gets specific.

Would Burawoy concede that Robert Nisbet, the great late conservative sociological theorist from the University of California at Riverside and Berkeley, was a critical sociologist who put the issues of the ultimate goals of sociological analysis on the table for a discussion? Few sociologists have been as critical of professional narrowness as Nisbet. He clearly was centrally concerned with the ultimate ends for sociology as a discipline and moral/intellectual enterprise (Nisbet, 1966; 1976). If C. Wright Mills, Alvin Gouldner, DuBois, Dorothy Smith, and Bourdieu are critical sociologists, but Nisbet is not, is "critical sociology" then just a less straightforward term for politically radical sociology? Would Burawoy include, in his critical sociology, intellectually serious but religiously conservative sociologists who raise fundamental questions about the moral obligations of social science research? Or Philip Rieff? Or Alan Wolfe's work, as he has moved from this New Left position in the 1960s to a more centrist liberalism that takes the questions of sociology's moral obligations very seriously indeed (Wolfe, 1989; 1998; 2003)? Deflem has dealt with these questions in an unhelpful way, but the basic question is not unreasonable. The authors of this article consider ourselves to be critical sociologists, but this position flows from our politics not from some generic notion of 'reflexivity" that serves to hide—rather than openly deal with—potential political biases. Expanding what we mean by "critical" in ways that do not refer exclusively to political positions (or by finding a less politically charged way of labelling this type of sociology) is an important first step to help us avoid political posturing and counterposturing so that public sociologies might be studied empirically. We will be engaging in this empirical analysis elsewhere, but here we offer an exploration of some of the issues we believe must be addressed.

Comparative Institutional Analysis

A major problem with Burawoy's analytic model is that is does not allow for an analysis of the institutional environments that shape the dynamics of public sociologies in a comparative context. Burawoy is fully aware of these processes, having written extensively in comparative sociology, often with a central concern for structures and institutional dynamics. Moreover, he goes to great lengths to emphasize the very particular institutional dynamics of American sociology. Sociology in the United States is a form of academic practice that is embedded in a unique system of higher education. American sociology relates, in important and complex ways, to the very distinctive state, social service institutions, business elites, and student clients that make up the institutional environment for sociology in the United States. Burawoy's simple two by two table, however, does not allow us to model in analytic ways how his categories of professional, policy, critical, and public sociologies are related to outside institutions. Moreover, all of this is different in distinct national contexts, something worth theorizing in more detail.

Defining public sociologies as inherently part of the reflexive axis of his model hides the extent to which the different institutional arrangements in distinct nations will shape the practice of public academic life. How are newspapers, electronic media and the university sector organized in different nations? How might this shape the nature of public debate? What is the role of the state in university life, in different nations? What is the relative size and resource basis of university sectors in distinct nations? How are distinct states and governance structures different, and how might this shape the ways in which policy sociology operates? What about the role of think tanks and social movements in different national environments? Burawoy is certainly aware of all these issues, and puts a particular stress on the uniqueness of the steeply hierarchical, combined public and private and resource rich American higher education system. Most sociologists in other countries are more public, *precisely* because they operate in societies where the university systems are different from that of American higher education. Burawoy makes these points in his highly persuasive speeches and writings, but for the purposes of greater analytical clarity and empirical research, it would be helpful to be able to capture these institutional dynamics within a general framework of how sociology is practiced that could be operationalized, measured and visually represented in a more complex way than Burawoy has done so far.

Comparing Disciplines

Then there is the issue of disciplines. Burawoy and Deflem share a common commitment to the health and growth of sociology as a discipline, but neither of them has outlined a theoretically informed approach to thinking about sociology in comparative context. Sociology, to be sure, is not the only discipline that has a professional, policy, critical, and public face, but Burawoy's model, in particular does not give us a way to think about this comparatively.

Burawoy's simple two by two table leads us to believe that, for example, the size of the various professional, policy, critical, and public wings in each discipline should be the same. Is that the case? Economics, one would think, has a far larger policy wing that does history or philosophy. But how many economists engage in "critical economics" where they debate the fundamental ethics of their professional activity? Is it difficult to imagine that the critical wing of sociology might be far larger in sociology than in economics? And might it be closer to the core of the discipline, while "critical economics" would be near the very edge of the legitimate boundaries of the profession? History as a discipline, in contrast, is likely to have a very large public component, as professional historians have long been involved in writing histories of presidents, kings and queens, military conflicts, and nations themselves, and more recently have focused on labor, gender, race, and local communities, all representing issues of some interest to the public. Historians, we are sure, do have a role to play in policy but it is at least worth hypothesizing that their policy wing is less developed than is the case in political science, certainly, but also sociology and economics. Psychology, to be sure, has a strong presence among the public, as the examples of *Psychology Today* and the various best-selling popular psychoanalysts and self-help writers remind (McLaughlin, 1998; McGee, 2005; Park, 2004).

In addition, it is worth theorizing and eventually researching the question of how the critical wings of different disciplines are related to their respective professional practices. Critical sociology, we would argue, could be placed graphically near the very center of sociology. What sociologist is unaware of C. Wright Mills' powerful critique of Parsons' grand theory and Lazarsfeld's abstracted empiricism, representative versions of professional and policy sociologies from sociology's golden era of the "1950s" (Mills, 1959)? In addition, while Dorothy Smith (e.g., Smith, 1991; 1995) might claim that her work as been marginalized within sociology, what other social science, with the possible exception of anthropology, discusses such sharp critiques of its own discipline's gender practices so prominently in its theory textbooks (for example, Bailey and Gayle, 1993; Farganis, 1996; Ritzer 2000a; 2000b)? No other major social science discipline debates its various institutional and epistemological crises as energetically and as often, with the possible exception of anthropology, as sociology does. This is related to the centrality of critical sociology relative to the comparative marginality of 'critical economics," "critical psychology," or "critical political science." Burawoy's two by two table with its instrumental and reflexive axis, does not allow us to think analytically about how disciplines differ according to the very categories he reifies in his model.

Conclusion: Towards Public Sociologies

We are not suggesting that there exist some universal patterns in the inter-relations among the major categories of sociological practice, torn out of national and historical context. We believe, for example, that critical sociology and policy sociology are both relatively large in Canada, with professional and public sociology relatively undeveloped in comparison to the United States (McLaughlin, 2005).[7] In addition we know, for example, that policy sociology in South Africa was highly involved in the development of the Apartheid regime throughout the 1960s and 1970s in a period where critical, liberal and especially black scholars were being jailed or repressed by the state in vicious ways (Ally, 2005). Policy, public and critical sociology seem highly developed in Great Britain, with a very small professional sociology core (Abrams, 1968; Fuller, 2000; Halsey, 2004; Platt, 2003). These national variations, alongside comparative analysis of different disciplines, make for a research project of some importance and scope, something to which we hope to contribute as part of a project on "Public Academics in Canada."

For some, Burawoy's vision of professional, policy, critical and public sociologies working together is a utopian vision, at best, or a cover for his own political agenda, at worst. We would like to convert the issue into various empirical and analytic questions, the most important being under what sociological conditions can these four faces of the sociological imagination live together productively in stable coalitions rooted in academic excellence that can anchor a strong discipline of sociology while contributing to the broader society?

Before engaging in this larger research project, we have tried to show here, however, that sociology in particular, does not need saving in the ways that Deflem is suggesting. Burawoy's agenda for public sociologies is a far more compelling vision for the discipline, albeit one with its own intellectual and analytic limitations. Dropping the reflexive axis from Burawoy's two by two table, thinking more deeply about what we mean by "critical," and embedding our analysis in a model that leaves room for national and institutional context and empirical comparative research on disciplines, provides for, we have argued, an analytic way forward in the coming debates on the future of public sociologies. The "audience" for academic works could be operationalized and measured comparatively (both in terms of nations and disciplines) while the level of "reflexivity" and "criticalness" strikes us as an empirical dead-end that would lead to more posturing than insight.

In any case, it is our view that the strength of sociology as a discipline will depend on preserving the unique, balanced and complementary space for policy, professional, critical and public sociologies outlined in Burawoy's (2005a) inspirational speech at the 2004 ASA meeting. The devil, of course, is in the details— something that ASA committee on public sociology has been working on, and sociologists around the country have been debating. We have offered here some thoughts on Burawoy's model that can lead towards the development of a road map for empirical research that can help us preserve sociology's unique moral and intellectual energy while being realistic about the institutional, academic and political context we must operate in. "Saving sociology," by attacking its public and critical wings is, however, just about the last thing we need to be doing as a discipline in the coming period.

Notes

1.   The authors would like to thank Jeffery Cormier, Scott Davies, Josse Johnston, Tony Puddephatt, Steven Brint, Jonathan Turner, Kyle Siler, Vincent Jeffries and Larry Nichols for their insightful and helpful comments on various drafts of this paper. We thank the department of sociology at McMaster University for hosting the event "Public Sociologies in Canada: A Dialogue" in the fall of 2005.

At the 2005 annual meeting of the Canadian Sociology and Anthropology Association in London, Ontario, Canadian sociologists Lisa Kowalchuk and Jeffrey Cormier organized two panels on the theme. In the first of these, panelists focused on the historical development and institutional incentive structures for publicly-oriented sociology in Canadian academe. Participants in the second panel analysed their own experiences in applying their sociological expertise and knowledge to various public realms. These panels were part of a larger Social Science and Humanities Research Council (SSHRC) funded project to study academics empirically as public intellectuals in Canada being undertaken by Neil McLaughlin, Lisa Kowalchuk and Jeffrey Cormier. Please address correspondence to Neil McLaughlin, Associate Professor, Sociology, McMaster University, KTH 620 1280 Main Street West, Hamilton, Ontario, L8S 4M4, Canada, (nmclaugh@ mcmaster.ca).

2. Interestingly, Burawoy says little about psychology, a discipline that we would argue is too rooted in methodological individualism and positivism to contribute in useful ways to public intellectual life. Psychology is a discipline, nonetheless, which does have a very large public face and competes with us very directly in our universities.

3. The categories are mechanical reflexivity, substantive reflexivity, methodological reflexivity, meta-theoretical reflexivity, interpretative reflexivity and ethnomethodological reflexivity (Lynch 2000).

4. We would define the teaching role as the public face of professional sociology, not as public sociology *per se*, a role that, for us, involves activity outside the formal professional work academics do as professors.

5. Burawoy's point about the complexity of each type of sociology is well taken, but his caveat about the pathology of dogmatism in critical sociology does not get around the fact that his model puts "critical" as *inherently* in the reflexive space.

6. Giddens (1990) points to the ongoing "monitoring of behaviour and its contexts" (37) as a "defining characteristic of all human action" (36). Modern social life raises this reflexive process to a new level, as "social practices are constantly examined and reformed in the light of incoming information about those very practices, thus constitutively altering their character" (38). Sociology is of particular significance in this process, as it is "the most generalized type of reflection upon modern social life" (41). By extension, then public sociologies should factor even more significantly in the modern process of reflexive monitoring. Of course, to the extent that expert knowledge becomes indistinguishable from "knowledge applied in lay actions" (45), the distinction between sociology and lay knowledge, and therefore, between sociology, public sociology, and lay knowledge is potentially non-existent in the end. No wonder that some have argued that Giddens has not been good for British sociology's institutional health despite the claim of Beck that more mainstream sociology is bound for the museum (Fuller 2000; Beck 2005).

7. At a recent discussion of public sociologies in Canada at McMaster University, Carl Cuneo made the case that Canadian sociology does indeed have a strong public sociology component, in the form of the networks of the Canadian political economy perspective centered around the journal *Studies in Political Economy*. This is arguable. While there are organic public sociologists in English Canada, we would make the case that the traditional elite public intellectual role is dominated by old fashioned "Tory" oriented scholars in the humanities, as well as philosophers and scholars from other disciplines, at least when compared to the United States. These are partly empirical questions, something being explored in our project on "Public Academics in Canada" sponsored by SSHRC. At the same event, Scott Davies made the case that it is important for Canadian sociology to "go professional" before going further down the policy, critical and organic public sociology paths. For different views from Canada, see Ericson 2005 and Hall 2005. The issue will play out quite differently in Quebec. Burawoy's discussion of public sociologies in Norway makes for particularly interesting reading for sociologists living in nations with relatively smaller populations and social democratic tradi-

tions. These are questions worth debating in both normative and empirical terms, in Canada and globally.

References

Abrams, P. 1968. *The Origins of British Sociology: 1834-1914.* Chicago, IL: University of Chicago Press.

Acker, J. 2005. "Comments on Burawoy on Public Sociology." *Critical Sociology* 31(3): 327-332.

Adorno, T. W., Frenkel-Brunswik, E., Levinson, D.J. and Sanford, R.N. 1950. *The Authoritarian Personality.* New York: Harper and Row.

Ally, Shireen. 2005. "Oppositional Intellectualism as a Reflection, not Rejection, of Power: Witts Sociology, 1975-1989," paper presented at the American Sociological Association meetings, Philadelphia, PA.

Anderson, E. 2002. "The Ideologically Driven Critique." *American Journal of Sociology* 107 (6): 15331550.

Aronowitz, S. 2005. "Comments on Michael Burawoy's 'The Critical Turn in Public Sociology.'" *Critical Sociology* 31 (3):333-338.

Bailey, G. and Gayle, N. 1993. *Sociology: An Introduction From the Classics to Contemporary Feminists.* Toronto: Oxford University Press.

Baiocchi, G. 2005. "Interrogating Connections: From Public Criticisms to Critical Publics in Burawoy's Public Sociology." *Critical Sociology* 31 (3): 339-352.

Beck, U. 2005. "How Not to Become a Museum Piece. *The British Journal of Sociology.* 56(3): 335-343.

Bourdieu, P. 1984. *Homo Academicus.* Stanford, CA: Stanford University Press.

_____, and Wacquant, L. 1992. *An Invitation to Reflexive Sociology.* Chicago, IL: University of Chicago Press.

Brady, D. 2004. "Why Public Sociologies May Fail." *Social Forces* 82 (4): 1629-1638.

Braithwaite, J. 2005. "For Public Social Science." *The British Journal of Sociology.* 56(3):345-353.

Brewer, Rose M. 2005. "Response to Michael Burawoy's Commentary: 'The Critical Turn to Public Sociology.'" *Critical Sociology* 31 (3): 353-360.

Burawoy, M. 2004a. "Public Sociologies: Contradictions, Dilemmas, and Possibilities." *Social Forces* 82 (4): 1603-1618.

_____. 2004b. "South Africanizing U.S. Sociology." *From the Left, Newsletter of the Marxist Section of the ASA.*

_____. 2004c. "Introduction: Public Sociologies: A Symposium from Boston College." *Social Problems* 51(1): 103-106.

_____. 2004d. "Manifesto for Public Sociologies." *Social Problems* 51(1): 124-129.

_____. 2005a. "2004 Presidential Address: For Public Sociology." *American Sociological Review* 70 (1): 4-28.

_____. 2005b. Provincializing the Social Sciences. G. Steinmetz, editor, *The Politics of Method in the Human Sciences: Positivism and its Epistemological Others.* Durham, NC: Duke University Press.

_____. 2005c. "The Critical Turn to Public Sociology." *Critical Sociology* 31 (3): 313-326.

_____. 2005d. "Rejoinder: Toward a Critical Public Sociology." *Critical Sociology* 31 (3): 379-390.

_____, Gamson, Ryan, Pfohl, Vaughan, Derber, Schor. 2004. "Public Sociologies: A Symposium from Boston College." *Social Problems:* 51:1:103-130.

Bute, M. 2005. "Public Sociology: Aristocratic or Populist?" Paper presented at the American Sociological Meetings, Philadelphia, PA.

Calhoun, C. 2005. "The Promise of Public Sociology." *British Journal of Sociology.* 56(3): 355-363.

Chriss, J.J. 1999. *Alvin Gouldner: Sociologist and Outlaw Marxist.* Aldershot, UK: Ashgate.

Deflem, M. 2004a. *Save Sociology.* http://www.savesociology.org. Accessed August 10, 2005.

_____. 2004b. *Sociology and Politics.* www.cas.sc.edu/socy/faculty/deflem/ savesociology/ 00socpolitics.html. Accessed August 10, 2005.

_____. 2004c. *Public Sociology.* www.cas.sc.edu/socy/faculty/deflem/savesociology/ 02publicsociology.html. Accessed August 10, 2005.

_____. 2004d. "There's the ASA, but Where's the Sociology?" *Footnotes* 32 (6): 9.

Derber, C. 2004. "Public Sociology as a Vocation." *Social Problems* 51(1): 119-121.

Duneier, M. 2002. "What Kind of Combat Sport is Sociology?" *American Journal of Sociology* 107 (6): 1551-1576.

Ericson, R. 2005. "Publicizing Sociology." *The British Journal of Sociology* 56(3): 365-372.

Etzioni, A. 2005. "Bookmarks for Public Sociologists." *The British Journal of Sociology* 56(3):373-378.

Farganis, J. 1996. *Readings in Sociological Theory: The Classic Tradition to Post-Modernism.* NewYork: McGraw-Hill.

Fuchs, S. 2002. "A Review Essay on *Making Social Sciences Matter: Why Social Inquiry Fails and How It Can Succeed Again.*" *Sociological Theory* 20 (1): 131-133.

_____. 2000. *The Professional Quest for Truth: A Social Theory of Science and Knowledge.* Albany: State University of New York Press.

Fuller, S. 2000. "A Very Qualified Success, Indeed: The Case of Anthony Giddens and British Sociology." *Canadian Journal of Sociology* 25 (4): 507-516.

_____. 2004. *Kuhn vs Popper: The Struggle for the Soul of Social Science.* Columbia University Press.

Gamson, W. 2004. "Life on the Interface." *Social Problems* 51(1): 106-110.

Ghamari-Tabrizi, B. 2005. "Can Burawoy Make Everybody Happy? Comments on Public Sociology." *Critical Sociology* 31 (3): 361-370.

Giddens, A. 1990. *The Consequences of Modernity.* Stanford, CA: Stanford University Press.

Gouldner, A. 1970. *The Coming Crisis of Western Sociology.* New York: Avon.

Gramsci, A. 1971. *Selections from the Prison Notebooks of Antonio Gramsci.* New York: International Publications.

Hall, J.A. 2005. "A Guarded Welcome." *The British Journal of Sociology* 56(3): 379-381.

Halliday, T. 1992. "Introduction: Sociology's Fragile Professionalism." T. Halliday and M. Janowitz, (eds.), *Sociology and Its Publics: The Forms and Fates of Disciplinary Organization.* Chicago, IL: University of Chicago Press.

Halsey, A.H. 2004. *A History of Sociology in Britain: Science, Literature, and Society.* Oxford: Oxford University Press.

Katz-Fishman, W. and Scott, J. 2005. "Comments on Burawoy: A View From the Bottom-Up." *Critical Sociology* 31 (3): 371-374.

Light, D. 2005. "Contributing to Scholarship and Theory through Public Sociology." *Social Forces* 83(4): 1647-1654.

Lynch, M. 2000. "Against Reflexivity as an Academic Virtue and Source of Privileged Knowledge." *Theory, Culture, and Society.* 17(3): 26-54.

McLaughlin, N.G. 1998. "Why Do Schools of Thought Fail? Neo-Freudianism as a Case Study in the Sociology of Knowledge." *Journal of the History of the Behavioural Sciences* 34 (2): 113-134.

_____. 1999. "Origin Myths in the Social Sciences: Fromm, the Frankfurt School and the Emergence of Critical Theory." *The Canadian Journal of Sociology* 24 (1): 109-139.

_____. 2004. "A Canadian Rejoinder: Sociology North and South of the Border." *American Sociologist* 35 (1): 80-101.

_____. 2005. "Canada's Impossible Science: Historical and Institutional Origins of the Coming Crisis in Anglo-Canadian Sociology." *Canadian Journal of Sociology* 30 (1): 1-40.

McGee, M. 2005. *Self-Help, Inc: Makeover Culture in American Life.* Berkeley, CA: University of California Press.

Mills, C.W. 1959. *The Sociological Imagination.* New York: Oxford University Press.

Neilsen, F. 2004. "The Vacant 'We': Remarks on *Public Sociology.*" *Social Forces* 82 (4): 1619-1627.

Newman, K. 2002. "No Shame: The View from the Left Bank." *American Journal of Sociology* 107 (6): 1577-1599.

Nisbet, R. 1966. *The Sociological Tradition.* New York: Basic Books.

_____. 1976. *Sociology as an Art Form.* London: Heinneman.

Oakes, G. and Vidich, A.J. 1999. *Collaboration, Reputation, and Ethics in American Academic Life: Hans H. Gerth and C. Wright Mills.* Chicago, IL: University of Illinois Press.

Park, D.W. 2004. "The Couch and the Clinic:The Cultural Authority of Popular Psychiatry and Psychoanalysis." *Cultural Studies* 18 (1): 109-133.

Pfohl, S. 2004. "Blessings and Curses in the Sociology Classroom." *Social Problems* 51(1): 113-115.

Platt, J. 2003. *The British Sociological Association: A Sociological History.* Durham, UK: Sociologypress.

Riesman, D. [1954] 1993. *Abundance for What? And Other Essays.* New Jersey: Transaction Press.

Ritzer, G. 2000a. *Modern Sociological Theory.* New York: McGraw-Hill.

_____. 2000b. *Sociological Theory.* New York: McGraw-Hill.

Ryan, C. 2004. Can We Be Compañeros? *Social Problems* 51(1): 110-113.

Schor, J. 2004. "From Obscurity to 'People Magazine.'" *Social Problems* 51(1): 121-124.

Scott, J. 2005. "Who Will Speak, and Who Will Listen? Comments on Burawoy and Public Sociology." *The British Journal of Sociology.* 56(3): 405-409.

Smith, D.E. 1991. *The Everyday World as Problematic: A Feminist Sociology.* Toronto: University of Toronto Press.

_____. 1995. *The Conceptual Practices of Power: A Feminist Sociology of Knowledge.* Toronto: University of Toronto Press.

Stacey, J. 2004. "Marital Suitors Court Social Science Spinsters: The Unwittingly Conservative Effects of Public Sociology." *Social Problems.* 51(1): 131-145.

Steinberg, S.1995. *Turning Back: The Retreat From Racial Justice in American Thought and Policy.* Boston: Beacon Press.

Swartz, D. 2003. "From Critical Sociology to Public Intellectual: Pierre Bourdieu and Politics." *Theory and Society* 32: 791-823.

Tittle, C. 2004. "The Arrogance of Public Sociology." *Social Forces* 82 (4): 1639-1643.

Turner, J. 2005. "Foundations of Sociology: In Search of the Disciplinary Core." Paper presented at the American Sociological Association meetings, Philadelphia, PA.

Turner, S. and Turner, J. 1990. *The Impossible Science: An Institutional Analysis of American Sociology.* London: Sage.

Urry, John. 2005. "The Good News and the Bad News." *Critical Sociology* 31 (3): 375-378.

Vaughn, D. 2004. "Public Sociologist by Accident." *Social Problems* 51(1): 115-118.

_____. 2005. "On the Relevance of Ethnography for the Production of Public Sociology and Policy." *The British Journal of Sociology* 56(3): 411-416.

Wacquant, L. 2002. "Scrutinizing the Streets: Poverty, Morality, and the Pitfalls of Urban Ethnography." *American Journal of Sociology* 107 (6): 1468-1532.

Walzer, M. 1988. *The Company of Critics*. New York: Basic Books.

Whitely, R. 1984. *The Intellectual and Social Organization of the Sciences*. Oxford Clarendon.

Wiggerhaus, Rolf. 1994. *The Frankfurt School: Its History, Theories, and Political Significance*. Cambridge: MIT Press.

Wolfe, A. 1989. *Whose Keeper? Social Science and Moral Obligation*. Berkeley, CA: University of California Press.

_____. 1998. *Marginalized in the Middle*. Chicago, IL: University of Chicago Press.

_____. 2003. *An Intellectual in Public*. Ann Arbor, MI: Michigan University Press.

Appendix:
Letter to the Editor by Mathieu Deflem

In response to the article, "Why Sociology Does Not Need to Be Saved," by Neil McLaughlin, Lisa Kowalchuk, and Kerry Turcotte, a few clarifications are in order—and not only because the title of the article is an apparent reference to my website campaign, "SaveSociology.org." In the article, my activities against public sociology are referenced in a very distorted and misleading manner. The authors suggest that the tone of my campaign is "problematic and divisive." I cannot see how my campaign can possibly be problematic—except perhaps for those who support public sociology—because it has garnered a lot of attention and fostered debate, to wit, for example, the article by McLaughlin et al. My campaign is also not divisive, but instead is oriented at clarifying the contours and foundations of a debate that is important to our discipline and profession. The divisions that have been made (e.g., the very notion of a public sociology) are not mine.

I am faulted for presenting a "vision of a purely 'scientific sociology'." Nothing could be further from the truth. Besides wondering what a non-purely scientific sociology might mean, I merely argue, in response to the attempted politicization of sociology by the recent wave of public sociology, that sociology is a social science. There is no specific socio-logical perspective that I defend in my campaign against public sociology other than taking a stance on what sociology should not be. The authors write of "the 'save sociology' perspective" when such does not exist. Moreover, the sociological perspectives I do defend are articulated in my substantive contributions in sociology and are not at issue here.

McLaughlin et al. argue that the presentation of public sociology on my website is "fragmented and brief." That is true inasmuch as my website merely seeks to expose the basic arguments I have against public sociology. But the website campaign does not comprise the whole of my concerns. Should the authors have relied on at least some of my numerous writings (all of which are linked from my website), they would have been able to entertain in an actual discussion of my ideas. But, most damaging to their article, they cite only one letter (Deflem, 2004b) and none of my other, more important writings (Deflem, 2005a, 2005b, 2005c, 2004a, 2004c). On formal grounds alone, the allegations leveled against me are without merit. For instance, I am being critiqued for activities that verge on "red-baiting." This is flat-out absurd, because my activities are oriented against any politicization of sociology, the specific form or direction of which does not interest me one bit, as I have argued explicitly elsewhere (Deflem, 2004c).

Finally, I must take special exception to the authors' contention that I would have launched into "personalized attack" in my relevant activities, specifically by attacking "the ASA staff." I deny this charge unequivocally. Not on one single occasion have I been personalized in any of my work in this context. Any criticisms I have launched have always focused on professional and intellectual positions, never on personal dimensions. Besides, I do not even know most of my fellow sociologists in this debate on a personal level. My contacts within the ASA, also, have been very numerous and professional, especially as I have served in a multitude of service functions in and for the association since I became a member in 1993. I would encourage McLaughlin et al. to be more thoughtful before they raise such a serious charge, especially when they do not even have one argument to support it.

References

Deflem, M. 2004a. "The War in Iraq and the Peace of San Francisco: Breaking the Code of Public Sociology." *Peace, War & Social Conflict*, Newsletter of the ASA section, November issue, pp. 3–5. ———. 2004b. "There's the ASA, but Where's the Sociology?" Public Forum. *Footnotes*, ASA Newsletter, July/August 2004, 32(6):9. ———. 2004c. Letter to the Editor ("The Proper Role of Sociology in the World at Large"). *The Chronicle Review*, October 1, p. B17. ———. 2005a. "Southernizing *Social Forces*." *The Southern Sociologist*, Newsletter of the Southern Sociological Society, Winter 2005, 36(3): 12–15. ———. 2005b. "Sociologists, One More Effort! A Propos Goodwin." *Comparative & Historical Sociology*, ASA Section newsletter 16(2): 4–6. ———. 2005c. "Comment" (on public sociology). *Contemporary Sociology* 34(1):92–93.

13

Third-Wave Sociology and the End of Pure Science

Michael Burawoy[1]

Pure science has been waiting in the wings for the storm of public sociology to pass. Thus far, the storm has not passed. Instead, it has shown unexpected force, bursting through old, poorly built levees. The army corps of pure scientists has finally entered the battle for sociology, but they have arrived too late, and their technology is inadequate and outdated. Their attempt to rescue sociology has an air of desperation. The three papers of Turner, Brint, and Boyns and Fletcher defend what the latter call the Strong Program in Professional Sociology (SPPS)—a program of dispassionate science and value-neutrality—but they do so, ironically enough, with a torrent of acrimony and recrimination, passion, and politics. They protest far too much, precisely because, as I shall argue, the time for SPPS has passed—if it ever existed—and necessarily so. In the contemporary world a sociology hostile to values, politics, diversity, utopias, and above all to publics no longer makes sense—if it ever did. It can be defended only by violating its own premises.

My response to these critics draws on the other papers in this symposium, but I begin by outlining the paradoxes of the Strong Program in Professional Sociology. Then, in the second section of this essay, I show that SPPS is not the universalistic project it claims to be but a specific response to the early development of American sociology. In the third section I show how SPPS belongs to a historical period, second-wave sociology, that has now been transcended. The fourth section turns to the essays of Jeffries; Putney, Alley and Bengtson; Bonacich; and Chase-Dunn. Rather than resurrecting a past already superseded, these

317

four essays point to the future, toward a third-wave sociology that integrates public sociology into our discipline. In their different ways they call on us to be accountable to rational and deliberative publics, such as communities of faith, the elderly, labor movements, and transnational organizations. In contrast to the first three, these last four contributions view engaging with publics not as a threat to professional sociology but a source of its vitality. Moreover, their diversity effectively counters the claim that Marxism is the true face of public sociology. The fifth and last section of my response engages the paper of McLaughlin, Kowalchuk, and Turcotte who reformulate my four-sociology matrix (policy, public, professional, and critical) by excising the critical dimension. I end, therefore, by defending critical sociology—the independent discussion of values and assumptions—as an essential accomplice of public sociology. Critical sociology is integral to third-wave sociology as the latter takes on the challenges of unconstrained market expansion.

I. The Strong Program in Professional Sociology (SPPS)

In *Backlash* Susan Faludi not only reveals the social basis of opposition to feminism but also exposes its "blame the victim" ideology according to which the women's movement is inherently self-defeating. Feminism, its critics claim, failed to deliver on its promises not because of entrenched opposition to its goals, but because women cannot cope with and do not desire their new won freedoms. In similar fashion the defenders of SPPS argue that public sociology will inevitably undermine its own goals. By putting a political foot forward it will undermine sociology's already precarious legitimacy among publics who are suspicious of moralizing. David Boyns and Jesse Fletcher go so far as to assert (with precious little data) that public sociology only masquerades as science, hiding its true identity as Marxism (assumed to be the antithesis of true science). Rather than building unity, the defenders of SPPS suggest, public sociology will bring down the whole house by further fragmenting and dividing our discipline. Far better, they argue, to retreat from the public sphere and insulate sociology so that its still immature science can develop a unified and coherent body of knowledge. Only then can it be deployed to influence people who really count, policy makers in the halls of power.

Of the three papers advocating SPPS, Jonathan Turner's is the most uncompromising. Calling for a linkage between professional sociology and policy sociology in a model of social engineering, he would have us use "sociological knowledge to solve problems that clients bring to us" (p. 40). Having vilified public sociology for its divisiveness, although again with precious little evidence, Turner himself proposes to split our discipline in order to sustain the purity of his social engineering. On the one side would be scientific sociology (or "social physics" as he prefers to call it), practiced by enlightened, objective experts, working away at the laws of society; on the other side would be the "activist sociology," the infidels practicing public sociology. He labels them "extremists," "ideologues," "inflammatory dogmatists," subject to the "tyranny of political correctness," "storm troopers" "manning the barricades," "signing petitions," and "shouting their morality." Who are these anonymous apostates? Do they include the public sociology contributors to this symposium: Vincent Jeffries? Norella M. Putney, Dawn Alley, and Vern L. Bengtson? Chris Chase-Dunn? Edna Bonacich? Innuendo and invective stand in place of the empirical examination of actually existing public sociology. One can only marvel at the irony of wild and unsubstantiated accusations coming from the pen of a devout believer in objective and dispassionate science.

Empirical examination of actual public sociologies would distinguish the normal from the pathological forms of sociological practice, pointing to the ways public sociology degenerates into populism or vanguardism. Without any evidence Turner simply reduces public sociology to its pathological forms and then pretends that this is the only form public sociology can take. In short, he first pathologizes the normal and then normalizes the pathological. Not content with this sleight of hand, Turner then accuses the apostates of "attack dogmatism," that is of making precisely the same error but in reverse, that they reduce professional sociology to the "tyranny of scientism" (p. 36). Here again evidence is missing, simply pointing a finger at supposedly hapless graduate students misled by unnamed and irresponsible faculty.

The point of the exercise is inescapable: having demonized public and critical sociologies, Turner is justified in expelling these vile bodies from the community of scientists. To put it in more neutral language, from Turner's point of view, the positive pole (the instrumental knowledge of professional and policy sociology) is in irreconcilable antagonism with the negative pole (the reflexive knowledge of critical and public sociology). In this Manichean view, one pole or the other must reign supreme: if the former then sociology is saved, if the latter it is doomed. My effort to hold them together in a single organic division of disciplinary labor is utopian.

But who is the utopian now? What is this pure science at the heart of SPPS? We do not hear a great deal about its principles, but we do know that it abjures any values. So much so that Turner himself rejects the theories of alienation in Marx, anomie in Durkheim, and bureaucratization in Weber as inaccurate evaluative representations of reality. He extends his assault on the canon to include both Merton and Parsons, accusing them of deploying normative concepts and thus violating the norms of pure science. Habermas's notion of undistorted communication, the telos of language, is condemned as pure philosophy unrelated to sociology that must only deal with what is, not with what might be or should be. In Turner's view concepts that reflect "moral biases ... almost always miss the point" (p. 33). They cannot be scientific, which would rule out such methodological devices as the ideal type. This radical empiricism, as Max Weber demonstrated long ago, is a futile exercise. To develop concepts that exactly mirror the infinite manifold of the concrete world is an impossible task. The essence of science must lie in simplification and thus the use of concepts that are necessarily one-sided, and in the case of the social sciences one-sidedness is driven by their value orientation. Social science without values is impossible.

Steve Brint's critique of public sociology is more measured. Like the others he criticizes public sociology for wrapping political activism in non-partisan clothing. My call for a joint endeavor of all four sociologies will encourage rather than prevent conflict; instead we must build up professional sociology as the moral and not just the structural core of the discipline. He departs from Turner, therefore, in recognizing the importance of one particular set of values—the moral passion that underpins the scientific enterprise. In other words, moral passion is necessary to produce value-neutral science, value-neutral research. But is Brint able to sustain such a position? Against my own valorization of civil society he argues, quite persuasively, that civil society contains both constructive and destructive forces. Remonstrating against the view of civil society as a harmonious, spontaneous defense of humanity, equally he insists that states and markets cannot be painted as evil incarnate. No less than civil society they too contain their progressive moments, promoting public welfare. His sociology, therefore, is no less imbued with values than my own. The question is, therefore, which values makes more sense today?

In my rejoinder below I argue that Brint's ecumenical view of the moral equivalence of state, market and civil society reflects a period that has been superseded,— the period of second wave marketization, when states defended society against markets, when state regulation of markets did promote greater welfare for all. Today, however, state and

یعنی SPPS و برنت که می گوید که آیا نهادهای مدنی اهمیت دارد؟ نظام و بازار هم در زندگی هفته اند!"
هم ارزشی اند و به دیده دقت می خورند که نظام بازار، کنترل می کند مردم رو خودش ...

markets are in collusion, jointly promoting the commodification of everyday life and the privatization of all things public. These circumstances require a fundamentally new approach to sociology—third wave sociology—that valorizes civil society above state and market. To defend the Strong Program in Professional Sociology today is not so much utopian as ideological, in Karl Mannheim's sense of the word, that is seeking to restore a regressive form of sociology. Like all ideologies SPPS did have its progressive period when it was indeed a forward-looking utopia (when Turner was a graduate student!). To this earlier period we turn first, before analyzing its subsequent degeneration.

II. The Genesis of Pure Science

The Strong Program in Professional Sociology is based in the notion of pure science in which theory arises from careful interrogation of data. Pure science presents itself as a natural and universal form of science, obscuring the conditions of its existence as well as the historical circumstances out of which it emerged. In American sociology the rise of pure science harkens back to a bygone era, the birth and consolidation of professionalization, stretching from the First World War to the 1960s. It is a reaction against the early antebellum sociology that defended slavery, and more emphatically against the crusading social reformers of the postbellum period who proposed all manner of cooperatives and communes to protect labor from the tyranny of markets. But pure science was also a rebellion against the grand speculative science of the successors to nineteenth-century social reform, the Social Darwinists of early twentieth-century American sociology (Lester Ward, William Graham Sumner, Franklin Giddings, and Albion Small). SPPS rejects the unity of science and morality that pervaded all these early periods.

Professional sociology has long insisted on the separation of science from morality, the turn from speculative to pure science—a social physics based on the empirical world. Sociology's contribution to the world, in this view, can consist only of laws induced from systematically collected data. This was the objectivism of the second generation of American sociologists—William Ogburn, Howard Odum, Stuart Chapin, and others. Their claim was not that sociology should be a science for science's sake but rather that it should be applied to the world through the mediation of the state. Ogburn after all presided over the research for President Hoover's 1933 Committee on Recent Social Trends; Samuel Stouffer was commissioned by the government to do his famous study of the American Soldier. After World War II, sociology was increasingly funded by the federal government and private foundations, developing important expertise in such areas as education and market research.

This policy research produced its own reaction in the formation of the Society for the Study of Social Problems in 1951, critical of sociology's close connection to elites. Even as this insurgent organization was critical of dominant interests, and focused on the problems of oppressed and marginalized groups, it was still a sociology linked to the state and in particular to its welfare apparatuses. Throughout this period, from the New Deal until the Civil Rights Movement, the idea of an articulate public remained dormant within sociology, having been buried by Walter Lippmann and then by the 1950s sociologists of mass society. Professional sociology's engagement with the world beyond was largely restricted to clients who could afford its expertise.

To be successful in the policy world it was important that sociology develop a coherent and unified science and this indeed was the project of post-World War II sociology, whether that unity was defined by theory (e.g., structural functionalism) or method (the application of new statistical techniques). It aimed to present a common front so as to more effectively influence policymakers. Unlike economics, however, it did not have that *sine qua non* of effective policymaking, namely the monopoly of knowledge over a well-defined object, which, in the case of economics, was the market economy. The idea of society remained as elusive as the systems analysis of structural functionalism remained short lived. In the final analysis sociology failed to construct a characteristic entity over which it had privileged, expert knowledge, and around which it could build unity. Without such an entity policy sociology could not compete with economics or political science and the unity to which SPPS aspired remained illusory.

What then is our discipline of sociology? If it is not defined by a distinctive object of knowledge then how do we define its unity? I argue its unity is defined by a "standpoint"—the standpoint of civil society—or rather the standpoints of civil society, since it is far from being a unified, homogeneous entity. Civil society was an invention coterminous with capitalism, arising to protect human community from the tyranny of the market. So long as commodification was held in check by the state, sociology could also collaborate with the state, but when the state itself turns against civil society, sociology has to concentrate on cultivating its relation to civil society, to the associations and movements that compose it. This, then, becomes the epoch of public sociology.

III. Three Waves of Sociology

To develop this perspective of sociology I draw on Karl Polanyi's *The Great Transformation* that has become a canonical text in the contemporary era of neoliberalism. Polanyi's understanding of the capitalist market—its political requirements, its destructive tendencies, its ideological representations, and the counterformations it inspires—lays the basis of a theory of civil society and its successive constructions within sociology. He provides the tools for a theory of sociology and its periodization, entirely absent from SPPS that cannot understand the conditions of its own possibility precisely because pure science eschews reflexive knowledge.

Karl Polanyi studied the origins, reproduction and consequences of market expansion from the late eighteenth century to the middle of the twentieth century. In a chain of elaborate causality he ties together the most micro processes to the most global forces. He puts to rest the mythology that markets are self-created and instead shows their dependence on the nation state, both in their origins and their reproduction. His most original contribution, however, lies in the analysis of the way markets sow the seeds of their own destruction by commodifying the uncommodifiable. Labor, money, and land are fictitious commodities, which lose their use value when they are subject to exchange. When labor is commodified— purchased by capital on a piece-meal basis only to be expelled when it is no longer needed—then it can no longer perform its function in production. It no longer generates the spontaneous consent and creative participation so necessary for capitalist production. Similarly, subjecting money to exchange means that its value is continually fluctuating, creating havoc for capital that requires a predictable context within which to organize production and make profit. Finally, the commodification of land—and we might generalize to the environment—destroys its capacity to sustain human life.

In his analysis of first-wave marketization of the nineteenth century Polanyi focuses mainly on society's self-defense against the commodification of labor. Here he refers to the emergence of the factory movement to regulate the length of the working day, the trade union movement, the spread of cooperatives, and the Chartist Movement. For Polanyi Robert Owen—both his theory and his organization of the self-regulating community at New Lanark—epitomizes the creation of an industrial society against the market. In postbellum United States there were similar self-sustaining communities promoted by social reformers bent on

در فاز اول بازار سازی قرن ۱۹ جامعه به دنبال دفاع از خود در مقابل کالا یی شدن نیروی کار ...

خط تاکید و اضافه شدن در اصل ۱ ...

protecting society from the market. This was indeed the era of utopian sociology.

If first-wave marketization was *national* in origin but prompted *local* reactions, second wave marketization was *international* in origin, prompting *national* reactions. Second-wave marketization begins with the expansion of imperialism at the end of the nineteenth century, interrupted by World War I but moving forward with renewed energy during the 1920s. The pegging of currencies to the gold standard proved too much of a liability to national economies which sought to insulate domestic markets from the devastating effects of international trade. This was the era of national self-protection, or what Hobsbawm calls the age of extremes, from Fascism to Stalinism, from Social Democracy to the New Deal. During this period sociology is either destroyed or it becomes focused on policy questions of the emergent welfare state. This was a period of social rights that protected labor from the market: social security, unemployment compensation, pensions, labor legislation and minimum wages. Sociology deals with such familiar issues as inequality, educational opportunity, poverty, political stability, industrial organization, and the family, all with a view, implicitly if not explicitly, to developing state policies that regulate the destructive consequences of the market. Such a policy sociology calls for a unified discipline with a singular science—just like the Strong Program in Professional Sociology.

Polanyi thought that second-wave marketization spelled the end of market fundamentalism since it had led to such disastrous political forms as Fascism and Stalinism. At his most optimistic he anticipated a socialist future in which markets and states would be subordinated to a self-regulating society. Polanyi's warnings notwithstanding, today third-wave marketization is sweeping the earth, with the state no longer a bulwark to market expansion but its agent and partner. The state, either directly or indirectly through the market, takes the offensive against labor and social rights won in previous periods, establishing a very different terrain for sociology that can no longer collaborate with the state for a policy sociology. Instead sociology must directly defend civil society, against the twin forces of state and market. In other words, third-wave marketization makes public sociologies necessary.

When second-wave marketization swept the world in the early part of the twentieth century, it led first to the retrenchment of labor rights but then to a deeper reaction from the state (in the United States the New Deal) that brought social rights into existence, social rights that included rights of labor organization and regulation of working conditions and wages, but also a range of welfare rights—from unemployment benefits to pensions, from health insurance to minimum wages. Now third-wave marketization has turned against both labor and social rights, and the question is whether the reaction can subsume both under an even broader rubric. The obvious candidate for such a rubric is human rights, the rights of human beings to survive in community with one another, wherever they are, under whatever conditions. The progression from labor rights to social rights, and then to human rights corresponds to the succession of fictitious commodities: labor, money and the environment. Polanyi had little to say about the environment but the commodification of nature has reached new proportions threatening the survival of all, endangering the human species. There is, therefore, an elective affinity between the defense of human rights and environmental degradation.

Human rights can be a treacherous terrain, exploited by powerful nations, the United States in particular, to justify all manner of atrocities at home and particularly abroad. If human rights are defined in the narrow terms of political liberalism, it is well suited to the expansion rather than containment of the market. To ensure the protection of fundamental labor and social rights and to extend them to rights of universal survival, we must enter into a struggle over the very definition of human rights.

In this era of third-wave marketization, sociology turns toward civil society, above and below the nation state. Below the nation state sociologists forge a public sociology with local communities and even a policy sociology tied to local governments that now have to bear the brunt of the provision of social support—responsibility which the federal state has abdicated. Above the state, public sociology develops in close connection to transnational associations, organizations and movements. Third-wave marketization calls for a public sociology that knits together local publics into a global formation. The impetus of a global public sociology is transmitted back into professional sociology not only in the form of multiple research programs, attentive to the needs and interests of different publics, but also in an overarching sociology of publics.

These three periods of sociology should not be seen as separate and disconnected. Shaped in response to marketization, they also develop dialectically. If professional-policy sociology repudiates utopian sociology, public sociology combines the value stance so central to the latter with the disciplined engagement of the former. Third-wave sociology replaces the quest for a singular object of knowledge with the embrace of multiple such objects organized around the concerns of multiple publics. The corresponding plurality of research programs combines the value

Table 1
Three Waves of Marketization and Sociology

	First Wave of Marketization (1850–1920)	Second Wave of Marketization (1920–1970)	Third Wave of Marketization (1970 onwards)
Rights against the Market	Labor Rights	Social Rights	Human Rights
Social Defense against Market	Local Community	State Regulation	Global Civil Society
Contribution to Society	Utopian Sociology	Policy Sociology	Public Sociology
Unifying Principle	Vision	Object of Knowledge	Standpoint
Science	Speculative Science State Regulation	Pure Science	Value Science

commitments of early sociology with the knowledge-base of the empirical research of second-wave sociology. The Strong Program of Professional Sociology can only present itself at the forefront of sociology by collapsing public sociology back into first-wave utopian sociology, thereby missing public sociology's transcendence of first and second waves and its elective affinity to the challenges of the contemporary era.

If third-wave marketization calls for reactions on the level of a global civil society, how well are our sociological organizations doing? Do the structure and interests of professional sociology reflect the diversity of the publics we might reach? Looking at the American Sociological Association we see that it is indeed a plural organization—according to the defenders of SPPS disastrously fragmented—divided into 43 sections that in large part reflect the overlapping publics that are our potential audience, partners in dialogue. To be sure there are sections that speak mainly to sociologists—theory or mathematical sociology—but so many speak to actual or potential publics such as Medical Sociology, Mental Health, Children and Youth, Latino/a Sociology, Labor and Labor Movements, Racial and Ethnic Minorities, Religion, etc. Conceived of in this way professional sociology consists of multiple intersecting research programs, some more developed than others, each with its own theoretical frameworks rooted in value assumptions, and expanding through the engagement of empirical anomalies and internal contradictions.

The American Sociological Association is less effective when it comes to developing global perspectives, reaching out to transnational publics. Institutionally, American sociology is the most powerful in the world, yet it remains strangely parochial. It possesses far more resources than the International Sociological Association, which, it is also worth noting, is also divided into 53 Research Committees, reflecting a potential array of public sociologies on a global scale. We should not romanticize the ISA, however, since, as in so many transnational organizations, the presence of Europe and United States is hegemonic.

To summarize the argument so far. Disciplinary unity is no longer based on the quest for a <u>singular paradigm</u> but on the interconnections of multiple research programs. If the unity of *pure science* requires an authoritarian organization of sociology, what Durkheim might call a <u>mechanical solidarity</u> with a strong collective consciousness, the unity of *value science* is based on an <u>organic solidarity,</u> involving the interdependence and complementarity of multiple research agendas. But even the latter requires a type of shared collective consciousness, namely the standpoint from within civil society that opposes the tyranny of markets that threaten human survival. When values are the self-conscious foundation of sociological research, critical sociology has a particularly important role, engaging with and making manifest those value presuppositions, linking them to one another. I will return to this aspect of critical sociology in the last section. First, I will consider the diversity of public sociologies exemplified by the other papers in this volume and the synergy between public and professional sociology that they embody.

IV. Varieties of Public Sociology and Their Synergy with Professional Sociology

We can see now why the accusation that public sociology is a thinly disguised Marxism is baseless. The disciples of the Strong Program in Professional Sociology can only imagine a monolithic science, echoing the old aspiration of second wave sociology. They, thus, reduce my defense of pluralism to a political ruse for a Marxist takeover of sociology. This accusation is a projection of their own imperial ambition for a sociology with a singular, unified, homogeneous frame. To be sure I have never made a secret of my Marxist commitments and, undoubtedly, if I had a public sociology it would have a Marxist coloring. But I don't represent a distinctive public sociology. Instead I advocate a broad range of public sociologies, which I have never tried to reduce to Marxism. My sociological Marxism, with its emphasis on the restoration of the social, calls for a pluralistic professional sociology with multiple research programs, corresponding to multiple public sociologies. The history of twentieth century Marxism has tragically shown that when Marxism rules it petrifies. To sustain itself as science and critique Marxism has to occupy a minority position. The demonization of Marxism as dogmatic and supremacist is a relic of the cold war when sociology as pure science was an ideological front in the siege against Communism. That period is now over.

Any doubts about the plurality of public sociologies should be dispelled quickly by the essays in this volume, which range from an exploration of Sorokin's integralism and its connection to religious values, to the new science of social gerontology, to the study of labor movements, to transnationalism at the World Social Forum. There is as little doubt about the breadth of publics being engaged as there is about the diversity of their value orientations. These essays also demonstrate, contra SPPS, the possible synergies among three and sometimes all four types of sociological knowledge: professional, policy, public, and critical.

One common criticism of public sociology focuses on its failure to capture the imagination of publics with mentalities different from that of the sociologist. Vincent Jeffries's counters this criticism with his rendition of Sorokin's "integralism." He shows how Sorokin's life can be seen as a complex movement among the four types of sociological knowledge. Deeply involved in social issues of the time, Sorokin began systematizing sociology in Russia, immediately after the Bolshevik Revolution, and before the advent of professional sociology. In the United States his early work on social mobility was one of the first attempts at systematic analysis of social stratification. When he went to Harvard in 1931 to head the newly created department of sociology his projects became ever more ambitious, developing grand theories of history while attacking professional sociology's penchant for trivial empiricism. He tied the crises of the age to the rise of sensate culture, represented within sociology as the devotion to pure science. Sorokin's critical sociology was aimed precisely at the SPPS, with its absence of moral foundations. He resolutely opposed any policy sociology in the service of a client. His own "integralism" combined empirical, rational and intuitive knowledge as the basis of a public sociology for a new moral order. You might say he was one of the prophets of public sociology.

Jeffries especially admires Sorokin's later faith-based sociology, his theories of human goodness and the creative power of altruistic love. Social life, writes Sorokin, will be more effectively ameliorated through personal transformation than through "political campaigns, legislation, wars and revolutions, lockouts and strikes, and pressure reforms." Sorokin becomes ever more the public and critical sociologist than a professional sociologist, gathering behind him a band of devoted followers. It remains an open question as to how successful they will be in turning Sorokin's sociological legacy toward an organic public sociology engaged with communities of faith or toward a broader traditional public sociology in the lineage of Robert Bellah, Andrew Greeley, Christian Smith, Rodney Stark, or Robert Wuthnow.

If Sorokin's public sociology grew out of a dissatisfaction with professional sociology, then the field of social gerontology took the opposite trajectory. It grew up as a response to a particular public—the elderly—that becomes ever more important with the aging of the demographic structure of societies. The public impetus inspired theoretical developments that grew back into professional sociology. Norella M. Putney, Dawn E. Alley, and Vern L. Bengtson illustrate the complex synergy among all four types of sociological knowledge. For them the organic division of sociological labor is no utopia but the reality of a youthful disciplinary subfield whose latecomer status gives it access to a wide range of preexisting sociological theory. It has yet to develop an elaborate division of labor in which the core professional knowledge develops autonomously from policy, critical, and public knowledges. Social gerontologists might have difficulty grasping what all the fuss is about, why SPPS finds reflexive knowledge to be such a threat, when it appears to be the driving energy behind this subfield, as well as connecting it to other disciplines.

Our third case offers another example of the synergy of professional and public sociology. Edna Bonacich has a long history of working with the labor movement, starting with her own union on campus, AFT (American Federation of Teachers), then AFSCME (American Federation of State, Country, and Municipal Employees), garment workers when they were still organized by the ILGWU (International Ladies Garment Workers Union), truck drivers and most recently the WGA (Workers Guild of America). Her close engagement, a case of organic public sociology, reverberated into a policy sociology concerned with organizing strategies, such as the campaign against Guess, but also into professional sociology, concerned with the place of labor in the global economy.

Bonacich's autobiographical narrative emphasizes the precarious character of the dialogue between sociologist and public. She recounts her efforts to combine independence and trust, to deflect pressure to become a paid consultant for policy research, to avoid the appearance of omniscience while still offering unionists important insights. How to sustain such a delicate balance is an important issue and Bonacich has much to teach us, but here I want to attend to what she sidelines, namely how her public sociology has contributed to the accumulation of scientific knowledge. Bonacich made a big splash in the professional world in the 1970s with her theory of the split labor market, which, simply put, argued that racial orders spring from a class compromise between capital and high-priced white labor at the expense of lower-priced black labor. She applied this idea with appropriate specifications to the history of race and class in United States and South Africa.

Her public sociology, which came decades later, eventuated in a book written with Richard Applebaum, *Behind the Label*, that analyzed the plight of garment workers in Los Angeles. *Behind the Label* shows how the split labor market was transformed as capital went on the offensive against high-priced industrial labor while low-priced immigrant labor began to flex its organizational muscle. In a development unanticipated by her earlier research, global capitalism undercuts high-priced industrial labor, redirecting union campaigns to the more vulnerable sectors of the labor force, be they made up of women or immigrants, and often in the service sector—groups the labor movement once deemed unorganizable. The split labor market theory reflected the protectionist era of second wave marketization. Since then third-wave marketization has recalibrated the dynamics of the labor market, redistributing power within the working class. The public engagement of the new labor scholars, among whom Bonacich is a leader, has produced a new research program and a thriving new section of the American Sociological Association, Labor and Labor Movements. This is just one example of third-wave marketization generating a new public sociology in tandem with major advances in professional sociology.

Our fourth case is less developed than the others but no less important. In search of a public sociology on a global scale, Chris Chase-Dunn calls attention to waves of globalization and anti-globalization, and directs us to the literature on transnational social movements. He announces his yet-to-be-analyzed interviews with activists at the World Social Forum (many of whom, it turns out, have some social science background). In taking the World Social Forum as his research site, however, he risks romanticizing global civil society and missing the way it is decisively shaped by states and supra-state multi-lateral agencies. As other commentators have shown the ever-growing ranks of transnational organizations compete for limited resources from the same nation-states and foundations. This competition all too often forces them into a more conservative mode, as they tailor their projects to the preferences of these powerful actors. The thickening of global civil society, then, is as likely to bolster as to oppose the hegemony of states and the tyranny of markets.

To capture how third wave marketization absorbs or destroys opposition, it might be more pertinent to study the clash between insurgent elements of transnational civil society and the World Trade Organization. This body with its 149 member states governs through consensus so that the presence of protestors outside can often give confidence to dissident voices on the inside, thereby subverting the will of the dominant powers, as happened in Seattle (1999), Cancun (2003), and Hong Kong (2005). The WTO's mission (if not necessarily its effect) is to foster international trade, so that the Global South has found this to be a convenient place to protest, for example, the enormous subsidies the United States and the European Union give to their domestic agriculture. These subsidies sponsor the export of cheap food that has displaced farmers in the Global South, ruined local agriculture, and made basic human survival dependent on the North. If in this case the Global South is fighting for the expansion of markets, more usually it is defending itself against the invasion of markets. The General Agreement on Trade in Services (GATS), for example, WTO's new program to give multi-national capital access to public utilities, health services, higher education, etc. is a direct threat to the welfare of the Global South. Public sociology can join with professional sociology, as it does in South Africa, to study the effects of privatizing water, electricity, and health, and on that basis enter into a dialogue with elements of global civil society, arming them with the knowledge to challenge the capitalist giants now striding the earth. Herein lies an emerging research program for economic sociology, a shift from the static analysis of the embeddedness of markets (that is, the exploration of the conditions of existence of markets) to the more dynamic understanding of markets—in this case by investigating the causes and consequences of privatization and the deepening commodification of all facets of human existence.

In the age of third-wave sociology, second-wave sociology becomes a tool of critical analysis. Brint's warning against romanticizing civil society can be extended to global civil society as I noted above. No less important is Turner's stress on subjecting the claims of public sociology to empirical examination and his warning against the dangers of populism and vanguardism. More interesting and original, however, are the criticisms of Boyns and Fletcher. Especially important is their distinction between a *sociology for publics*, which is public sociology, and a *sociology of publics*, which would be an integral part of professional sociology.

If public sociology requires a sociology of publics, where might we begin? We have some possible building blocks for such a sociology—from Lippmann to Dewey, from Park to Arendt, from Habermas to Fraser, from Sennett to Warner, from Blumer to Eliasoph, from Du Bois to Collins—but we don't have a coherent sociology of publics. We need to ask such basic questions as: What is a public? What are the dimensions of variation of publics: thin versus thick, passive versus active, local versus global, hegemonic versus counter? How have publics varied historically and geographically? To study public sociology comparatively, as McLaughlin, Kowalchuk, and Turcotte propose, we need to map national terrains of publics and their arrangement into public spheres. What would that entail? How have publics interacted with and shaped one another? As Brint asks, what is the relation between civil society and publics? How are publics distorted by mass media? What does it mean to engage with different publics and are some disciplines better equipped to do so than others? These are questions for a research program in a sociology of publics, a program driven by the development of public sociology, a program that should be at the core of tomorrow's professional sociology.

V. The Critical Foundations of Public Sociology

We have attended to the policy, public and professional dimensions of third-wave sociology but what about the critical dimension? Critical sociology generates the four-sociology scheme, which does not arise *ex nihilo* but from two sets of questions, both well entrenched in critical thinking: Knowledge for whom? Knowledge for what? If the first question generates the distinction between academic and extra-academic audiences, the second (analytically) separates knowledge for efficient means from knowledge for ultimate ends. This latter distinction between instrumental and reflexive knowledge recognizes intellectuals, sociologists among them, as inherently part of the world they study.

Reflexivity, reflecting on who we are and what we do, becomes imperative as third wave marketization's offensive against society, even denying its very existence, has placed sociology in a weakened, defensive position. At the same time, this inescapable reflexivity comes not at the cost of instrumental knowledge but is its necessary accompaniment. Third-wave sociology counterpoises reflexive to instrumental knowledge, but never to the exclusion of either. It refuses the post-structuralist reduction of all knowledge to reflexive knowledge no less than pure science's reduction of all knowledge to instrumental knowledge. Sociology is neither a branch of literature nor a branch of physics.

While not joining the backlash against public sociology, Neil McLaughlin, Lisa Kowalchuk, and Kerry Turcotte nonetheless want to dispense with the instrumental—reflexive axis. To do so, however, is to cut out the core of third-wave sociology. Their strategy of excision is to turn the empirical world against the ideal type. But being normative as well as descriptive, ideal types are not so easily refuted. Let us take a look at their argument. McLaughlin, Kowalchuk, and Turcotte correctly point out that there is much public sociology that is not itself reflexive. Their examples are such well-known writers of public sociology as William Julius Wilson, C. Wright Mills, and David Riesman. To be sure they may not always be engaged in dialogue but they certainly stimulated dialogue. Still an argument could be made, as Boyns and Fletcher do, that these classics are better understood as the public face of professional sociology rather than as core works of public sociology. The distinction is an important one, based on whether the work in question was designed and produced in conjunction with and accountable to some real or virtual public or whether it became "public" as a by-product of professional research. Public sociology proper is not the popularization of professional sociology but the product of a distinctive dialogical practice of sociology.

McLaughlin, Kowalchuk, and Turcotte go still further, however, and argue that not only traditional but also organic public sociology is non-dialogic. Here they provide precious little evidence. Would they deny the dialogic moment to the two examples of organic public sociology in this volume—the new labor studies, exemplified by Edna Bonacich and the research program in social gerontology? To be sure, there is no perfect dialogue even here, but that doesn't deny the importance of the aspiration to reciprocal interchange. In fact the failure to achieve this goal only underlines its importance as a regulatory principle. Thus, to argue that organic public sociology fails to realize its own ideal is not to disqualify the ideal but to compel us to think more deeply about its conditions of possibility. As Bonacich herself is at pains to point out, reciprocity between sociologist and public is hard to achieve and always precarious but this does not put the objective in question. Falling short of an ideal is not a warrant for dismissing it but for redoubling our efforts to reach it.

Ideal types are important as enduring standards of evaluation and aspiration but they are also internally complex. Each type of sociological knowledge has its own internal divisions: professional sociology has its critical and public dimensions, just as critical sociology has its professional side, a careerist moment necessary simply to survive in the academy. Thus, Adorno and Horkheimer, titans of critical theory, had to search for sponsors of their research, but that reality does not invalidate their critical theory. To the contrary it underlines the truth of their critical theory—even the most committed reflexivity cannot escape instrumental action. That is to say, instrumentalism pervades intellectual life, invades the academy—which is precisely why it is so important to sustain the distinction between instrumental and reflexive knowledge.

The key point can be summarized as follows: instrumental knowledge is concerned with orienting means to given ends, while taking the larger world as given and unproblematic. In the academic context we generally accept existing frameworks of sociology and spend most of our time working within them rather than inventing new research programs, while in the extra-academic context instrumentalism means serving clients who define the problems and issues of research. Reflexive knowledge, on the other hand, problematizes the foundations, and especially the value foundations, of our discipline, or reveals the assumptions behind policy research sponsored by the rich and powerful. The Frankfurt School was bound up with a critique of second wave marketization, whether it was totalitarian reactions of the state (Fascism and Stalinism), the commodification of mass culture or the administration of needs by the welfare state. Its reflexivity sought to rescue human values in a sea of instrumentality, or, in Habermas's framework, to save the life world from colonization by the system world.

Third-wave marketization poses these questions even more starkly as the state loses its autonomy *vis-à-vis* the market. Nothing seems to be protected from the twin forces of marketization: commodification and privatization. The production of knowledge itself—not just in the media but also in our universities—is increasingly subject to market forces. Increasingly, the rich and prestigious universities organize corporate campaigns for buildings and research, advertising campaigns for admissions, recruitment campaigns for prestigious faculty, and so forth, while the rest of higher education is denuded of funds, subjects staff and faculty to speed-ups and cut-backs, while hiking fees for students. Public entities everywhere are under assault, from state services that are privatized and outsourced, or simply disappear, to the public spheres of political debate, increasingly subjugated to the dictates of the corporate media. The degradation of everything public and the valorization of almost everything private put public sociology on the back foot, battling against the grain.

To eliminate the distinction between instrumental and reflexive knowledge—between the logic of means and the logic of ends, between the logic of efficiency and the logic of reason—just because there is a real tendency toward the stifling of reflexive knowledge, whether critical or public, is to surrender to third-wave marketization. It implicates one in the destruction of all things public—public life, public spaces, public services, and public education. In retreating from values, pure science has no basis for contesting the destruction of the conditions of its own existence. What we share as sociologists—pure scientists as well as public sociologists—is the defense of our profession, that is, the maintenance of an arena of autonomy against the corrosive powers of privatization and commodification. In this we have much in common with other publics beyond the university. Public sociology is the recognition of such a common interest in human freedom, and thus a commitment to human rights that reach beyond the university, human rights that are embedded in the standpoint of civil society. It is part of the art of public sociology to build bridges and transcend differences between otherwise disconnected worlds.

Note

1. Thanks to Erik Wright for his comments and suggestions.

بوروی مسله ی که ای داره در مهم ظیر ای عموی روا ز

بین می بره، همی ارزش ها رو.

علم نمی تونه هیچ چیز درباره ی ارزش بگه پس نمی تونه جلوش واسته

علم کامل می تونه جلوش واسته نه علم انزی کر.

About the Contributors

Dawn E. Alley is a doctoral candidate in gerontology at the University of Southern California, Davis School of Gerontology. Her main areas of interest include the epidemiology of frailty and social disparities in late-life health, gerontological theory, and longitudinal research methods. She can be reached at alley@usc.edu.

Jill Niebrugge Brantley, a widely published scholar in the fields of gender and the history of sociology, is scholar in residence at American University in Washington, D.C.

Sean McMahon is associate professor of history at Lakeland Community College (Florida), with a specialization in American intellectual history. He has published a book and several articles about pioneering sociologist Edward A. Ross, while also carrying on research about the history of the State of Florida.

Chet Ballard is professor of sociology at Valdosta State University and was president of the Association for Humanist Sociology in 2000. Address for Correspondence: Department of Sociology, Valdosta State University, Valdosta, GA 31698. E-mail: cballard@valdosta.edu

Vern L. Bengtson holds the AARP/University Chair in Gerontology and is professor of sociology at the University of Southern California. He received his BA from North Park College in philosophy and his MA and PhD from the University of Chicago. He has published twelve books and over 200 articles in gerontology, the sociology of the life course, family sociology, social psychology, and ethnicity and aging. He has been elected president of the Gerontological Society of America and has been granted a MERIT award for research from the National Institute on Aging.

Edna Bonacich is professor of sociology and ethnic studies at the University of California, Riverside. She can be reached at edna.bonacich@ucr.edu.

David Boyns is an assistant professor in Sociology at California State University at Northridge. He specializes in sociological theory and its fundamental role in facilitating sociological research. His recent work is directed toward the investigation of forms of epistemology in sociology, in particular the role of the scientific process. He can be contacted at david.boyns@csun.edu.

Steven Brint is professor of sociology at the University of California, Riverside. Among other works, he is the author of *The Diverted Dream* (with Jerome Karabel), *In an Age of Experts*, and *Schools and Societies*. His work has won prizes from the American Educational Research Association, the Association of Colleges and Universities, and the American Sociological Association. He is currently at work on a book, *Creating the Future*, about efforts to organize universities for purposes of developing new technologies, new modes of expression, and new social relations. The second edition of *Schools and Societies* was published in 2006 by Stanford University Press. He can be reached at brint@ucr.edu.

Christopher Chase-Dunn is Distinguished Professor of Sociology, and director of the Institute for Research on World-Systems, at the University of California, Riverside. He is the author of *Rise and Demise: Comparing World-Systems* (with Thomas D. Hall), *The Wintu and Their Neighbors* (with Kelly Mann), and *The Spiral of Capitalism and Socialism* (with Terry Boswell). He is co-editor (with Walter Goldfrank) of *The Journal of World-Systems Research*. He is currently doing research on global elite integration in the nineteenth century and on the growth/decline phases and upward sweeps of empires and future global state formation. He can be reached at chriscd@ucr.edu.

Robert Prus is professor of sociology at Waterloo University, Canada. Professor Prus has published numerous articles and books on sociological theory (especially symbolic interactionism) and the sociology of deviance, and has recently examined the roots of American pragmatism in classical Greek scholarship.

Mathieu Deflem is associate professor of sociology at the University of South Carolina. His research specialties include international policing, terrorism and counterterrorism, criminal justice, abortion, and Internet technology.

Jesse Fletcher is a doctoral student at the University of California, Riverside. His primary interests lie within the creative combination of theory and methodology for the furtherance of scientific sociology. He is a musician, and would very much like to be involved in the revitalization of the sociology of music in America. He can be contacted at socalsociophile@yahoo.com.

Vincent Jeffries is professor of sociology at California State University, Northridge. His current work involves developing a theoretical tradition derived from Pitirim A. Sorokin's idea of integralism. He is also working on a study of the influence of the virtues in long-term marriages. He can be contacted at Vincent.Jeffries@csun.edu.

Lisa Kowalchuk has done research on Salvadorean social movements around land reform and public service privitization. She is an assistant professor in the Sociology and Anthropology department at the University of Guelph (Ontario). Her latest article, "The Discourse of Demobilization: Shifts in Activist Priorities and the Framing of Political Opportunities in a Peasant Land Struggle," appears in *The Sociological Quarterly* 46(2) 2005.

Patricia Madoo Lengermann is Research Professor of Sociology at The George Washington University. Jill Niebrugge-Brantley is Scholar in Residence at American University. E-mail: patleng@attglobal.net

Neil McLaughlin teaches sociological theory at McMaster University and publishes in the sociology of culture, intellectuals, and knowledge. In addition to studying both Canadian intellectual life and sociology, he is working on *The Concept of the Global Public Intellectual* and the issue of marginality and the social origins of creativity.

Lawrence T. Nichols is Professor of Sociology, and former chair of the Division of Sociology and Anthropology, at West Virginia University. Co-author of books on alternate dispute resolution and corporate social responsibility, he has published widely in the fields of white-collar crime, social problems theory, and the history of sociology. He has also served as editor of *The American Sociologist* since 1998.

Norella M. Putney is an NIA postdoctoral fellow at the Ethel Percy Andrus Gerontology Center at the University of Southern California. Her publications focus on intergenerational relations, aging families, the life course and human development, and theories of aging and the family. She can be reached at putneyh@usc.edu.

Kerry Turcotte is a doctoral candidate in sociology at McMaster University. Her current work involves the analysis of blame-laying by public intellectuals. Her broader research agenda includes what she calls "sustainable" forms of interpersonal violence, the sociology of knowledge and creativity, and sociological theory.

Jonathan H. Turner is Distinguished Professor of Sociology at the University of California, Riverside. He is primarily a theorist, and his substantive interests include the history and structure of American sociology. He can be reached at jonathan.turner@ucr.edu.

Michael Burawoy is professor of sociology at the University of California, Berkeley, and he is former president of the American Sociological Association. His numerous articles and books have focused on economic sociology in a broad international and comparative perspective. Since his presidential address to the American Sociological Association in 2004, he has been deeply engaged in the debate over his proposed model of public sociology.